ADVANCE PRAISE FOR *MASSACRE*

"*Massacre* is an absorbing and very moving read. John Merriman has found exactly the right unemotional tone and mastery of detail—including many new stories heretofore unpublished—to produce the best popular history of the Commune, in English or French, in a generation."

> **—Steven Englund, author of *Napoleon: A Political Life***

"Dream of emancipation, nightmare of repression—the Paris Commune was a focal point of the political imagination of nineteenth-century Europe. John Merriman's new book brings vividly to life the hopes and fears, the passions and hatreds, and the social and political struggles that inspired a famous revolutionary regime and led to its violent destruction."

> **—Jonathan Sperber, author of *Karl Marx: A Nineteenth-Century Life***

MASSACRE

MASSACRE

THE LIFE *and* DEATH
of the PARIS COMMUNE

JOHN MERRIMAN

BASIC BOOKS

A Member of the Perseus Books Group

New York

Published by Basic Books,
A Member of the Perseus Books Group

Books published by Basic Books are available at special discounts for bulk purchases in the United States by corporations, institutions, and other organizations. For more information, please contact the Special Markets Department at the Perseus Books Group, 2300 Chestnut Street, Suite 200, Philadelphia, PA 19103, or call (800) 810–4145, ext. 5000, or e-mail special .markets@perseusbooks.com.

Text design by Cynthia Young

Library of Congress Cataloging-in-Publication Data
  Merriman, John M.
    Massacre : the life and death of the Paris Commune / John Merriman.
      pages cm
    Includes bibliographical references and index.
    ISBN 978-0-465-02017-1 (hardcover)—ISBN 978-0-465-05682-8 (ebook)
  1. Paris (France)—History—Commune, 1871.   2. Social conflict—France—Paris—History—19th century.   3. Violence—France—Paris—History—19th century.
  4. Massacres—France—Paris—History—19th century.   5. Paris (France)—Politics and government—19th century.   6. Paris (France)—Social conditions—19th century.
  7. France—Politics and government—1870–1940.   I. Title.

DC317.M365 2014

944.081'2—dc23

                                                    2014023988

10 9 8 7 6 5 4 3 2 1

For Don Lamm

CONTENTS

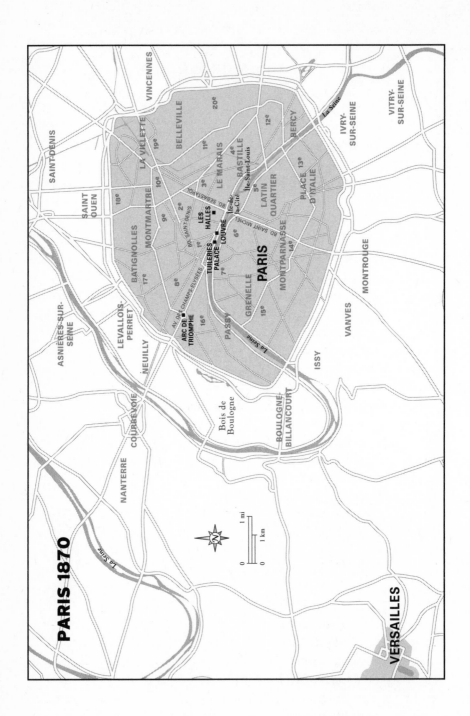

PROLOGUE

O N MARCH 18, 1871, Parisians living on Montmartre awoke to the sounds of French troops attempting to seize the cannons of the National Guard. The troops acted under the orders of Adolphe Thiers, the conservative head of a provisional government recently ensconced in Versailles, once the residence of the Bourbon monarchs of the Ancien Régime. Thiers, fearing the mobilization of angry and radicalized Parisians, wanted to disarm their city and its National Guard, whose ranks comprised, for the most part, workers desirous of a strong republic and angered by the capitulation of the provisional government in the disastrous war against Prussia that had begun the previous July and brought about the fall of the Second Empire.

Despite the efforts of the French army, the men and women of Montmartre, Belleville, and Buttes-Chaumont courageously prevented the troops from taking the cannons. Seeing about 4,000 soldiers arrive on Montmartre, then halt to await the arrival of the horses necessary to haul the weapons down the hill, women sounded the alarm. Working-class residents of the butte overlooking the French capital prevented the heavily armed troops from hitching the cannons to horses and, in keeping with the tradition of revolutionary defiance, began to build barricades. Soldiers started to fraternize with the people of Montmartre. The 6,000 troops sent to Belleville, La Villette, and Ménilmontant fared no better. Parisians would keep their cannons.

Thwarted, Thiers withdrew his forces from Paris to Versailles, where he planned to regroup and eventually retake the city. Thousands of wealthy Parisians joined him there. In Paris, left-wing militants proclaimed a "Commune" of progressive self-government that brought freedom to Parisians, many of whom believed themselves "masters of their own lives" for the first time. Working-class families from proletarian neighborhoods proudly strolled into the *beaux quartiers* of the capital, imagining a more just society and prepared to take steps to make it a reality. Their progressive Commune would last a mere ten weeks before Thiers's troops annihilated it during the last bloody week of May.

The birth and destruction of the Paris Commune, one of the most tragic, defining events of the nineteenth century, still resonate today. In the streets of Paris, Thiers's army gunned down thousands of ordinary men, women, and, occasionally, children. Soldiers killed many for their defense of the Commune; others died because their workers' attire, remnants of a Parisian National Guard uniform, or manner of speaking marked them for death. The massacres by French troops of their countrymen anticipated the demons of the century to follow. You could be gunned down simply because of who you were, because you had the nerve to demand freedom. This may have been the ultimate significance of Bloody Week, May 21 to 28, 1871, the biggest massacre in nineteenth-century Europe.

PARIS WAS A SURGING CITY of great social contrasts and contradictions during Napoleon III's Second Empire (1852–1870). On one hand, the capital led a rapidly growing French economy. Artisans in small workshops dominated industry, producing the *articles de Paris*—high-quality gloves, and other luxury goods that came to epitomize French manufacturing. Imperial financial institutions helped boost industrial production in and around Paris, bringing unparalleled prosperity to people of means, who attended lavish social events and theatrical performances, traversing the city and the Bois-de-Boulogne in carriages while ordinary people walked to work. Powerful trains, their engines spewing steam, carried wealthy passengers from the burgeoning capital to Deauville and other increasingly elegant towns on the Norman coast.

The economic boom and the incredible wealth it brought to Paris diverted attention from widespread poverty and divisions in the city. Napoleon III and Baron Georges Haussmann plowed spacious boulevards through the tangle of medieval Paris. Fancy restaurants and cafés welcomed those who could afford to frequent them. In the dilapidated and overcrowded districts of eastern and northern Paris, working people living in miserable tiny apartments or rooming houses struggled to get by. For them, the hard times never seemed to end.

By the late 1860s, Napoleon III faced mounting political opposition, so much so that many Parisians anticipated a disastrous end to his reign. France already had a lengthy history of class strife. Three revolutions had chased monarchs from the French throne over the previous sixty years. So far, none had brought to France the stability found across the English Channel in Great Britain.

Napoleon III, however, was confident that he, unlike his immediate predecessors, would hold onto power. Born in 1808, Louis Napoleon Bonaparte, the son of Napoleon's brother, had grown up in a Swiss chateau amid artifacts of his uncle's rule. Certain of his destiny to build on his famous family's dynastic heritage, which he identified with the fate of France, he added to his ambition a shrewd political opportunism combined with notoriously bad judgment. The July Monarchy of King Louis-Philippe of the Orléans family (a junior wing of the Bourbons, the French royal family) maintained its policy of forcing the family of Napoleon Bonaparte to remain in exile. Louis Napoleon had attempted to invade France with a handful of followers in 1836, when he marched into a Strasbourg garrison and was arrested, and then again four years later, when he landed on the coast near Boulogne-sur-Mer, with the same embarrassing result. Imprisoned in 1840 in northern France, he escaped in 1846 dressed as a worker. These fiascos earned him a reputation as something of a buffoon who surrounded himself with sleazy, inept cronies. Short and increasingly corpulent, he resembled his uncle—to whom his enemies compared him, calling him "the [Napoleonic] hat without the head" and poking fun at his "fish eyes."

Yet, for all his early failures, Louis Napoleon was surprisingly optimistic and believed that economic progress under his rule could benefit all Parisians, wealthy and poor alike. With his usual modesty, he wrote from prison, "I believe that there are certain men who are born to serve as a means for the march of the human race. . . . I consider myself to be one of these."[1]

The February Revolution in 1848, one of the many revolutions that swept Europe that year, brought an end to the Orléans monarchy, and Louis Napoleon quickly returned to Paris, winning election as president of the Second French Republic in December 1848, nine months after the overthrow of King Louis-Philippe. After orchestrating the repression of the Left, the "prince president" ended the Second French Republic with a coup d'état on December 2, 1851, because his term in office would have expired the following year. Parisians awoke to martial law; the democratic-socialists in the National Assembly, whose members were elected from the provincial *départements*, found themselves under arrest.

But some Parisians refused to submit to another empire without a fight; Louis Napoleon's coup d'état sparked an ill-fated uprising in working-class neighborhoods in central and eastern Paris. In France, more than 125,000 people, the majority of them peasants, took up arms to defend the republic, particularly in the south, where secret societies had built networks of underground support. But the insurgents stood no chance against columns of professional soldiers and soon fled for their lives. In a precursor to the aftermath of the Commune in 1871, almost 27,000 people—whether they had participated in the revolt or not—were brought before courts-martial, "Mixed Commissions" consisting of senior military officers and judicial and administrative officials. Thousands received sentences ranging from deportation to Algeria or Cayenne, to imprisonment in France, to exile. The following year Napoleon III declared the Second Empire.[2]

The emperor found his Bonapartist following among wealthy individuals who had supported Louis Philippe in the name of social "order" during the Orleanist July Monarchy that ruled between 1830 and 1848.[3] The financial system under Napoleon III served to enrich those already in power. Napoleon III's family received 1 million francs (roughly $3 million) from the treasury each year. Random relatives also received large sums from the state simply for existing. Millions of francs in special funds disappeared into the emperor's deep pockets; an English mistress received a hefty sum as well. But the new emperor did not please everyone. As the rich became richer, many in Paris and the provinces continued to struggle and held "Napoleon le Petit," as Victor Hugo dubbed him, in contempt. Workers had no legal recourse against their employers, who were backed by gendarmes and troops.

In fact, an increasing number of Parisians benefitted not at all from Napoleon III's regime. The population of Paris almost doubled during the 1850s and 1860s, rising from a little more than 1 million in 1851 to almost 2 million by 1870. Each year during the Second Empire, tens of thousands of immigrants poured into the capital from the Parisian Basin, the north, Picardy, Normandy, Champagne, and Lorraine, among other regions, mostly male laborers even poorer than the Parisians and attracted by the possibility of construction work. These new residents, many of whom had left precarious economic situations in the rural world, accounted for virtually all of this rapid urban growth. Many were underemployed, if not unemployed, and crowded into *garnis* (rooming houses) on the narrow, grey streets in the central districts or in shacks in the emerging industrial suburbs. The central arrondissements, always densely packed, reached an astonishing 15,000 people per square kilometer in the Fourth Arrondissement in the Marais, where population density was three times today's. Tens of thousands were indigent, depending, at least to an extent, on charity. Some simply slept wherever they could. In 1870, almost half a million Parisians—one-quarter of the population—could be classified as indigent.[4]

As the deterioration of the old medieval center of Paris became more pronounced, elites became more frantic about "the urban crisis." Most artisans had moved away from the Ile-de-la-Cité, leaving about 15,000 men, mostly day laborers, crammed into the island's rooming houses. Notre Dame towered over these small, jam-packed buildings. A police report noted the presence of "an enormous number of down-and-out people, men and women, who survive only through plunder and who find refuge only in the bars and brothels that pollute the *quartier*." On the Right Bank, much of the First Arrondissement, centering on the great market of Les Halles, the Marais, including the Third and Fourth Arrondissements, and the Eleventh and Twelfth Arrondissements to the north reflected the grim texture of urban life. A good part of the Fifth Arrondissement on the Left Bank, with its many scrap-metal and cloth sellers, was also very poor. The miserable, disease-ridden faubourg Saint-Marceau, one of the most destitute parts of Paris, reached into the Thirteenth Arrondissement, where ragpickers plied their trade and tanners tossed animal remains into the Bièvre River.[5]

Central and eastern Paris formed, according to one observer, "a gothic city, black, gloomy, excrement- and fever-ridden, a place of darkness, disorder, violence, misery, and blood." Horrible smells emanated from "appalling alleys, houses the color of mud" and from stagnant, putrid waters. In Paris, an unhealthy place like other large cities, more people died every year than were born. Only about a fifth of the buildings had running water. Keeping out the cold during the freezing winters was a perpetual challenge. People of means, living in relative ease in the *beaux quartiers* of western Paris, felt they resided uncomfortably in a sordid capital of immorality and vice, its dark, dank *quartiers* the preserve of the "dangerous and laboring classes," even if these privileged individuals had never actually seen these neighborhoods. Popular literature helped cement this image in the upper-class imagination, depicting Paris's poor neighborhoods as the haunts of "the dregs of society."[6]

To accommodate the exponential growth in Paris's population and limit the deterioration of its center, in 1853 Napoleon III summoned Baron Georges Haussmann, prefect of the *département* of the Seine, to plan the rebuilding of the city. Of Alsatian origins and born in the capital, Haussmann moved into the bureaucracy after completing law school, serving as subprefect and then prefect in several provincial *départements*, where, during the Second Republic, he had lent his administrative skills to political repression. An energetic man with a talent for organization, Haussmann seemed the perfect Parisian bureaucrat and was eager to use the emerging field of statistics to his advantage in launching his great projects. But the elegantly dressed Haussmann was also an arrogant, vain, aggressive bully willing to do anything in his power to ensure that France never again became a republic.[7]

In many ways, then, Haussmann was the ideal man to realize Napoleon III's dream of rebuilding the French capital as an imperial city. The emperor and the prefect of the Seine had three goals. First, they wished to bring more light and air into a city ravaged by cholera in 1832 and 1849 (and again in 1853 and 1854, after Haussmann's grand projects had begun) and to build more sewers to improve the city's sanitation. Second, they wanted to free the flow of capital and goods. The first French department stores—Bon Marché, Bazar de l'Hôtel-de-Ville, Le Printemps, Le Louvre, and La Samaritaine—would stand on Haussmann's wide boulevards, along with glittering brasseries and cafés, which became the face of modern Paris, although small shops remained essential to the urban economy.[8]

Third, the emperor and his prefect wanted to limit the potential for insurgency in traditional revolutionary neighborhoods. The boulevards themselves would become an obstacle to the construction of barricades by virtue of their width. On eight occasions since 1827, disgruntled Parisians had erected barricades in the city, most recently during the February Revolution and then during the June Days of 1848, when workers rose up to protest the closing of national workshops that had provided some employment in a time of economic distress. Barricades went up again in Paris following Louis Napoleon Bonaparte's coup d'état. Protestors managed to block the advance of professional armies of the state by hurriedly constructing barricades on the narrow streets of central and eastern Paris, using wood, cobblestones, and just about anything else they could find. Napoleon III had no intention of letting that happen again.[9]

Haussmann's boulevards reflected the determination of the Second Empire's leaders to impose their version of social order on Paris. The prefect of the Seine did not mince words: "Bringing order to this Queen City is one of the first conditions of general security." Some of the boulevards indeed tore right through the insurgent *quartiers* of the June Days. The boulevard Prince Eugène provided troops relatively easy access into "the habitual center . . . of riots."[10]

The new boulevards of Paris thus embodied the "imperialism of the straight line," intended not only to quash uprisings but also to display the modernity and might of the empire. They provided power alleys down which troops could march in showy processions, as had earlier examples of classical urban planning, from Philip II's Madrid to Peter the Great's St. Petersburg to Frederick the Great's Berlin. The rue de Rivoli, completed in 1855, led visitors to the international exposition on the Champs-Élysées, which featured 5,000 exhibits, many celebrating the city's technological innovations. The "capital of the world" had emerged as a spectacular "permanent exposition," or what novelist Théophile Gautier called "A Babel of industry . . . A Babylon of the future."[11]

The National Assembly provided funds for the enormous series of projects, augmented by a tax on goods brought into the city, assessed at the customs barriers (*octrois*) that ringed Paris. But as costs soared, Baron Haussmann found other resourceful ways to raise money, working around the Corps Législatif to do so. He demanded capital outlays from contractors, who would in principle be paid with interest once they had completed their work. Haussmann then turned to issuing "proxy bonds," backed by funds now owed by these contractors. The imperial rebuilding of Paris left the capital with a debt of 2.5 billion francs. By the late 1860s, the prefect of the Seine had raised 500 million francs. The emperor was well aware of Haussmann's financial machinations but remained committed to his grand plans for Paris, which would continue to create jobs and build the prestige of his empire.[12] Yet the financing strategy was rather like a balloon mortgage that could burst at any time.

The rebuilding of Paris also entailed the destruction of 100,000 apartments in 20,000 buildings. The "Haussmannization" of Paris sent many Parisians packing for the urban periphery because they had been pushed out of rented apartments, their homes had been destroyed, or prices had skyrocketed in a city that was already extremely expensive. In some places in the central arrondissements, such as Ile-de-la-Cité, the population actually fell as people moved toward the periphery. About 20 to 30 percent of the Parisian population moved, mostly into nearby or neighboring *quartiers* but also into the inner suburbs, which Paris had annexed on January 1, 1860, to increase tax revenue as well as to ease the government's policing of this restive periphery. Newcomers from the provinces had also moved to the inner suburbs, particularly Montmartre in the Eighteenth, La Villette in the Nineteenth, and

Belleville in the Twentieth Arrondissements. These districts became the residences, temporary or permanent, of an increasingly large number of poor workers, as did the growing suburbs beyond the city's walls.[13]

Rather than staving off class strife, however, the rebuilding of Paris accentuated the contrast between the more prosperous western arrondissements and the poor eastern and northeastern *quartiers*, the so-called People's Paris. The flowering of western Paris had begun a half century before with the establishment of businesses and banks there. One could also find arcades and passageways of glass and metal—"veritable gallery-streets"—whose shops anticipated the new department stores. But under Napoleon III, the bourgeoisie's day had truly arrived.

In the Ninth Arrondissement, for example, the quartier of Chaussée d'Antin, the center of what Balzac described as "the world of money," became a residence for the kings of finance and their ladies. The residence, or *hôtel*, of the Guimard family, built in 1772, was converted into a store selling the latest consumer novelties. Nearby stood another elegant residence that became the headquarters of one of the railroad companies whose trains were slowly transforming France. The Grand Hôtel and its Café-de-la-Paix on the boulevard des Capucines stood a few steps from Charles Garnier's new Paris Opera, construction of which began in 1861. When Empress Eugénie asked the Parisian-born architect about his intended style for the new opera house, he supposedly replied without hesitation, "Pure Napoleon III."[14] On the place Saint-Georges stood the sizable residence of Adolphe Thiers, who packed his mansion with objets d'art from around the world.

Nearby, the Champs-Élysées and the Eighth Arrondissement on the western edge of Paris also flaunted the privileges granted by wealth. Carriages and horses carried the rich out to the Bois-de-Boulogne, where *tout Paris* frolicked. Magnificent private residences lined the avenue. Nearby stood elegant circuses (*cirques*), café-concerts (where revelers could go to drink and listen to live music), and restaurants. A lavish private residence had been purchased by Empress Eugénie's mother, who of course could not live just anywhere. The Champs-Élysées fit the bill.[15]

On the other side of the Seine, the boulevard Saint-Germain, partially completed in 1855, paralleled the river. As it cut through the Seventh and Sixth Arrondissements, the boulevard also sported private residences offering privacy and elegance, many dating from the eighteenth century. Across the street, the Café Flore set up shop late in the

Second Empire, bringing together, then as now, a clientele with money to spend.

A WORLD AWAY FROM the opulence of western Paris, although not far as the crow flies, the rue de la Goutte d'Or bisected a proletarian neighborhood. In his *L'Assommoir*, Émile Zola describes Gervaise—a character who ultimately drinks herself to death—as she looks up at number 22:

> On the street side it had five floors, each one with fifteen windows in a line, the lack of shutters of which, with their broken slats, gave the huge wall-space a look of utter desolation. But below that there were four shops on the ground floor: to the right of the doorway a huge sleazy eating-house, to the left a coal merchant's, a draper's and an umbrella shop. The building looked all the more colossal because it stood between two low rickety houses clinging to either side of it. . . . Its unplastered sides, mud-coloured and as interminably bare as prison walls, showed rows of toothing-stones [stone links projecting from the end of a building so that more could be quickly added and linked up] like decaying jays snapping in the void.[16]

Like Gervaise, many working-class Parisians began to feel alienated from the city they loved amid the dramatic and devastating changes orchestrated by Haussmann in the interests of the upper classes.[17] Indeed, this sense of not belonging arguably contributed to an emerging sense of solidarity among those living on the margins of the capital. And even as western Paris was transformed into a gleaming city of wide boulevards and lavish apartments, ongoing industrialization was remaking eastern and northern Paris and its periphery. The edge of the city offered more space, access to railroads and the canals of northern Paris, and a labor force perched at its gates, making it an ideal location for manufacturing. Larger factories, some predating the Second Empire, were to be found in the inner suburbs annexed in 1860, including the Cail metallurgical factory in Grenelle, which employed about 2,800 workers. Entrepreneurs in the inner suburbs produced candles, soap, perfumes, and sugar, bringing raw materials into northern Paris via the Ourcq canal.

The populations in the industrialized parts of Paris shot up with the construction of new factories. The population of the Twentieth Arrondissement, for instance, grew from 17,000 in 1800 to 87,000 in 1851 and continued to soar. Montmartre, which had only about 600 inhabitants in 1800, had 23,000 in 1851 and 36,500 five years later. Chemical and metallurgical production transformed La Villette, which had grown from about 1,600 inhabitants in 1810 to more than 30,000 by 1860. Beyond the walls of Paris, the arrondissement of Saint-Denis grew from 41,000 in 1841 to an astounding 356,000 in 1856 as industries leapfrogged beyond the city.[18]

IN 1834, ONE OF LOUIS-PHILIPPE'S ministers had warned that the factories being built on the edge of Paris could "be the cord that will strangle us one day."[19] During the Second Empire, the staggering population growth in Paris's working-class neighborhoods accentuated Parisian elites' fear of ordinary workers living on the geographic and social margins of their city. Paris had annexed Belleville, a neighborhood of nearly 60,000 people on the northeastern edge of Paris, along with the other inner suburbs. Whispers that "Belleville is coming down the hill!" reflected the anxiety felt in the *beaux quartiers* below.[20]

Louis Lazare, a royalist critic of the Second Empire and the rebuilding of Paris, argued that instead of dispensing millions of francs on the wealthier neighborhoods, the regime would have been wiser to spend the money on the "dreadful Siberia" of the periphery. Lazare warned, "Around the Queen of Cities is rising up a formidable *cité ouvrière*."[21]

Conservative Louis Veuillot shared a critique of Haussmannization with republicans, who rejected the authoritarian structure of the empire and its privileged elite. The Catholic polemicist embraced the memory of old Paris, destroyed by modernity, materialism, secularism, and state centralization. He saw the new boulevards as "an overflown river which would carry along the debris of a world." Paris had become a "city without a past, full of minds without memories, hearts without sorrows, souls without love!" He lamented, "City of uprooted multitudes, shifting piles of human dust, you can grow to become the capital of the world, [but] you will never have citizens."[22]

ANTICLERICALISM AMONG THE RANKS of both middle-class radicals and the urban poor also infused mounting opposition to Napoleon III's regime. The Catholic Church was extremely visible in the Paris of the Second Empire, yet increasingly absent from the lives of Parisian working families. If the Second Empire had seen a revival of fervent Catholicism in parts of France, particularly after the sighting of the

Virgin Mary at Lourdes in 1856, Paris, other large cities, regions like the Limousin and Ile-de-France, and large parts of the southwest had undergone "de-Christianization"—a marked decline in religious practice. In Ménilmontant in the Twentieth Arrondissement, only 180 out of a population of 33,000 men performed their Easter duty, the obligation to receive Holy Communion. The Church's situation was even bleaker in the working-class suburbs,[23] perhaps unsurprisingly as the Church told the poor that they should resign themselves to poverty in the valley of tears that is this world—their reward for their suffering awaited them in Heaven.

Intellectual currents during the middle decades of the nineteenth century also challenged the Catholic Church's declared primacy of faith over reason. Positivism, based on the belief that rational inquiry and the application of science to the human condition were advancing society, was becoming more popular in universities across Europe. Pope Pius IX's *Syllabus of Errors* (1864), which denounced modern society, seemed to associate the Church with ignorance and a rejection of human progress. Popular literature, including works by Victor Hugo, George Sand, and Eugène Sue, sometime presented the Catholic clergy in an unfavorable light. Anticlericals believed French peasants to be under the thumb of the clergy, who whispered instructions in the confessionals.

If the parish clergy provided useful functions—baptisms, marriages, and burials—the religious orders lived in isolated contemplation and prayer ("They eat, they sleep, they digest," went an old refrain). Moreover religious orders, particularly the Jesuits, were closely identified with the conservative political role of the Church, whose archbishops and bishops had supported Louis Napoleon Bonaparte's coup d'état.

Many Parisians particularly objected to the Church's dominant role in primary education. During the Second Empire, the number of religious orders rose in Paris from six to twenty-two for men and from twenty-two to an astonishing sixty-seven for women. The number of men in religious orders increased from 3,100 in 1851 to well over 20,000 by 1870; the number of women rose from 34,200 to more than 100,000 in 1870. In 1871, 52 percent of Parisian pupils attended schools run by religious orders and staffed by teachers who had not taken the examinations required of lay teachers. The Church's virtual monopoly on the education of girls stood out; yet literacy remained lower among women than men.[24]

THE HARDSHIP FACING the working poor also contributed to mounting opposition to the imperial regime. As prices soared above wages, and the gap between the wealthy and the workers increased, workers found ways to combat these injustices. Although unions remained illegal (and would be so until 1884), the late 1860s brought the creation and toleration of more workers' associations, which were basically unions—this at a time when employers, particularly in larger industries, were seeking to reduce costs by attacking the shop-floor autonomy of skilled workers by aggressively posting rules and regulations, increasing mechanization, and hiring more unskilled workers. In 1869, at least 165 workers' associations in Paris had about 160,000 members. Cooperative restaurants offering meals at reduced prices catered to more than 8,000 diners. Workers' associations began to organize producers' cooperatives (in which workers in a trade would own tools and raw materials, thereby circumventing the existing wage system). These associations' aims were political and even revolutionary, as well as economic. Indeed, many workers believed that workers' associations would ultimately replace the state itself.[25]

A number of Parisian women emerged as militants, demanding rights and better working conditions. Countless women worked at home—many living in barely lit attics—in the putting-out system of textile work, an important component of large-scale industrialization in France. Female workers earned about half as much as their male counterparts in workshops and factories. Yet calls for female suffrage were few and far between; the emphasis remained on economic issues and the struggles of working-class families and single women to survive. In a manifesto penned in July 1868, nineteen women demanded that every woman be given "possession of the rights which belong to her as a human person." A year later, female militants organized the Society for Affirming the Rights of Women. They advocated for women's right to divorce and published a plan for a democratic primary school for girls, with the goal of the "conquest of equality" and "moral reform."[26]

It seemed, briefly at least, that these efforts would pay off. Beginning with an amnesty in 1859 for those punished for resisting the coup d'état or espousing militant republicanism or socialism, Napoleon III's Second Empire entered a somewhat more liberal phase. The legalization of strikes in 1864 led to a wave of work stoppages. Laws in 1868 made press censorship less oppressive. A spate of republican newspapers began to publish, notably *La Marseillaise* and *La Lanterne*, which had a circulation of up to 150,000 copies.[27]

However, despite its new liberal facade, Napoleon III's Second Empire remained a police state, focusing attention on perceived threats to the regime. The prefecture of police stored information on as many as 170,000 Parisians. In two decades, the number of police had increased from 750 to more than 4,000, employing countless spies. The municipal police force was 2,900 strong, backed by garrisoned army units.[28]

Still, there was a vibrant culture of resistance to Napoleon III. Anyone entering the most popular cafés of the Latin Quarter would encounter a variety of republican and socialist militants determined to bring about a change in regime as they dreamed of creating a government committed to social and political justice. In those days, the *brasserie* Chez Glaser appeared as if still under construction; two large chunks of cement at the base of metal poles, seemingly the only things keeping the place from collapsing, greeted clients. Small tables of white marble and a billiard table in the rear of the small hall awaited the thirsty. Glaser, an Alsatian schoolteacher dismissed by the government for his republican views, had, like most of his customers, little use for Napoleon III's Second Empire.

Other major watering holes for militants included the Café Madrid on the boulevard Montmartre on the Right Bank and, on the Left Bank, the Café de la Salamandre in the place Saint-Michel, the nearby Café d'Harcourt, and Café Théodore on the rue Monsieur-le-Prince. A *cabinet littéraire* (a bookstore that rented books) on the rue Dauphine also brought together critics of the regime, including, from time to time, the naturalist painter Gustave Courbet, a fixture in the Latin Quarter.[29]

A police report described Courbet with the compelling accuracy of one of his own self-portraits: "Physically, he has lost his romantic allure." He was "big, fat and stooping, walking with difficulty because of back pain, long greying hair, with the air of the mocking peasant, and badly dressed." English resident Ernest Vizetelly described Courbet as "peasant-like in appearance, puffed out with beer, good-humoured." Denis Arthur Bingham, another British observer, saw the painter as "a good-natured country farmer. . . . Courbet was always treated by his friends as an overgrown child, and he behaved as such."[30] Born in Ornans in Franche-Comté in eastern France, the accent of which he proudly retained, Courbet had been a friend of the anarchist Pierre-Joseph Proudhon, who came from the same region and shared his contempt for the Second Empire. Proudhon held that the purpose of art was "the physical, intellectual, and moral perfecting of humanity."

Courbet, the *maître d'Ornans*, sought the same freedom in painting that he dreamed of for individual French men and women.[31]

Courbet emerged as a feisty opponent of Napoleon III. Turned down by the Salon, the annual government exhibition of approved academic painting, in 1863, he insisted he had become a painter "in order to gain his individual liberty and only he could judge his painting." In 1870, the government offered Courbet the Legion of Honor. In his letter refusing the award, the painter stated that the government "seemed to have taken on the task of destroying art in our country. . . . [T]he state is incompetent in such matters. . . . I am fifty years old and have always lived as a free man—let me end my existence free."[32]

MOST PARISIANS DID NOT FEEL FREE. Unlike all 36,000 other cities, towns, and villages in France, Paris did not have a mayor. The post had been abolished in 1794 and again in July 1848. Now Parisians could not even elect representatives to the municipal councils of the city's twenty arrondissements; rather, the emperor appointed them. Each arrondissement had a mayor and deputy mayor, also appointed by the government. All this generated calls for self-determination. In 1869 and 1870, demands for municipal autonomy merged with republicanism. In the dance halls and warehouses on the edge of Paris, the idea of one day establishing a "Commune," in which Parisians would have political rights and Paris would stand as a beacon of liberty, gained strength.[33]

RAOUL RIGAULT HAD BECOME a well-known opponent of the imperial regime. He was also a prominent personage in the cafés and brasseries of the boulevard Saint-Michel during the late 1860s. He ate, drank, and socialized with young women, some of whose charms he rented for cash. With a bock—a strong beer—in hand, he held court, providing acid commentaries on the Second Empire. Obsessed with the French Revolution, Rigault considered himself the living incarnation of the radical Jacques-René Hébert, whose life and writings he studied carefully when he left his table to cross the Seine to visit the Bibliothèque Nationale. There he took a place at one of the long rows of seats toward the front, always on the left side, of course. He could recite by heart passages penned by Hébert, his hero, the uncompromising revolutionary, guillotined in March 1794 at the order of the Committee of Public Safety.[34]

Parisian through and through, Rigault was born in the capital in 1846, his father, Charles-Édouard, a respectable republican. Following the coup d'état, the family took up residence in northwestern Paris's Seventeenth Arrondissement, whose residents where somewhere between elite and proletarian. Expelled from the Lycée Imperial in Versailles, he nonetheless passed the *baccalauréat* examination in both science and literature. In 1866, Rigault's father kicked him out of their home after a particularly nasty argument. Moving into an attic room on the rue Saint-André-des-Arts and earning a little money by giving math lessons, Rigault first began to hang out at the Café Buci, discussing politics or playing billiards. He began calling everyone he met *citoyen* or *citoyenne*, including "citizen prostitutes," as had the sans-culottes of the Revolution. Rigault and other young political radicals organized and published several short-lived newspapers, one of which the police seized and shut down in 1865 for containing an article that "outraged religion." The offending article had Raoul Rigault written all over it.[35]

Rigault's café life, interrupted by short spells in jail, brought him premature corpulence. He was of average height, with "prying eyes" peering from behind his pince-nez. Dressing as shabbily as possible and carrying his snuffbox, Rigault welcomed visitors with a shower of spit that flew from his mouth as he harangued and coughed. Some drops caught on his bristly, thick, chestnut-colored beard, which complemented long, unruly hair. Those who encountered him noticed that his lips contributed to a seemingly "ironic," even provocative, pose, his glare piercing and inquisitorial, "full of sardonic cheekiness." Rigault's voice rose from resonant to thunderous when the subject turned to politics and class struggle. His temper was notorious; he once shouted at his opponent during an argument, "I am going to have you shot!"[36]

Developing an obsession with the organization and personnel of the police, Rigault studiously followed agents, including the omnipresent police spies (*mouchards*) on their rounds, noting their habits, strengths, and weaknesses, as well as their addresses. By dressing as a lawyer, he obtained entry to the court in the Palace of Justice, which considered political crimes, and took careful notes on policemen who testified. Rigault collated the information he gathered or observed in a large file.

Like many other young militants, Rigault joined Karl Marx's International Workingman's Association, created in 1864 and banned in France in 1868.[37] In late 1865, he helped organize a student gathering in the eastern Belgian city of Liège. The next year police arrested him following a raid on a boisterous gathering in the Café Buci—which they subsequently closed for several months—on charges of having formed a secret society known as "the Renaissance." Although Rigault refused to swear an oath to tell the truth that invoked Jesus Christ, he was freed because this was his first arrest.

In 1865 Rigault became attracted to Blanquism through Gustave Tridon, a French revolutionary socialist. "Blanquists" were followers of Auguste Blanqui, *Le Vieux* (the Old One), a professional revolutionary and consummate man of action who had spent about half his life in prison for his role in a series of conspiracies. He held that a tightly organized band of left-wing militants could one day seize revolutionary power.

In order to attend student political meetings in its lecture halls, Rigault enrolled in medical school, not far from his favorite cafés and brasseries. Over the next few years, Rigault's dossier in the Prefecture of Police grew. At the dance hall Folies-Belleville, he found eager listeners among craftsmen and semiskilled workers. In a speech on December 1868, he called for the recognition of *unions libres* (unrecognized unions), arguing that any obstacles to "the union of a man and a woman" violated the laws of nature. Rigault taunted the ever-present police spies, who scribbled down what was said. That year he published a prospectus for a newspaper, informing readers, "God is the absurd." Later that year, he published an article in *Le Démocrate*, predicting that if atheists came to power, they would not tolerate their enemies. When, during one court appearance, the prosecuting attorney contemptuously referred to Rigault as a "professor of the barricades," his target replied, "*Oui! oui!*"[38]

After one arrest, Rigault managed to escape by reaching the roof of a building, running to the Gare de Lyon, and jumping on the first departing train. He got off in Moret-sur-Loing, near Fontainebleau, and for two days wandered through a forest. Rigault came upon Auguste Renoir standing before his easel. The Impressionist painter saw several deer suddenly scatter and heard noises in the brush. A young man "of an appearance not terribly engaging appeared. His clothes were torn and covered in mud, his eyes wild and his movements jerky." Renoir, believing Rigault to be a madman escaped from an institution, grabbed his cane to defend himself. The man stopped several feet from him and said, "I beg of you, Monsieur, I am dying of hunger!" Rigault explained his situation, and Renoir, who had republican sympathies, went to town and bought him a painter's smock and a box of paints, assuring him that people in the vicinity would ask no questions; peasants there were now quite used to seeing painters.[39]

Back in Paris, Rigault helped effect an alliance between the "citizen proletarians" and the radical intelligentsia, linking the traditionally revolutionary faubourg Saint-Antoine and the new workers' bastions of Montmartre and Belleville with the Latin Quarter. At the same time, he helped find funds for upstart newspapers to replace those that had shut down or failed, collecting news and accounts of political trials and publishing torrid denunciations of individuals he considered imperial lackeys. In four years, Rigault faced ten judicial condemnations in court—or the *bordel* (whorehouse), as he liked to call it.[40]

Thus in the late 1860s, Paris came alive with the surging political mobilization of ordinary people. A law of June 8, 1868, permitting freedom of association initiated the frenetic period of the "public meeting movement." Crowds flocked to dance halls, café-concerts, and warehouses, most on the plebeian periphery of Paris, to listen to speeches and debate political themes previously forbidden. From 1868 through mid-1870, almost 1,000 public meetings took place. As many as 20,000 people participated on a single night. Workers remained the principal constituency of the political meetings, although these gatherings drew middle-class Parisians as well. The police, to be sure, were also in attendance, copying down what was said and thereby providing historians with an incredibly rich account of these "parliaments of the people."[41]

AT THE BEGINNING OF 1870, in the wake of continued liberal political mobilization and electoral victories, Napoleon III appointed a new cabinet led by Émile Ollivier, a moderate republican; it was considered a government of conciliation. Yet this brief accommodation between the government and the republican opposition came to an end amid escalating republican militancy. It was no coincidence that the rapprochement ended during a stalled economy that brought hard times. When the financing of Haussmann's grand projects became a public scandal, contributing to growing opposition to the regime, the balloon popped, and on January 5, 1870, Napoleon III dismissed the baron as prefect of the Seine, a position that Ollivier had made one of the conditions of his acceptance of a role in the government. Resentment against Napoleon III mounted, amid strikes and more public meetings. In this precocious springtime, it became possible to imagine a new political world.[42]

RIGAULT WAS ENTERING THE Bibliothèque Nationale when he heard the news that on January 11, 1870, Prince Pierre Bonaparte had shot his friend Victor Noir dead during a duel following insults the prince had given two journalists. "*Chouette! chouette!*" (Cool! cool!), Rigault intoned, because a Bonaparte would finally stand trial. On January 12, 1870, political opponents of the regime transformed Noir's funeral into a massive demonstration against the empire attended by 100,000 people. Gustave Flourens, one of about 3,000 French Blanquists, attempted to turn the demonstration into an insurrection. Rigault also helped organize and lead the march, which included a few workers bearing pistols or iron bars under their blue tradesmen's smocks. Confronted by readied soldiers, the crowd dispersed. A court acquitted the emperor's cousin, condemning the two journalists to prison sentences. The acquittal did not surprise members of the Left; instead, it galvanized them.

IN AN ATTEMPT TO BOLSTER SUPPORT for his empire, in May 1870 Napoleon III resorted to that old Bonapartist—and later Gaullist—tactic of organizing a plebiscite with sneaky wording to attempt to reassert his authority. It asked French men if they approved of the liberal changes undertaken by the empire. A *non* could thus indicate opposition either to the emperor or to liberal reforms, such as the relaxation of censorship. Nationwide, 7.4 million men voted *oui*, and 1.5 million *non*, but in Paris the no vote carried by 184,000 to 128,000. Thus, in the capital the plebiscite fell far short of achieving its intended effect. The announcement of the results led to bloody demonstrations and pitched battles with the police, bringing several deaths.[43] The Second Empire and its opponents in Paris seemed on a collision course.

CHAPTER I

WAR AND THE
COLLAPSE OF THE EMPIRE

IN 1870, NAPOLEON III foolishly pushed France into war with Prussia and its South German allies, a war that would undermine his power, strengthen antigovernment sentiment, and lead to the collapse of the Second Empire. At issue was the candidacy of Prince Leopold—a member of the Prussian royal Hohenzollern family—for the vacant throne of Spain. If a Prussian became king of Spain, Hohenzollerns, rivals for European continental supremacy, would flank France, leaving potential enemies on the other side of the Pyrenees as well as across the Rhine.

But the French emperor had other reasons for wanting a war. The growing strength of republicans and socialists in France had further weakened his empire, which was still reeling from a foreign policy fiasco in Mexico in 1867, when the forces of President Benito Juárez defeated those of the French and executed Napoleon III's protégé, Maximilian, Mexico's would-be emperor. Napoleon III may have assumed that war with Prussia would bring a relatively easy victory and thereby enhance his prestige. It would not be the first time he had used war to that end; Napoleon had used French victories in the 1853–1856 Crimean War and against Austria in 1859 to remind his people and the rest of Europe of the strength of his empire. When dining with army officers in Châlons-sur-Marne in 1868, he provocatively hoisted a glass of German Rhineland Reisling and announced, "Gentlemen, I hope that you yourselves will shortly be harvesting this wine," as he nodded toward the east.[1]

In 1866, Napoleon III had badly underestimated the strength of the Prussian army and assumed that Habsburg Austria would emerge victorious in a short war that year for political supremacy in Central Europe.

He made the same mistake four years later. The creation of the North German Federation, dominated by Prussia following Austria's defeat, shifted the balance of power. Even after Prussia's victory, however, the French emperor had made forceful demands for territorial compensation in response to the increased might of a rival for power perched across the Rhine from Alsace. Specifically, he insisted on Prussian acquiescence to the possible annexation by France of Belgium and Luxembourg, which Britain and the other powers successfully opposed. Prussian chancellor Otto von Bismarck rejected written French demands.

In July 1870, under great French pressure, Prince Leopold withdrew his candidacy for the Spanish throne. Napoleon III demanded that King William I of Prussia formally apologize to France and promise that the Hohenzollerns would never again attempt to place one of their own on the throne of Spain. The French ambassador to Prussia, Count Vincent Bénédetti, aggressively and rudely put forward this insistence to the Prussian king in the spa town of Bad Ems. Bismarck responded with a telegram, later released to the press and known as the Ems Dispatch, forcefully embellishing what had occurred. Bismarck, whose father was a Prussian noble (Junker), had entered the Prussian bureaucracy after completing law school, where he had gained more prominence for his dueling scars than for his academic success. As prime minister of Prussia, he mastered domestic and international politics with his brand of realpolitik, the pursuit of national self-interest based on a shrewd assessment of all possibilities. The Ems Dispatch was a calculated maneuver to prime his country for war. The "Iron Chancellor" was now confident that a victorious war against France would lead to the unification of the German states under Prussian leadership.[2]

The story quickly spread in Prussia and other German states that the French ambassador had arrogantly insulted the king. In both Prussia and France, the mood was bellicose. Many ordinary Parisians also seemed to want war, including some republicans. Crowds sang "La Marseillaise," then forbidden in imperial France due to its association with republicanism and the French Revolution. One publisher's decision to produce a "French-German Dictionary for the Use of the French in Berlin" reflected the popular mood and the expectation of victory.[3] Egged on by his foreign minister, the duc de Gramont, and the Empress Eugénie, as well as a segment of the public, Napoleon III declared war on July 19, 1870.

The German states of Württemberg, Hesse, Baden, and Bavaria joined the Prussian side. France went to war without allies. Bismarck revealed to the British the document in which Napoleon III had demanded the annexation of Belgium and Luxembourg, an attempted power grab that Bismarck knew would anger the British and ensure their neutrality. Newly unified—at least in principle—Italy had not forgiven France for the absorption of Nice in 1860 following a plebiscite and was unwilling to come to her aid now. Gramont foolishly assumed that Austria would join France against its former enemy once French armies had moved into the Prussian Rhineland and Palatinate in southwestern Germany, but Austria stayed out of the fray.

Although it would face the Prussians alone, the French army seemed confident of victory. In addition to reaping victories in the Crimean War and against Austria in 1859, French troops had expanded imperial interests in Southeast Asia, giving the officer corps more experience in battle. The army hoped it could conveniently discount the debacle in Mexico of three years earlier.

But military complacency had set in, and traditional routines took over. The officer corps was ridden by cliques, intensified by tensions between aristocrats and men of ordinary social origins and expectations—members of the lower middle class, workers, and peasants. Furthermore, experience garnered in one-sided military campaigns in North Africa and Southeast Asia did not translate easily to European warfare.[4]

To make matters worse, French mobilization for war was chaotic. Trains carried regiments stationed all over the country to often distant mobilization points, a disorganized, inefficient, and painfully slow process. Reservists, summoned from their homes, had to be transported to regimental depots. The army of Alsace was notably short of supplies and funds, and some troops were openly hostile to their officers. Even proper topographical maps were unavailable or hard to locate. Commanders had only two-thirds the number of soldiers anticipated and lacked the massive reserves available to Prussia and its allies.

Prussian mobilization plans, on the other hand, were well in place. The military had taken control of Prussia's railways, public and private, and modernized them with particular attention to wartime needs. In contrast, the French high command had given little consideration to the crucial role of railroads so necessary for the rapid and efficient mobilization of troops. French troop trains moved on a single track and thus could only make transports in one direction at a time. Each day fifty Prussian trains pushed toward the front along double tracks on five main lines; the French managed to convey twelve.

Yet the French army had a new breech-loading rifle, the chassepot, which was superior to the rifles of the Prussian army because soldiers could carry many more of its smaller-caliber bullets. French troops also had an early version of the machine gun (*mitrailleuse*), rather like the Gatling gun of the American Civil War. A soldier fired its thirty-seven barrels, or "gun tubes," in rapid succession by quickly turning a hand crank. The gun soon picked up the nickname the "coffee grinder."

Not only did French commanders have little idea of the cohesive and organized Prussian general staff relentlessly overseen since 1857 by Helmuth von Moltke, but, incredibly, France had no head of the general staff. In principle the emperor commanded the army, and he assumed that his being Napoleon's nephew was enough. Napoleon III, unlike von Moltke, appears to have had no specific plan for waging the war against Prussia.

Within eighteen days after the declaration of war, Prussia and its South German allies had nearly 1.2 million troops at or near the border. One French general reported in panic by telegraph, "Have arrived at Belfort. Can't find my brigade. Can't find the divisional commander. What shall I do? Don't know where my regiments are." Demoralized French troops, many of them unwilling conscripts ill at ease among professional soldiers who had seen it all, seemed apathetic, playing cards and drinking heavily to bolster their spirits amid food shortages. Commanders were notoriously uninterested in their soldiers' conditions. Recently recalled reservists lacked sufficient training and sometimes commitment.[5]

Prussian tactics, developed in the war against Austria four years earlier, emphasized the quick and coordinated movement of units toward enemy positions, thus extending the field of battle. French commanders believed that sturdy lines of troops, armed with chassepots and machine guns, supported by artillery fire, would carry the day over the Prussian "needle-gun" with its inferior range. They seem to have been oblivious to the fact that the sturdy steel Prussian cannons, produced by the Krupp factories, were more powerful and accurate than the older French bronze artillery pieces and could be fired more rapidly. Moreover, von Moltke had made his batteries more mobile and thus responsive to changes in the enemy's positions. He had also gone to great length to modernize the cavalry, purging incompetent officers, despite their credentials as Prussian nobles. In contrast, aristocrats retained their privileged place in the French officer corps, no matter their incompetence.[6]

THE EMPEROR LEFT PARIS for Metz on July 28, appointing Empress Eugénie to serve as regent in his absence. On July 31, the French Army of the Rhine moved forward in a preemptive strike. French troops crossed the border and captured Saarbrücken, left virtually undefended because Prussian armies commanded by von Moltke had bigger fish to fry. This was the last French victory of any consequence. Two Prussian armies then moved into northern Lorraine and a third into northern Alsace. Prussian forces won hard-fought victories at Wissembourg on August 4, at Spicheren near the northern Vosges mountains the next day while Marshal Achille Bazaine's regiments were camped but nine miles away, and then at Woerth the day after that.

France's defeats were not overwhelming, and her enemy suffered many casualties; nonetheless they forced the French armies back. Prussian cannons rained shell after shell upon the French, with Prussian soldiers well out of range of French machine guns. Marshal Patrice de MacMahon retreated to Châlons-sur-Marne, and Bazaine, now named commander in chief, fell back to the fortress of Metz. Chaotic and sometimes ill-informed French orders flew back and forth. Bazaine moved his army in the direction of Verdun but found the route cut off by von Moltke.[7]

On August 18, the Prussian army, 188,000 strong, moved against French forces two-thirds that size under Bazaine's command. In the Battle of Gravelotte, fought just west of Metz, the Prussians inflicted 20,000 casualties (against 12,000 on the German side). Demoralization and acrimony followed the French armies after such defeats. In Saverne, tipsy soldiers insulted officers whom they found sitting comfortably in a café. Yet another loss made matters worse. The Prussian army besieged Metz, defeating the army commanded by MacMahon, who was trying to relieve Bazaine. There, some senior officers, disenchanted with Bazaine, plotted to organize, without the marshal's approval, an attempt to break out of Metz and engage the Prussians in battle. But the French commander got word of the plan, and it collapsed. For republicans, the incident took on a political tone because Bazaine, like other French commanders, had reached high military office through blatant imperial patronage.

As a Prussian siege of Paris now seemed inevitable, General Louis Trochu suggested to Napoleon III's war council withdrawing Bazaine's army to the outskirts of Paris, beyond the city's fortifications, to hold off the Prussians there. Six days later, the emperor arrived in

Châlons-sur-Marne to preside over a military meeting to determine whether to follow Trochu's plan. There he found confirmation of just how dire the army's situation had become: ostensibly beaten soldiers lounged about, "vegetating rather than living," as one officer put it, "scarcely moving even if you kicked them, grumbling at being disturbed in their sleep."[8] Napoleon III's army seemed resigned to defeat.

In Paris, where anxiety about a looming Prussian siege mixed with anger at the French military's miserable defeats, the atmosphere presented an opportunity to the political Left. On August 14, a group of Blanquists stood ready for revolution. Now, led by a young student, Émile Eudes, a group of Blanquists forced their way into a fire station at La Villette in northern Paris. Their attempt to spark an insurrection came to nothing when the firemen held on to their weapons and workers did not step forward to assist them. The insurgents rapidly retreated to their peripheral bastion of Belleville.[9]

On August 17, the emperor named Trochu military governor-general of the Paris region. The conservative's nomination seemed sheer provocation to most Parisians. Napoleon III had rejected Trochu's idea that Bazaine's forces return to defend Paris, believing that such a move would suggest near defeat and potentially endanger his empire. Instead of defending Paris from a Prussian siege, it seemed, the emperor was taking pains to check civil unrest, a move that only angered an already anxious populace. Nonetheless, Trochu immediately returned to Paris with 15,000 Parisian Mobile Guards (*Gardes Mobiles*), newly created companies of reservists, to ensure security in the capital.

French morale continued to falter. The arrival of Mobile Guards near the front increased tensions, in part because they had little military experience. They lounged around Châlons-sur-Marne and other camps in their shiny new uniforms, which contrasted with the increasingly tattered apparel of regular soldiers. Moreover, a number of senior officers with strong ties to the empire were now in the mood for peace, in part due to concern for their careers should more defeats follow. The ongoing French military catastrophe accentuated political tensions that had increased in the late 1860s between Bonapartist loyalists and republicans.[10]

After sending Trochu to Paris, the emperor ordered MacMahon to move his army from Châlons-sur-Marne to Reims, then changed the destination to Montmédy on the Belgian border. Napoleon III accompanied MacMahon, intending to organize a new army and march on Metz to relieve Bazaine's besieged forces. No French troops now stood between the Prussian armies and Paris, and Trochu, upon his arrival in Paris, found that the government had made almost no preparations to defend the capital.

Napoleon III's plan was quickly derailed. On August 30, von Moltke's army attacked, inflicting heavy casualties and forcing the army of 100,000 men to retreat to the fortress town of Sedan, near the Belgian border. The French army was surrounded. Napoleon III, weakened by illness, could barely stay on his horse. On September 1, the French army tried to break out of Sedan but suffered round defeat by the Prussians, losing more than 17,000 killed and wounded, with another 20,000 captured. The next day, the emperor and 100,000 of his soldiers surrendered.

As imperial armies floundered, the political truce, brought on by the war, between the empire and the republican opposition quickly evaporated. In Paris, revolution already appeared a distinct possibility, not least because the city's National Guard had grown in strength during the war and become an increasingly organized and militant republican force. As of September 12, national guardsmen received 1.50 francs per day, or *trente sous*; they later received an additional seventy-five centimes for a spouse and twenty-five for each child. Poorer families depended on this paltry sum to purchase food. National guardsmen elected their company officers, who in turn elected battalion commanders, workers and lower-middle-class men largely unknown outside their neighborhoods.[11]

The Left considered the National Guard—which had grown to 134 battalions during the Franco-Prussian War, incorporating somewhere between 170,000 and 200,000 men, perhaps more—a balance against the professional army, recently used by the imperial regime before the war to repress strikers. The majority of the units drew from the ranks of working-class Parisians, although fancy *quartiers* boasted elite units. Although the National Guard may not have had access to many chassepots, which the regular army held, it was armed and had cannons.

On September 3, Empress Eugénie received a terse message from Napoleon III: "The army has been defeated and surrendered. I myself am a prisoner." Her situation was not much better. Shouts against the empire already echoed in the streets, although many Parisians remained unaware of the defeat at Sedan. Eugénie offered provisional authority to Adolphe Thiers, who had served as prime minister from 1830 to 1840 under the Orleanist July Monarchy, but he refused, saying that nothing further could be done for the empire.[12]

Late on September 3, deputies of the imperial Legislative Body (Corps Législatif) meeting in the Palais Bourbon could hear shouts outside for the proclamation of the republic. In a general tumult, the moderate republican Jules Favre proclaimed the end of the empire well after midnight. Twenty-six deputies named a "government commission," with members yet to be determined, while maintaining Trochu as governor-general of Paris.

On the morning of September 4, a crowd moved from the place de la Concorde across the Seine to the Palais Bourbon. A count described the people he watched with condescension as belonging to "the most diverse classes," including women, "who, as always, were noteworthy for their enthusiastic, violent, and hysterical performances."[13]

Sutter-Laumann, an eighteen-year-old republican, went down from Montmartre to the boulevards, where he found people in a state of noisy agitation. Not long before, he had been arrested and beaten for giving a speech to a public gathering in an old dance hall on the boulevard Clichy. Now the word "treason" was in the air. On hearing that the Prussians had taken the emperor prisoner at Sedan, he walked to the place de la Concorde and sat on a sidewalk to reflect. "A triumphant clamor" moved toward him, shouting for a republic. The young man described his emotions as reflecting "a triple drunkenness: that of patriotism, that of wine, and that of love."[14]

At the Palais Bourbon, troops and the crowd eyed each other warily. Conservative national guardsmen drawn from nearby neighborhoods were also there, their bayonets glistening in the sun. Then, as late-arriving deputies appeared, someone opened the gates. Parisians stormed into the Palais Bourbon. There, debate raged: Favre's early-morning proclamation of the end of the empire competed with proposals put forth by the government and by Thiers, calling for the nomination of a "commission of the government and of national defense." Léon Gambetta, a radical anti-imperial activist, proclaimed a republic. Crowds then crossed the Seine, moving toward the Hôtel de Ville, that "superb Louvre of revolutions" that had come to symbolize revolutionary Paris. A number of prominent radical Jacobin republicans and socialists were already there, including the old *quarante-huitards* (Forty-Eighters), veterans of the Revolution of 1848.[15] Jacobins were an amorphous group of nationalist republicans, inspired by the French Revolution and the role Paris had played in it, who espoused direct democracy and believed that the centralized state ought to look out for citizens' welfare.

Later on September 4, Gambetta proclaimed the republic for a second time, cheered by the throngs below. The crowd had forced the release from prison of Henri Rochefort, a strident but erratic opponent of the imperial regime. The republican crowd saluted him in triumph. Gambetta proclaimed himself minister of the interior, and Favre took on the role of minister of foreign affairs. Rochefort joined the list as the only member of the Left. Two days after Napoleon III's defeat at Sedan, his Second Empire had collapsed and the Third Republic been established.

WITH PRUSSIAN ARMIES moving toward Paris, challenges plagued the new republic from the start. Serious divisions between moderates and radicals became immediately apparent, as Paris assumed the right to speak for the rest of the country, much of which was far more conservative than the capital. The extremely moderate political composition of the provisional Government of National Defense particularly outraged those Blanquists present, but their voices were barely audible in the chaos.[16]

Most Parisians believed that only a republic could save France. Members of the Government of National Defense—a name designed to suggest political neutrality—feared another Parisian insurrection and were determined to elbow aside radical republicans and socialists. A Bonapartist wrote in his diary that "the internal dangers were dreaded as much as the Prussians."[17] The new administration kept Trochu on as the interim president of the government to reassure conservatives and moderates; he made clear his commitment to "God, Family, and Property." In the meantime, Paris took on a festive air, its people confident that republican unity, unlike the regime of Napoleon III and Eugénie, would ultimately defeat the Prussians.

Empress Eugénie fled Paris, leaving behind empty jewel boxes tossed to the floor in haste, as well as an unfinished, elegantly prepared meal that "revolutionaries" finished upon storming into the Tuileries.[18] Fearing both Prussian troops and a republic, many other wealthy residents also took the easy way out, leaving the more prosperous western arrondissements for the safety of country houses. As they did workmen replaced Paris signs announcing "rue du 10 décembre," the date Louis Napoleon Bonaparte had been elected president in 1848, with "rue du 4 septembre," still the name today. Hammers pounded out the "N" for "Napoleon" on bridges and stone monuments.

The Left mobilized quickly. Raoul Rigault, who had been hiding in Versailles from the police, arrived in Paris on September 5, the day after the proclamation of the republic. That day, members of "vigilance committees," which radical republicans had created in each arrondissement demanded elections for a municipal government. Ten days later, a red poster (*affiche rouge*) repeated this demand. Rigault and other Blanquists began feverishly planning an insurrection. They rushed to the Mazas prison near the Gare de Lyon, freeing Eudes and several other political prisoners. Rigault then went to the prefecture of police and installed himself as head of security. He combed through documents in the police archives to uncover the names of those who had worked as imperial police spies, in the hope of later punishing them. Given his obsession with the police, Rigault was the perfect person for the job. Blanqui described his ardent disciple as having "a vocation. . . . He was born to be Prefect of Police."[19]

Now, as Prussian armies neared Paris, France was a divided, fledgling republic. Many on the left believed the circumstances might provide an opportunity to establish a radical, progressive republic. Reconstituted Parisian political clubs joined the chorus. Plebeian Paris led the way. On September 6, Jules Vallès, a radical journalist, organized a club in Belleville. It met in the Salle Favié, a bastion of the public meeting movement before the war. In Montmartre in the Eighteenth Arrondissement, André Léo (Victoire Léodile Béra, a writer who took the names of her twin sons) and Nathalie Le Mel (a bookbinder, a frequent orator in the public meeting movement, and one of the founders of a consumers' cooperative in Montmartre) were among the militant women devoted to the cause of defending Paris, working-class families, and the republic. There the *mairie* (the town hall of the arrondissement) provided some social services in response to letters written by working-class women asking for assistance and reflecting the women's suffering as they tried to make do for themselves and their families with the help of friends and neighbors.[20] In the Thirteenth Arrondissement, the Club Démocratique Socialiste announced it would study "all of the social and political problems related to the emancipation of work and of workers," while remaining vigilant against any attempt to restore monarchy. With Prussian forces besieging Paris, the Arrondissement Vigilance Committees selected "delegates" to a Central Vigilance Committee dominated by left-wing republicans and socialists. The Central

Committee of the Twenty Arrondissements held its first meeting on September 11. It gradually evolved into the equivalent of a party of the Left, committed to the republic and to continuing the war. Blanquists were active in the Central Committee, meeting in clubs in Montmartre and in the Sixth Arrondissement.[21]

In September the word "Commune" began to be heard in the context of the "revolutionary nationalism" that followed the outbreak of the war. The historical precedent was the "revolutionary Commune" that took power in August 1792, when foreign states had laid siege to France. Now demands for popular sovereignty and Parisian self-government emerged as part of the definition of a desirable "Commune," even as Prussian troops threatened the capital. For the political Left, the Commune's role would include undertaking major social reforms. Thus the word "Commune" had different meanings for different people, depending on their allegiances.[22]

On September 15, the Central Committee of the Twenty Arrondissements signed a wall poster calling for the arming of all Parisians and "popular control" over defense, food supply, and lodgings. This was part of an explosion of demands for municipal autonomy in the early days of the republic, a desire that had emerged in the context of heavy-handed imperial centralization under Napoleon III. Calls for municipal autonomy were even louder given the threat of a Prussian invasion. In the tradition of the French Revolution and, most recently, of the public meeting movement that had begun in 1868, republicans believed that popular organization alone would permit the defense of Paris against enemy troops surrounding the city. Political clubs and the vigilance committees therefore called for an "all-out war" (*guerre à l'outrance*) in defense of Paris. To make things a little easier for ordinary Parisians readying for war, on September 30 the Government of National Defense declared a moratorium on the payment of rents and instructed the municipal pawnshop (Mont-de-Piété) to return pawned items worth less than fifteen francs at no cost.[23]

The armies of Prussia and its allies laid siege to Paris beginning on September 19, while other enemy forces moved away from the city toward the Loire River. On October 10, a Prussian force of 28,000 men attacked a position held by the reconstituted French Army of the Loire, its numbers swollen by a flood of volunteers. The Prussian troops carried the day and captured Orléans. The French army withdrew, grew in strength to about 70,000 men, and retook that city. However, the arrival of more Prussian troops from northeastern France led to more French defeats in the Loire River region and at Le Mans on January 11 and 12, 1871.[24]

In the meantime, the Prussians had allowed Napoleon III to depart for exile in Great Britain, the third French head of state (following King Charles X after the Revolution of 1830 and King Louis-Philippe after that of 1848) to be sent packing across the English Channel.

The Government of National Defense named new mayors for each arrondissement. The Republican Central Committee of the Twenty Arrondissements demanded participation in decisions concerning the defense of Paris. National Guard units began to tighten their organization and imposed their authority in the neighborhoods from which they had been recruited.

One Parisian, Félix Belly, opened up an office hoping to attract 30,000 women, enough to fill ten battalions, each comprising eight companies. Members of these all-female defense units would wear black pants and blouses, as well as black hats with orange bands, and they would promise not to drink or smoke. Belly's egalitarian battalions never materialized, however. He briefly needed protection from neighbors who complained about noise, and the plan quickly evaporated when Trochu banned the new units.[25]

The young republican Sutter-Laumann, conscripted into the army, described the strange sense of security that existed in Paris during the siege. Army strategists had assumed that the exterior forts would keep the Prussian troops at bay, but they would soon be proven wrong. Sutter-Laumann's baptism by fire occurred during a sortie on the route de Neuilly-sur-Marne, followed by several other episodes of fighting. The Parisian population began to manifest "considerable irritation," Sutter-Laumann noticed, as Prussian troops easily fended off the sorties.[26]

In early October, Gambetta, the minister of the interior, courageously flew over the Prussian lines in a balloon and raised a sizable army that continued the fight the enemy. Then incredible news arrived from Lorraine. On October 27, Bazaine inexplicably surrendered his army of 155,000 soldiers at Metz, virtually ending any hope of relieving the besieged Parisians and defeating the Prussians and their allies. Rumors of treason abounded, particularly when the French commander's secret negotiations with his Prussian counterparts became known.

Parisians were quick to react. On October 31, Sutter-Laumann heard shouts of "Long live the Commune!" in the faubourg Saint-Denis, as Paris, hungry and freezing, held out. Angry workers charged down the hill from Belleville and other plebeian *quartiers* into central Paris and to the Hôtel-de-Ville, goaded by members of radical clubs and vigilance committees who called for insurrection. Blanquists stormed into the Hôtel-de-Ville. Gustave Lefrançais, a National Guard officer, jumped on a table and declared the end of the Government of National Defense, just two months after it had been proclaimed. The militants announced a new government headed by old names from the Revolution of 1848: Félix Pyat and Charles Delescluze, as well as the inveterate revolutionary Auguste Blanqui. Gustave Flourens arrived with some national guardsmen and pushed Lefrançais off center stage, adding new members to the government. Flourens and Lefrançais hated each other, and the latter simply went home. Rigault had arrived as well, and Blanqui ordered him to take men to the prefecture of police to secure it.

Soon, however, the workers returned to their *quartiers* in north and northeastern Paris, many thinking that they had succeeded in overthrowing the provisional government, and only Flourens's group of guardsmen remained at the Hôtel-de-Ville. Trochu and Jules Ferry, another member of the provisional government, took advantage of the crowd's departure and the next day regained control of the municipal building. Blanqui barely escaped a manhunt organized by the police of the reestablished Government of National Defense.[27]

Following the October 31 attempted insurrection, militants organized even more political clubs, driven as much by political desires as by despair during the ongoing siege. Hunger gnawed as soaring food prices defied arrondissement officials' best efforts to deal with the situation by handing out ration cards and distributing what food they could find. Club speakers denounced hoarders and made more heated demands for a "revolutionary Commune." The results of a plebiscite on November 3 and municipal elections two days later may have reflected the ascendancy of moderate voices, but they did nothing to still the militancy of the Left, increasingly based in working-class *quartiers*. Some arrondissement mayors encouraged the creation of producers' cooperatives and vigilance committees that played a role in the allocation of food and weapons. Blanquists and other revolutionaries began to form their own clubs, firming up the relationship between militant intellectuals like Rigault and Parisian workers.[28]

At the beginning of the siege, Parisian families rode the train around Paris's walled circumference and picnicked near the ramparts, until they realized that Prussian shells could actually kill them. The Scientific Committee of the Government of National Defense received many suggestions early on about how Parisians might extricate themselves from the siege. The ideas submitted were laughable and included letting loose "all the more ferocious beasts from the zoo—so that the enemy would be poisoned, asphyxiated, or devoured." One writer proposed the construction of a "musical *mitrailleuse*" that would lure unsuspecting Prussian soldiers by playing Wagner and Schubert, then mow them down; another advocated arming Paris's thousands of prostitutes with "prussic fingers"—needles filled with poison that would be injected into the Prussians at a crucial moment during a close encounter.[29]

But reality set in after Bazaine's surrender, as the siege continued and the weather worsened. Sixty-five balloon flights over enemy lines transported the only mail going in or out of Paris. Pigeons carried messages beyond the Prussian lines. By late October, all became deadly serious, as the weather became unbearably cold—the Seine froze—and food supplies dwindled. A military attempt to break out of Paris—a "*grande sortie*"—and inflict damage on enemy forces failed miserably on October 31, the same day as the failed political insurrection. The French lost more than 5,000 troops, twice more than their German adversaries.

Edmond de Goncourt wrote in his journal on December 8, "People are talking only of what they eat, what they can eat, and what there is to eat. . . . Hunger begins and famine is on the horizon." Signs advertising "canine and feline butchers" began to appear. Pet owners had to guard their dogs, rather than the reverse. Mice and even rats became meals; one American claimed that the latter tasted rather like a bird. Slices of zoo animals, such as bear, deer, antelope, and giraffe, ended up on Parisian plates. The very elderly and very young suffered most, with the sight of small coffins being carried through the streets becoming increasingly common.[30]

The long siege had further isolated Paris—politically as well as economically—from the provinces, particularly the west of France. In Paris the conservative *L'Opinion Nationale* on January 1 regretted that some *quartiers* had fallen into the hands of "*Communeux*," reflecting a bourgeois fear that "evoked the Terror" of the French Revolution. For conservatives who remained in Paris, any mention of a "Commune" took on a terrifying aspect.[31]

On the morning of January 6, Parisians awoke to see another bright red poster plastered on the buildings; it read, "Make way for the Paris Commune!" Rigault was among the signatories of this *affiche rouge*. The Club Favié of Belleville approved the resolution: "The Commune is the right of the people. . . . [I]t is the *levée en masse* [mass conscription] and the punishment of traitors. The Commune, finally . . . is the Commune." In club meetings the term "Commune" was still used to refer to municipal rights, but now with an even more progressive turn, with Paris and its teeming working-class neighborhoods imagined as the center of a democratic and social republic. The vigilance committee of the Eighteenth Arrondissement proclaimed, "The *quartiers* are the fundamental base of the democratic Republic."[32]

Another military defeat heightened calls for a Commune. On January 19, a force of 100,000 troops commanded by Trochu attempted to break out of Paris and defeat Prussian forces. The catastrophic result—more than 4,000 men killed or wounded—led to a frenzied demonstration that verged on insurrection on January 22. Crowds shouted against Trochu. Blanquists called for the proclamation of a Commune, as Blanqui himself sat in a café near the Hôtel-de-Ville, from whose windows shots, ordered by the moderate republican Gustave Chaudey, a friend of Rigault, greeted the demonstrators. The gunfire left five dead on the pavement below, including another of Rigault's friends, Théophile Sapia, his blood drenching Rigault. The crowd quickly dispersed, but this latest mobilization of the Left and the violence that followed only increased the gap between the militants and conservatives in the Government of National Defense.[33]

ON JANUARY 28, the Government of National Defense agreed to an armistice with the Prussians and their allies that would finally end the siege. Jules Favre signed the surrender two days later, meeting Bismarck in Versailles. Paris had held on for four months, but Prussian cannons had destroyed parts of the city, and Parisians had suffered enormously. Unsurprisingly, most Parisians remained opposed to any concessions to the Prussians, although Bismarck now allowed convoys of food to enter the capital. The harsh terms of the armistice outraged Parisians, as well as many other Frenchmen. France would owe an enormous indemnity to the new German Empire, proclaimed, to France's great humiliation, in the Hall of Mirrors at the Château de Versailles. Even worse, according to the Treaty of Versailles signed by Thiers and Bismarck on February 26—later formalized by the Treaty of Frankfurt on May 10—France would cede the relatively prosperous region of Alsace and much of Lorraine to Germany.[34] Léon Gambetta resigned in disgust from what remained of the Government of National Defense on March 1. Prussian forces remained camped around Paris, with ready access to the city.

After the armistice, the French Government of National Defense, which had utterly failed in its mission to defend France, immediately called for elections for a new National Assembly, which would create a new regime. Despite protests from republicans that such a short time between military capitulation and elections would favor monarchists, the latter were scheduled for early February. Republicans and socialists, now clearly threatened by the possibility that monarchists would dominate the new National Assembly, organized a Central Committee of the National Guard to defend the republic.[35] They appeared ready to take matters into their own hands.

The national elections on February 8, with their somewhat aberrant results due to the exceptional circumstances and lack of preparation, returned overwhelmingly conservative, monarchist deputies to the National Assembly, which would meet in Bordeaux, not Paris. In sharp contrast, thirty-six of forty-three deputies elected from Paris were republicans, most of whom believed that France, led by their city, should keep fighting the Prussians. Yet in Paris, revolutionary candidates won only 50,000 of 329,000 votes (15.2 percent) and returned only seven of forty-three representatives. *Le Rappel*, on February 8, commented, "It is no longer an army you are facing. . . . [I]t is no longer Germany. . . . It is more. It is monarchy, it is despotism."[36] On cue, on February 17, 1871, the National Assembly meeting in Bordeaux voted to give Adolphe Thiers executive powers.

Although perhaps identified with the Parisian bourgeoisie, Thiers, born out of wedlock in Marseille in 1797, remained Provençal in some ways. His father, Louis, a hustler who compromised the family's status and wealth, had disappeared. With the help of a partial scholarship, Thiers entered lycée in Marseille in 1809. Absorbed by liberal politics, in November 1815 he began law school in Aix-en-Provence.

When the newspaper *Le Constitutionnel*, a moderate royalist newspaper critical of the Bourbon monarchy, offered him a position, Thiers moved to Paris. A contract to write a history of the Revolution earned him money, and he made useful salon contacts in the capital.

Relatively small at five feet, two inches and anything but handsome, Thiers had little patience for anyone else. The poet Lamartine recalled, "He speaks first, he speaks last, he doesn't pay much attention to any reply." Thoroughly from the Midi, he spoke quickly and colorfully, with a Marseillais accent leaning on the last syllable, accompanied by rapid gesticulations for emphasis. He had a solemn voice as orator and seemed to an admirer "graced with an almost divine authority." Ambitious and hardworking, he had a reputation for garrulousness and cutting retorts. He may also have had a Napoleon complex, if indeed there is such a thing. Even a friend noted that Thiers reacted to anyone who "refused him blind confidence" with outrage and verbal violence.[37]

THE ELECTION OF A NATIONAL ASSEMBLY dominated by monarchists and led by Thiers, whom many people on the left had reason not to trust, increased tension and galvanized revolutionaries in Paris. On February 15 a crowd of working-class Parisians stormed into the archbishop's palace. Archbishop Georges Darboy asked what the people intended, telling them that if they were eying the furniture, it all belonged to the state. As for the books, he pointed out, they were precious to him but not to them. All that remained was his life. The Parisians left him alone.[38]

On February 20, three days after the National Assembly granted Thiers executive powers, André Léo left Paris to try to convince peasants that they too would suffer under a monarchist-dominated National Assembly, in opposition to which the Left within Paris also began to unite. The Central Committee of the Twenty Arrondissements and members of Karl Marx's International Workingmen's Association found much to agree on. For his part, Rigault also reached out to moderates with the goal of building a coalition capable of seizing power. A Revolutionary Socialist Party, based in radical clubs, and the arrondissement vigilance committees, emerged during these heady days, its adherents expressing determination to achieve social equality in Paris. A Declaration of Principles announced that it sought "by all possible means the suppression of the privileges of the bourgeoisie, its downfall as the directing class, and the political advent of workers—in a word, social equality."[39]

Of course, German troops still surrounded much of the capital, their cannons stretching beyond the northern and eastern walls of the city. Not enough stood between them and entry into Paris, should signs of resistance to the armistice materialize. Republicans in Paris were wary of Prussian troops, and not simply because they posed a military threat. Parisian republicans also feared that they could well help restore the monarchy.

Radical Republicans were right to question the future of republicanism under Thiers. He had earlier indicated that he supported a restoration of the monarchy, although he did not say which one: Bourbon, supported by the Legitimists, or Orleanist, in the person of a son of Louis-Philippe, overthrown in 1848. This explains why the National Assembly, dominated by monarchists, elected him "head of the executive authority of the republic" when it convened in Bordeaux in February 1871. But Thiers also enjoyed increasing support from conservative republicans. In 1850, he had expressed the belief that "the republic is the regime that divides us the least." This now seemed particularly true, given the mistrust between Legitimists and Orleanists. Legitimists would accept a restoration on their terms, insisting that the white flag of the Bourbons be maintained. With the heir to the Bourbon throne, the count of Chambord, childless, the Legitimists suggested that on his death the throne could pass to the Orleanists, with a transition to the tricolor flag. The Bourbon pretender refused. Amid the tension between the two families, Thiers tried to assure moderate republicans that he was not "the instrument of a plot formed in the National Assembly to abolish the Republic."[40] Yet most Parisians suspected Thiers of intending to do just that, even if the government he established did not reflect monarchist domination of the National Assembly. Moreover, three commanders of the army—conservative Bonapartists Joseph Vinoy, Patrice de MacMahon, and Gaston Galliffet—would unquestionably prefer a monarchy to a republic.[41]

The collective memory of previous revolutions remained powerful in Paris, and the next demonstration against the National Assembly occurred on an important date. On the anniversary of the Revolution of February 24, 1848, a huge crowd formed at the place de la Bastille, surrounding the Victory Column erected following the July Revolution of 1830. Two days later, passersby saw an undercover policeman observing them near the Seine. They grabbed him and—egged on by shouts of "Into the water! Into the water!"—tied his arms and legs and threw him into the river from the quai Henri IV. When he bobbed to the surface, they pushed him under until he drowned. Many Parisians hated the police, and assaults on policemen had occurred from time to time.[42] On this occasion, however, the attack took on political significance. That evening, a crowd of Parisians outnumbered soldiers watching over National Guard cannons at the place Wagram and hauled the guns up to the heights of Montmartre. Meanwhile, crowds rushed the Saint-Pélegie prison to free political prisoners. To put down the rioting crowds, General Vinoy, commander of the Paris region, called up what he considered reliable units of the National Guard, most of whom openly opposed the new government. Few men responded.

The Parisian National Guard was not a professional military force, instead consisting of ordinary men proud to defend their city and the *quartiers* from which they had been mobilized. Indeed, it seemed that during the Franco-Prussian War, the remnants of the empire feared the largely plebeian National Guard more than the Prussian army. The abolition of the French army, which had disappointed all of France with its defeat in the war, was essential to the Commune's vision of the new Paris, in which the National Guard would ensure the defense of the capital.

The new Central Committee of the National Guard had emerged as a revolutionary authority in the weeks after the armistice. It demanded that the National Guard retain its weapons, including, above all, its cannons, some of which the units had purchased themselves and many of which now stood on Montmartre or in Belleville. One committee member insisted that the National Guard represented "an inexorable barrier erected against any attempt to reverse the Republic."[43] Clearly, given its composition, the provisional government of Thiers could not count on the National Guard as an effective repressive force in the face of mounting popular political anger and mobilization. Of 260 National Guard battalions in Paris, only about 60 could be counted to defend "order" as Thiers defined it.[44]

THE ARRIVAL OF GERMAN TROOPS IN PARIS on February 27 reminded seething Parisians yet again of the stunning French military defeat and humiliating armistice terms. Four days later citizens who happened to be near the Arc de Triomphe watched in anger as several French officers climbed out of carriages with German ladies on their arms. Republican Paris radicalized, infuriated by the ostensible cowardice, if not duplicity, of Thiers and the Government of National Defense in capitulating. Paris seemed to be moving in a very different direction from much of the rest of France.[45]

Demonstrations occurred almost daily at the place de la Bastille, as Parisians prepared for the departure of German troops following their triumphant march down the Champs-Élysées on March 3. The presence of tens of thousands of French troops, many undisciplined and eagerly awaiting demobilization, also stretched Paris's resources.

Many officers were young and recently promoted. As with the men under their command, their loyalty to Thiers and the National Assembly was not assured. Political allegiances mattered little to French soldiers distracted by poverty and hunger. One observer witnessed "the most lamentable of spectacles. Soldiers wandering about . . . their uniforms sullied, disheveled, without weapons, some of them stopping passersby asking for some money."[46]

Soon after the Prussian troops departed, the new government passed laws that seemed a blatant affront to struggling Parisians. On March 7, the National Assembly ended the moratorium declared by the Government of National Defense on items deposited at the municipal pawnshop, which could now sell any goods not reclaimed. But reclaimed with what? Most Parisians had no money. The London *Times* reported that "2,300 poor wretches had pawned their mattresses, and starving seamstresses had pawned 1,500 pairs of scissors. . . . How many necessities to existence were stored away in these cruel galleries? . . . [T]he gaunt secret frowning on us from every loaded shelf . . . starvation!" The Assembly also ended the moratorium on the payment of bills of exchange (promissory notes requiring that funds owed be paid), adding that holders must redeem them with interest during the next four months. This move had devastating consequences for Parisian businessmen of modest means. At least 150,000 Parisians immediately defaulted on bills they owed. Of 260 National Guard battalions in Paris, only about 60 could be counted to defend "order" as Thiers defined it. Worse, the assembly ended the moratorium on the payment of rent—families who could not pay up could be expelled. This hit ordinary Parisians hard—the vast majority of the population rented their lodgings. Not satisfied with these moves against the poor, the assembly ended the daily stipend of 1.50 francs for national guardsmen, leaving tens of thousands of families without enough money to buy food and fuel.[47]

On March 10, the National Assembly decided to meet in Versailles, formerly the capital of kings. The fort of Mont-Valérien stood nearby to offer protection. In Thiers's provocative words, "Honesty would not allow me to promise the Assembly complete safety in Paris." Thiers immediately met with mayors or municipal council members from Lyon, Marseille, Toulouse, and other major cities. He blamed Paris for revolutionary activity, while assuring the other cities' leaders of his support for a republic as a way of undercutting their possible support for the insurgent capital.[48]

When Thiers and his government set up shop in Versailles, the Germans had only recently departed the former capital of the Bourbon monarchs. Versailles in some ways resembled, in the words of conservative republican Jules Simon, a city of "German taverns, [with] the smell of tobacco, beer, and leather." The orderly Prussians had destroyed nothing, leaving only a few signs in German at the railway station and on the walls of the barracks.[49]

Versailles opened its arms to Thiers, the National Assembly, and the wealthy *beau monde* fleeing an increasingly turbulent Paris. Viscount Camille de Meaux was struck by the contrast between between the somber thoughts of those so preoccupied by the challenges facing France in the wake of humiliating defeat and the fancy folk in Versailles heated up by good meals in the former capital of the Bourbons. Government officials, deputies, diplomats, military officers, journalists, and people seeking posts swarmed through boulevards practically deserted since 1789. The Château de Versailles became sort of a "ministerial beehive" that took over vast rooms of marble and superb salons decorated with renowned paintings and magnificent ceilings.[50]

Despite the wealth of most of those arriving in Versailles, whose population jumped from about 40,000 to about 250,000, it became difficult to find suitable lodgings. Newcomers complained of poorly furnished rooms with hard beds, but the restaurants of the capital of the Bourbons welcomed diners with empty stomachs and full wallets. During the first week of the Commune, people trying to leave glutted the railway stations of Paris—it seemed like *le grand départ* of the summer months in normal times.

Exiled Parisians found in Versailles "their newspapers, their restaurants, their clubs, their gentlemanly relations, and even their bankers." Charles Laffitte ran into a friend from Paris's exclusive Jockey Club now dressed in relative "tatters." High financiers turned up in the salons of Versailles, including Baron Rothschild. Hector Pessard, editor in chief of *Le Soir,* described "the artillery of Veuve Clicquot firing popping [champagne] corks against restaurant ceilings." However, at the beginning he found only "a mob . . . uniquely preoccupied with particular interests." More troops arrived every day in Versailles, and France's elite bought them drinks and cigars. On Easter Sunday, the Abbé du Marhallac'h, deputy from Morbihan, said Mass before a huge throng on the plateau de Satory, raising the host on an altar complete with military trappings, "a truly grand spectacle . . . under a radiant sky, around a priest who blesses and who prays."[51]

Paris, just a few months earlier home to France's government and its wealthiest families, had come under the control of ordinary people who demanded municipal rights and social reform. France's defeat in the Franco-Prussian War had brought an end to Napoleon III's regime, and the long siege of Paris that followed his surrender only angered the city's citizens, long critical of their emperor. Radicalized by the war, working-class Parisians and republican and socialist intellectuals alike would no longer stand for centralized government oppression. When Thiers and the National Assembly, dominated by monarchist and conservative members, seemed poised to reinstate a monarchy, Parisian republicans—supported by potentially revolutionary National Guard units—were prepared to run the city themselves.

CHAPTER 2

THE BIRTH OF
THE COMMUNE

With Adolphe Thiers's government convening in the grand chateau of the Bourbon monarchy, republicans had even more reason to worry about a possible monarchist restoration. The government's move to Versailles, for centuries identified with the close alliance of the Bourbon monarchy and the Catholic Church, further inflamed popular opinion. Thiers had once asserted, "I want to make the clergy's influence all powerful, because I am counting on it to propagate that good philosophy that teaches man that he is here below to suffer, and not that other philosophy that tells man the opposite; take pleasure."[1] On March 11, 1871, the Versailles government banned six newspapers of the Left. This news reached Paris after word came that a court-martial had condemned to death in absentia Auguste Blanqui and another popular revolutionary, Gustave Flourens, for their roles in the attempted insurrection of October 31 during the Prussian siege.

Parisians mobilized against the provisional government sending out decrees from Versailles, and government troops spent much of late February and early March reacting to riotous crowds. General Joseph Vinoy's forces, limited by the armistice with the Prussians to 12,000 troops and 3,000 gendarmes, had already dispersed several demonstrations. Vinoy, who had left a seminary to enter the army as a young man and whose temperament was as chilly as the Alps of his native region of Dauphiné, believed "ringleaders," "the lowest of the low," and "guilty agitators" were taking over Paris, intent on "pillage" and sowing "disorder." The US ambassador, Elihu B. Washburne, realized that the government was losing control of the capital; on March 16, he sent a dispatch to Washington relating that "the insurrectionists of Paris are gaining in power and strength every hour."[2]

On March 17, Thiers decided to move against the Parisian militants. He would send troops early the next morning to capture the National Guard cannons, most of which had been moved to Montmartre (171 cannons) or Belleville (74 cannons), *quartiers populaires*—predominantly neighborhoods of workers—from which they could dominate the city. Thiers made his decision for economic as well as political reasons. He explained, "Businessmen were going around constantly repeating that the financial operations would never be started until all those wretches were finished off and their cannons taken away. An end had to be put to all this, and then one could get back to business." A crowd had thwarted Thiers's troops' first attempt on Montmartre on March 12. To the citizens of that *quartier*, the National Guard's cannons represented Paris's right to arm itself. They would stop at nothing to keep the guns from government troops. Thiers's officers, meanwhile, hurriedly prepared a plan to occupy the city.[3]

On Montmartre, the cannons still stood in two rows on the heights and on a plateau further down the butte. Four days after the first attempt, national guardsmen countered soldiers once again trying to retrieve some of the guns under Thiers's orders. Thiers decided to have the cannons brought down early on March 18 in order to "disarm Paris" and its "revolutionary party." The task at hand was exceedingly difficult, requiring soldiers to seize the cannons and haul them down the steep, narrow cobblestone streets through hostile neighborhoods.

On the evening of March 17, Thiers's head of the Paris National Guard, General Louis d'Aurelle de Paladines, an old Bonapartist suspected of having switched allegiance to the Bourbons, convoked commanders of about thirty or forty conservative National Guard units and ordered them to have their men ready the next morning. At about 4:30 A.M. on March 18, troops under Vinoy were in place to begin bringing down the National Guard cannons from Montmartre. Soldiers commanded by General Claude Lecomte also went up to Montmartre from the north. A column of about 4,000 men under the command of General Bernard de Susbielle was to set up a command post at the place Pigalle. Another column was to take control of Belleville, while a division was to remain below and ensure control of the neighborhoods between the Hôtel-de-Ville and the place de la Bastille.[4]

Very early in the morning, as women in these neighborhoods went out to buy bread, they found themselves face-to-face with soldiers clad in the red pants, blue tunics, and red-and-blue caps of the regular army. Georges Clemenceau, mayor of the Eighteenth Arrondissement, angered to see soldiers when he left his apartment at about 6 A.M., expressed his "extreme surprise and disappointment" to one of the commanders. Thiers had ordered the military operation without notifying the arrondissement mayors, who had tried to achieve the peaceful surrender of the cannons without a show of force by Thiers's provisional government. For the moment, however, all was calm, and some residents of Montmartre chatted amiably with troops in a light Parisian rain.[5]

From the place Clichy, soldiers commanded by Susbielle and led by gendarmes who knew the streets of Montmartre, moved to secure the cannons standing near the Moulin de la Galette and the Château Rouge, as well as to occupy the Tour Solferino. General Lecomte's soldiers were to take control of the cannons standing near the large dance hall at Château Rouge. Troops blocked entry to the Church of Saint-Pierre, preventing the ringing of the tocsin to alert Parisians and republican National Guard troops to the threat. By 6 A.M., General Lecomte's force held the butte of Montmartre. Soldiers set up posts on the eastern and southern slopes of the hill to facilitate the descent of the cannons in case of trouble, pushing aside the national guardsmen assigned to protect them. They posted a proclamation from Thiers explaining that reclamation of the cannons was "indispensable to the maintenance of order." The proclamation also stated that Thiers wanted to eliminate the "insurrectionary committee," which he insisted existed, whose members were almost all unknown and promulgated "Communist" doctrines while preparing to turn Paris over to pillage.[6]

In the meantime, residents of Montmartre got into several churches, climbing into steeples to sound the tocsin. Parisians poured into the streets. At the place Saint-Pierre, soldiers filled in small trenches dug to thwart easy movement of the guns, while onlookers, including men in work clothes, expressed hostility. Although troops had arrived several hours earlier, the guns were still in place. About 2,000 horses needed to haul the cannons down from Montmartre had not yet turned up; nor did they have enough coupling attachments to hitch the horses to the guns.[7]

In Belleville, word spread that line troops had come to take the cannons, including some standing in the park of Ménilmontant. Several strongly republican National Guard units were already afoot, arriving at the rue Puebla as troops were hauling cannons toward the rue de Belleville. Belleville residents and National Guard troops began to construct impromptu barricades to prevent troops from moving the guns through the streets. Many of the soldiers had turned their rifles upside down, signaling that they would not use them. When government drums began to beat, summoning National Guard units considered reliable, no guardsmen came to join their commanders.

At the *mairie* of Belleville, an English correspondent for the London *Times* came upon a platoon of cavalry armed with three *mitrailleuses* and stationed near the cannons with horses standing nearby, looking like it intended to fight. But hostility quickly evaporated into fraternization, as nearby residents began building a barricade and the troops made no move to stop them. Finally at about 11 A.M. the small detachment headed toward Buttes-Chaumont, where it stopped. Going back to Montmartre, the Englishman noticed that "there was not a red trouser [the color of the French soldiers' pants] to be seen, excepting here and there a straggler making a fraternal speech to an admiring audience. . . . These streets, so deserted in the morning, excepting here and there a slinking warrior, were now swarming with them, drums were beating, bugles blowing, and all the din of victory."[8]

The uneasy peace between soldiers and guardsmen did not last for long. A confrontation erupted after troops surprised guardsmen, who opened fire, wounding a cavalryman. One national guardsman, a man called Turpin, challenged gendarmes and was shot and mortally wounded. Several other guardsmen were captured and held in the Tour de Solferino. A few managed to get away and spread the alarm. Soldiers and horses managed to begin hauling two convoys of guns down the hill from Montmartre. A crowd stopped a third on the rue Lepic, but soldiers managed to clear the way, and the convoy made it all the way down and across the Seine to the École Militaire on the Left Bank. Elsewhere, nothing went smoothly for the troops. A detachment moving toward the Moulin de la Galette found its way blocked by national guardsmen who called out to the troops to join them. One guardsman gave an officer a rifle-butt blow to the head, while some soldiers made their way quickly down the hill. At the place Pigalle, shots from national guardsmen killed a captain who had ordered his troops to clear the area.[9]

When Clemenceau went to the National Guard headquarters at about 7:30 A.M., he came upon Louise Michel, who had been active in the Eighteenth Arrondissement's vigilance committee. She left hurriedly and ran down the hill: "I descended the Butte, my rifle under my coat, shouting: Treason! . . . believing that we would die for liberty. We were risen from the earth. Our deaths would free Paris."[10]

Louise Michel, born in a village in Haute-Marne in eastern France, was the illegitimate daughter of a domestic servant and a young man of vaguely noble title. Her mother and her father's parents raised her in a crumbling chateau near the village of Vroncourt-la-Côte. There she became interested in traditional customs, folk myths, and legends. Increasingly hostile to Catholicism, she was influenced nonetheless by "the shadowy depths of the churches, the flickering candles, and the beauty of the ancient chants." As a child she gave fruit, vegetables, and small sums to poor people; as a young adult she became a school-teacher, first in a nearby village and then in Paris. With her oval face and "long, thin and tight-lipped mouth," she could seem hard, almost masculine. Known to history as "the Red Virgin," Michel embraced the cause of women's rights, proclaiming that one could not separate "the caste of women from humanity."[11]

WHEN MORE HORSES finally arrived, some of the soldiers began try-ing to move more guns down from Montmartre. But the women who had been out in the neighborhood had returned home to awaken their men, so the formerly sparse gatherings of curious bystanders had now swelled into an angry crowd. Men, women, and children blocked the soldiers' descent, trying to cut the horses' harnesses and hurling bottles and rocks at the troops. An observer saw "women and children swarm-ing up the hillside in a compact mass; the artillerymen tried in vain to fight their way through the crowd, but the waves of people engulfed ev-erything, surging over the cannon-mounts, over the ammunition wag-ons, under the wheels, under the horses' feet, paralyzing the advance of the riders who spurred on their mounts in vain. The horses reared and lunged forward, their sudden movement clearing the crowd, but the space was filled at once by a backwash created by the surging mul-titude." A national guardsman climbed onto a milestone and yelled, "Cut the traces!" Men and women sliced through the harnesses with knives. The artillerymen, quickly giving up on moving the cannons, climbed off their horses, and some began to fraternize with people in the crowd, accepting the meat, rolls, and wine offered by women. Sol-diers who abandoned the cannons and broke ranks became "the object of frenetic ovations" from the crowd.[12]

On the eastern side of Montmartre, angry residents also prevented troops under the command of Lecomte from taking the cannons down the hill. The general believed that a brigade commanded by General Susbielle would attack from the other side of Montmartre, trapping the insurgents between them. When sentries reported that the national guardsmen were advancing toward them, Lecomte confidently announced that his troops would take care of them. But his soldiers, rather than attempting to fight the insurgents, stopped and began to discuss the situation with guardsmen and other residents. An officer named Lalande even affixed a white handkerchief to his sword. At Buttes-Chaumont, troops waited in vain for the anticipated horses. National guardsmen, however, turned out to construct barricades, and the soldiers withdrew.

On Montmartre, General Lecomte stepped forward to take charge. The general ordered his troops to fire into the crowd of men, women, and children three times. But the troops did not obey. A woman challenged the soldiers, "Are you going to fire on us? On your brothers? On our husbands? On our children?" Another insulted them, reminding the line troops of their defeat at the hands of the Prussians. Lecomte threatened to shoot any man who refused to fire, asking if his soldiers "were going to surrender to that scum?" Louise Michel recalled that a noncommissioned officer left the ranks, "placed himself before his company and yelled, louder than Lecomte, 'Turn up your rifle butts!' The soldiers obeyed. . . . [T]he Revolution was made."[13]

Captain Lalande informed Lecomte that he would have to surrender. The general sent an officer down the rue Lepic to bring back reinforcements, but troops charging a crowd there had met with shots that killed another officer and wounded several of his men. National guardsmen rushed forward and took Lecomte and several other officers prisoner, holding them at a police post at Château-Rouge.[14]

Mayor Clemenceau was eager to obtain General Lecomte's release, fearing that he might be harmed as a furious mob had gathered outside the police post. Guardsmen took Lecomte and a few other prisoners back to the modest house that served as the headquarters of the neighborhood's National Guard on the rue de Rosiers, searching in vain for members of the Central Committee who could decide what to do. However, the members had departed, believing the prisoners safely held by the National Guard. Guardsmen arrived at the headquarters with another prisoner: General Clément Thomas, who had preceded Aurele de Paladines as commander of the National Guard. The crowd quickly recognized Thomas, reviled by working people for his role in the slaughter of insurgents during the June Days of 1848. As he was wearing civilian clothes, they took him for a spy. The crowd of men and

women pulled Thomas and Lecomte into a garden behind the building. Both were shot, Lecomte after pleading for mercy on behalf of his
wife and five children.[15]

The Central Committee of the National Guard moved into action,
albeit somewhat belatedly due to uncertainty about what was going on.
By 10 A.M. about a dozen members had gathered. They sent representatives into neighborhoods where National Guard battalions were known
to be hostile to the provisional government. Early in the afternoon,
guardsmen commanded by Émile Duval, the son of a laundress, occupied the Panthéon and prefecture of police. Eugène Varlin, a printer
and socialist, led 1,500 guardsmen from Batignolles and Montmartre
down into the *beaux quartiers*, controlling the place Vendôme, where
the National Guard headquarters stood in the midst of the conservative
neighborhood. That evening, a red flag flew from the Hôtel-de-Ville,
where the Central Committee now gathered, for the moment the de
facto government of the fledgling Commune of Paris. A spontaneous
defense of National Guard cannons had quickly evolved into an insurrection and then a revolution. As Benoît Malon, a member of the International Workingmen's Association, put it, "Never has a revolution so
surprised revolutionaries." Louise Michel proclaimed, "The eighteenth
of March could have belonged to the allies of kings, or to foreigners, or
to the people. It was the people's."[16]

THIERS REALIZED THAT THE ARMY did not have enough troops to
crush the insurrection. He first ordered Vinoy to pull his troops back
behind the Seine and to occupy the bridges on the Left Bank; then
he ordered a complete evacuation of Paris by all government officials,
followed by troops. Of about 4,000 policemen, more than 2,500 joined
line troops heading for Versailles. Paris was left with virtually no officials or functionaries, no magistrates or police. Many Parisians of
means had already begun to desert the city. The next day, Thiers cut all
correspondence between Paris and the provinces.[17]

During the February Revolution of 1848, Thiers had advised the Orleanist regime to move the army outside Paris, regroup, and then return
to crush the working-class insurgents. Prince Alfred Windischgraetz
had done the identical thing that same year in Vienna. With several
hundred thousand French troops in prisoner-of-war camps in Germany, and with the potential unreliability of many line troops, Thiers
could not contemplate an immediate assault on Paris. He wanted time
to rebuild his forces.

Thiers ordered the evacuation of troops from the forts of Mont-Valérien, Issy, Vanves, and Montrouge, each well beyond the ramparts of Paris. Soon after, he realized that giving up Mont-Valérien, southwest of Neuilly, had been a grave mistake and reoccupied it; his troops turned back a halfhearted assault by National Guard forces. The officers of the now twice-defeated army gathered in Versailles, shocked by events and utterly humiliated.

RAOUL RIGAULT HAD RETURNED TO PARIS on February 18, the day after the National Assembly elected Thiers head of the executive authority. The police were looking for him, and he lay low until mid-March. Having dined late in the Latin Quarter at the *brasserie* Glaser the evening before, Rigault woke up late on March 18 to hear the news that the people of Montmartre had prevented the troops from carrying off the National Guard cannons and had shot Generals Lecomte and Thomas. The fervent disciple of revolution had missed the whole thing! Rigault ran to the prefecture of police and, finding that Émile Duval had already assumed police functions there, pushed him out of the way and began to set up shop. Rigault then began to sign orders for the liberation of political prisoners. Blanquists were chomping at the bit, impatient to organize a military march on Versailles. However, the Central Committee of the National Guard hesitated, as did Jacobins and many members of the International.

Montmartre, Belleville, and other peripheral plebeian neighborhoods claimed the March 18 victory as their own, proclaiming it a revolution that would challenge the existing conservative provisional government. They poured down from the heights to parade triumphantly on the place de l'Hôtel-de-Ville and the boulevards of central Paris. Organization and militancy would remain firmly rooted in neighborhood action.[18]

Edmond de Goncourt witnessed the explosion of popular joy and energy that erupted on March 18: "All around me people are talking of provocation and making fun of Thiers. . . . The triumphant revolution seems to be taking possession of Paris: National Guards are swarming and barricades are being put up everywhere; naughty children scramble on top of them. There is no traffic; shops are closing." The next day he walked near the Hôtel-de-Ville. Disdaining ordinary people, he snarled,

> You are overcome with disgust to see their stupid and abject faces, which triumph and drunkenness have imbued with a kind of radiant

swinishness. . . . [F]or the moment France and Paris are under the control of workmen. . . . How long will it last? Who knows? The unbelievable rules . . . the cohorts of Belleville throng our conquered boulevard . . . going along in the midst of a somewhat mocking astonishment which seems to embarrass them and makes them turn their victors' eyes toward the toes of their shoes, worn mostly without socks. . . . The government is leaving the hands of those who have, to go into the hands of those who have not. . . . Is it possible that in the great law underlying changes here on earth the workers are for modern societies what the Barbarians were for ancient societies, convulsive agents of dissolution and destruction?[19]

In Ernest Vizetelly's description, the most prosperous neighborhoods of Paris had been invaded by men "with faces such as were only seen on days of Revolution."[20]

Yet, in some ways, life in Paris went on as if nothing had changed. Shops opened as usual the next day, and in some neighborhoods people simply walked around the remaining barricades. Eugène Bersier, a Protestant pastor, recalled that no one could really believe that Paris was in midst of an insurrection. He watched National Guard battalions from Belleville, Montmartre, and the southern suburb of Montrouge, "poor lost souls who believe that they have saved the Republic," parade through central Paris. A week later, Auguste Serraillier, a thirty-year-old shoemaker and member of the Council of Marx's International, reported that the only abnormal occurrence was the closing of workshops—employers appeared to be organizing a lockout in order to undercut the Commune. Even the conservative historian Hippolyte Taine had to admit that nothing scary or dramatic had followed the people's victory of March 18. He watched national guardsmen playing *boules*, passing the hat for money to buy some sausage and a little wine.[21]

As the drama unfolded on Montmartre, Paul Vignon, the son of a magistrate and himself a lawyer who had served as a national guardsman during the Prussian siege, had taken his mother to the Gare Montparnasse so that she could return to their family home in the Norman town of Falaise. Returning to the Palace of Justice, he heard shouts coming from the direction of the quai de la Mégisserie. He then learned what had happened up on Montmartre, far from his comfortable existence. He saw two gendarmes in shirts torn during struggles with a crowd shouting for the Commune and against the army. Within hours, most conservative national guardsmen had left their ranks. Only "the lazy element" was left of his National Guard unit, Vignon claimed—those continuing to serve for the 1.50 francs per day they would receive. Vignon contended that a kind of fever had hit ordinary Parisians. The Franco-Prussian War had wrenched them away from their normal occupations, and they now seemed to believe that no leaders were necessary in a world of total equality, without a "ruling class," in which the kind of luxury to which he was accustomed would be "a stigma."

Édouard, Paul's father, told his wife two days later, "After the Prussians, now its Belleville and Montmartre who want to stage their political drama." For wealthy Parisians like Paul and Édouard Vignon, the insurgency was at first of no great concern, just another Parisian episode with which to contend. Indeed, the capital seemed astonishingly calm, particularly the Vignons' bourgeois *quartier* in central Paris, where faces were "sad, gloomy."

Paul briefly set about trying to organize conservative National Guardsmen who were "frankly reactionary." His father also believed it their duty "to increase the number of *honnêtes gens.*" The Vignon family quickly adopted the vocabulary of social and spatial stigmatization, juxtaposing the Communard "rabble"—for example, "the low-life of Belleville"—with the *honnêtes gens* of the upper classes—"hardworking" men of property—in the fancy neighborhoods. Édouard and his son would bide their time and looked to Thiers and the National Assembly to put an end to the mess.[22]

ON MARCH 19, ÉMILE DUVAL warned the Central Committee that resistance against events was afoot, particularly in the conservative First and Second Arrondissements. He demanded that steps be taken to prevent conservative National Guard units from reaching Versailles. Members of the committee protested that they did not have a mandate to defend Paris and refused to transform the body formally into even a provisional revolutionary authority. Yet they agreed to order detachments of guardsmen to ensure security at key points, such as the Bank of France and the Tuileries Palace. Paris had to be defended.[23]

Members of the committee issued a proclamation ending the state of siege imposed by Thiers and Vinoy and called on Parisians to organize elections to ensure the existence of the republic. Although unwilling to serve formally as a provisional government, the Central Committee remained the only real authority, although some of its members were quite unknown to the average Parisian. François Jourde, a committee member from Auvergne who had been a clerk for a notary and then a bank, later related the surprise and confusion that had followed such a swift victory: "We did not know what to do: we did not want to take possession of the Hôtel-de-ville. We wanted to build barricades. We were very embarrassed by our authority."[24]

Édouard Moreau, a twenty-seven-year-old Parisian Blanquist who made artificial flowers, presided over the Central Committee. Moreau's fine features, including long blond hair, earned him the nickname "the Aristocrat." The committee also included the Blanquists Émile Eudes and Duval. Rigault and other Blanquists would run the prefecture of police and looked to Auguste Blanqui as a potential savior and leader, despite his being a prisoner of the government of Versailles on an island near Morlaix in Brittany. Rigault put it this way: "Nothing can be done without the Old One," Blanqui.[25]

The committee, led by Moreau, sent a list of demands to the National Assembly in Versailles, demanding that Parisians be granted the right to elect mayors of each of the city's twenty arrondissements, that the prefecture of police be abolished, that the army in Versailles be kept out of Paris, that the National Guard be allowed to elect its officers, that the moratorium on the payment of rents arbitrarily ended by the National Assembly be resumed, and finally that the National Assembly officially proclaim the republic. Eudes declared that since March 18 Paris "has no other government than that of the people and this is the best one. Paris is free. Centralized authority no longer exists." The concept of the Commune as a governing entity gained ground when the first issue of the *Journal Officiel de la Commune* appeared on March 20. A strident assessment congratulated "the proletarians of the capital [who] amidst the failures and treasons of the ruling classes have understood that the hour has struck for them to save the situation by taking the direction of public affairs into their own hands." The term "Commune," as we have seen, was in the air during the Prussian siege and after the French defeat. Now the success of the men and women of Montmartre in preventing Thiers's troops from seizing the National Guard cannons encouraged insurgent Parisians to believe that the creation of a progressive and even autonomous authority in the capital, the Commune of Paris, was within reach.[26]

For the moment, however, the majority of arrondissement mayors and deputy mayors and the deputies representing Paris in the National Assembly refused to meet with the Central Committee, believing that to do so would be tantamount to recognizing it as a legitimate authority. A minority of mayors, however, met with the Central Committee at the Hôtel-de-Ville, including Clemenceau, the mayor of the Eighteenth Arrondissement. Clemenceau insisted that the body did not represent Paris and tried to persuade its members to return the cannons to the government of Thiers and to recognize the authority of the existing mayors. He hoped that the latter could negotiate with the National Assembly. The more conservative arrondissement mayors limited their demands to achieving municipal autonomy.[27]

The monarchist-dominated National Assembly met in a secret session on the evening of March 22 to determine how to respond to the uprising in Paris. Thiers and Jules Grévy, a very conservative republican, dominated the proceedings. The monarchist Right found support for its demand for calls for volunteers from the provinces to defend "order and society." One member reflected the prevailing mood, insisting, "The criminals who now dominate Paris have attacked Paris: now they attack society itself." No concessions were to be made to "a riot." Thiers and Grévy made clear that while the assembly rebuilt a "serious army," they were willing to give what they considered an illegal, insurgent authority time to set itself up in order to make legitimate a bloody repression. Thiers relished the fact that the possibility of civil war hung over the gathering. When someone challenged Thiers, asking if he would push Paris to that extreme, shouts came from the assembly, "It has already begun! It's here!" The conservative National Assembly revolted against Paris, and not the other way around. Only days after the people of Paris had taken control of their city, Thiers and the National Assembly were readying for a war that they understood as "a class war" between the bourgeoisie and Parisian workers.[28]

Meanwhile many of those elite Parisians who would proudly title themselves "the men of order" followed Thiers to Versailles or retreated to safer places outside the capital. Conservative republicans in Versailles who at first found themselves in the difficult position of having to choose between a monarchical restoration and the Commune could now back Thiers, who promised to crush "the vile multitude" in Paris he so detested.

For conservative republicans, the word "Commune" had become a synonym for "communism." These so-called men of order could convince themselves that the members and supporters of the Commune, dubbed the Communards, primarily intended to confiscate and divide up the property of the wealthy. Thiers, like other anti-Communards, was convinced that members of the International were largely responsible for the insurrection of March 18.[29]

While Thiers and the National Assembly prepared to rebuild the army, counterrevolution was afoot in Paris. Thiers appointed the conservative Admiral Jean-Marie Saisset commander of the National Guard of Paris, a decision sure to outrage many ordinary Parisians. The Bonapartist faithful, the Society of the Friends of Order, and "loyal" national guardsmen began to gather around the Bourse, the Opera, and the elegant Grand Hôtel in Paris, rallying around Saisset. On March 21, a demonstration of about 3,000 Friends of Order began on the boulevard des Capucines and marched through several boulevards and streets in conservative neighborhoods. Versailles loyalists dominated *quartiers* between the *grands boulevards* down to the market of Saint-Honoré and around the Palais-Royal, the Banque de France, and the rue Montmartre. Saisset organized another demonstration at the place Vendôme the following day. The choice of location—in front of the headquarters of the National Guard—was provocative. When Saisset was about to speak, counterdemonstrators fired shots in his general direction. Twelve-year-old Gaston Cerfbeer, living on the rue Saint-Honoré near the rue Royale, looked down to see "men of order . . . running like madmen, beneath our windows."[30]

About twelve people were killed and a number of others were injured in the melee. Saisset's disorganization and lack of charisma, as well as rumors that key Orleanists hoped the demonstrations would constitute a first step toward a restoration, which most Parisians did not want, helped bring the bloody incident to a close. But rather than putting an end to the counterrevolution, the deaths only solidified strong anti-Communard sentiment among conservatives remaining in Paris.

In the meantime, the National Assembly refused to use the name "Republic" in its proclamations. The government immediately adopted a discourse of denigration, describing Parisians as "wretches," "brigands," "pillagers," and "bandits." In mid-April, the assembly reacted to Paris's claims with a new law on municipalities, stating that in the future the capital would still have no mayor and would instead come under the direct administration of the prefect of the Seine. The assembly would appoint municipal councilmen, responsible only to the central government that appointed them, for five-year terms.[31]

PARIS'S INSURRECTION STIRRED SOME provincial cities. Crowds in Lyon had proclaimed the republic in August 1870 before Paris did so on September 4, reflecting political radicalization during the last years of the empire. Demonstrators called for continued war against

Prussia—now Germany—municipal autonomy, and social reform. On March 22, representatives from Lyon, Bordeaux, Rouen, Marseille, and several other cities met with the Central Committee to listen to an account of the Parisian movement for rights. That day, insurgents seized power in Lyon. Marseille, Narbonne, and Saint-Étienne, a center of manufacturing, and the small Burgundian industrial town of Le Creusot rose up on March 24, followed by Limoges in early April. All proclaimed short-lived, varied "Communes." Benoît Malon and militant socialist, feminist, and novelist André Léo, penned her "Appeal to the Workers of the Countryside," 110,000 copies of which reached the provinces: "Brothers," the text read, "they are fooling you. Our interests are the same!"[32]

Some prominent moderate Parisian republicans, such as former deputy Édouard Lockroy, a member of the municipal council who had represented the *département* of the Seine in the National Assembly, and Jean-Baptiste Millière, another deputy, joined Clemenceau in attempting to negotiate a compromise with Thiers. On March 23, however, Thiers turned away the delegation of mayors and deputies representing Paris. He was playing for time, saying, "Once already I have pulled France drowning out of a revolution; I am not young enough to do it a second time."[33]

Three groups, the League of the Republican Union for the rights of Paris, the National Union of Commerce and Industry, and the Freemasons, continued to pressed for conciliation, hoping that recognition of the republic by the Versailles government and an affirmation of the rights of Paris would lead to a settlement. Thiers insisted that because the Commune had no legitimacy, there was nothing to negotiate. To the National Union of Commerce and Industry, which claimed to represent 6,000 merchants and manufacturers, Thiers stated his demand that the Communards relinquish their arms—in other words, surrender.[34]

THE TERM "COMMUNE" had in these days several meanings. The manifesto of the Central Committee of the Twenty Arrondissements, released several days after the events of March 18, defined "the Commune . . . [as] the base of all political states, as the family is the embryo of societies. [The Commune] should be autonomous . . . [with] its sovereignty complete, just like the individual in the middle of the city." With an eye toward economic development and a guarantee of security, Paris should "federate itself with all other communes or associations of communes that make up the nation. . . . It is this idea . . . which has just triumphed on March 18, 1871."[35]

Much more than municipal autonomy was at stake, however. Many Parisians believed that the assertion of municipal rights represented the first step toward achieving a "democratic and social Republic." The manifesto asked for the organization of "a system of communal insurance against all social risks," including unemployment and bankruptcy, as well as a systematic investigation into all possibilities for procuring capital and credit for individual workers in order to end endless "pauperism."[36] Thus, whereas some militants limited their demands to municipal rights, others insisted on meaningful social reforms.

On March 23, the Paris branch of the International Workingmen's Association threw its support behind the Commune. Its proclamation, written by Albert Theisz, a bronze worker, optimistically asserted, "The independence of the Commune will mean a freely discussed contract which will put an end to class conflict and bring about social equality." It also echoed prevalent republican demands put forth during the Second Empire: obligatory, free, and secular education; the right of assembly and to form associations; and municipal authority over the armed forces, police, and public health. As the socialist printer Eugène Varlin put it, "Political revolution and social reforms are linked, and cannot go one without the other."[37]

The Protestant minister Élie Reclus captured the hope of many Communards that social reforms could improve their lot: "Lazare, always starving, is no longer content with the crumbs that fall from the table of the rich, and now he has dared ask for his part of the feast." Like his anarchist geographer brother Élisée, Reclus believed that the future of humanity lay in a close connection with nature, without a state. He believed that if workers could organize themselves into associations of producers, they could eventually emancipate themselves from bosses. Yet, although some 300,000 Parisians were now without work in the wake of the war and siege, various associations of workers bravely started up. At the Council of Federated Trade Unions, one orator asked, "What difference does it make to me that we be victorious over Versailles, if we don't find the answer to the social problem, if the worker remains in the same conditions?"[38]

Louis Barron, a washerwoman's son, former soldier, and writer, wanted "a social revolution" so long awaited by many in his generation. He described the world of work from which the Commune took its strength: "The vast working-class faubourgs, by which one slowly reaches Butte Montmartre or Buttes-Chaumont, these Aventine hills of Paris, reflect the mysterious, tumultuous, and sad movement of these industrial neighborhoods. . . . Ordinary people live in these streets, mixing together, walking about, discussing, arguing, killing time. For these thousands of men used to working with tools every day in order to earn enough to eat, unemployment, even if absolute famine is not a consequence, is as difficult as if utter dark impoverishment followed in its wake."[39] Hundreds of thousands of Parisian workers would look to the Commune to bring out reforms that would better their lives.

MUNICIPAL ELECTIONS, postponed for four days while some of the mayors unsuccessfully sought a negotiated settlement with Versailles, were held on March 26, with the goal of electing the governing council of the Commune. Rigault stood as a candidate in the generally reactionary Eighth Arrondissement, which included the Church of the Madeleine, where some of the wealthiest families married and held baptisms, and the Champs-Élysées.[40] He assumed that his reputation and newly acquired status as head of the police would win him the election even in such a reactionary district, and he was right.

The elections reflected the increasingly divided social and political geography of Paris. They were weighted by population, with the plebeian Eleventh—the most populous, with almost 150,000 residents—and the Eighteenth Arrondissements each electing seven people, while the Sixteenth—the smallest, with 42,000 residents—received two representatives. Only about half of men voted, due in part to the fact that thousands had fled the city but also because many were unfamiliar with the candidates or had been dissuaded by Thiers's call for people not to participate.

The candidates of the revolutionary Left did well in the plebeian arrondissements of eastern and, above all, northeastern Paris, where Blanquists, members of the International, and Jacobins constituted a majority. In Belleville, Gabriel Ranvier, a shoemaker's son, clerk, national guardsman, and anticlerical, was reelected mayor of the Twentieth Arrondissement, where he became known as "the Christ of Belleville." He had a reputation for drinking to political change with fruit syrup and not wine, spoke frequently in the warehouses of *quartiers populaires*, and spent time in prison for his role in the attempted insurrection of October 31. Like others of similar background, he was determined that Paris should lead the way in the struggle to create a just republic.[41]

The men now wielding authority in the Commune had little or no administrative experience, but they stepped together—debating and quarreling from the beginning—into the unknown. No dominant figure emerged to lead the Commune, and problems of overlapping authority and rivalries persisted. It was up to the mayors, deputy mayors, police, and national guardsmen in each arrondissement to enforce any decrees the Commune issued. Of course, not all local mayors and police willingly supported the Commune, meaning that, limited in its effective authority, the Commune had to rely on officials, policemen, and national guardsmen, no matter how republican they were.[42]

The Commune's first and most pressing task, however, was defending Paris against the Army of Versailles, which was readying for a fight against Communards. Debate raged between "realists" and "idealists," with "realists" insisting, much to the chagrin of "idealists" eager to establish a just society, that no real reforms, social or political, could be achieved with determined enemies poised for attack. The first decree of the new administrative body of the Commune on March 29 reminded citizens that they were "masters of [their] own lives," warning that "criminals" were "fostering a hotbed of monarchist conspiracy at the very gates of the city. They are planning to unleash civil war."[43]

On March 28, the victorious new authority in the French capital officially proclaimed the Paris Commune at the Hôtel-de-Ville, as drums, bugles, and artillery salvos fired into the air from the nearby quay saluted victory over tyranny. The newly elected members of the governmental council of the Commune stood on a platform, while the National Guard marched past a vast, excited crowd. The color red was everywhere—in scarfs, belts, cockades, and the flag waving from Hôtel-de-Ville. Rigault had trimmed his beard and was shockingly well dressed, reveling in his status as head of the police. Jules Vallès described the proclamation of the Commune as "making up for twenty years of Empire, six months of defeat and betrayals." The Commune had, from the beginning, the overwhelming support of most Parisians.[44]

The Central Committee of the National Guard had announced that with the elections of March 26, it would cede power to those elected to the Commune. Yet, the very next day, the Central Committee began to reorganize, after sixteen of its members had been elected. The Central Committee, which continued to hold regular meetings, saw itself as the "guardian of the revolution." It warned Parisians to be wary of those favored by fortune, because only rarely did they consider "the workers as brothers." Arguably a kind of dual sovereignty existed, held by the

Central Committee of the Federation of the National Guard, formally established on March 20, and the "Commune," the elected governing body of the Commune proclaimed on March 28.[45]

THE COMMUNE IMMEDIATELY faced challenges both internal and external. First and most immediately, it required funds to operate. Second, not everyone who supported the Commune agreed on the extent of the transformation in Paris it was to oversee; political divisions remained. Third, while German forces surrounded the northern and eastern ramparts and forts, Thiers's army, headquartered at Versailles, held the territory to the south and west of Paris. The Germans posed no immediate threat, but Thiers's army was already planning its attack on Paris.

How was the Commune to find the money to pay national guardsmen 1.50 francs a day for their service, as well as the many municipal employees? The Commune also had to find a way to make good on its promise to finance some care for the poor. As in other cities and towns in France, the bulk of municipal revenues came from money collected at the *octrois* (customs barriers) that surrounded Paris. Monies seized at the Hôtel-de-Ville when the empire disappeared into the night counted for something. But many more financial resources were required.

The Commune named François Jourde as its delegate for finance. On March 19 Jourde and Eugène Varlin went to the Bank of France to ask politely for a loan of 700,000 francs, which they received. The Commune also received credit worth well over 16 million francs, a paltry sum compared to the 258 million francs Versailles received on credit from the Bank of France, making possible the reconstitution of the French army. The Rothschild banking family also loaned money to the Commune.[46] Attached to legalism, the Commune did not confiscate funds in the Bank of France, which it easily could have done, but it did begin to mint its own coins in mid-April.[47]

For the moment, the Commune's provisional authority proposed no concrete economic or political program other than affirming that France was a now a republic. Yet the Commune immediately took important measures in the interest of working- and middle-class Parisians. It forbade the expulsion of tenants unable to pay their rent, which reassured those frustrated and angered by the National Assembly's sudden abolition of the moratorium on rents that had kept people in their homes during the siege. Gustave Flaubert, for one, expressed his indignation as a property owner who wanted rents owed paid immediately. He would not have been happy to hear the comment of one man who informed his landlord in the Eleventh Arrondissement that "the Commune would triumph, and would put renters in the place of landlords." The Commune reassured businesses by coming up with a compromise in the interest of debtors and creditors, phasing repayments over three years, whereas the Versailles government had allowed only four months to pay back debts. The Commune also suspended the sale of items exchanged for cash at the municipal pawnshop, another measure important to many Parisians.

The Commune Council, which included about sixty-five men, many of whom were also officials in their own arrondissements, met fifty-seven times during the Commune's existence. Overlapping administrations, committees, delegates, ideological differences, and personal rivalries, however, undermined its efforts.[48] (Élie Reclus found the governing council the Commune's least reassuring aspect.) In each of the *mairies* of the arrondissements, smaller versions of the meetings at the Hôtel-de-Ville took place, with each mayor, deputy mayor, and commission overseeing local affairs. The very structure of what amounted to a federation of arrondissements meant that coordinating a unified policy at the level of the Commune proved difficult, if not impossible. National Guard units and the existence of the Central Committee of the Federation of the National Guard served to decentralize authority and further complicate coordination of policies ordered by the Commune itself. From the beginning, competing authorities and two opposing visions plagued the Commune. On the one hand, Proudhonians, anarchists who therefore opposed the very existence of states, saw the Commune as essentially embodying popular democracy and municipal autonomy. The Jacobins, meanwhile, favored a more authoritarian and realistic structure that seemed increasingly necessary, given the challenging military situation.[49]

Further diffusing its authority, the Commune established executive commissions, the equivalent of ministries, each run by a delegate. Commissions were to convene twice a day at the Hôtel-de-Ville, and these long and increasingly contentious meetings often lasted well into the night and wasted considerable time discussing issues of little to no importance. A few members seemed caught up in the ceremonial aspects of their limited authority. In an effort to dispel this emphasis on appearance and ceremony, Varlin suggested that the Commune refuse to pay for the fancy uniform complete with military stripes ordered by Eudes. He explained, "The Commune does not have money for luxurious clothing."[50]

The Commune's administrative body quickly decided that it was not democratic to call someone "minister of war," so that person became "citizen delegate to the Ministry of War." Besides war, the other commissions dealt with subsistence, finance, foreign affairs, public services, education, general security, justice, and labor and exchange. Léo Frankel, a small, bespectacled Hungarian watchmaker and member of the International, headed the latter. Speaking French with a strong accent, Frankel lived near the faubourg Saint-Antoine, in the heart of artisanal Paris. He insisted that because workers had made the Revolution of March 18, the Commune would mean nothing if it did not do something for them.[51]

WHILE THE COMMUNE was busy setting up its government, Adolphe Thiers was beginning to rebuild the French army in Versailles.[52] This would be a challenge. More than 300,000 soldiers and officers who had surrendered at Sedan and Metz were still interned in the German states. The Army of the East, camped in Switzerland, largely consisted of Mobile Guard soldiers awaiting demobilization. By early April, the number of troops reached only 55,000, including those released from German internment, and the three corps had taken the appropriate name of the Army of Versailles. The Volunteers of the Seine provided another 6,000 men. Yet Thiers bided his time, convinced that well more than 100,000 might be needed.[53]

Marshal Patrice de MacMahon seemed the perfect commander in chief for the Army of Versailles. A Legitimist hoping for a Bourbon restoration, MacMahon, a decorated veteran of campaigns of conquest and slaughter in Algeria, shared the belief at Versailles that the Commune threatened social order. The marshal's surrender at Sedan had only somewhat compromised his sterling reputation, for he had been wounded early in the battle.

On April 6 Thiers named as commanders Paul de Ladmirault, Ernest de Cissey, François du Barail, Justin Clinchant, and Félix Douay. Thiers appointed Joseph Vinoy, who had led the unsuccessful effort to capture the National Guard cannons, to command the reserve army. All were politically conservative, including two Legitimists, two Bonapartists, and a conservative republican (Ladmirault). The French officer corps remained upper-class and status proud, retaining the belief that noble blood guaranteed dedication and competence. Senior French officers had rallied to Louis Napoleon and then to his second incarnation as Napoleon III, in part because they feared republicans and socialists.

It should come as no surprise, then, that they were keen to take up arms against the Parisian Communards.[54]

Whereas conservative republican Jules Simon had described the Versaillais army in its first weeks as being "like a Tartar horde," officers now imposed discipline. Cases of insubordination and, above all, politically motivated dissent—such as when soldiers arriving from Bordeaux shouted for the Commune—were dealt with harshly. Units considered even vaguely sympathetic to Paris were sent to far-flung duty in France or the colonies.

Morale among soldiers, laid so low just a few months earlier, improved dramatically. It helped that Thiers took a personal interest in improving living conditions for troops, increasing their wine ration by four and tripling that of eau-de-vie. Troops were also bombarded by propaganda attacking the Communards. After first denying soldiers access to newspapers, the National Assembly in April voted to provide troops with copies of *Le Gaulois* and *Le Soir*, which denounced the Commune for challenging the regime of property, religion, social hierarchy, and authority. These organs presented the Communards as the dregs of society, ex-convicts, drunks, vagabonds, and thieves, foreigners turned loose by virtue of fiendish plots organized by the International, perhaps in cahoots with Germany.[55]

Once the German Empire and the provisional government of France had signed the Treaty of Frankfurt on May 10—by which France had to cede to Germany Alsace and much of Lorraine, pay off an enormous indemnity of 5 billion francs, and recognize William I as emperor of Germany—Bismarck released captured French soldiers to join the Army of Versailles. These troops would make up a quarter of the force of 130,000 men available to Thiers. Officers were anxious to restore the pride of the French army after the abject humiliation of the catastrophic war against Prussia, although some who had served in the Army of National Defense were squeezed out. With their careers on the line, returning officers quickly hitched their wagons to the Versailles caravan. Thiers had no military experience, but this in no way dissuaded him from trying to impose his will on the commanders of the Army of Versailles. Each morning he insisted on meeting with MacMahon and the others, but not with their titular superior, Adolphe Le Flô, minister of war, or with Vinoy, whose reputation the events of March 18 had stained.[56]

Thiers and the Army of Versailles's planned invasion of Paris would not be easy. The city had held out for more than four months during the Prussian siege against an imposing army. An encircling wall with ninety-four interspersed, fortified bastions, each capable of housing cannons and machine guns, protected the capital. A moat thirty feet deep and forty-five feet wide provided another serious obstacle to an invading force. During the Prussian siege, the Government of National Defense had constructed additional fortifications beyond the southwestern side of the ramparts, using embankments provided by the railway that ran around the exterior circumference of Paris. Drawbridges could close the gates of the city.

Moreover, a series of exterior forts, connected in places by trenches and redoubts, had been built during the July Monarchy: Issy, Montrouge, Vanves, Bicêtre, and Ivry. Communard forces controlled these, with the major exception of the enormous fort of Mont-Valérien west of Paris, which the Versaillais had retaken. Ironically these forts had been constructed at Thiers's instigation. Their placement had generated heated debate, as republican critics noted that their location seemed to reflect a preoccupation with firing into Paris, against insurgent workers—such as those who had risen up on several occasions following the Revolution of 1830—rather than a desire to construct a useful defense against invading forces. The German army controlled the areas beyond the northern and eastern walls of Paris, including the exterior forts (with the exception of Vincennes to the east, which the Communards held). Supposed German neutrality saved the Communards from having to worry about a Versaillais attack from those directions.[57]

THE COMMUNARD DELEGATE for war who would have to prepare for a Versaillais attack was Gustave Cluseret, a Parisian-born graduate of the elite military school of St. Cyr. Though not yet fifty, Cluseret had impressive military experience: he had been wounded in Algeria and fought as a commander of the Mobile Guard against the insurgents during the June Days of 1848. He then moved to the Left and was placed on inactive duty before fighting for the North in the American Civil War, after which he became an American citizen. Increasingly committed to social revolution, he returned to France in 1867 and was briefly jailed in 1868 after writing an article that displeased imperial authorities.

Cluseret had, in the words of Louis Rossel, another Communard commander, "a coarsely handsome face" but was "curt, uncivil in his manner," leading to accusations that he was dictatorial in his methods. One of the commander's secretaries described a mood of "perpetual improvisation, fundamental incoherence, a chaos trying in vain to organize itself and . . . a mob-scene where everyone commands and no one obeys." But Cluseret understood the daunting problems of trying to defend Paris with undisciplined National Guard forces vulnerable to the indecision and arguments of their commanders. The National Guard was organized into companies formed within arrondissements, bringing together neighbors, workmates, and friends. Each company now elected a delegate to serve as a sort of "political and military policeman," searching for disloyal officers, with the right to call meetings to discuss matters deemed important.[58] That National Guard companies elected such delegates added to the layers of command and increased the difficulty of the overall commander's tasks.

Cluseret believed that if the National Guard could hold off the Versaillais, the Commune could reach some sort of negotiated settlement with the government at Versailles. The first step, however, was ensuring that the National Guard was ready for the task at hand. With that in mind, he reorganized some National Guard units and reminded arrondissement authorities that he had ultimate authority over battalions. On April 7, a decree obliged all men between nineteen and forty to serve in the National Guard. Cluseret urged guardsmen to police their neighborhoods and force men avoiding service to join up. The delegate for war created a War Council in each National Guard legion, a kind of court-martial, with the goal of imposing discipline and thus to counter Versaillais attempts to subvert moral. A court-martial tried one commander who stood accused of refusing to lead his men against line troops at Neuilly. He was condemned to death but never executed.[59]

The limits of his own authority and an increasingly obstructionist National Guard leadership rendered complicated Cluseret's attempts to create a real army out of National Guard troops. He denounced the meddling of the Central Committee of the National Guard, which accentuated the division of authority undermining the Commune. The Central Committee continued to send out commands to arrondissement municipalities, ignoring Cluseret's efforts to centralize his authority. A spate of official proclamations appeared, some extremely contradictory. When on one occasion Cluseret assumed that 1,500 national guardsmen would be awaiting his orders at the Gare Saint-Lazare, he found only 200 "who did not want to march." Only about 80,000 men were ready to fight by mid-May, if that.[60]

Cluseret anticipated that Thiers's army would attack the western gates at Point-du-Jour, Auteuil, and Passy. With this in mind, he established a battery at Trocadéro and another near Passy at the Château de la Muette, not far from the Bois-de-Boulogne. Yet, during the siege to come, they did no real damage to the Versaillais forces.[61]

IN LATE MARCH, the Versaillais sent out an exploratory patrol toward the ramparts and then well beyond the southern fortifications to assess Communard defenses. Thiers believed it would take thirty days to gain control of the immediate area around the ramparts and to set up cannons there. He remained committed to blasting the ramparts with cannon fire in preparation for an assault, insisting on selecting the targets.[62]

The first fighting took place on March 30, just two days after the Commune's proclamation, when Versaillais troops moved toward Courbevoie, which lies across the Seine from Neuilly, on an exploratory mission. Coming upon a small Communard perimeter post, Versaillais line troops hesitated. General Gaston Galliffet immediately ordered the artillery to fire, and when they grumbled, he harangued them, pistol in his hand. He then charged forward on his horse, taking some prisoners, as Communard guardsmen fled. Versaillais soldiers grabbed a red flag and threw it at Galliffet's feet in triumph. The general's ability to rally his troops may have been a turning point; the army, at first unwilling to attack their fellow Frenchmen, now seemed prepared for an assault on the Communards of Paris. Thiers ordered Galliffet's battalion to return without attempting to take the pont de Neuilly and Porte Maillot, but the skirmish had the intended effect. Commune forces retreated in a panic, whereas the army's performance reassured Thiers. He sent off a telegram informing provincial authorities that "the organization of one of the finest professional armies ever possessed by France is being completed at Versailles; good citizens can take heart."

On April 2, Thiers ordered two army brigades, backed by artillery and commanded by Galliffet, to attack a concentration of national guardsmen at the *rond-point* at Courbevoie. A military surgeon general called Pasquier went forward to negotiate with the Communards. His uniform gave him the appearance of a gendarmerie colonel, and shots rang out from the Communard side, killing him. The fighting that ensued ended with a Versaillais victory, but because Thiers's troops then fell back, some Communards conceived of the encounter as a victory. It was anything but that, as the Army of Versailles now held Courbevoie, a key point in the defense of Paris. Pasquier's death became an early cornerstone of Versaillais propaganda.[63]

About thirty Communards were taken prisoner at Courbevoie, as *fédérés*—the name derives from the Federation of the National Guard—returned in haste to Paris, reaching the avenue de Neuilly and then Porte Maillot. Vinoy's orders were unambiguous: all soldiers, men from the Mobile Guard, or sailors taken prisoner were to be shot. When news of such executions reached the Hôtel-de-Ville, the Commune Council decided to order a major sortie against the Versaillais. The Blanquists Eudes and Émile Duval were the principal proponents for an attack. Late on April 2, the Commune informed the National Guard that "royalist conspirators" had attacked, launching civil war.[64]

The willingness, even eagerness, of the Versaillais troops to carry out summary executions of captured Communards marked an early turning point in the history of the Paris Commune. It left little doubt in the minds of determined Communards that the government and armies of Adolphe Thiers were capable of unrestrained violence and that Paris had to be defended at all costs.

The Commune's leadership quickly assembled a force perhaps numbering 20,000 but probably fewer. At 5 A.M. on April 3, four columns marched out of Paris toward Versailles, two from the right side, one commanded by Jules Bergeret, which was to go around Mont-Valérien, and the other under Gustave Flourens, instructed to cross the pont d'Asnières. A third column, under the command of Eudes, was to march through Issy and Meudon, while a fourth commanded by Duval would move through Châtillon. Thiers's line troops were ready, having been informed by spies in Paris.[65]

One Parisian on his way out of the city took note of the disordered and paltry forces marching toward Versailles. A colonel in the French army, who had managed to go back and forth to Versailles, had deemed it "prudent" to return to the capital of the Bourbons. He had heard someone refer to him as a *mouchard* and believed that his comings and goings were being noted. As the colonel prepared to leave Paris, a "great rumor" swept down the boulevards that Communard forces were going to move on Versailles. The colonel watched the national guardsmen leave in near total disorder, each carrying sausage, bread, and a liter of wine, some drunk and singing as they went along. Resourceful merchants plunged into their ranks, selling strong eau-de-vie. He could hear some guardsmen shout out that "*Père* Thiers" should be hung. National guardsmen assured him that they would be 100,000 in number. They seemed far fewer than that.[66]

Communard leaders had reassured national guardsmen that the Versaillais soldiers would not engage and would point their rifles to the ground, as some troops had done on March 18 on Montmartre. But now every sign indicated that the line troops would indeed fight. Once beyond the ramparts, Communard fighters faced incessant shelling by Versaillais cannons firing from the heights of Mont-Valérien. Only the column commanded by Eudes had any success, and even it had to fall back on Clamart late in the afternoon because of insufficient artillery cover.[67]

Émile Duval and Gustave Flourens were captured during the fighting. Flourens had taken refuge in an inn. Gendarmes burst in and (falsely) accused him of having shot a gendarme who had earlier come looking for Communards. A gendarme who recognized Flourens dragged him outside and hacked him to death on the banks of the Seine. The loss of Flourens, a highly educated and energetic force within the Commune, was disastrous. A general had promised that Communard fighters who surrendered would be spared. But when he arrived and asked who commanded the *fédérés*, Vinoy barked out orders that Duval and his chief of staff should be shot immediately. A soldier removed Duval's boots from his body and, as he rode away, yelled, "Who wants Duval's boots?" As the Communard columns fell back, Galliffet ordered at least three other prisoners shot.[68]

Sutter-Laumann, the young socialist living on Montmartre, heard in Paris that Vinoy's forces had moved against the *rond-point* of Courbevoie and that the Versaillais had executed captured national guardsmen. He returned hurriedly to Montmartre to see if his battalion had been summoned to action and found his neighborhood in a state of alarm. Drums and trumpets were sounding "with a lugubrious air that made one shudder." He learned that his unit, which included his father, a corporal, had left two hours earlier. Sutter-Laumann caught up with them along the Seine. No one seemed to have the slightest idea where they were heading. Yet rumor had thousands of guardsmen moving on Versailles. Could the taking of Versailles not be ensured?

In the distance, they could see the silhouette of Mont-Valérien. Suddenly its cannons opened up. They approached Meudon, its chateau and park stretching behind it, with Fort Issy off to the left. Amid fighting and losses, they reached the village of Clamart, greeted with machine-gun fire. The National Guard battalion retreated as it had arrived, in chaos, and then received orders to march to Châtillon. Sutter-Laumann decided to return to the village of Issy. Absolutely exhausted, he came upon guardsmen amusing themselves with target practice, even as Versaillais troops seemed headed in their direction. There Sutter-Laumann learned of the fiasco at Châtillon and the killing of Flourens and Duval.[69]

Sutter-Laumann and other colleagues found themselves under attack between Vanves and Issy. Their numbers fell from fifty to thirty, then to about eight, as guardsmen scurried off to safety. By a miracle, he managed to meet up with his father, separated from his own battalion, and the two made it back to Paris together. For his part, Sutter-Laumann was now convinced that the Commune's defeat was inevitable. The sortie of perhaps as many as 20,000 national guardsmen, supported by the forts of Issy and Vanves, had been unable to dislodge two or three regiments of Versaillais line troops.[70]

The overall result was a disaster, and the Communard forces retreated into Paris. On April 4, the Versaillais launched a counterattack against the columns of Duval and Eudes, capturing the plateau of Châtillon and the pont de Neuilly. For the moment Communards forces still held the forts of Issy, Montrouge, Bicêtre, and Ivry. But as of the evening of April 12, the Versaillais held Sèvres, Châtillon, Meudon, and Saint-Cloud. The Commune had lost about 3,000 fighters killed or captured.

DESPITE DEFEAT at the hands of Versaillais troops and the unforeseen challenges of governing Paris, Communard confidence still abounded in the early weeks of spring. Louis Barron remembered, "The Parisian movement . . . is carried along purely by its own momentum. . . . I recklessly allow myself to be swept along in its current. . . . I hardly ever think of the dangers of the morrow." Barron had to "admit that the cheerful bravado of the participants, their frivolous chatter, their wildly ostentatious dress, their taste for brilliant colors, plumed hats and impassioned speeches all help to distract me from my brooding fears."[71] With Thiers reconstituting the French army in the royal chateau at Versailles, there was much to fear indeed.

CHAPTER 3

MASTERS OF
THEIR OWN LIVES

Paris was free. Ordinary people from *quartiers populaires* strolled through western Paris's fancy neighborhoods, which many of them had never seen before unless they had worked as domestics or day laborers. Other working families, expelled from central neighborhoods by Haussmann's grand projects, reappropriated streets they had once known very well. But with Adolphe Thiers readying his troops in Versailles, how long could it last?

On Easter Sunday, the Luxembourg Gardens seemed as crowded to Ernest Vizetelly "as in the calmest days of peace." And so were the principal boulevards of Paris, at least until cafés shut, as ordered, at 11 P.M. In many ways, during the first half of April, life in Paris seemed to go on very much as before. The Louvre and Bibliothèque Nationale reopened. The Bourse carried on, despite the fact that most of the big investors had left Paris. The Café de Madrid, Vizetelly observed, was "swarming with delegates and staff officers."[1]

Concerts held in the Tuileries Gardens celebrated the Commune. Louis Barron noted the social mix at the gatherings, which brought together elderly proletarians and "the white and fat figures of well-nourished bourgeois, along with the little, laughing faces of young women." He was amused to see people from all social classes greeting each other enthusiastically with the words "*Ah! Citoyenne . . . Ah! Citoyen!*" More surprisingly, the Tuileries Palace, where Napoleon III and his family had lived so recently, had been opened to the public, with the entry fee of fifty centimes going toward the care of those wounded fighting the Versaillais. Women flocked to the apartments of the empress, imagining the luxurious life Eugénie led there. Those hostile to the Commune were likely to miss the continued laughter of young children as they watched the Guignol puppets at the lower end of the Champs-Élysées.[2]

The Commune was something of a "permanent feast" of ordinary people who celebrated their freedom by appropriating the streets and squares of Paris. Revolutionary songs echoed, well entrenched in the collective memory. *Le peuple* (the people) of Paris sang "La Marseillaise," "Le Chant du Depart," and "La Carmagnole." Édouard Moriac remembered that "everyone wanted to see the spectacle of the day" as Parisians rushed to watch the cannons being hauled off to battle, forgetting perhaps that a bloody clash with Thiers's troops was all but inevitable. The Commune placed enormous importance on political symbolism, and the destruction of several symbols of "reaction" and "injustice" took place in a festival-like atmosphere that made it possible for some to ignore the increasingly grim situation.[3]

In one such display of symbolic destruction, national guardsmen from the Eleventh Arrondissement burned a guillotine at the place Voltaire on April 7, just below the prison of La Roquette, where executions took place every year. Several thousand people were there. John Leighton watched: "When nothing remained but a heap of glowing ashes, the crowd shouted with joy; and for my own part, I fully approved of what had just been done as well as of the approbation of the spectators."[4]

The almost frenetic proliferation of newspapers, brochures, pamphlets, political posters, manifestos, wall posters, and caricatures that flooded Paris reflected popular excitement about and engagement with the Commune. Ninety newspapers appeared during its existence, including the Jacobin *Le Vengeur* and the Proudhonist *La Commune. La Sociale* was largely the work of André Léo, aided by Maxime Vuillaume. Other newspapers published only a few editions. Jules Vallès's *Le Cri du Peuple* turned out 50,000 to 60,000 copies per issue, sometimes more. Boys wearing red caps peddled *Le Bonnet Rouge* on the boulevards.[5]

Père Duchêne, which published as many as 60,000 copies a day, was one of the more popular newspapers, though its tone, insults, and sheer vulgarity offended even many loyal to the Commune.[6] Like its namesake during the French Revolution, *Père Duchêne* borrowed the biting argot of working-class Parisians. It also adopted the revolutionary calendar that began in 1792, so 1871 was the year 79. On 3 Germinal, *Père Duchêne* denounced "the reactionary good-for-nothings (*jean-foutres*) who spread disorder in Paris." Yet, despite the violence of the newspaper's denunciation of wealthy men of property, Vuillaume, another anti-imperial militant who had written his first piece for the newspaper in 1869, called for class collaboration. His articles reflected the sentiments of most Parisians, who read newspapers and wall posters while discussing politics and the current situation, but did so in good order and, for the most part, good humor.

We must view the publication of so many newspapers during the Commune against the censorship of others. Just as General Joseph Vinoy had shut down a spate of newspapers less than a week before the Commune's proclamation, the Central Committee in late March banned *Le Figaro* and *Le Gaulois*, both closely tied to Thiers. At least twenty-seven newspapers were shut down after March 18. On May 5, it was the turn of *France*, *Le Temps*, and *Le Petit Journal*; later ten more disappeared.[7]

There were signs too of a new efflorescence of art during the Commune. Claiming authority given him following the proclamation of the republic on September 4, the great painter Gustave Courbet had announced on March 18, coincidentally, the convocation of an assembly of artists. Courbet demanded artistic freedom from constraints and tastes imposed by the state. He exclaimed, "Paris is a true paradise. . . . [A]ll social groups have established themselves as federations and are masters of their own fate."[8]

Courbet stood in the Sixth Arrondissement as a candidate for the elections to the Commune the next day but came in sixth, falling one position short. When by-elections took place on April 16 to replace members of the Commune who had not accepted the Commune's mandate, had been elected in more than one arrondissement, or had resigned, Courbet was elected, becoming mayor of the arrondissement a week later.[9]

Courbet celebrated his newfound artistic freedom as he ate and drank. Barron paid a visit to the "master of Ornans" in his apartment on the rue Serpente in the Sixth Arrondissement. He found the painter seated before a pungent platter of cabbage and sausages, which he consumed with glass after glass of red wine. They went down to the boulevard Saint-Germain. The café terraces were full of students and loving couples, while the usual flâneurs strolled by, breathing in the sweet smells from the flowers of the nearby Luxembourg Gardens. Yet, in the far distance, one could just hear the sound of gunfire. Courbet seemed briefly preoccupied and hoped that the Parisians would not let themselves be taken, noting, "It's true that the French in the provinces are celebrating the carnage inflicted on the French of Paris."[10]

Courbet moved quickly to organize and codify freedom for and promotion of the arts in Paris. The artist announced a fifteen-point proposal on April 7. In his fiery speech he insisted that Paris had saved France from dishonor. He called upon artists, whom Paris had "nursed as would a mother," to help repair France's "moral state and rebuild the arts, which are its fortune." In the amphitheater of the Medical School, four hundred artists elected a committee of forty-seven members drawn from painting, sculpture, architecture, lithography, and the industrial arts, with thirty-two of them to be replaced after one year. Besides Courbet, who was elected president of the new Federation of Artists, Jean-François Millet, Camille Corot, Édouard Manet, and Eugène Pottier (author of "The Internationale") were members. The establishment of the federation and the large number of artists who participated in its assembly reflected the dramatic increase in the number of artists in Paris: from 350 in 1789 to 2,159 by 1838 to 3,300 in 1863. Parisian artists, like members of other professions, had feared for their livelihood under Louis Napoleon. In the arts, too, the Commune offered hope.[11]

The federation took on responsibility for the conservation of monuments, museums, galleries, and relevant libraries and put forward the idea that the Commune should pay for the training of exceptionally promising young artists. It would soon abolish the Academy of Beaux-Arts, long considered an appendage of "official" taste. A week later, the federation produced a blueprint for the future administration of the arts in Paris. Its committee would soon cashier the directors and associate directors of the Louvre and the Musée Luxembourg, believed sympathetic to Versailles. The federation became increasingly concerned with protecting the artistic treasures of the Louvre from damage by Versaillais shells; indeed, it had already sent some paintings to distant Brest for safety. Courbet ordered that windows in the Louvre be secured and placed guards around the museum.[12]

The Commune appointed Courbet to the Commission on Education on April 21, in part because the commission was nominally responsible for overseeing the federation. Courbet described his work: "To follow the wave that is the Paris Commune, I do not have to reflect, but only to act naturally."[13]

On April 29, the Commune named Protestant Pastor Élie Reclus director of the Bibliothèque Nationale; like Courbet with the Louvre, he sought to ensure that Versaillais shelling did no harm to its rich collections. When he arrived at the great library on May 1, he had to summon a locksmith to open the office of the previous director, who had bolted for Versailles. Twelve days later Reclus notified all employees that he would fire anyone who did not sign a paper pledging allegiance to the Commune.[14]

WHILE THE FINE ARTS seemed poised to flourish under the Commune, Paris's theaters staggered on as best they could, given the severity of the situation facing the city. The Commune abolished monopolies and subsidies to the theaters of Paris, seeking to encourage the creation of cooperative associations instead. The Comédie Française had shut down on the evening of March 18, the day the people of Montmartre succeeded in keeping the National Guard cannons from troops, but reopened ten days later with the help of a loan. In the immediate confusion, some other theaters also closed for a time. A reduced troupe of actors in Parisian theaters—some had left the city—put on fifty-one performances during the Commune, closing only on April 3, for whatever reason (causing a brief panic in the neighborhood because it seemed that something dire had occurred), and during the Easter holidays later that week. However, fewer tickets sold, generating barely enough income to cover the lights and heating. The most relevant production may have been staged at Gaité in late April. It portrayed in unflattering terms men who managed to avoid serving in the National Guard.[15]

With May came faltering morale and fewer theatrical performances. On May 1, the Comédie Française filled only thirty-eight seats. No one likes to play to a largely empty theater, and the director adopted the strategy of giving away tickets so that on some nights five hundred people attended. At least eleven other theaters staged performances during the Commune, including the Folies-Bergères. When Catulle Mendès purchased a ticket to a performance, the theater was almost empty. The actors went through their lines quickly, accompanying them with slow gestures. They seemed bored and in turn bored those who had bothered to come. Cafés on nearby boulevards shut down for lack of a post-theater crowd.[16]

Musicians in Paris played on, thanks to the support of the Commune, which named a commission to oversee their interests. When the director of the Opera stalled on organizing performances, the Commune named a new director of the Conservatoire de Musique, composer Daniel Salvador, the son of Spanish refugees. The Commune encouraged music that was "heroic in order to exalt the living, funereal to mourn the dead." Charles Garnier's Opera stood unfinished—it would open in 1875—and became a food storage facility. The old Opera continued with barely half its musicians. On May 13, Salvador summoned professors at the Conservatoire to a meeting at Alcazar in the rue du faubourg Poissonnière, but only five turned up. One asked Salvador if he understood that he was risking his neck by casting his lot with the Commune. Salvador replied that he knew that very well but had to act according to his principles.[17]

REVOLUTIONARY MUSIC and symbols could not gloss over great differences in the political inclinations of the men leading the Commune. Former 1848ers were prominent among them. Such Jacobins—including Félix Pyat, Charles Delescluze, and Charles Beslay, the senior at seventy-five years of age—tended to be older than the others. A Breton from Dinan, Beslay had begun a factory producing machines in Paris during the July Monarchy. He supported workers' rights, unlike Thiers, whom he had joined in opposing the Bourbon regime in its last years. Pyat, the son of a lawyer from Vierzon, had studied law but devoted himself to politics and writing political pamphlets and plays. The blowhard Pyat was anything but a man of courage, having hidden on a coal barge during the demonstrations that followed the funeral of Victor Noir. Pyat had a "rasping laugh" and the "bilious eyes of a man whose childhood had been unhappy."[18]

Devoted republicans, Jacobins seemed to romanticize a return to previous revolutions—hence their choice of the color red and the Phrygian cap, associated with the sans culottes of the French Revolution, as symbols. Raoul Rigault referred to them disparagingly as "the old beards of [18]48." Jacobins tended to assess the situation facing Paris in terms of the politics of previous revolutions, particularly that of 1789, when foreign invasion and civil war threatened revolutionary gains. Both Jacobins and Blanquists continued to respect centralized revolutionary authority; however, unlike the Blanquists—above all, Rigault, who had become excessively focused on seizing and exercising power—Delescluze and other Jacobins remained committed to retaining essential freedoms despite the threatening military situation. As we have seen, Rigault also made constant reference to the French Revolution and was obsessed with militants of the extreme Left during those heady days. Jacobin and Blanquist militants were prominent in the governing body of the Commune and in the Central Committee of the National Guard; indeed, following the elections of April 16 about fifteen members belonged to both groups.[19] Therefore, when the members of the Commune's elected governing body began to meet, the political divisions surfaced immediately and contentiously. Unlike the Jacobins, the Blanquists did not want the sessions of the Commune's Council publicized, fearing that within an hour or so Thiers and his entourage would know everything discussed, particularly military strategy, which the followers of Blanqui, professional revolutionaries, considered their specialty. Moreover, Rigault proposed that Blanqui be named honorary president, but Delescluze, among others, protested vigorously. He could not stand Rigault's authoritarian posture and denounced the proposition as "monarchical."[20]

In an effort to reconcile political tensions and make clear that the judicial abuses of the Second Empire would be left in the past, the Commune asked Eugène Protot, the son of Burgundian peasants, a lawyer, and once a delegate to the congress of the International in Geneva and now Communard delegate for justice, to move civil and criminal proceedings along more rapidly and to undertake measures to guarantee "the freedom of all citizens." But Protot's efforts had little effect on the deep divide between Blanquists and Jacobins, in no small part thanks to Rigault's obsession with perceived threats to the revolution. Gustave Lefrançais and some other delegates advocated abolishing the prefecture of police in order to put an end to seemingly arbitrary arrests undertaken by Rigault. The Blanquist fought against this measure tooth and nail, insisting that Thiers might well have a thousand spies in Paris.

However, Rigault's fears were not unfounded. Conspiracies against the Commune were afoot from the beginning. Within a couple of weeks, anti-Communard organizers began to distribute armbands (*brassards*)—conservative rallying marks that were at first white, the color of the Bourbons, and later tricolor—in conservative neighborhoods. Those who had them awaited the day when they could come into the open and crush the Commune.[21] On one occasion the militant Internationalist Jean Allemane, a printer by trade, got through the lines to Versailles in a failed attempt to infiltrate Thiers's government. Upon his return, he related his short trip to Paris in the company, by chance, of two loose-tongued Versaillais secret agents. When one of them observed that entering revolutionary Paris was as easy as slicing butter with a knife, Allemane quickly realized his mistake and had them arrested upon their arrival. Thiers and his entourage also tried to bribe well-placed Communards, apparently with some success.[22]

In an effort to counteract this threat, Rigault, named civil delegate for general security on March 29, appointed committed young

Blanquist disciples to fill the empty offices of the prefecture of police. Rigault's team compiled files, followed up on their agents' reports, and oversaw policing. One young Blanquist, Théophile Ferré, a twenty-five-year-old Parisian and "a dark little man, with black, piercing eyes," seemed omnipresent. A detractor referred to the former clerk as strange looking, "but what is funnier is when he speaks; he raises up on the points of his feet like an angry rooster and emits sharp sounds, which constitute what one can improperly call his voice." P.-P. Cattelain, head of security, tried to understand how political passion could translate into such enormous hatred in Ferré, who "inspired respect by his honesty and fear by his temperament as a ferocious friend of the revolution." He could be unforgiving of those he believed stood in the way of revolution. Cattelain said that despite Ferré's small size, he feared him and believed that he would himself kill someone he suspected of treason. When several men robbed a house on the Champs-Élysées, Ferré told Cattelain to have "these wretches who dishonor the Commune" shot. Then he changed his mind and sent them into battle with the National Guard; one was wounded and later died.[23]

Gaston Da Costa—"Coco"—served as faithful Rigault's assistant, the *chef du cabinet* of general security. Da Costa was a tall and pleasant twenty-year-old with long, tousled blond hair who had studied mathematics, earned the *baccalauréat*, and once considered applying to the elite École Polytechnique—as had his mentor Rigault. The latter asked Da Costa, known in the Latin Quarter in the late 1860s as "Rigault's puppy," to reorganize the prefecture of police. He was among those who tried, with limited success, to convince his boss to organize the prefecture in a less incendiary way. Rigault's fear of the enemy within took hold. He greeted every Communard military setback with shouts of "Treason!" Soon "a single sign of [Rigault's] hand [was] sufficient to cause any one's arrest, while no one knew what might become of his prisoners."[24]

Already unpopular among Jacobins as well as Parisians with ambivalent attitudes toward the Commune or hostility toward its uncompromising policing efforts, Rigault and his companions' raucous lifestyle did little to soften their image and provided fodder for propagandists in Versailles. In their free moments, they downed food, wine, and eau-de-vie, having moved one of their favorite brasseries from the boulevard Saint-Michel into the prefecture of police. Nor had Rigault's appetite for female companionship faded with the advent of revolution. He was often in the company of Mademoiselle Martin, a young actress. All this gave rise to rumors in Versailles of "orgies" at the prefecture of police. The long workday finished—not without a break for food, drink, and frivolity—Rigault and the others went out to dine and drink some more. His critics howled at the restaurant bills he allegedly ran up with Da Costa. One breakfast on May 10 costing 75.25 francs allegedly included two great Burgundies and *Chateaubriand aux truffes*; five days later, 62.85 francs paid for cigars and bottles of Pommard, Veuve Clicquot, and Nuits-Saint-Georges.[25]

Communard general Gustave Cluseret described Rigault's obsession with the police: "He could not knock down a bock—and he drank many—without talking about the police." US citizen Lili Morton, enthusiastic about the Commune, soured slightly when she met Rigault. Needing a pass to leave Paris, she went to see him carrying a letter of introduction, but the head of the police received her rudely and interrogated her "diabolical[ly]." The American got her passport but left repulsed by the "wicked expression . . . [in Rigault's] cunning eyes."[26]

Rigault, for all his faults, was devoted to the cause and aided Communards whenever he could. Cattelain remembered his boss as an "ardent revolutionary, sometimes brutal, but always subject to sentiments of humanity" and emphasized "the extreme instability of his character." He could be vicious but also compassionate. Every day people showed up asking to see him. Women came to beg for help: their families did not have proper lodging and were hungry. Some even turned up asking for help even though their men were fighting on the side of Versailles. The Commune provided spouses of national guardsmen seventy-five centimes per day, but that was not enough. Rigault gave some of them rooms in the Lobau barracks. Having been aided by Auguste Renoir when he was on the run from imperial police several years earlier, Rigault also made it possible for the Impressionist to get out of Paris to paint in the countryside.[27]

Maverick journalist Henri Rochefort, though no fan, admitted that Rigault was "made of the stuff from which veritable revolutionists are cut out." He sacrificed all for the cause of revolution. Rigault was fearless—no danger caused "his face to pale." He was the kind of man who could tell someone, "I'm very fond of you, but circumstances unfortunately compel me to have you shot. I am, therefore, going to do so!"[28]

Rigault set up eighty neighborhood police offices and had at his disposal a brigade of two hundred agents tasked with sniffing out Versaillais spies. In the morning, at least when he was awake, Rigault convoked a sort of council that went over reports that had come in during the past twenty-four hours. Political policing remained, predictably, Rigault's central focus. About 3,500 people were arrested during the Commune, among them 270 prostitutes. The prisons of Paris were full. Rigault had ordered the arrest of over four hundred people between March 18 and 28, even though many, including Georges Clemenceau, were quickly released.[29]

As the weeks passed, the arrests of those accused of working for Versailles increased and included a member of the International Workingmen's Association who had been an imperial police spy. Rigault's political opponents within the Commune objected to his dictatorial methods. Tensions mounted between Rigault and the Central Committee. Rigault responded memorably to a critic, "We are not dispensing justice, we are making revolution."[30]

On April 13 Rigault drew more fire when he ordered the arrest of Gustave Chaudey, former deputy mayor, follower of the anarchist Pierre-Joseph Proudhon, former editor of *Le Siècle*, and a friend. Chaudey was also a friend of Courbet, who had painted a portrait of him in 1870 and protested his arrest. Chaudey had ordered Breton guardsmen to fire from the Hôtel-de-Ville on demonstrators on January 22, killing several people, including Rigault's friend Théophile Sapia. Élie Reclus, who described Chaudey as haughty and something of a mediocrity, suggested that the journalist had been incarcerated by the Commune, to which he had rallied, because he had forcefully opposed all "who do not appear to be acting in good faith."[31]

WHO WERE THE COMMUNARDS? British journalist Frederic Harrison assessed the Communards in Paris, writing, "The 'insurgents' . . . are simply the people of Paris, mainly and at first working men, but now largely recruited from the trading and professional classes. The 'Commune' has been organized with extraordinary skill, the public services are efficiently carried on, and order has been for the most part preserved." In his view, the Commune, while being "one of the least cruel, has been perhaps the ablest revolutionary government of modern times."[32]

The average Communard was the average Parisian: young, between twenty-one and forty years of age, with the largest number men aged thirty-six to forty. Three-fourths had been born outside Paris and arrived in the waves of immigration, above all from northeastern France but also from the northwest, along with seasonal migrants from the Creuse in the center; 45 percent were married, and 6 percent were widowers, although many workers lived in *unions libres*, which the Commune legitimized. Only 2 percent had secondary education. In a time of increased literacy, only about 11 percent were illiterate, although many ordinary Parisians enjoyed only basic reading and writing skills.[33]

Most Communards hailed from the world of Parisian work and included artisans and craftsmen who produced *articles de Paris* and jewelry. Their numbers included skilled and semiskilled workers—many working with wood, or in shoemaking, printing, or the small-scale production of metals—as well as construction workers, day laborers, and domestic servants. Shopkeepers, clerks, and men in the liberal professions were also well represented. They were among "the people" who had suffered during the siege and felt threatened by monarchist machinations.[34] Of female Communards, 70 percent came from the world of women's work, particularly textiles and the clothing trades. Some courageously provided food and drink to Communard fighters or served as doctors' assistants tending to the wounded. Louise Michel saw no problem with incorporating prostitutes into the corps of women nursing injured fighters: "Who has more right than these women, the most pitiful of the old order's victims, to give their lives for the new?" The Commune accorded pensions to widows and children, whether "legitimate" or not, of men killed fighting for the Commune.[35]

However average or ordinary most Communards were, many observers—foreign and local alike—saw the Commune as a pitched conflict between classes. During his relatively short time at the US Legation, for instance, Wickman Hoffman took note of "the class hatred which exists in France." For the American, it was "something we have no idea of, and I trust that we never shall. It is bitter, relentless, and cruel; and is, no doubt, a sad legacy of the bloody Revolution of 1789, and of the centuries of oppression which preceded it."[36]

Hippolyte Taine, a conservative historian, was sure that the Commune was a proletarian revolution. On April 5 he wrote that most fundamentally the "present insurrection" was socialist: "The boss and the bourgeois exploit us, therefore we must suppress them. Superiority and special status do not exist. Me, a worker, I have abilities, and if I want, I can become the head of a business, a magistrate, a general. By good fortune, we have rifles, let's use them to establish a republic in which workers like us become cabinet ministers and presidents."[37]

Edmond Goncourt and his brother Jules had assessed, shortly before the latter's death a year earlier, that "the gap between wages and the cost of living would kill the Empire." A workman had indeed reason to ask, "'What good does it do me for there to be monuments, operas, café-concerts where I have never set foot because I don't have the money?' And he rejoices that henceforth there will be no more rich people in Paris, so convinced is he that the gathering of rich people into one places raises prices."[38]

The economic and political divisions in Paris's *quartiers* did seem to bear out the Commune's origins in class conflict. The more plebeian neighborhoods of Paris led the way in support of the Commune. The social geography of Paris reflected a divide between the more prosperous western half of the city and the People's Paris of the eastern districts, as well as between the center and the proletarian periphery. Baron Georges Haussmann's massive urban projects during the Second Empire had only intensified the divide, but with the uprising on March 18, the periphery had arguably conquered the *beaux quartiers*. This is not to say that there were none who opposed the Commune in poorer arrondissements like the Eleventh, Twelfth, Eighteenth, Nineteenth, and Twentieth or that there were no devoted Communards in the relatively more privileged Sixth, Seventh, and Eighth Arrondissements. It does indicate that social geography counted for much.

The Second Arrondissement embodied the social and political divide that existed even within relatively prosperous districts. The western parts of the arrondissement were more bourgeois, more anti-Communard, and highly suspicious of proletarian Belleville and its national guardsmen and the Vengeurs de Flourens, a military unit named in honor of the martyred Communard, who came down to parade in the conservative *quartiers* below. In the early weeks of the Commune, many residents advocated conciliation and a negotiated settlement and voted for moderate representatives in the election of March 26. The more plebeian eastern neighborhoods of the Second Arrondissement sent delegates to the Commune; the middle-class residents to the west did not. Around 12,000 people required living assistance in the arrondissement and were more likely to be guardsmen whose families' depended on the 1.50 franc daily payment. A mechanic put it this way: "I have seven children, and my wife was ill. I had no other means of feeding my family."[39]

Given the needs of its plebeian supporters, the organization of work remained a significant goal for Communard militants. The "Declaration of the French people" of April 19 called for the creation of institutions that would provide ordinary people with credit, facilitating "access to property" and "freedom of labor." Ideas and even concrete projects for the "organization of work" were in the air, amid confidence that the defense of the National Guard cannons on March 18 had inaugurated a new era, full of possibilities that would make Paris and the world a better place.[40]

Thus the "social question"—the condition of the poor and how to help them—remained important to many ordinary Parisians. The idea that revolution could bring about reforms that would reduce or even eliminate the considerable differences in conditions of life, opportunities, and expectations remained entrenched in the collective memory of Parisian workers. As Eugène Varlin stated, "We want to overthrow exploitation of workers by the right to work [*le droit au travail*] and the association of workers in corporation." Workers hoped that newly established cooperatives would reflect the organization of the Commune itself: decentralized and locally governed. The anarchist Proudhon's influence was apparent in many workers' organizations in many trades. The Proudhonists and Blanquists imagined that France, like Paris, would evolve into a federation of communes, becoming a free country just as Paris had for the moment become a free city (*ville libre*). Such echoes could be heard at the meeting of women in Trinity Church on May 12, when a speaker thundered, "The day of justice approaches with giant strides. . . . [T]he workshops in which you are packed will belong to you; the tools that are put into your hands will be yours; the gain resulting from your efforts, from your troubles, and from the loss of your health will be shared among you. Proletarians, you will be reborn."[41] This was a time of big dreams.

The regulations established by a workshop set up in the Louvre to repair and convert weapons reflected how some workers envisioned manufacturing operating in the future. Foremen and chargehands (who supervised lathes) were to be elected, just as the National Guard units elected officers. The regulations also laid out the responsibilities of the administrative council, to consist of the manager, the foreman, a chargehand, and one worker "elected from each workbench," which would set salaries and wages and ensure that the workday did not exceed ten hours.[42]

On April 16, the Commune ordered a survey of workshops abandoned by employers who had fled Paris so that workers' cooperatives could ultimately take them over, which indeed happened in a few instances. A small cooperative iron foundry started up in Grenelle. Members moved into one workshop after four days and another after two weeks. The cooperative, employing about 250 workers, produced shells crucial to the city's defense against Thiers. Workers elected "managing directors"—not a very socialist term—led by thirty-nine-year-old Pierre Marc, who had inherited a foundry from his father. The cooperative paid rent to the previous owner of the shop, and its workers earned less than their counterparts employed by the Commune's Louvre shell factory. Producers' cooperatives were thus organized along traditional class lines, and workers were expected to show up with their *livret*, a record book of employment, which they had been required to have with them since 1803, despite wide resentment of this obligation.[43]

In addition to reorganizing Paris's workers, the Commune also endeavored to improve their working conditions. The abolition of night baking by a decree issued on April 20 was one such concrete social measure in the interest of labor taken by the Commune. The debate centered on advantages for bakers and the fact that workers' virtual nighttime enslavement benefited "the aristocracy of the belly." Some master bakers resisted, fearing the loss of clients, and the application of the measure was postponed until May 3, with another decree the next day threatening to seize bread produced before 5 A.M. and distribute it to the poor. Many Parisians still demanded warm croissants first thing in the morning, however, making it difficult for the Commune to enforce the measure. Other Communard decrees established a maximum salary for municipal employees (6,000 francs a year), prohibited employers from taking assessed fines from workers' wages (an increasingly common practice during the Second Empire), and established labor exchanges in each arrondissement.[44]

Given the circumstances and ideological divisions among Communard leaders, it is not surprising that no full-fledged attempt to transform the economy took place, despite the role of socialists who ultimately wanted workers to control the tools of their trades.[45] Yet most Communards accepted the idea of private property. Moreover, for Blanquists, a complete social revolution would have to wait until political power was secured.

Even though the structure of the economy remained relatively unchanged, the status of women improved by leaps and bounds. Indeed, the solidarity and militancy of Parisian women, who had suffered such hardship during the Prussian siege, jumps out as one of the most remarkable aspects of the Paris Commune. Women, taking pride in their role as *citoyennes*, pressured the Commune to attend to their rights and demands and pushed for an energetic defense of the capital. *Citoyenne*

Destrée proclaimed in a club, "The social revolution will not be operative until women are equal to men. Until then, you have only the appearance of revolution."[46]

Such militants considered the condition of women a reflection of the "bourgeois authoritarianism" of the defunct empire and of the enemies gathering their forces at Versailles. Here, too, the Commune seemed to offer exciting possibilities for change. Élisabeth Dmitrieff, who had helped organize cooperatives in Geneva and then arrived in Paris in late March as a representative of the International, stated, "The work of women was the most exploited of all in the social order of the past. . . . [I]t's immediate reorganization is urgent."[47]

The economic disadvantage faced by ordinary female workers infused women's demands. Many *communardes* remained more interested in improving their lives than in achieving political equality, a demand strikingly absent from women's discourse. As Louise Michel explained, "[A woman] bends under mortification; in her home her burdens crush her. Man wants to keep her that way, to be sure that she will never encroach upon his function or his titles. Gentlemen, we do not want either your functions or your titles." Many women were doubly exploited—by their family situations and by their employers. One woman denounced bosses as "the social wound that must be taken care of" because they took advantage of workers, whom they considered "a machine for work," while they lived it up. Dmitrieff called for the elimination of all competition and for equal salaries for male and female workers, as well as a reduction in work hours. She also demanded the creation of workshops for unemployed women and asked that funds go to aid nascent working-class associations.[48]

Dmitrieff, born Elisavieta Koucheleva in the northwestern Russian province of Pskov in 1850, was the illegitimate daughter of an aristocrat and a German nurse twenty years his junior. Élisabeth entered into a *mariage blanc* (a marriage of convenience) to get out of Russia, after having been active in a student group in Saint Petersburg. She carried funds from her sizable dowry into exile in Geneva in 1868. Dmitrieff went to London, where she met Karl Marx and his family. Immediately following the proclamation of the Commune, Marx sent her to Paris, and she sent reports on the situation back to him.

Dmitrieff cut quite a figure. She wore a black riding costume, a felt hat with feathers, and a red silk shawl trimmed in gold. A police description put her at about five feet, three inches tall, with chestnut hair and gray-blue eyes. Léo Frankel was probably but one of the Communards who fell in love with her. Dmitrieff combined a precocious feminism with a socialism influenced by Marx and a firm expectation that revolution would some day come to Russia.[49]

Like Dmitrieff, some women during the Commune wore clothing that reflected their determination to effect change. Some garments were colorful, indeed flamboyant, with the color red omnipresent—for example, in sashes. Other women wore men's clothing and carried rifles. Lodoïska Caweska, a thirty-year-old Polish woman, rode at the head of soldiers, adorned in "Turkish pants, high-buttoned shoes with a red cockade, and a blue belt from which hung two pistols."[50]

On April 8, Dmitrieff sought to rally *citoyennes* in defense of Paris in the tradition of the women who had marched to Versailles in October 1789. Three days later, mothers, wives, and sisters, including Dmitrieff and Nathalie Le Mel, published an "Appeal to the Women Citizens of Paris": "We must prepare to defend and avenge our brothers."[51]

That evening, the Union des Femmes was constituted, led by a council of five women, with Dmitrieff as general secretary. The union called on women to form branches in each arrondissement. Saluting the Commune as representing "the regeneration of society," the organization asked women to build barricades and to "fight to the end" for the Commune. It set up committees in most arrondissements as recruiting centers for volunteers for nursing and canteen work and barricade construction.[52]

The Union des Femmes also took the fight for equal rights to Paris's factories. The manufacture of National Guard uniforms, the vast majority of which women produced, was one Parisian industry that kept going full steam. The Commune had first signed contracts with traditional manufacturers for the production of uniforms, but a report determined that under this arrangement female workers were earning less than under the Government of National Defense. The Union des Femmes demanded the award of all future contracts to workers' producers' cooperatives and that the Tailors' Union and delegates from the Commission of Labor and Exchange negotiate piece rates.[53]

The Commune gave women in the Union des Femmes, which included perhaps as many as 2,000 women, unprecedented public responsibilities, but the response was not all positive. Some Communard leaders and other men reacted with uncertainty and even outright hostility. An official of the Tenth Arrondissement told the female administrator of a welfare hostel that members of the union committee "were to be kept away from all administrative agencies."[54] Yet, without question, women made essential contributions to the Commune, encouraging the military defense of Paris, and caring for wounded Communard fighters.

ALTHOUGH THE COMMUNE concerned itself mainly with the well-being of its citizens, the new government also faced the daunting task of demonstrating its stability and legitimacy to foreigners residing in or visiting the city. About 5,000 US citizens who had been living in Paris before the Commune found themselves surrounded by Versaillais troops. US Ambassador Elihu B. Washburne feared that it would be a long time "before these terrible troubles in Paris are ended." Including tourists passing through, the number of US citizens in Paris during the Commune may have reached 13,000. They read the newspaper *American Register.* Most resided on the Right Bank on the Champs-Élysées or in the Sixteenth Arrondissement. Many spoke no French but benefited from a strong dollar. They had the reputation for being "without polish," even boorish, and "arrogantly aloof."

Most Americans seem to have sided against the Commune. W. Pembroke Fetridge disparaged it as "the most criminal [act] the world has ever seen . . . a revolution of blood and violence" led by "ruthless desperados . . . the refuse of France . . . bandits . . . atheists and free-thinkers . . . madmen, drunk with wine and blood." Yet two Americans residing in Paris could find no fault with the way the city operated. Marie Putnam described the "apparent orderliness of the Commune." Frank M. Pixley of California remembered, "I was present in the city of Paris during the entire period that the Commune held sway. . . . And yet during the five weeks—weeks of menace from without and suffering within—I saw and heard of no single act of pillage and murder."[55]

Indeed the Commune's leaders trumpeted a "revolutionary morality," knowing that their constituents and foreign observers alike would scrutinize them closely. They held themselves to a high standard of honesty and accountability, intended to contrast starkly with the rampant corruption of Napoleon III's Second Empire. Communard leaders went out of their way to demonstrate that they ran a tight ship and could account for all expenditures. Inspired by the goals of equality and decentralization, the Commune rejected high salaries for officials, while affirming the principle of electing functionaries. The idea was that public servants would listen to citizens, who in turn would be actively involved in their government; a poster in the Second Arrondissement called for "the permanent intervention of citizens in communal affairs through the free expression of their ideas and free defense of their interests." Administrators of the Commune were considered responsible to ordinary people, as their representatives and delegates.[56]

The ability of the Commune to provide public services in the wake of the prolonged Prussian siege and the government's overthrow was also essential to demonstrate its legitimacy. The sudden departure of so many officials and employees complicated the situation. Yet the Commune's municipality managed well enough, providing water, light, and postal service, cleaning streets regularly, disposing of garbage properly, and collecting taxes. An American woman had received her tax bill and went to see an official, relating that in view of events, her family was having trouble coming up with the money owed. The Communard replied that this would be no problem, much to the American's relief. She was forced to admit that "Communards were not as bad as all that." The cemetery service continued to function as always—and would have increasingly more to do.[57]

Some observers insisted that crime seemed less of a problem in Paris during the Commune than before or after. On March 23 a poster warned that thieves arrested in *flagrant délit* would be shot, but none were. Relatively few thefts seem to have been reported, and probably only a couple of murders occurred in a city that, despite the departure of so many, remained a teeming place. Charles Beslay attributed this to the spontaneous emergence of a "revolutionary morality." Yet some evidence suggests that thefts may have actually increased. We just do not know. The prefecture of police forbade begging, which Rigault admitted on April 17 had "taken on a considerable extension"; the police banned gambling, and a decree warned cheats and hucksters to stay away from markets. The Commune outlawed prostitution, making some arrests and pushing the industry into corners, although venereal disease proliferated, as it had during the Prussian siege. A decree in May reimposed on prostitutes the old draconian regulations, including the resented obligatory medical inspections. Despite Rigault's ban on the serving of drinks to anyone "in a state of drunkenness" (ironic, considering the source), alcoholism continued its ravages in the City of Light, which could well have been called the City of Drink.[58]

The Commune also wanted to ensure that food was available and affordable. To that end, it established a Commission on Subsistence on March 29. The annual Ham Fair took place April 4–6; pigs and charcuterie went on sale as they had since medieval times. The price of food rose, but the situation did not come close to the extreme short-ages that had compounded the disastrous effects of the freezing weather during the Prussian siege. Once German military authorities allowed the Commune to open the gates leading to their zone of occupation, more provisions entered the city. Some arrondissement *mairies* pur-chased and then sold meat at about cost. Yet Henri Dabot, who lived in the Latin Quarter, complained that his cook could not find what she wanted at the market and that a modest little rabbit, which before would have gone for two francs (almost a day's wage for a worker in ordinary times), now cost five. Courbet drank a little glass of Gentiane liqueur "to forget having to eat black bread and horsemeat." However, for ordinary people who did not have cooks, prices put some commod-ities increasingly out of range. In early May an employee of the pre-fecture of police reported that Parisians were complaining about rising food costs. Denunciations of hoarders became common, and officials ordered some stores searched.[59]

Arrondissement *mairies* became hubs of activity during the Com-mune; in addition to selling food at or near cost, they handled matters of local governance that brought in a steady stream of citizens. Paul Martine, a former *normalien* (student at the prestigious École normale) and lycée teacher, related the creative chaos of the *mairie* at Batignolles in the Seventeenth Arrondissement: "First came our tumultuous de-liberations in the large hall where the municipal council met, then the public crowding the door with demands of all kinds. Then came those carrying news, the dissatisfied, foreigners, and people who wanted to declare births, deaths, or ask to be married. And this while the cannons rumbled, day and night, all around the ramparts. We were there almost permanently." Martine often slept on one of the mattresses placed in the corner, as the "hall of the municipal council was transformed into a dormitory."

Depending on supplies, the *mairie* of each arrondissement pro-vided national guardsmen and indigents with coal, wood, and bread. Beginning early in the morning, "an uninterrupted procession of poor women, without work and bread, and whose husbands had been killed in the fighting" arrived asking for vouchers to exchange for food when-ever stocks permitted. The *mairie* undertook *soupes populaires* (soup kitchens) when sufficient provisions were available. Couples arrived asking to be married: Benoît Malon sometimes performed the brief cer-emonies. Malon, who had eight national guardsmen arrested for theft on April 25, also oversaw burials of Communards killed in fighting outside the ramparts or by Versaillais cannon fire, sad events followed by angry calls for vengeance and the death of Thiers and the "bombers of Paris!"[60]

Sutter-Laumann's father had begun working in the *mairie* of the Eighteenth Arrondissement at the beginning of the Prussian siege. His son now found work there. Sutter-Laumann and his father received 1.50 francs per day for National Guard service. This was barely enough to live on, so the salary of five francs per day for each of them from their work in the *mairie* helped out. The younger Sutter-Laumann dispensed vouchers for bread and meat to poor residents of the district from 8 A.M. until 5 P.M. Though not difficult, the work was "odiously monotonous and fatiguing," because of 40,000 people inscribed on the registers in that poor district alone, perhaps 10,000 showed up. The help the *mairie* could provide was quite small; many women demanded more, "half imploring, half threatening."

Sutter-Laumann made it a point to attend battalion meetings and club gatherings. The clubs epitomized popular sovereignty at work. The Club of Saint-Nicolas-des-Champs insisted that the Commune respond directly to all its proposals, even if doing so took two hours per day. The belief that Commune officials should attend such public meetings was widespread. Some clubs admitted participants at no charge; others levied small fees ranging from five to fifteen and occasionally twenty-five centimes per person. Those in attendance rose to speak and debate, frequently amid noise and, depending on the subject, heckling. The defense of Paris became an increasingly frequent theme. At a club meeting in Saint-Ambroise in the Eleventh Arrondissement, Citizen Jubelin recalled "the dreadful threat looming over our intelligent people, the convict settlements of Lambessa and Cayenne that await us if we should fail." He added that he would die in the defense of his rights. On May 9 at a meeting of the same club, Citizen Roussard rose to denounce "the young dandies and others who are too cowardly to join the ranks of the National Guard" and demanded their immediate incorporation into the Commune's fighting force. Several days later Citizen Lesueur related that his National Guard battalion had fallen apart because a few men had deserted, after which "everyone" had fled. He blamed the men who "wore the stripes" and should be leading but were "staying to the rear."[61]

Of 733 people identified as participating in political clubs (*clubistes*), 113 were female (15 percent), and 198 held some position within the Commune (27 percent). The average member was somewhat older than the average Communard and most likely hailed from the most working-class neighborhoods. Organizers saw the clubs as a means of popular education and a way to maintain vigilance against the Versaillais fifth column within the walls of Paris.[62]

On April 16 Sutter-Laumann asked for two days off from his work in the *mairie* so that he could join his battalion, which was heading out to reinforce troops in Asnières. The city lay directly in the line of fire of Versaillais cannons appropriately placed at a chateau in Bécon across the Seine. Sutter-Laumann was fortunate to return with his life. Near Gennevilliers, the Versaillais advanced, approaching so near that he could easily distinguish the uniforms of gendarmes from those of line troops. The national guardsmen retreated under enemy fire, leaving fallen comrades behind. Those reaching the Seine earlier had destroyed the bridge, fearing the Versaillais would use it to cross the river. Sutter-Laumann swam across and returned to Paris.[63]

THE COMMUNE FACED staunch critics from the start, as well as the nearly impossible challenge of governing a divided city, still reeling from months of siege, even as it prepared for a Versaillais attack. But while ordinary citizens like Sutter-Laumann and his father were willing to wait for the new government to work out its kinks—and even take part in its ministries—the Versaillais threat would test their patience. And for all its efforts, the Commune would quickly lose (if indeed it had ever had) the confidence of many foreign visitors and most of the bourgeoisie remaining in the city.

Englishman Ernest Vizetelly was one foreigner who noticed that the mood in Paris was shifting. It had become somber, or "more dismal" as Vizetelly put it. Most workshops had shut down, except those turning out uniforms or other items for the National Guard, and "there were no spring fashions and no bargain days." The wine shops, however, seemed always to be open. One evening Edmond de Goncourt went out to dine and asked about the *plat du jour* (dish of the day). "There isn't one, nobody's left in Paris," a waiter replied, referring to his usual clients. Another large restaurant had no diners, and "the waiters spoke only in low tones," while well-heeled clients were dining well in Versailles. On April 17 Goncourt also caught wind of the bourgeoisie's disgruntlement. He wondered, "Are things going badly for the Commune? I am astonished today to find that the population has come back to life." He noted occasional shouts against the Commune, including those of a man in a grey overcoat "who goes on up the boulevard defying the angry rowdies and turning around to shout aloud his disdain for the Communards." Five days later he observed, "The whole length of the Rue de Rivoli there is a procession of the baggage of the last bourgeois making their way to the Lyon railroad station." He went to the zoo and there thought he had found "the sadness of Paris. The animals are silent."

The Commune's defeat at the hands of the Versaillais in skirmish after skirmish did little to restore faith in the new order. In central Paris, Goncourt watched as four hearses adorned with red flags went by, one carrying "a man, half of whose face and nearly all of whose neck have been carried away by a shell, with the white and blue of one of his eyes running down his cheek. His right hand, still black with powder, is upraised and clenched as if it clasped a gun."[64] The bodies of those killed by Versaillais shells were taken to the Hôtel-de-Ville to await identification by family and friends. Unidentified corpses were photographed in the hope that someone would come looking for a missing person. It was all so grisly. A national guardsman penned a letter to a newspaper reflecting his disgust at returning exhausted from fighting at Issy and Vanves to find the cafés on the boulevard Saint-Michel full of revelers cavorting "with *drôlesses* [female jokers]," carrying on as usual while other Parisians risked their lives for the Commune.[65]

Within the ramparts of the besieged French capital, many upper-class Parisians who had been unable to get out or believed the Commune would collapse more quickly than it had awaited their liberation. These included members of the Vignon family, who worried most about their property. They had money, jewelry, and other valuables in another apartment in the Tenth Arrondissement, now under the supervision of domestic servants. They also owned a house in the village of Clamart just south of Paris, but all was well there. Henri, Paul Vignon's brother, was safely lodged in Versailles, and from there Henri assured his mother in Falaise in Normandy that "all the honest and sensible people are deserting Paris." In Versailles, Henri got up late, purchased the Versaillais newspaper *Le Gaulois* to read the government's slant on the news—for example, that many foreigners were involved in the Commune—ate lunch, hung around the chateau, dined again, and went to a café. Henri reassured his mother that he was receiving an indemnity from Versailles of ten francs a day. In any case, he assured her, the family remained well-off, and money was not a problem.

The Sixth Arrondissement seemed as calm as Falaise. Paul could write his mother while sitting in a quiet café. Édouard, Paul and Henri's father, was more than sixty years old, so he did not have to worry about being conscripted into the National Guard of Paris. Paul had managed to avoid service in his unit, which for the moment did not have any officers. He noted that there was no problem getting about in Paris, even on streets where barricades were going up.[66]

Ten days into the Commune, Édouard Vignon became alarmed about the situation in Paris, which he described by letter to his wife as the absolute power "of the most perverse that society can offer." He did not think that the *honnêtes gens* (men of property) would let themselves be pillaged and massacred. Édouard lamented that all talk of reconstituting a National Guard "of order" remained only that. For his part, Édouard's son found measures taken by the Commune to be increasingly "absurd," notably the law on rents and the abolition of conscription and thus of a professional army.

Paul could also imagine reaction by the *honnêtes gens* against these "bandits." His reflections reveal the emerging biological discourse differentiating the "healthy" part of the population and those so corrupted that they had to disappear. Paul distinguished people of property from those without. The family property was a constant theme in the correspondence of the Vignon family. Édouard received a worrying order from a justice of the peace to take items of value from their apartment in the Tenth Arrondissement, which had been "sealed" until lawyers could adjudicate ownership after the recent death of a relative. The residence was near enough to Montmartre that it might suffer "an indiscrete visit from ill-intentioned men." Édouard moved the nicest furniture to a room well inside the apartment and took things of value to the apartment in the Sixth Arrondissement, where he believed there was nothing to fear because of the social composition of the *quartier*. He carried family deeds and titles to be locked away. To the Vignon family, the Commune put at risk "all of society, the future of France, and especially private fortunes," including Thiers. Édouard mused about moving his family and fortune to the mountains of Switzerland; he was not the last French person of means to consider such a decision.

For the moment, Paul could not complain. He was pleased to have heard that "the members of the Council of the Commune have begun to eat each other, a good sign." Paul reassured his mother on April 1, "We continue to enjoy the most perfect tranquility. I walk about all day, looking for ways of occupying my time." Paul went to a café every day to see his friends, read in the garden of the Cluny Museum or in the Luxembourg Gardens, and played whist. He strolled the boulevards alone or with his father. Paul observed clergy walking through his neighborhood without the slightest problem. His National Guard unit, commanded by "Citizen Cook Lacord," operated under the principle of inertia, stronger than resistance.

In the meantime, the Vignons' two domestics took care of one of their apartments, going to daily Mass and asking God "to bestow the most precious blessings on our excellent masters and on their dear family." The servants noted wistfully that "Monsieur's newspaper" was no longer to be found, only *Le Cri du Peuple* and *Père Duchêne*, of which the Vignons did not approve. Their concierge was under pressure from the Commune to make empty apartments available to Parisians whose homes had been blown apart by Versaillais shells. Each day the domestics told the concierge that they were expecting friends of the Vignon family to arrive at any time. The servants had worries of their own, with a brother-in-law and brother in the Army of Versailles. "Monsieur is really so good," they wrote, "to think of our dear soldiers."[67]

Paul avoided walking on or near streets close to his apartment, afraid of seeing men with whom he had served during the siege who might ask why he was not in uniform. One day, he went to the Palace of Justice to pick up some papers and ran into a lawyer of vague acquaintance, who knew that Paul had served in the National Guard during the Prussian siege and encouraged him to join up again. The lawyer could make sure that he would retain his former rank of captain, adding that Paul would see "that the Commune is an honest and legitimate government." Paul refused, telling him very coldly that he knew what he had to do and was not about to join the Commune. Miffed, the lawyer turned around quickly and walked away.[68] Despite run-ins like this, Paul decided not to try to leave Paris for the time being, thinking that fleeing could well be more dangerous than remaining in the city.[69]

At the very end of March, the railway line to Versailles along the Right Bank of the Seine had been cut, but the train on the other side of the river continued to operate. Paul's brother Henri had no difficulty getting from Versailles into Paris on March 30 to spend the evening with his father and brother. Likewise, Paul got to Versailles without problem to visit his brother. However, many Parisians were not so fortunate in exchanging news and even visits with their families. The Versaillais seized letters sent from Paris via Saint-Denis "by the thousands"; some got through, but many—indeed most—did not. Édouard worried that his and Paul's letters might no longer get out of Paris, as during the Prussian siege. At the same time, he rejoiced that increased surveillance by the Versaillais and Germans might prevent Communard propaganda directed at the provinces from getting out. Thiers's government, unsurprisingly, was at the same time bombarding the provinces and other countries with fanciful accounts of happenings in Paris.[70]

The failure of the Commune's forces to defeat the Versaillais at Courbevoie on April 2 pleased the Vignon family. National guardsmen retreated down the avenue de Neuilly and into Paris, followed by Versaillais shells. Henri left his father and brother and headed back to Versailles via Sceaux. Nearing the valley of the Bièvre, he heard sounds of combat uncomfortably near. Henri came upon peasants who advised against his chosen route, warning that he would soon find himself in the middle of the fighting. Finally reaching Versailles, he watched as Communard prisoners arrived under escort. About 20,000 people waited to have a look at them; they greeted the troops and gendarmes with enthusiastic shouts and insulted and even struck the national guardsmen. The presence of guards prevented the Versaillais crowd from going so far as to massacre the captured soldiers. The soldiers made clear, however, that they wanted nothing more than to storm Paris and "take care of these revolutionaries." Henri wrote his mother that the Communards had suffered losses of between 1,000 and 1,500 men and that the Army of Versailles had only 25 wounded. The Versaillais troops' decision "to give no quarter" pleased the Vignons. Captured Communards who had "deserted" from the regular army were immediately shot, which Henri considered an "energetic and good example."[71]

The victory at Courbevoie renewed Édouard Vignon's confidence in the French army. Once it had reached full strength, Édouard was sure it would show the Parisians a thing or two. The bourgeois was not disappointed that attempts at conciliation or some sort of negotiated settlement had failed. Yet he assured his wife that she should not fear for Paul and Henri—they would not be forced to march. Édouard believed that when the Versaillais launched an assault on Paris, "the brave national guardsmen of order" would rise up and complete the rout of the "bandits." Then they would only need "to reestablish order with severity." He had heard that the National Guard fighting at Châtillon and Clamart had encountered not gendarmes but rather regular French troops, easily identified by their red pants. National guardsmen had reason to be discouraged.

Henri excitedly related to his mother news of a successful Versaillais attack on the barricades at the pont de Neuilly on April 6; one had included an overturned omnibus, another a toppled railroad car. The Army of Versailles crossed the Seine and occupied the first houses of Neuilly. Communard defenders taken prisoner had been killed. As Henri explained, "The *mot d'ordre* (watchword) is to take no prisoner, to shoot everyone who falls into their hands." He assured his mother that "foreigners" were playing a major part in the Commune and repeated reports that the British government had assured the Versailles government that 5,200 pickpockets were on their way across the English Channel to Paris to add to the chaos in the capital.[72]

Henri amused himself by once or twice going with the Versaillais troops on expeditions near the walls of Paris. He found such excursions a little dangerous but "truly admirable." He could judge for himself the effectiveness of the artillery duels between the two sides. As the Communards returned fire from Point-du-Jour, he and his friends decided it would be prudent to return to Versailles. But Henri was convinced that his exile would soon end. After all, Thiers had announced that the Versaillais would soon be in Paris.[73]

IN EARLY APRIL, it remained fairly easy to get in and out of Paris. Céline de Mazade remained there for the first six weeks of the Commune to oversee the operation of her husband's textile manufacturing company, which had factories in the Oise north of Paris and a warehouse in the capital. Her husband, Alexandre, stayed away from the capital to avoid conscription into the National Guard. Husband and wife supported Versailles and complained that the Commune was hurting business. Good labor had become difficult to find. Yet, at least in the beginning, Céline de Mazade managed to leave Paris regularly and to ship silk out of the capital to the company warehouses, sometimes with the help of bribes. She was not the only one to rely on that method to move in and out of the city.[74] As Thiers's propaganda continued to flood in, accompanied by wounded soldiers returning from battle, wealthy and foreign-born Parisians—even those who had held out—began to see the appeal of escape.

The US Legation was jammed with French citizens asking for passports. By late April, Ambassador Elihu B. Washburne had provided more than 1,500 *laissez-passer* (diplomatic passes) to Alsatians, who could now claim to be German subjects. He became increasingly pessimistic about the entire situation, reporting on April 20, "Fortune, business, public and private credit, industry, labor, financial enterprise, are all buried in one common grave. It is everywhere devastation, desolation, ruin. The physiognomy of the city becomes more and more sad . . . and Paris, without its brilliantly-lighted cafés, is Paris no longer."[75]

But for those who could not claim foreign citizenship in order to escape the city and avoid service in the National Guard, bribery was the best, if not the only, option. The ongoing fight with Versailles troops meant that the National Guard was in dire need of men to fight, so they did everything in their power to round up those shirking their duty. National guardsmen demanded information from concierges, who lived in the buildings they tended, and searched apartments, looking for men trying to avoid service. Those between twenty and forty who were discovered hiding and resisted were hauled off and told that they would be put up front during the next skirmish. The Commune cut off their daily wage in the hope that spouses might pressure them to serve. Yet some men still managed to leave by bribing guards to look the other way. John Leighton noted that one could go to the Gare du Nord and claim to be seventy-eight years old, and a guard might well reply in playful jest, "Only that? I thought you looked older." Leighton heard that some residents of Belleville and Montmartre were earning "a nice little income" helping people get out, such as by aiding them in climbing over the walls.[76] Wickham Hoffman, secretary of the US Legation, also managed to go back and forth to Versailles, where he had found lodgings, thanks to his embassy. In Paris, Versaillais shells hit his Paris apartment building eight times. Hoffman travelled to and from his office in the capital with passes easily obtained from both sides. But as he had to go through German-held Saint-Denis in order to get back into Paris by train, the trip grew from twelve to thirty miles, taking three-hours each way. Friends asked him to bring their horses and carriages to Versailles on his trips. He noted, "If the Communist officers at the gates were close observers, they must have thought that I was the owner of one of the largest and best-appointed stables in Paris." His principal complaint during the Commune was that his landlady had run out of his favorite champagne.[77]

PAUL VIGNON, like 200,000 other upper-class Parisians who had already fled, realized in mid-April that the time had come to leave Paris. In his apartment building on the rue de Seine, the concierge took Paul aside and told him that a junior officer in the National Guard had come by with a notebook containing a list of names, asking about men under age forty living there. When the concierge hesitated, the officer said he was aware that the man had knowingly provided false information in the past, adding that the Commune wanted to make an example of people who did this in order to reduce the number of draft dodgers (*réfractaires*). The concierge took a real chance, saying that two brothers of the age to serve, *les citoyens Vignon*, who had been in the 84th battalion during the war, normally residing there but had left for the provinces. The National Guard officer departed, saying he would find out whether this was in fact the case. Paul Vignon profusely thanked the concierge but knew he could delay no longer.

The challenge now was to get out. Increased Communard security had made it more difficult to leave Paris. The gates were closely guarded, and only civilians with passes stamped by the Commune could leave. Paul had heard that some young men had managed to escape hidden beneath laundry in the wagons of washerwomen or even, somehow, encased in giant slabs of meat, thanks to sympathetic butchers. But guards had heard about that trick and were stabbing meat being transported with their bayonets. Several young department store clerks got away by jumping a guard at the customs barrier post and quickly fleeing. A few other hardy souls had thrown ropes from the top of the ramparts and climbed down at night.

The Vignon family's devoted servant had heard that a young Swiss man had loaned his papers to a Parisian, and she said she could get hold of them. Paul and his father accepted the proposition. Soon Paul was in possession of a Swiss birth certificate in the name of Schmitt, who was approximately his age, along with a passport stamped at the Swiss embassy.

Early the next morning Paul Vignon, his father, and the domestic—who would return to Paris with the papers once they had arrived in Saint-Denis—went to the Gare du Nord armed with Paul's new identity. Guards would not stop Paul's father, because of his age, or the domestic servant, as women could pretty much come and go as they pleased. Paul went up to the window to buy three second-class tickets so they could (for once) "travel democratically" in order not to attract unusual attention. Communards did not travel first-class. They registered their two crates of belongings without problem and walked into the waiting room.

The travelers showed their papers to a guard at the door, who stepped back to let them pass. But a young National Guard lieutenant suddenly appeared and asked politely to see their documents. He announced that Paul's papers were not in order because they lacked the stamp of the prefecture of police. Paul replied that this was not necessary because they bore the stamp of a representative of Switzerland—"my country," he lied—and no such requirement had been in place when his brother had left. The lieutenant told him that because so many men avoiding military service were trying to leave Paris, a new regulation had been decreed. Paul reminded him that as a foreigner, he should be allowed to go, but the young lieutenant would not relent. Paul told his interrogator that he would find the head of surveillance for the railway station, who would presumably take care of the matter.

When he arrived at the station's police office, Paul discovered that the suspicious national guardsman had taken a back stairway and was already there. The surveillance officer assured Paul that he did not doubt his Swiss nationality for a minute, but he had received explicit instructions that he could not ignore. There was nothing to be done. If Paul made a scene, they might well have a look at his luggage and see that as a good Parisian bourgeois, he had had is initials "P.V." embroidered on his clothes and inscribed on his cane. He could not go to the prefecture of police because for four years he had been attached to the appellate court and often had dealings with officials there. Someone might recognize him. He and his father would have to find another way.

By good fortune, they did. A railroad employee had brushed by Paul a bit close as he paced back and forth in the station. When Paul reacted by looking directly at him, the man asked if they were being prevented from leaving for Saint-Denis. Paul started to tell his story when the man cut him off: they should follow him and give him a small bribe in cash. If Paul gave the guard on duty twenty francs—a considerable sum—he could be arrested for bribery if ensnared. So he took out two francs, handed them over, and went quickly through the door to the quay while the railroad official looked the other way.

Paul, his father, and their servant entered the closest second-class train compartment they found. Paul's heart was pounding. Their traveling companions would be six *femmes du peuple*, not the sort Paul and his father had traveled with before. One of the women suddenly warned him to be careful—before the train left, Communard guards would pass through the cars. She noted that he looked too young to be leaving Paris. Paul recounted his now quite tired story about being Swiss and how the Communard authorities could not prevent him from leaving, and so on. "Believe me!" the worthy woman replied, telling him to slide under the bench of the compartment so that the women could conceal him with their clothes. He did so, and an instant later a guard looked in. The train pulled out, and twenty minutes later his new acquaintance said that he could come out from under the bench; she had seen a German soldier on the quay of the train station in Saint-Denis.

Now no longer within the Commune's jurisdiction, Paul and his party got off the train, giving each of the working-class women "a warm handshake." The Vignons' domestic servant returned to Paris with the Swiss papers. Paul and his father immediately went to eat a "copious" lunch upon leaving the station. They then left for Falaise. Not long thereafter, Paul Vignon was in Versailles. It seemed to him that he should show "some zeal" about working again. He found Versailles full of deputies and senators, as well as a bevy of job seekers, men like him who had abandoned Paris. Still, Paul managed to find a post in Thiers's government.[78]

THE PARIS COMMUNE brought most Parisians, such as Sutter-Laumann, hardship but also hope. For others with more comfortable existences, like the Vignon family, the Commune was to be endured until the Army of Versailles could put an end to the pretentions of ordinary Parisians. With the capital surrounded militarily, civil war impinged on daily life, as shells fell on western Paris and casualties mounted amid growing, gnawing fear.

Gradually some Parisians who had been willing to give the Commune a chance because they were republicans or favored the program for municipal autonomy began to turn against it. The quarrels among Communard leaders, for instance, disgusted lower-middle-class Parisians. In an attempt to combat dwindling support, Communard propaganda, in the *Journal Officiel* and on wall posters, transformed *fédéré* losses into great victories over depleted Versaillais forces taking many casualties. In the propagandists' telling, battalions and entire regiments of Versailles line troops were abandoning Thiers and joining the Commune.[79] There was no truth to these reports, and Parisians, even those devoted to the Commune, could not have ignored the mounting casualties resulting from the skirmishes.

Yet growing opposition to arbitrary arrests, hostage taking, and the occasional requisition of supplies did not turn all hesitant public opinion toward Thiers. In fact, Thiers continued to do everything possible to earn the hatred of Parisians. The Versaillais leader had agreed to the devastating armistice, and his cannons were inflicting great damage on Paris—more than that caused by the Prussian siege—and killing

innocent citizens. His commitment to the republic was at best equivo-
cal. Charles Beslay wrote a letter to Thiers, whom he had once known
fairly well, calling on him to resign. The Communard moderate saluted
this third revolution of the century in Paris, "the greatest and the most
just," and accused Thiers of opposing in obvious bad faith the social
transformation that had been occurring over the past half century in
Europe. If Versailles was now stronger, Beslay and many others firmly
believed, Paris at least had right on her side.[80]

In a grand demonstration of Parisians' hatred of Thiers, newspapers called for the demolition of the house of the "bomber" who was
launching destructive shells into Paris while denying doing so. On the
morning of April 15, Communard leaders with national guardsmen
turned up at the door of Thiers's house on the place Saint-Georges.
The concierge almost fainted when she saw "grim-looking visitors"
but quickly turned over the keys. A quick search revealed objets d'art,
paintings, and books that Thiers had assiduously collected over the
years. They found Italian Renaissance bronzes, porcelain from centuries past, ivory carvings, engraved rock crystals, and Chinese and Jap-
anese jade carvings. Courbet proposed that the objets d'art belonging
to Thiers should be enumerated. When Thiers learned in Versailles that
his beloved house was to be demolished, he became quite pale, fell into
an armchair, and burst into tears. Thiers, one could easily conclude,
loved objects, not people.[81]

Destroying Thiers home did little to assuage the fears of Communards like Élisabeth Dmitrieff, who worried about the fate of the
Commune in which she had invested so much effort. Would there be
time to establish unions for female workers as she hoped? Sick with
bronchitis and a fever, with no one to replace her, Dmitrieff knew time
was of the essence. On April 24 she wrote the General Council of the
International, "I work hard; we are mobilizing all the women of Paris.
I organize public meetings; we have set up defense committees in all
arrondissements, right in the town halls, and a Central Committee as
well."[82] She had worked tirelessly for the cause, but would it be enough?
Increasingly, it seemed the future of the Commune relied not on Communards like herself but on powerful forces beyond Paris—and beyond
her control. Razing Thiers's house would have no impact on efforts to
defend the city against the Versaillais hordes. Thiers no longer had his
mansion, but he had a powerful army moving ever closer to the ramparts of the capital.

CHAPTER 4

THE COMMUNE
VERSUS THE CROSS

T HE SUMMARY EXECUTION of Communard commanders Émile Duval and Gustave Flourens on April 2 changed the story of the Paris
Commune. From the Commune's point of view, the Versaillais had no
right to execute captured prisoners. It had demanded that its fighters be
treated as "belligerents" and thus cared for, as specified by the Geneva
Convention of 1864, passed in response to the bloody Crimean War of
1853 to 1856 and the 1859 war between France and Austria. But Adolphe
Thiers and his government continued to insist that Communards taken
prisoner were insurgents, indeed bandits and criminals, and deserved no
protection under any kind of international law.

At the meeting of the Commune on April 4, Raoul Rigault insisted
that action be taken in response to the killing of Duval and Flourens.
Now, with the support of Édouard Vaillant, he proposed that hostages be taken, suggesting the incarceration of the archbishop of Paris,
Georges Darboy, and other ecclesiastics. Four days earlier, Darboy had
received warning of his impending detention. When Rigault gave the
order, he barked, "Get me two cops and go arrest the priest!"[1]

BORN IN 1813 IN THE SMALL TOWN (2,500 people) of Fayl-Billot in
Haute-Marne in eastern France, Darboy was the oldest of four children
whose parents owned a small grocery and haberdashery. Their neighbors worked the land or produced baskets and other wickerwork sold
in or beyond the region. The Darboy family's world centered on the
village church. Early on, the parish priest decided that Georges was
destined for the priesthood.

Georges entered the Little Seminary in Langres in 1827 with about two hundred other boys; the classrooms were so cold that the ink sometimes froze in winter. Four years later, Darboy entered the Grand Seminary in Langres, announcing that he would always stand ready to die for his religion, as had a good many priests and nuns during the Terror of 1793 and 1794 during the French Revolution. Ordained in 1836, Darboy became a professor of philosophy and later theology at the Grand Seminary. Always fascinated by history and its relationship to theology, he believed that the Church had to adapt to new social and political realities.

Darboy became more and more preoccupied with the growing indifference to the Church among large segments of the population and the staggering difference in religious practice between women and men, with the former more likely to attend Mass. He lamented that people were more concerned with "terrestrial things." Could not the sciences, in which he had become keenly interested, help reawaken faith? And should the Church not trumpet its historical role in France?[2]

Darboy's intense study and quest for personal perfection took a physical toll, leading even to suffering, a kind of private *calvaire* (ordeal), that would bring him grace in the mission of saving himself and others. Pale and small, the priest had a reserved, nervous, pensive, and even melancholy aspect. His hair, greying prematurely, as if drained of color by worry, hung down limply over very narrow temples. An English contemporary said of him, "His nose is too big, his lips are too thick, his chin is too heavy, and he is lacking in finesse and grace." Yet, as an admirer put it, "a flower does not require a dazzling casing."[3]

In 1845, Denis Affre, the archbishop of Paris, summoned Darboy to the capital and named him chaplain of the prestigious Collège Henri IV. Darboy described himself as "happy, free, and cheerful" in Paris, with "its atmosphere, its chaos, its ideas—its all-consuming life." Yet the poverty of the working poor, comprising the majority of Parisian residents, appalled him as he walked through the city.[4]

On a rainy February 22, 1848, Paris exploded in revolution when a movement for political reform culminated in street demonstrations and troops shot several protesters dead. The July Monarchy collapsed, and like his Bourbon predecessor, Charles X, King Louis-Philippe hightailed it for England. Darboy immediately threw his support behind the Second French Republic. The young priest believed that the February Revolution would usher in better relations between the Church and ordinary people. Then the June Days uprising rocked the capital, as demonstrations by workers turned into full-scale insurrection. As fighting swirled around the Panthéon, Darboy gave the last rites to several dying workers. Over the ensuing year, as the revolutionary Left grew in strength, Darboy's enthusiasm for the republic faded.

Darboy remained concerned about the plight of poor Parisians, however, and hoped to address the anticlericalism stemming at least in part from the profound disparity in wealth between privileged and plebian parishes. When the new archbishop of Paris, Marie-Dominique Sibour, assigned Darboy to survey the parishes of the diocese of Paris, he discovered the obvious. Those in the wealthy western districts enjoyed virtually inexhaustible resources; religious ceremonies there took place with splendor and pomp. Such ostentation augmented popular anticlericalism in the poorer neighborhoods, where churches were spartan, often almost bare, and fewer and fewer faithful attended.[5]

Darboy's primary battle, however, was with the Vatican, and his refusal to submit to Pope Pius IX pushed him closer to Napoleon III. As a young man, Darboy had accepted Gallicanism, the doctrine that the authority of the ninety-one French bishops should take precedence over that of the pope.

As a major figure in France's most important and visible diocese, Darboy got to know one of the best-connected clergymen, Abbé Gaspard Deguerry, *curé* of the Church of the Madeleine, where the elite held their marriages and baptisms. A large, imposing, outgoing man who gave the impression of holding court, Deguerry served as confessor to Empress Eugénie, who, like her husband, Napoleon III, apparently had lots to confess.[6]

In 1859, the emperor named Darboy bishop of Nancy, making him the first openly Gallican bishop appointed during the first seven years of the Second Empire. The Vatican went along with the nomination, having no choice, because the Concordat signed with Napoleon in 1802 gave the French state the right to name bishops. The new bishop insisted that the Church could not exist independently of social and political conditions and that the temporal authority of the pope simply did not correspond "to modern realities." In his view, "the great days of the Papacy as a political institution are no more."[7]

When the archbishop of Paris died on the last day of 1862, the emperor selected Darboy to replace him, ignoring the opposition of the Vatican. Learning in Fayl-Billot of his appointment, Darboy's mother said, "Archbishop of Paris, that's nice, but archbishops of Paris do not last very long."[8] Since Darboy's move to Paris, three archbishops had died—two violently.

In his new role, Darboy became even closer to the emperor. Pleased with Darboy's loyalty, Napoleon III named him to the Senate, the only bishop or archbishop so honored, and to the emperor's private advisory council. In 1864, Darboy became grand chaplain at the emperor's residence at the Tuileries, where imperial occupants surrounded themselves with adoring wealthy people. The archbishop married and baptized members of the imperial family and oversaw the First Communion of the prince imperial. Such flamboyant events made him uncomfortable, because it clearly identified him with fancy folk, among whom, as the son of provincial shopkeepers, he never really felt at home. When Napoleon III awarded Darboy the Legion of Honor, the archbishop reassured his parents that he had not been struck by "the sickness" of seeking imperial honors.[9]

THE FIRST VATICAN COUNCIL commenced in December 1869, summoned to approve the pope's planned proclamation of papal infallibility, which he assumed would mark the end of Gallican opposition to papal prerogatives. French Ultramontanes were pleased, insisting that the pope was "Christ on earth." In Rome Darboy emerged as a leader of the opposition to papal infallibility. On July 13, the pope got his way: the bishops supported the new doctrine, but a third of French bishops voted against it or abstained. Darboy left for Paris without voting, later sending in his formal acceptance of a doctrine he had vigorously opposed.[10]

Archbishop Darboy's first reaction to the proclamation of the Commune had been scathing: "This is a parade without dignity and a mindless parody without soul." In the wake of the first military defeats suffered by Communard forces on the afternoon of April 4, about thirty national guardsmen entered the courtyard of the archbishop's palace. National Guard captain Rével carried the official summons signed by Rigault ordering him to "arrest Monsieur Darboy, so-called archbishop of Paris." Révol told Darboy that no harm would come to him and that he could return to his residence after a simple visit to see the prefect of police, who wished to inquire about some shots supposedly fired from the windows of a school operated by the Jesuits. The archbishop's sister asked to come along, but Darboy refused. Ernest Lagarde, a forty-five-year-old vicar, went with him.[11]

Led through various offices, some in chaos, with an overflow of people smoking, shouting, and drinking, Darboy was taken to Rigault. The delegate for security, renowned for his lack of sartorial attention, now surprisingly sported a military cap replete with military decorations and sat elegantly in an elevated armchair before a large table covered in green cloth. The sight of men in clerical garb seemed to enrage him: "So, it's you, Citizen Darboy! Well, there! Now it's our turn!" When the archbishop referred to the new head of the police and his colleagues as "my children," the immediate, sharp response was, "We are not children—we are the magistrates of the people!" The archbishop asked why he had been arrested. Rigault snapped that for 1,800 years "you imprison us with your superstitions!" It was time for this to cease: "Your *chouans* [counter-revolutionary peasant insurgents in western France in 1793 and 1794] massacred our brothers! Well, each one his turn. Now it is we with the force, the authority, and the right; and we are going to use them." He promised that the Communards would not burn the clergy alive, as the Church had done in places during the Inquisition: "We are more humane. No. . . . We will shoot you." When Darboy evinced a small smile, Rigault told him that in two days he would be shot; would he be smiling then?

Rigault and his Blanquist friend Théophile Ferré accused the archbishop of having stolen "the assets of the people." Darboy rejoined that the possessions used for religious services belonged to the church councils. Rigault and Ferré were utterly unwilling to acknowledge Darboy's position as archbishop, the properties of the Church, or even the existence of God. When the archbishop was eventually allowed to see another priest briefly, the authorization referred to him as "Prisoner A, who says he is a servant of somebody called God."

The archbishop's sister, Justine, was also incarcerated. Darboy was transferred to the Conciergerie prison, which during the French Revolution had hosted Louis XVI and Marie-Antoinette, among others, before they were guillotined.[12]

On April 5, the Commune, following the Versaillais execution of captured prisoners, passed the Law on Hostages by a vote of 5–4, a move that legalized the arrest and incarceration of more clergymen. Article 5 of the law announced that since the government of Versailles had put itself outside the laws of war and of humanity, the Commune would retaliate by ordering the execution of three hostages.[13]

Rigault wasted no time. The next day, he arrested more ecclesiastics, beginning with the *curé* of Saint-Séverin, along with several Jesuits, at their residence on the rue de Sèvres. The following day, he seized seven Jesuits from a school in the Fifth Arrondissement for making the unfortunate decision (in Rigault's eyes) to welcome with open arms the sons of the old nobility and wealthy middle classes. He also incarcerated the parish priest of Saint-Jacques-du-Haut-Pas, accused of asking the women of his congregation to convince their husbands not to take up arms to defend the Commune. The number of clergy arrested during the Commune may have exceeded 300, a tiny percentage of the more than 125,000 priests, nuns, and religious brothers living in Paris at the time.[14]

Gaspard Deguerry lived on the rue Saint-Honoré, near his Church of the Madeleine. A group of *fédérés* knocked on the door of the presbytery and, at least according to the concierge, came in and helped themselves to wine. After donning civilian clothing, Deguerry managed to slip away and hide in a nearby house. But he was found and immediately arrested, accused of resisting the Commune's April 2 decree separating Church and state. A national guardsman allegedly told him, "We are soon going to procure for you your paradise."[15]

Within the Commune, the hostage decree accentuated tensions between republican moderates, who still hoped for some sort of compromise with the Versailles government, and Rigault and the hard core (*les durs*). Rigault had already ordered the arrest of a number of moderates who displeased him. Eugène Protot, the delegate for justice, demanded a full explanation of the reasons for arrests, outraged that prisoners could have no visitors and that even members of the Commune could not see them. Rigault remained adamantly opposed to allowing prisoners to receive visitors, but he lost the point in the end.[16] Over his objections, the Commune voted on April 7 that prisoners could receive visitors.

On April 8 a bitter exchange occurred between Rigault and more moderate Communards. Arthur Arnould, a member of the Commune who advocated abolition of the prefecture of police, denounced Rigault. He had the support of Charles Delescluze and Jean-Baptiste Clément, who accused Rigault of moving the Commune toward a dictatorship. When the meeting upheld, by a vote of 24–17, the previous day's declaration permitting members of the Commune to see prisoners, Rigault and Ferré tendered their resignations from the Commission for General Security, which were not accepted. However, the Commune voted to replace Rigault as delegate for security with Frédéric Cournet, a moderate. Still, Rigault maintained his status as a member of the governing body of the Commune and head of the prefecture of police; three weeks later he was also named public prosecutor. The uncompromising Rigault believed that by dispensing "revolutionary justice," he could help save the Commune.[17]

THE ARRESTS OF DARBOY, Deguerry, and other priests followed the summary executions of Flourens and Duval and were, nominally at least, a reaction to them. But the arrests would never have occurred had the Commune not unleashed a wave of popular anticlericalism in Paris. As Darboy himself realized soon after he arrived in the capital, anticlericalism had been building for decades in France. Religious practice continued to decline in Paris and other large cities, as well as in a good many regions. Moreover, the Catholic Church remained closely identified with its opposition to the French Revolution and support for monarchy. The Communards viewed construction of an essentially secular society as an overarching goal. Élie Reclus, himself a man of the cloth, a Protestant minister, did not mince words, capturing on April 8 the popular mood: "Plot or no plot, it is certain that the enormous clerical establishment stands as an even more threatening army than that of Versailles, more dangerous in that it operates in the shadows," working against the Commune.

From the outset, the Commune had done everything in its power to undermine the power of the Church and the clergy. On March 29, the day after its rise to power, the government of the Commune had proclaimed free and obligatory primary education, but that was not all. A New Education Society and the Friends of Instruction soon sent delegates asking that the Commune consider "the necessity . . . of preparing youth to govern itself by means of a republican education" and demanding that religious teaching be eliminated from schools. In the Third Arrondissement, a poster bragged that lay education was a "fait accompli." Paul Martine went around with an arrondissement delegate to check on schools in the Fourth Arrondissement but admitted that the idea of tossing out clerical personnel repelled him. In the militant Twentieth Arrondissement, however, a Freemason oversaw "a muscular program of laicization."[18]

On April 2, Palm Sunday, the Commune formally voted for the separation of Church and state, ending government subsidies for religious institutions. It also decreed the confiscation of the property of religious orders (*congrégations*). The battle between the red flag and the cross was on. On the rue de Grenelle, a crowd stormed into a school taught by a congregation and shut it down.

Within several weeks, many members of religious orders had left their teaching posts and asked that lay teachers be appointed to replace them. The Commune raised the salaries of teachers and their assistants and awarded equal pay to male and female teachers. Schools for girls run by lay teachers sprang up in several neighborhoods.[19]

A proposal later submitted suggested that new, secular nurseries for infants and young children "should be scattered throughout the working-class areas, near the large factories," each accommodating up to a hundred infants and young children. Several such nurseries had already been established.[20] A professional school of industrial arts started up, with a young woman as director.

By mid-May, the Commune had banned all religious teaching in lay schools. All religious markers were promptly removed, including crucifixes in schoolrooms (some had already been taken away during the Government of National Defense), whose presence clearly reflected the once central role of the Church in French education.[21] Édouard Moriac watched with horror as on the rue des Martyrs a "band" of about two hundred "toddlers" marched behind a drum and a small red flag: "They sang at the top of their lungs 'La Marseillaise.' This grotesque parade celebrated the opening of a lay school organized by the Commune."[22]

The Commune also took measures to secularize hospitals and prisons. A decree of April 22 mandated removal of all religious symbols from medical facilities. Moreover, it forbade members of religious congregations from coming to minister to patients. Four days earlier, religious brothers had been expelled from the now quite busy medical facility at Rond-Point de Longchamps, despite the opposition of wounded guardsmen. Augustinian sisters continued to help out at the Hôtel-Dieu, wearing red belts over their black cassocks, their altars and crucifixes covered over by flowers. Although kicked out of prisons and hospitals in principle, chaplains were allowed to return to visit patients and prisoners during the day. They continued to sign official documents, including baptismal certificates. Nuns were removed from charitable institutions in some places but continued their work elsewhere.[23]

For the most part, the Commune was not forcing secularization upon the people of Paris. The Church's close association with people of means had long drawn popular ire; the birth of the Commune merely unleashed it. Many ordinary Parisians now saw priests as "a particular type of bourgeois." If humble priests labored away in plebeian *quartiers* where churches were increasingly empty, ornate processions, ostentatious ecclesiastical accouterments, and attendance by the elegant faithful characterized churches such as Notre-Dame-des-Victoires and *Curé* Gaspard Deguerry's Church of the Madeleine in western Paris. Letters written to *Père Duchêne* denounced the Church for its "social parasitism." Irenée Dauthier, living in the Tenth Arrondissement, first asked editors and readers to excuse her writing and spelling errors, then asked why bishops and abbeys had such enormous revenues. Was this not so they could have "a more gourmand table than that of the king?" In a city where about a quarter of all couples were unmarried, the Church, which normally charged 2 francs to register a birth, demanded 7.50 francs (about two days wages for many) to register an "illegitimate" birth. A Parisian commented bitterly, "Baptisms, marriages, burials—you have to pay for everything."[24]

Anticlerical discourse abounded in political clubs, which in early April began to meet in at least twenty-four of the fifty-one churches in Paris. Not only were churches by far the largest indoor places in which large numbers of people could meet—as had been the case during the French Revolution—but their use represented the Communards' appropriation of public space, fully sanctioned by the government of the Commune. Some of the clubs originated after the establishment of the republic on September 4, 1870, and had been banned by General Joseph Vinoy on March 11. Others started up during the Commune. Parisians listened to speakers debating the themes of the day, including the high cost of food, the rights of women and workers, the state of primary school education, the role of the clergy, and the leadership of the Commune.[25]

The transformation of churches into clubs sometimes led to confrontations with the faithful. At Club Saint-Ambroise, a woman loudly protested against a meeting being held in the church, and militants escorted her to the door amid laughter. On May 6, local residents showed up with official orders that Saint-Sulpice was to be used for a club. Some of the expelled faithful vigorously protested, and a brawl erupted. National guardsmen from Belleville, camped nearby, responded to protect *clubistes* singing "La Marseillaise."[26]

Unsurprisingly, the faithful resented the presence of political clubs in their churches. *Clubistes* were overtly critical of the Church and persistent in their attacks. Club speakers demanded the seizure of property belonging to the congregations, insisted that the clergy pay rent to the

Commune for the use of ecclesiastical buildings "to stage their comedies," and demanded that the proceeds go to helping widows and orphans of the Commune. The Club of Faubourg Saint-Antoine asked that church bells be melted to make cannons, as during the French Revolution.

Female speakers focused their critiques on the Church's out-size influence on women, marriage, family life, and education. They were particularly strident in their denunciation of marriage. At the great Gothic Church of Saint-Eustache near the central market of Les Halles, a woman warned *citoyennes* that marriage was "the greatest er-ror of ancient humanity. To be married is to be a slave." In the Club of Saint-Ambroise, a woman rose to announce that she would never permit her sixteen-year-old daughter to marry and that the latter was doing quite well living with a man without the blessing of the Church. The club in Saint-Germain l'Auxerrois approved an enthusiastic resolu-tion in favor of divorce.[27]

Louise Michel presided over a gathering of women three times a week on the grande rue de la Chapelle. There she proposed "the imme-diate abolition of organized religion and its replacement by a more se-vere morality," which for her entailed "treat[ing] all others and oneself with justice." During club meetings some women mounted the pulpits to denounce the clergy with rhetorical violence. At Club Saint-Sulpice, sixteen-year-old Gabrielle thundered, "We must shoot the priests. . . . Women are harmed by going to confession. . . . I therefore urge all women to take hold of all the priests and to burn their ugly mugs off. . . . The same for the nuns!"[28]

In the eyes of most *clubistes*, the clergy and the bourgeoisie were one and the same, which made it easy to denounce both groups. Speakers denounced those with top hats and fancy "black suits" as bourgeois re-actionaries. At one club, a shoemaker demanded the arrest of all reac-tionaries who employed domestics. At another such gathering, a woman related that near the Bourse a well-heeled lady had insisted that there were no "citizens" in the neighborhood, only "ladies and gentlemen." People of means, particularly property owners, became "vultures." A mil-lenarian—and at times violent—tone crept in, as at Club of the Deliver-ance, where a speaker saluted "the arrival of the day of justice [which] is rapidly coming. . . . Proletarians, you will be reborn!"[29]

PARIS'S CHURCHES, now adopted by political clubs, were utterly un-recognizable, to the delight of most Parisians but much to the chagrin of others. At the club meeting in Saint-Michel in Batignolles, children played while members of the Commune sat adorned in red sashes in places usually reserved for ecclesiastical dignitaries at Mass, who would have been attired quite differently. Instead of hymns the organs played "La Marseillaise" and "Ça ira," that revolutionary classic. Citizen Vicar Marguerite was assured on May 17 that the organist would be paid on the condition that he played "patriotic airs."[30]

Early in May, Maxime Vuillaume visited the Club Saint-Séverin, a block from the Seine, with a friend. The entry to the church was almost totally dark, but some light beckoned from the middle of the nave. Gas lamps hung from the pillars. Those presiding over the meeting sat behind a table; a red flag stood nearby. An orator suggested that brigades armed with instruments capable of shooting fire should take care of the Versaillais who threatened their city. A woman followed him as speaker, but Vuillaume and his friend were looking around and did not catch the gist of what she had to say. About a hundred people, including a dozen or so women, listened. Many of the men wore National Guard uniforms. Two sitting alongside a pillar ate bread and sausage and drank wine. "Let's go," implored Vuillaume's friend. "Midnight Mass would be more fun." As they left, the club session ended with the singing of "La Marseillaise." The next morning, someone swept out the church, and Mass went on as usual.[31]

Paul Fontoulieu, a hostile visitor, found as many female speakers as male when he attended a session of the club in the Church of the Trinity. The issue up for debate was how to reform society. Lodoïska Caweska, known as "the Polish Amazon," spoke first; the audience received her discourse coolly. Then another female orator of about thirty called for the establishment of producers' cooperatives. One after another, women rose to speak, their words sometimes straying from the intended subject. "Solutions" included shooting those who would not fight. In a brief speech, Nathalie Le Mel insisted that the day of reckoning was approaching, and everyone, women included, should do their duty, fight to the end, and be prepared to die.[32] Her speech met with lengthy applause. The final speaker drew cheers by presenting a "grotesque" (in Fontoulieu's eyes) parody of a Mass. As people filed out of the church, the female president of the assembly reminded those in attendance that the neighborhood remained full of monarchists and Versaillais.[33]

Entering the Church of Saint-Eustache, the Englishman John Leighton was "agreeably surprised to find the font full of tobacco instead of holy-water, and to see the altar in the distance covered with bottles and glasses." In a lateral chapel, someone had dressed a statue of the Virgin Mary in the uniform of a *vivandière* (a woman supplying national guardsmen with provisions) and placed a little pipe in her mouth. Leighton was "particularly charmed" by the "amiable faces of the people I saw collected there. . . . It was quite delightful not to see any of those elegant dresses and frivolous manners, which have so long disgraced the better half of the human race." As for the men, "it was charming to note the military elegance with which their caps were slightly inclined over one ear: their faces, naturally hideous, were illuminated with the joy of freedom."

Edmond de Goncourt encountered the smell of garlic when he entered a church, as the bells, which usually announced Mass, intoned for the opening of a club meeting. Goncourt listened as one speaker demanded the institution of the Terror "so that heads of traitors may roll immediately on the square." Another related the discovery of 10,060 bottles of wine in the seminary of Saint-Sulpice, and a third asked, "What do I care whether we are successful against Versailles if we don't find solutions for social problems, if workingmen remain in the same condition as before?"[34]

In most clubs, however, those in attendance respected the establishment in which they were meeting. For instance, Communards were told not to smoke pipes in Saint-Eustache. Goncourt noted that men took their hats off as they entered. Yet some visitors to churches behaved provocatively. At Saint-Vincent-de-Paul, Communards imbibed wine from chalices previously reserved for Mass. National guardsmen and prostitutes may have amused themselves in Notre-Dame-des-Victoires. In Saint-Leu, on April 14, thirty or forty *fédérés* donned ecclesiastical robes and mocked the Mass, singing "filthy songs . . . accompanied by the most grotesque gestures." A certain Kobosko offered "Communion" to the "faithful," replacing hosts with brioches, and at the accompanying dinner revelers downed 130 bottles of wine. In another church a man bathed his dog in a holy water vessel, and a few Communards relieved themselves in such places. Such acts shocked practicing Catholics. The Commune and most Communards defiantly rejected organized religion.[35]

Occasional pillaging did occur. Twelve convents reported damaged or lost property. In Saint-Médard, paintings were ripped, the organ and ornaments broken, and confessionals overturned. In Notre-Dame-des-Victoires, Communards beheaded what was left of a saint's relics. Overall, however, there were surprisingly few such cases, certainly in comparison with what occurred during the radical phase of the French Revolution. Items taken from the Cathedral of Notre Dame on Good Friday and piled into wagons to be taken away were saved when someone ran to notify members of the Commune at the Hôtel-de-Ville, who ordered them returned to the sacristy.[36]

Parisian ecclesiastics saw their role decrease dramatically during the Commune. Baptisms and First Communions declined. Marriages diminished in number, in part because so many men were in the National Guard and so many better-off Parisians had fled the city. During the Second Empire, civil burials had not been very common; now they took place almost every day, complete with red flags. Mass attendance fell off, and fewer coins were tossed into the collection basket as it was passed.[37]

The orders to close their doors affected thirty-four of sixty-seven churches in Paris. Notre-Dame-de-Lorette was transformed on May 13 into a barracks and six days later into a jail for those arrested for avoiding National Guard service. Saint-Pierre-de-Montmartre became a workshop for the manufacture of uniforms, then a storage place for munitions and, briefly, a school for girls. The Church of Saint-Merri was transformed into a medical facility.

The Communard press kept anticlerical discourse in full throttle. *Père Duchêne* led the way, denouncing the clergy as parasites with an inordinate passion for "the good life" and borrowing the image of the overfed priest or monk using the sacrament of confession to "coax" women. The Church stood accused of bringing young girls into convents—"places full of vice"—where they suffered exploitation as their wages undercut those of working women. Implicit in the anticlerical tirades were suggestions that the kidnapping of minors, rapes, and homosexuality threatened the families of ordinary people. Allusions to secret passageways beneath convents and monasteries abounded, contributing to an obsession during searches with their cellars. *La Sociale* reported that 2,000 rifles and considerable munitions had been found in that of Notre Dame, and *La Montagne* claimed that monks had been arrested following the discovery of gunpowder in the tabernacles of their churches. None of this was true, but rumors generated headlines and animated street discussions.[38]

One search led to a shocking story that spread rapidly through Paris. In the basement of the convent of the Dames de Picpus, guardsmen came across what to them looked like instruments of torture and human remains. The sisters explained that they had cared for three of their own suffering from mental problems. The rumored "instruments of torture" were in fact nothing more than several "orthopedic beds." A doctor established that the nuns had died of natural causes, and for whatever reason, their remains had been kept in the convent, awaiting a final destination. Yet newspapers continued to offer "revelations" of clerical misdeeds at Picpus and elsewhere, as suggested by headlines like "The Confessions of a Breton Seminarist," "The Revelations of a former *Curé*," "Tonsured Sadists," and "The Corpses of the Church of Notre-Dame-des-Victoires."[39]

The National Guard took reports of hidden stashes of weapons seriously. Laurent Amodru, the fifty-four-year-old vicar of Notre-Dame-des-Victoires, had just finished hearing confessions at about 4 P.M. on May 17 when he learned that men from the 159th National Guard battalion had surrounded the church. A young officer whom he asked what they were doing replied that they had authorization to search the church for weapons. The priest answered that there were certainly none to be found and asked that the search, if it must indeed be done, be finished before Mass at 7 P.M. The guards glanced apprehensively at the women in the church. Amodru claimed later that he was lucky not to have been killed by a drunken guardsman assigned to watch him in the sacristy during the search; two other guardsmen protected him. Although he survived the search, Amodru was promptly arrested and taken to the Conciergerie, then to Mazas prison and finally to La Roquette prison.[40]

Not all Communards were prepared to denounce the Church. Some people loyal to the Commune expressed their opposition to anticlerical measures, particularly the removal of nuns from medical facilities and the searches of some convents. On Good Friday, April 6, national guardsmen entered the Church of Saint-Eustache and demanded that Abbé F. Simon go with them to the neighborhood police station. There a young magistrate questioned the priest, assuring him that he knew of his good reputation in the *quartier*. The priest's nephew complained to members of the Commune about the arrest. On hearing of the arrest of their priest, the market ladies of Les Halles went to Rigault to insist that Abbé Simon be freed. Slightly taken back by their anger, Rigault asked, "And if I refuse to release your papist (*calotin*)?" The market ladies' response reflected their earthy toughness: "Then we will gut you on the first possible occasion on a block at the market, like the fine top-round that you are!" Rigault ordered the priest released. Abbé Simon returned to his church in triumph and at the next Mass preached a sermon about forgiving one's enemies. In *Le Cri du Peuple*, Jules Vallès thundered that when arrested during the Second Empire, he had not had a nephew to ask for his pardon.[41]

Despite rumors of opulence and high living (which, in any case, focused on male ecclesiastics), some "visitors" were impressed by the poverty of the nuns and their work for the poor, on whose behalf, after all, the Commune had come to power. And when national guardsmen searched the residence of the fathers of the Holy Spirit, the exchange quickly became cordial, with the guardsmen helping the priests distribute what meager resources were available to the poor.

On occasion guardsmen sent to search a church ran into a priest they knew in their *quartier*. Communards walking into Saint-Roch may well have been hostile to organized religion, but they recognized the priest because he had given them First Communion. Some Communards helped priests escape or tipped off religious institutions that a search was coming. Others provided ecclesiastics with identification papers. And for all their criticisms of the Church, many did not reject their personal faith. Some *fédérés*, for instance, donned religious medallions before going into battle.[42]

In Saint-Nicolas-des-Champs, a priest said Mass every day in a chapel, and a club met in the main part of the church most evenings. The clergy thus ended up comfortably sharing space with the *clubistes*, with Masses, baptisms, and funerals held at different times than the club meetings, most of which took place at night. The Church of Saint-Pierre in Montrouge, where a warning had been posted outside that "churches are the lairs of those who have murdered the morals of the masses," was split into two sections, one for the clergy and the other for a club, over whose meetings a hairdresser presided. Masses were celebrated in Saint-Roch, although the Englishman Ernest Vizetelly reported that "they were more than once disturbed by the insurgents, as on one occasion when a band of inebriate Guards rushed into the church while some forty young girls received First Communion."[43]

With increased tension stemming from the military situation, popular anticlericalism became more determined. In face of such opposition, the clergy remained united, helping each other when possible and taking the place of colleagues who had been imprisoned. Ecclesiastics kept religious ceremonies low-key. In the Church of Saint-Merri, bells did not toll, the organ remained silent, singing stopped or was muted, and flowers were not put in place. The Carmelites on the rue d'Enfer stilled their bells, and the nuns of Marie-Répartrice suspended catechism. The parish of Saint-Pierre-du-Petit-Montrouge held services clandestinely in a nearby house.[44]

AFTER THREE DAYS in a holding cell in the prefecture of police, Archbishop Darboy was transferred to Mazas prison, along with Abbé Deguerry. Louis Bonjean, who had served as president of both the imperial Senate and the Court of Appeals, joined them. Identified with the repression of political opponents during the empire, he had been one of the first Rigault ordered arrested.[45]

The Mazas prison, an enormous compound resembling a fortress, consisted of twelve buildings, each containing one hundred cells; a large, dome-capped central pavilion housed the administrative office and a chapel. The cells were small, each with an iron bed attached to the wall. Strict rules forbade singing, talking loudly, or communicating with other prisoners.[46]

The immediate goal behind incarcerating such high-profile hostages was to discourage the Versaillais from executing further Communard prisoners. Following the arrests, Rigault sent Gaston Da Costa, his right-hand man, to ask Darboy and Deguerry to write letters to Thiers protesting such killings. Within days after seizing the hostages, the leadership of the Commune decided to try to arrange an exchange of prisoners with Versailles. Auguste Blanqui, in prison in Morlaix in Brittany, still seemed just the kind of revolutionary leader who could galvanize Paris. For his part, Rigault was obsessed with bringing "the Old One" back to Paris.[47]

On April 8, Darboy wrote Thiers, stating that "humanity and religion" demanded that he request an exchange of prisoners for Blanqui. The archbishop directly referred to the "barbaric acts . . . the atrocious excesses" of the Versailles troops, including the execution of wounded fighters. He entreated Thiers to use his influence to put an end to the civil war. The previous day Deguerry had written to the members of the Versailles government, asking them to stop executing prisoners, which could only lead to more hostage taking and perhaps the retaliatory killings the Commune now threatened.[48]

When Thiers did not respond, Rigault asked Benjamin Flotte, a veteran of the 1848 revolution and a friend and disciple of Blanqui, to visit Darboy and propose that he write a second letter. On April 10, Flotte and Lagarde, Darboy's *grand vicaire* (vicar-general), visited the archbishop, who immediately raised the subject of his sister's arrest;

Flotte promised she would be freed (this did not occur until April 28). Darboy wrote Thiers again on April 12, proposing the release of Blanqui in return for his, Deguerry's, and Bonjean's freedom. Rigault refused to let Deguerry leave prison to personally deliver the letter, which was entrusted instead to Lagarde, who arrived in Versailles on April 14.

Thiers had no intention of permitting the exchange, fearing that Blanqui's release would provide the Communards with a leading figure to rally around. Thiers denied that his troops were carrying out executions, adding that all insurgents who turned over their weapons would be spared. He expressed doubt that the archbishop's letters were genuine. When Lagarde returned to see him a third time, Thiers informed him that the Versailles Council unanimously opposed the exchange. He then sent Lagarde a hand-delivered message instructing him to carry a sealed letter to Darboy, presumably with his decision.

Lagarde, however, remained in Versailles. Even though Darboy had instructed him to return to Paris at once, he asked for more time. The vicar-general finally sent news from Versailles that a delay was inevitable. Darboy wrote on April 19 insisting that he remain in Versailles no more than another day. But Lagarde stayed on. An April 23 article in *Le Cri du Peuple* revealed attempts to negotiate an exchange and criticized Lagarde for betraying his promise to Darboy by lingering in Versailles. *La Sociale* denounced Lagarde as a liar, coward, and traitor, which did not enhance the clergy's image among Parisians. The Commune's *Journal Officiel* published the correspondence on April 27.[49]

US Ambassador Elihu B. Washburne had remained in Paris to assist American citizens still in the capital. He now found himself "plunged into the most terrible events of the century."[50] Washburne, whose residence Versaillais shells had hit twice, knew of Archbishop Darboy's plight. On April 18 he had received letters from various ecclesiastical authorities, including Papal Nuncio Flavius Chigi and Lagarde, asking him to intervene. The ambassador had obtained the release of several Sisters of Charity by going to the prefecture of police, so he must have believed he would have similar success in Darboy's case. At 10:30 A.M. Gustave Cluseret accompanied him to the prefecture, where the ambassador asked to see Rigault. An employee smiled and responded that Rigault was sleeping, having just returned from a long night out. When Rigault awoke, he signed a document—without even reading it—authorizing Washburne "to communicate freely with Citizen Darboy, archbishop of Paris." Cluseret commented, "So here is the man to whom the proletariat has given one of its most important posts!"[51]

On April 23 the American ambassador—the first person from the outside to see him since his arrest—took the archbishop a bottle of Madeira. Darboy expressed no bitterness toward his captors, adding that the Communards "would be judged to be worse than they really were." He would await "the logic of events." On April 22, the Commune had enacted a decree specifying that juries drawn from among national guardsmen would consider the cases of individual hostages; at the same time it ordered the prosecutor of the Commune—this would be Rigault in a few days—to take more.[52]

Five days later, Darboy sent Lagarde another message, this time via Ambassador Washburne: the vicar must return to Paris immediately. Five days later, Washburne wrote a US official to inform him that he considered the archbishop's life "in the most imminent danger," relating that a group of national guardsmen had gone to Mazas intending to shoot Darboy before a Communard official intervened. Lagarde may have had legitimate reasons for delaying in Versailles. Perhaps he believed that his return to Paris would lead directly to the execution of Darboy and the other hostages. He may also have been in contact with Félix Pyat, who thought that a large ransom might secure the archbishop's freedom. Lagarde may have written to Jules Simon about these possibilities several days earlier, expressing hope for a return to moderate influence in the Commune. Moreover, General Cluseret seemed to favor releasing the hostages, which would have encouraged Darboy's supporters. On May 2, Lagarde promised to leave Versailles; yet two days later was still there. Whatever his reasons for tarrying, he never communicated them to Washburne or Darboy. Several days of optimism quickly evaporated.[53]

On May 11, Archbishop Darboy penned a memorandum to Thiers, which reached him through Chigi. He confessed that he did not know as yet what answer Thiers had given to Lagarde, who had sent "only vague and incomplete reports." Darboy described the possible exchange, which Ambassador Washburne would guarantee, adding, "The resistance of Paris is a military resistance entirely, and the presence of M. Blanqui could add nothing to it." For his part, the American ambassador assured Thiers that they had nothing to lose from an exchange and that Darboy's life probably depended on it.[54]

Lagarde did take some action to aid Darboy. He contacted the lawyer Étienne Plou, who would plead the archbishop's case directly to the Commune. Rigault allowed the lawyer to see the hostages twice. But on May 11 Plou wrote Ambassador Washburne to complain that Ferré had prevented him from seeing Darboy.[55] Two days later, Flotte, still in Paris and visiting Darboy, was admitted to see Thiers, who again insisted that the exchange was simply impossible, adding that the question had twice "agitated" his Council and that he did not believe Darboy's life to be in any danger. He said that he would raise the subject the next day with the Commission des Quinze, his advisory group.[56]

The next morning, Thiers informed Flotte that no exchange would be possible, because to "turn over Blanqui to the insurrection would be to provide it with a force equal to an army corps." Flotte reminded Thiers of the seventy-four other hostages being held at Mazas and said that if Thiers signed an order releasing Blanqui, he would bring them all to Versailles the next day. Thiers was probably overstating Blanqui's importance. The Old One was indeed old and also ailing, and his influence arguably derived from his legend and imprisonment in a distant place. If he returned to Paris, he would not necessarily have provided the Commune with much leadership. Few Communards besides Rigault and Flotte had ever even met him.

Back at Mazas, when Flotte related what had transpired, Deguerry said, "This is a man without a heart," believing the refusal to be a calculated maneuver on Thiers's part. Thiers may well have believed that the execution of Darboy and other hostages would greatly discredit the Commune. The killing of the archbishop would also justify continued reprisals against the Communards.[57]

As days became weeks and brought no sign that his release was imminent, the archbishop seemed almost indifferent to his earthly fate. Darboy wrote to his brother that he was doing well enough, had all that he needed, and "was not being treated as badly as [his family] might have heard." The prison doctor, however, warned that if the archbishop's conditions did not improve, he would not last a fortnight. Darboy was transferred to a larger cell with a small table and chair, more air, linen from his residence, and food from the outside. He was even provided with theology books and had in his cell a cross given to him by Archbishop Affre and a large sapphire ring, a gift from Archbishop Sibour.[58]

Two individuals presented Darboy with proposals for his escape. A young man, Count Anatole de Montferrier, managed to get in to see Darboy and described for him a complicated plan involving fake safe-conduct passes. The archbishop quickly declined. Then one of his guards offered to help him escape, but Darboy replied that his flight would be "the signal for the massacre of the priests," and he would rather be shot than have others killed in his place.[59]

The summary execution by Versaillais forces of Communard commanders Flourens and Duval raised the stakes for the Paris Commune, as well as for Archbishop Darboy and the other hostages being held in Mazas prison. All the pieces were in place for a dramatic military confrontation as Versaillais line troops edged closer to the ramparts of Paris.

CHAPTER 5

THE BATTLE TURNS AGAINST THE COMMUNARDS

THE VERSAILLAIS BEGAN BOMBARDING PARIS on April 2. Methodist pastor W. Gibson heard a national guardsman say the next day, "Soon we will be crushed!"[1] The shelling intensified on April 12. Five days later, Gibson concluded, "It appears, from what has transpired in the Assembly of Versailles, that there are many among the deputies who would be glad to see Paris bombarded and the city burnt to the ground." Indeed, by May 21, Versaillais shells had indiscriminately killed hundreds and perhaps thousands of Parisians, as well as destroyed hundreds of buildings in neighborhoods in the western and central districts within the reach of the army's artillery. Ironically many of these *quartiers* were openly opposed to the Commune or at least neutral. The might of Thiers's army was backing the Commune into a corner, and recovery seemed increasingly unlikely.[2]

British resident John Leighton was outraged that the Versaillais, with whom he felt a certain class sympathy, were "not content with" battering forts and ramparts and killing Communard soldiers but also targeted "women and children, ordinary passers-by [including] unfortunates who were necessarily obliged to venture into the neighbouring streets, for the purpose of buying bread." US diplomat Wickham Hoffman agreed: "It must always be a mystery why the French bombarded so persistently the quarter of the Arch de Triomphe—the West End of Paris—the quarter where nine out of ten of the inhabitants were known friends of the Government."[3]

For Parisians who had just lived through the Prussian siege, this was much worse. The Prussians had never bombarded medical facilities. The Versaillais did. Adolphe Thiers proclaimed to provincial France that the Communards were pillaging property in Paris as Versaillais cannons obliterated rows of houses on the Champs-Élysées. Thiers then denied shelling the capital.[4]

Some Parisians flocked to the Arc de Triomphe on April 6 to observe the goings-on, as they had during the first week or two of the Prussian siege. One enterprising man charged those who wanted a better view a fee to watch from atop a pile of chairs. From the Arc de Triomphe, Leighton saw "a motionless, attentive crowd reaching down the whole length of the Avenue de la Grande Armée, as far as Porte Maillot, from which a great cloud of white smoke springs up every moment followed by a violent explosion. . . . [S]uddenly a flood of dust, coming from Porte Maillot, thrusts back the thick of the crowd, and as it flies, widening, and whirling more madly as it comes, everyone is seized with terror, and rushes away screaming and gesticulating."[5]

The first Communard funeral for victims of the Versaillais bombardment took place on April 6, immediately after the siege began. Horses hauled giant hearses through the boulevards of Paris. Charles Delescluze, a member of the Commune's governing council, gave a funeral oration for the martyred Parisians, concluding, "This great city . . . holds the future of humanity in its hands. . . . Cry not for our brothers who have fallen heroically, but swear to continue their work!" Less ceremonial funerals would become a daily occurrence. The Commune awarded annual pensions of 600 francs to the widows of men killed in the fighting and 365 francs to their children.[6]

Among the killed and wounded were boys, including thirteen-year-old Eugène-Léon Vaxivierre, who continued to man a cannon although injured. A shell wounded another boy, Guillaume, as he fired an artillery piece with his father. Charles Bondcritter, fifteen, was killed after remaining at his cannon for ten days.[7]

On the avenue des Ternes, now well within range of Versaillais artillery, a mournful funeral procession moved slowly along. Two men carried the small coffin of a young child. The father, a worker dressed in his blue smock, walked sadly behind, with a small group of mourners. Suddenly a shell, fired from Mont-Valérien, crashed down, destroying the small coffin and covering the funeral entourage with human remains. Leighton wryly commented, "Massacring the dead! Truly those cannons are a wonderful, a refined invention!"[8]

Thiers's army was indeed ruthless. On April 11 Versaillais troops pushed Communard forces back at Asnières and moved into the plateau of Châtillon to the south of the capital. This permitted the army to move cannons closer and bombard the exterior forts and ramparts of Paris. As Communards fled back across a railway bridge partially destroyed by Versaillais shells, Ernest Vizetelly watched gendarmes on horses as they "picked off men who had fallen," some drowning in the Seine.[9]

Alix Payen, whose husband, Henri, was a sergeant in the National Guard, volunteered as an *ambulancière* (aide on an imporovised medical facility) because she did not want to be separated from her husband. She was with him at Fort Issy caring for the wounded during the fighting there. One Communard fighter found Alix shelter in a family tomb in a cemetery. While tending to the wounded, she met a mixed bag of Communards, representing the range of the Commune's supporters. With them at the shelter, for instance, was "a real Parisian from the faubourg, cheerful, sarcastic, a little bit of a thug and as chatty as a magpie." Another was a professor at the Collège de Vanves, "very well-educated and a poet. He improvised verses inspired by our situation." The man had suffered a "brutally unhappy love affair," which had left him so devastated that Communard fighters considered him "a little crazy."

On April 12, the Communard fighters let the Versaillais approach, then fired on them. Afterward, all was quiet for a time. Henri Payen and the poet, hoping to take advantage of the lull, wanted to organize a concert to cheer the wounded. Alix took a collection and went nearby to buy some flowers. A mulatto woman who, like Alix, had accompanied her husband into battle sang some songs. During the concert, someone shouted, "A wounded man!" and Alix ran to help an artilleryman hit by a shell while the woman sang on. More and more shells began to rain down on Issy, killing or wounding twenty-six Communards. Their position untenable, the troops retreated to the entrance to Levallois-Perret, their flag riddled by Versaillais bullets. The period of intense Versaillais shelling had begun.

As wounded Communards began to stream into Paris, the city scrambled to find places to house and treat them. Each arrondissement had a medical facility; the one at Porte Maillot was swamped with wounded Communards because it was near the fighting beyond the western walls. Civilian hospitals cared for the wounded as well, although many fighters simply wanted to be carried home. A medical facility occupied a lecture hall at the Sorbonne. Bodies were stacked in the Medical School, which was empty of students, primarily because most of them opposed the Commune, although some teaching took place elsewhere. British and American organizations also helped care for the Communard wounded. Near the faubourg Saint-Honoré, the Union Jack and the flag of the Red Cross flew at the English medical facility with its fifty beds. A British Protestant organization had six to eight hundred beds in Paris. An American facility also helped out.

The wounded faced the horrors of inadequate care. At Beaujon Hospital, all fifteen men who had had limbs amputated died of pyaemia or gangrene. Grossly overcrowded hospitals and medical clinics (*ambulances*) lacked suitable dressing and sterilization supplies. Despite all this, British doctor John Murray insisted that the Commune was looking after the population as best it could. Yet Murray feared that poverty and hard times would lead to an outbreak of cholera, "which is assuredly approaching."

Dr. Murray recalled the sad case of a woman mortally wounded by a shell while caring for the Communard injured at Issy. She passed away after thirty-six hours of suffering. Her friends wanted to arrange a funeral service presided over by a priest, which Commune hesitated to allow, then permitted. But no priest could be found. A Protestant minister was present and performed the service instead.[10]

In one large facility, Doctor Danet cared for between 1,500 and 2,000 men. He had difficulty finding enough people to tend to the wounded and lamented that in some cases the Commune's leaders hindered rather than helped doctors. One day, Delescluze, Gustave Courbet, and Jules Miot, another Jacobin member of the Commune's administrative council, showed up. Danet had been denounced for having the wounded trade their filthy National Guard uniforms for simpler hospital garb. Some national guardsmen had somehow concluded that this measure aimed to prevent them from visiting wounded comrades in other facilities. Danet complained that some Communards failed to realize that a hospital was not a restaurant and came to eat and drink. He had thrown some out, and they had denounced him. Courbet told Danet that he was too "severe" and raged at him in "his booming voice."[11]

With the number of casualties increasing daily, the Commune began to rally women to the defense of the city. On April 11, Parisians awoke to read in their newspapers an appeal to *citoyennes*, announcing that "the decisive hour has arrived" and calling on women to take up arms. Élisabeth Dmitrieff and seven other female organizers of the Union des Femmes proclaimed that women should be prepared to fight and, if necessary, to die for the cause. A group of women formed their own fighting legion, the Amazons of the Seine. Ernest Vizetelly went to their recruiting office to see these ladies for himself. His account, like others essentially hostile to the Commune and women's role in it, emphasized the women's (in his view) nonfeminine physical characteristics, describing them as "mostly muscular . . . from five-and-twenty to forty years of age, the older ones being unduly stout, and not one of them, in my youthful opinion, at all good-looking."[12]

Women conducted public demonstrations intended to rally flagging spirits in the struggle against Versailles. A mobilization of perhaps eight hundred women took place in early April at the place de la Concorde in front of the statue of Strasbourg, a city already incorporated into the German Empire. Women in Belleville proposed to march toward the armies of Versailles to see whether soldiers would really fire on them. The answer: they would do so eagerly.[13]

During skirmishes in April, women battled the Versaillais army outside the ramparts. In several cases, female fighters shot at, sometimes hitting and killing, troops of the line. Atop the city walls, a crowd of onlookers supposedly applauded a woman supplying food to Communard fighters who shot and killed a gendarme chasing her. Whereas rumors and Versaillais reports of entire battalions of women engaged in the fight may or may not be true, the participation of ordinary women is undeniable.

Women who supported the Commune without taking up arms were equally instrumental. Those who supplied food to Communard fighters or worked as doctor's assistants contributed enormously to the Commune's defense. Doctor's assistants wore red crosses and, often purchasing medical supplies themselves, cared for the wounded and dying. The Union of Women for the Defense of Paris and Care of the Wounded actively recruited women to serve in both essential capacities. Anti-Communard commentators mocked them; for instance, one cartoon depicted a *cantinière* (canteen worker) as a silly, flippant creature dispensing liquor to drunken Communards. Maxime du Camp described female doctor's assistants handing out eau-de-vie and not the "simple medication that would have healed." Some faced the condescension of national guardsmen. Men forced nine such women to return to Paris, rejecting their presence at the front. Louise Michel commented acidly, "If only they would let me take care of the wounded. You would not believe the obstacles, the jokes, the hostility!"[14]

Michel cared for the wounded as an *ambulancière* but had also volunteered to sneak into Versailles and assassinate Adolphe Thiers. "I thought that killing M. Thiers right in the [National] Assembly would provoke such terror that the reaction against us would be stopped dead," she later admitted. At first quite serious about carrying out her plot, Michel left for Versailles and got through because she was respectably dressed. But she could not get near Thiers and returned to Paris.[15]

Michel also fought with the 61st National Guard battalion at Issy and Clamart in early April. Nothing seemed to frighten her. A decent shot, she later wondered, "Was it sheer bravery that caused me to be so enchanted with the sight of the battered Fort Issy gleaming faintly in the night, or the sight of our lines on night maneuvers . . . with the red teeth of the machine guns flashing on the horizon[?] . . . It wasn't bravery, I just thought it a beautiful sight. My eyes and my heart responded, as did my ears, to the sound of the cannon. Oh, I am a savage all right. I love the smell of gunpowder, grapeshot flying through the air, but above all, I'm devoted to the Revolution." In a calmer moment, she and a friend read Baudelaire together, sipping coffee in a spot where several of their comrades had been killed. Just after they left, a shell crashed to earth, shattering their empty cups. Later a bullet grazed her, and she fell, spraining an ankle. For Louise Michel, who always conveyed the impression of sadness and melancholy, the Commune's struggles "became poetry."[16]

The Commune sought to rally Paris's women and nurse its wounded fighters back to health, but neither effort would prove enough. Daunting problems threatened to undermine the defense of Paris, and instability in the Commune and the National Guard did not help matters. The Communards had constructed no well-planned, sturdy defense network within the ramparts of besieged Paris. The confusion of competing authorities and the chaos engendered by the election and reelection of National Guard officers worked against the Commune. Some officers were happy to flash glittering symbols of their status but did little more. Unreliability and insufficient training in the officer corps, as well as difficulty getting often hard-drinking Communard guardsmen to accept military discipline, were constant issues. Jealousies and rivalries between officers contributed to the turmoil. Insubordination remained chronic and the distribution of weapons and munitions erratic. Perfectly capturing increasing lack of confidence in National Guard commanders, a cartoon in a Communard newspaper depicted a hungry man in a restaurant exclaiming, "Waiter, two or three more stuffed generals!"

"We are out of them."

"Very well, then a dozen colonels in caper sauce."

"A dozen?"

"Yes! Directly!"[17]

Furthermore not all guardsmen were absolutely committed to the Commune, and some performed their duties at a minimum, more out of loyalty to their comrades than to their companies or battalions. One of these, Émile Maury, born in Colmar, now lived in the *quartier populaire* of Popincourt. He had joined the National Guard during the Franco-Prussian War, which he had viewed as a patriotic struggle because of his Alsatian origins. Maury had turned up when the roll of the drums summoned him on the night of April 12, after a demonstration by the Friends of Order. In late April, when called to service again, he instead visited his mother in her small shop. In his view, only "the very needy, the rabid, and the curious" in his unit actually marched out of Paris to fight; he was none of these. From near the Church of the Madeleine, he could hear shells exploding near the Arc de Triomphe. On another occasion, he did venture out to Porte Maillot with part of his unit. When a Versaillais shell fell near him, he took refuge under a carriage door on the right side of the avenue and then at the Gare de la Porte Maillot. After this "baptism by fire," he took an omnibus back to Paris and went to assure his parents that he was fine, cynically describing his "brilliant expedition." At the end of April, he feared that everything would finish badly for the Communards, referring to them in the third person as though he no longer counted himself among them. Such indifference, however widespread, compromised the defense of Paris.[18]

Attempts to achieve some sort of negotiated settlement revived briefly but failed utterly. The Freemasons sent a delegation to Versailles on April 21. Thiers sent them away, saying, "A few buildings will be damaged, a few people killed, but the law will prevail." On April 29 a demonstration of 10,000 people, many wearing masonic symbols, moved from the place du Carrousel near the Louvre to the Hôtel-de-Ville. Masons planted their flag on the ramparts. On May 8 a poster appeared on the walls of Paris calling for reconciliation and criticizing the intransigence of the Commune's leaders, drawing a violent response from the Union des Femmes.[19]

ADOLPHE THIERS remained convinced that superior cannons sufficed to achieve victory. Versaillais shelling of Paris became increasingly incessant. Fifty-two guns opened fire on Fort Issy and Fort Vanves from Châtaillon, Breteuil, and the heights of Bagneux on April 25. Thiers's insistence that a private contractor mount eighty enormous naval guns at Montretout to increase firepower probably delayed the Versaillais assault on Paris, annoying his generals. At one point, fed up with Thiers's insistence that he knew it all, Marshal Patrice de MacMahon announced that his constant interference would make it impossible for the marshal to remain in his post. Thiers backed down.[20]

CONFRONTED WITH AN increasingly precarious military situation and the Versaillais threat to Fort Issy, on April 28 the aged Jacobin Miot suggested the creation of a five-member Committee of Public Safety. This was a self-conscious throwback to 1793, when the republic was under assault from counterrevolutionary forces within France and from the armies of the crowned allies of the Bourbons. The Paris of 1871 bore some striking similarities with that of the revolutionary era. Jacobins, including Delescluze, Félix Pyat, and others who referred constantly to the French Revolution, generally favored the proposal. So did Blanquists, including Rigault: it fit in nicely with Blanquist ideology and with his own obsession with the Revolution. A "minority," which included Gustave Lefrançais, Gustave Courbet, Eugène Varlin, and Benoît Malon, opposed the constitution of the Committee of Public Safety.

On May 1, the Commune approved the proposal by a vote of 34–28. The minority called the step dictatorial, while the majority insisted that, as in 1793 and 1794, the war necessitated such a move. For his part, Courbet concluded that the Committee of Public Safety represented a "return, dangerous or useless, violent or inoffensive, to a past that should teach us, but without us having to copy it." *Le Prolétaire* echoed the minority: "You are servants of the people: do not pretend to be sovereigns, for the role befits you no more than it did the despots who came before you."[21]

Members of the Committee of Public Safety included Blanquists Armand Arnaud, Léon Meilliet, and Gabriel Ranvier—by far the most able—as well as Charles Gérardin and Félix Pyat. The Committee immediately butted heads with the Central Committee of the National Guard, whose continued existence undermined the War Delegation's attempts to centralize its authority over the National Guard. On May 1, General Gustave Cluseret became a scapegoat for the Commune's inability to transform the National Guard into an organized fighting force; at the behest of the Committee of Public Safety, he was falsely accused of treason, although acquitted by a vote of 28 to 7, arrested, and incarcerated in the Conciergerie, the Gothic prison on the

Ile-de-la-Cité. Three days later, the Central Committee challenged the Committee of Public Safety, demanding that it replace the War Delegation with new members. In the Commune's view, the Central Committee clearly sought to take over the defense of Paris.[22]

In response, the Commune chose Louis-Nathaniel Rossel to replace the imprisoned Cluseret. Born in the Breton town of Saint-Brieuc in 1844 into a military family of republican Protestants from the Cévennes mountains in the south, Rossel had graduated from the elite École Polytechnique. A critic described him as speaking "too rapidly, the words gushing from his mouth in a most disorderly manner." Rossel had served as chief of Cluseret's staff but claimed that his boss was jealous of him. He noted cynically that "men are soon worn out in revolutionary periods," and that Cluseret was such a case. The Central Committee feared eclipse by Rossel, who had supported the idea of the Committee of Public Safety, in part as a way to get rid of Cluseret. On April 30 the Commune named Rossel delegate for war.

The Central Committee may have been wary of Rossel, but it was inaction and infighting among the Commune's leadership that stymied his plans for the defense of Paris. The Executive Commission summoned Rossel, demanding to know his overall strategy. Instinctively anxious that the "amateurs" of the Commune would get in the way of serious reform and hoping to work around them, Rossel had met secretly with Maxime Vuillaume and Communard general Jaroslaw Dombrowski, a member of the minor Polish nobility, to discuss a possible plan to create a dictatorship in the interest of defending the Commune against Versailles. Rigault apparently agreed with the idea of a coup d'état but, single-minded as ever, wanted to wait for the possible exchange of his hero Blanqui. In the meantime, Rossel now had to deal with the War Delegation of five members, only three of whom did any work. As for the Central Committee, he observed with frustration, it "was incapable of managing anything." Yet Rossel went along with the delegation's plan to administer the Commune's military structure, while he oversaw the actual defense of Paris. Commanders of the National Guard promised that twenty-five battalions of five hundred men would be ready to fight. In the meantime, Versaillais attacks on the night of May 3 moved them closer to the ramparts of Paris, and they took many Communard prisoners.[23]

In his first move as the new delegate for war, Rossel ordered more barricades erected, particularly to protect major strategic points within Paris. He named Napoleon Gaillard, a shoemaker sometimes credited with inventing rubber overshoes and a member of the International Workingmen's Association, to oversee the construction of these barricades, including the one protecting the key artery paralleling the Seine, the rue Rivoli, at the corner of Saint-Denis. Rossel described the average barricade as "a wall of cobblestones between 4 1/2 and 5 feet high and 3 to 4 1/2 feet thick." At the place de la Concorde, Gaillard's enormous "chateau"—constructed at a cost of about 80,000 francs—connected the rue Saint-Florentin to the Tuileries Gardens. Built of sandbags and barrels and fronted by a ditch about sixteen feet deep, it stretched across the enormous *place*. One small passageway cut through was "so narrow that only one person could pass at a time." Gaillard later proudly posed in front of it, wearing a splendid uniform with gold decorations and shiny boots.

Yet several newspapers, including *Le Cri du Peuple*, complained about the lack of speed with which such defenses were going up. An American family living on the avenue Friedland, which had only a hastily constructed and relatively flimsy barricade, even hired a taxi to behold Gaillard's masterpiece.[24] No such giant barricade had ever before graced the squares and streets of Paris. Fearing a seemingly inevitable battle of frightening proportions, people living nearby began to leave their apartments.

While the new barricades were being built, Rossel ordered Polish general Walery Wroblewski to organize the defense of the remaining exterior forts and the ramparts. For example, Wroblewski appointed commanders to take responsibility for specific sectors in Paris, naming Napoleon La Cécilia to the area between the Seine and the left bank of the small Bièvre River. The hope was that barricades would slow a Versaillais advance, possibly demoralizing the invading troops. However, the Commune still lacked a coordinated structure of defenses to defend central Paris against the certainty of an invasion by the powerful reconstituted army of Versailles. Imposing defensive impediments were particularly lacking in western Paris.[25]

Versaillais forces continued to gain ground beyond the ramparts of Paris, inflicting huge casualties on Communard fighters and, in defiance of the Geneva Convention of 1864, killing Communard prisoners and women alike. Capturing a chateau and the railroad station at Clamart on May 2, they executed former soldiers as deserters. This allowed the Army of Versailles to set up another huge battery, which rained shells on Fort Vanves. Near there the soldiers of "order" shot two young women aiding doctors, including seventeen-year-old Armande

Communard defenses (CORBIS)

Lafort, gunned down despite the pleas of the wounded men in her care. A week later, Versaillais forces stormed a defended windmill in Cachan, just south of Paris, and then took two barricades in Bourg-la-Reine, south of Paris, killing one hundred defenders and taking fifty prisoners. The next day, shelling of Porte Dauphine, Porte Maillot, and Point-du-Jour took on a new intensity.[26]

Versaillais forces made further advances toward the western ramparts of Paris on the night of May 3, taking some prisoners. In the wake of a Versaillais victory at Moulin Saquet, between Fort Montrouge and Fort Ivry to the south of Paris on May 3 and 4, the victorious soldiers mutilated some of the three hundred or more Communards killed in the fighting. Already weakened by weeks of more conventional shelling, and after putting up stiff resistance in and around the village of Issy, the *fédérés* abandoned Fort Issy on May 8 after two weeks of fighting, with up to ten Versaillais shells thundering during each minute of the previous day and the loss of about five hundred men killed or wounded.[27]

In Paris news of the fall of Fort Issy led to what US Ambassador Elihu B. Washburne called "a day of panic," despite the Commune's official denials. The next day Versaillais cannons pounded the gates of Auteuil and Passy, and an eventual entry seemed possible through Point-du-Jour on the western edge of the capital, where the Seine met the ramparts of Paris. The great battery at Montretout opened fire on May 8. Three days later Thiers promised the *honnêtes gens* that his troops would enter Paris within eight days. Communard forces abandoned Fort Vanves on May 13. A successful defense would have required 8,000 men; the Commune could muster but 2,000, if that. Firing from Forts Issy and Vanves, Versaillais cannons could now inflict even greater damage on the capital, forcing more defenders from the ramparts. The Army of Versailles now held the entire Bois-de-Boulogne. Within a week Thiers's army was ensconced on the other side of the fortifications.[28]

Rossel planned an attack to retake Fort Issy, lost by his predecessor. Upon his arrival at the place de la Concorde on May 9, he expected to find about 12,000 national guardsmen ready to march; he encountered only a few battalions, comprising no more than 7,000 guardsmen. Diminishing numbers of available, committed national guardsmen, as well as a lack of discipline and centralized authority, compounded the enormous material disadvantages confronting the defenders of Paris.[29]

Immediately after the place de la Concorde fiasco, Rossel, who had angered Communard leaders by releasing the news of the fall of Fort Issy, resigned. The Commune convened in a secret session to try to resolve tensions between the minority and the majority. Old quarrels and hatreds came pouring forth. Although the Military Delegation of the Commune continued to support Rossel, the majority on the Committee of Public Safety denounced the delegate for war. Pyat accused him of dictatorial methods, demanding his arrest on the charge of treason. Under guard, Rossel requested a cell in Mazas prison and then, with the help of his friend Gérardin, managed to get out of the Hôtel-de-Ville and hide in Paris until June 8.

The members of the Commune elected new Committee of Public Safety members drawn from the majority, including Émile Eudes, Gabriel Ranvier, and Charles Delescluze. Pyat was not reelected. The reconstituted committee then decided that the next delegate for war would be a civilian: Delescluze, who had seemed on the verge of joining the minority. He had absolutely no military background and managed to find Rossel to sound him out on the military situation.[30]

Even from hiding, Rossel continued trying to run Paris's defense. He sent Napoleon Gaillard suggestions for how to organize the defense. He warned that the Versaillais would attack the ramparts via the

Point-du-Jour and Fort Issy and reminded Gaillard that the only "seriously revolutionary forces" were those of the Eighteenth, Nineteenth, and Twentieth Arrondissements. Rossel had confidence in the determination of the remaining national guardsmen, insisting that ordinary people of Paris fought not just for their thirty *sous* but "for a settlement of the social question." However, he believed that if National Guard units fell back to defend their own neighborhoods, the overall defense of what was left of Communard Paris would be compromised. He recommended that the National Guard unit of the Eighteenth Arrondissement, considered particularly reliable, be sent permanently to the Fourteenth and Fifteenth Arrondissements to reinforce the defense of Grenelle, Vaugirard, and Montrouge, that the guardsmen of the Nineteenth be posted at La Muette near the western ramparts, and that the Twentieth, widely considered the most reliable, go to the Point-du-Jour. His informed advice fell on deaf ears.[31]

On May 15 the minority published a scathing protest, attacking the majority for leading the Commune toward dictatorship and away from meaningful social and political reform. The members of the minority announced that because of their devotion to "our great communal cause, for which so many citizens are dying," they would withdraw to their "perhaps too neglected" arrondissements, adding that "the principles of serious and social reform" seemed to have fallen to the wayside. They issued a statement calling for the twenty-two members of the minority to return to their neighborhoods and attend to important tasks there. The majority reacted by suspending four members of the Commune, including Varlin. In a flurry of verbal violence, *Père Duchêne* denounced the minority as "deserters in the face of the enemy who merit nothing more than an execution squad!"[32] These acrimonious disputes compromised the defense of Paris, eroding the trust of the people of the besieged capital.

Karl Marx's daughter Jenny was in Paris during the Commune. She, like Rossel, understood just how precarious the situation had become for the Commune. On May 12, she related to her father that the end of the Paris Commune loomed because of the lack of military planning (accentuated by an inveterate resistance toward "everything that is military") and open dissension among leaders. She wrote chillingly, "We are on the verge of a second June massacre."[33]

Thiers's flat refusal to agree to an exchange generated outrage in Paris and calls for the archbishop's execution. *La Montagne* insisted that "not one voice would be heard to damn us on the day when we shoot Archbishop Darboy . . . and if they do not return Blanqui to us, [Darboy] will indeed die." Addressing a club, Louise Michel demanded the execution of a high-profile hostage every twenty-four hours until Citizen Blanqui arrived in Paris. On May 15, Citizen Widow Thyou stood up in the Club of Saint-Ambroise and demanded that within twenty-four hours all people with any connection to the Church be shot, from parish priests down to those filling vessels with holy water.[34]

WHILE THE COMMUNE'S leaders quarreled and Versaillais troops neared the city, Paris's elites waited, hoping that the Commune would come to an end with no trouble to themselves. Others took a more active role and joined in the fight against the Communards. Gustave des E. was very much in the former camp. As May arrived, his peaceful existence in Paris continued, even as Versaillais troops drew nearer to the fortifications. A wealthy forty-eight-year-old bachelor trained in law but who had never worked, he was just the kind of person to hate the Commune. A carriage was always available to take him to the Cercle des Arts at the corner of the boulevard des Italiens and the rue de Choiseuil. His club offered very comfortable salons for conversation, and some members referred to it jokingly as the "Circle of Grocers," playfully differentiating bourgeois members from artists, if there were any to be found there. Most members were magistrates and lawyers, "all friends of calm and good manners."[35] Living on the rue Auber near Charles Garnier's uncompleted Opera, he had a servant and a very good cook to tend to his daily needs. Food was never in short supply. On May 4, he bragged that for lunch he had dined on a beautiful filet of sole, boiled mutton with vinaigrette, asparagus—very much in season for those who could afford it—and dessert. Paris might be suffering under siege, but he found it *drôle* that he could still eat so very well. The evening before, he had put away "the most succulent duckling and [later] today a delicious roast with a famous ham with spinach." His cook did the shopping, purchasing enough food to last for three or four days, including an entire leg of venison. Fine vegetables and butter were still available—at least to Gustave.

One day his brother's valet refused to carry mail to Saint-Denis, having, on his last trip there, been threatened with arrest by a Prussian soldier. In Gustave's *quartier*, things began to go downhill. He resented that, as of May 14, all Parisians had to carry an identity card. Moreover, nearby churches had been transformed into political clubs, and there were only lay teachers in the local schools. More people in the neighborhood had gone off to Versailles or somewhere else.

Convinced that Karl Marx's International controlled the fate of Paris, Gustave was sure that, for the most part, the Communards consisted of "adventurers, the ambitious, and the down-and-out." On a Saturday, national guardsmen came through the neighborhood searching for men dodging conscription into the National Guard. Gustave felt a little humiliated that they did not ask for his papers, because he did not look younger than forty, the maximum age, in principle, for obligatory service. Like a few neighbors, he hung an American flag from a window, hoping to confuse Communard officials.

By mid-May, once the Versaillais had advanced close to the ramparts, Gustave was forced to acknowledge that his life might be at risk. Increased Communard security now made it more difficult for him to get out of Paris. Moreover, it was inadvisable to stray too far away from one's *quartier*, especially the prosperous one in which he resided, and especially to go into the peripheral districts, such as Montmartre. Ordinary people saw Versaillais spies everywhere, and if someone like Gustave were stopped, "a bad quarter of an hour could follow." After noting all this in his journal, he returned to his favorite theme—what he had eaten: "Yesterday, it was a first-rate mackerel, a filet of venison with small white onions with cream." Cannon fire in the distance provided seasoning. His little cat slept through it all. If fighting came to central Paris, he would simply remain inside his apartment. Besides, he had enough to eat for several days at least. He had just polished off "an exquisite filet purchased for 55 *sous*."

While elite Parisians like Gustave relaxed, others left Paris to take up arms against the Communards. When the Commune began on March 18, Albert Hans, a veteran of military campaigns in the Crimea, Southeast Asia, and Mexico, had been working in an infirmary in Paris. To his satisfaction, his infirmary separated those still suffering wounds sustained during the Prussian siege from the *fédérés*. To his annoyance, an "insurgent" wounded at Asnières benefited because, as he had been an artillery officer, he was put with the regular army officers. Hans mocked the wounded man's lack of education and the fact that—at least in his view—he had been a "bad worker" before becoming a club orator.[36]

Hans managed to leave Paris and join the Volunteers of the Seine, part of the Versaillais National Guard of Order being organized in Chartres under the command of Gustave Durieu, who had fought as an officer against Mexican patriots and joined the Confederate forces as a lieutenant in the US Civil War. The Volunteers of the Seine would expand to 6,000 men.[37]

On April 20, the Volunteers of the Seine were attached to the First Corps of the Versailles army. At first Hans was upset that only about 120 of some 1,500 original Volunteers had shown up. The army had performed well during the Prussian siege, but Hans was convinced that the "appalling disease of indiscipline," which plagued the French army following its humiliating defeat, had surfaced in the regiment. But well into the second month of the Paris Commune, morale and efficiency had returned with the enlistment of former soldiers from Lorraine released by the Prussians.

Hans was ready to make war on the Communards. If the Volunteers of the Seine included a good many Parisians, most did not hail from the ranks of ordinary residents. Hans sang the praises of the son of a banker who proved to be "one of the most determined and most devoted" of the Volunteers. The notion of battle against an inferior people, so present in the emerging colonial discourse, became an increasingly common trope of "the war on Paris" and its insurgent plebeians. In Hans's assessment, all the Volunteers of the Seine belonged to "the great family of conservatism," sharing a determination to crush the Paris Commune.

On the night of May 12–13, the Volunteers of the Seine moved into position in the Bois-de-Boulogne, amid rumors in the ranks that the time to enter Paris was approaching. Hans's Volunteers were sent to the suburb of Asnières. Near the pont de Clichy, they dug in across the river from insurgent positions. After a nighttime reconnaissance excursion on May 14, *fédéré* shells from Communard cannons at a wide bend in the Seine landed near them. Hans concluded that envious hatred of those "who own property" drove the Communards to take reprisals against those few residents of the western suburb who remained.[38] The Volunteers of the Seine were, along with the regular line troops, ready to take their revenge.

In Versailles, meanwhile, Thiers was more prepared than ever to crush the Communards by any means necessary, including taking advantage of information provided by spies based in Paris. He had faced a no-confidence vote on May 11 after false rumors circulated that he was considering a compromise that would permit Communard leaders to escape. Thiers won by a vote of 490–9, and the renewed support only made him more ruthless. He now spoke even more menacingly of his obligation to order "dreadful measures," because he knew, from the bottom of his heart, that he represented what was "right" against "the crimes" of the Communards.[39]

Thiers made good use of Parisian spies, and the number passing information back to Versailles seemed to have increased dramatically. Charles Lullier, a drunken, unstable National Guard commander, attempted to lure *fédéré* officers to the Versailles side with money provided by Thiers. A clandestine Versaillais military organization, led by Colonel Charles Corbin, was also at work within Paris. Thiers's efforts did not always succeed, however. Versaillais troops, among them Albert Hans and the Volunteers of the Seine, moved into the Bois-de-Boulogne, where they were vulnerable to Communard shells, fully expecting that treason paid for handsomely by Thiers would open the gate. The gate remained shut.[40]

Thiers had tried to bribe General Dombrowski to sell out the Commune for a huge sum (rumored to be 500,000 francs), asking him to free up several gates in the ramparts to let in Versaillais troops and arrest various Communard leaders. He had no luck. Dombrowski, "a small, thin, blond man, curt, nervous, with an energetic, thin, and military bearing," had served as secretary of the Polish section of the International and was a veteran of the unsuccessful 1863 uprising against Russian rule in Congress Poland. False rumors here and there alleged that Dombrowski was a Prussian agent, perhaps because part of historic Poland lay within Prussia. Dombrowski's friend Bronislaw Wolowski went to Versailles to meet with Minister of the Interior Louis Picard and told him that Dombrowski would never betray the Commune. The Polish general considered Thiers a friend of imperial Russia and thus his enemy, and Dombrowski believed that he could help Poland by delivering France from "the wolves who exploit it." Picard asked Wolowski to try again with Dombrowski. To hedge bets, Wolowski asked for passports, if need be, for Dombrowski and other Polish officers, should they decide leave Paris. In this case, a train would be waiting in Saint-Denis to take the Poles to the frontier.[41]

ALTHOUGH THIERS failed to win over Dombrowski and was therefore denied easy access into Paris on May 12, he would not be held off for long. The Commune, having ignored Rossel's keen advice on how to defend the city, instead focused its efforts on destroying prominent symbols of the old order. These public destructions, while cathartic and popular among working-class Parisians, did nothing to slow or ward off the Versaillais.

Communards had been calling for the destruction of Adolphe Thiers's house in Paris since mid-April, and it finally came tumbling down on May 15. When John Leighton walked past, workmen had already begun to knock down the right side of the building; "a pickaxe was leaning against a loosened stone; the roof had fallen in. . . . The fire rose higher and higher." Twenty wagons carted books and objets d'art away from the house before it crashed to the ground. Gustave Courbet picked some small statues and other items of artistic value off the floor and transported them to safety. He reproached the workers for not having taken an inventory. Courbet opposed a proposal to sell Thiers's art to the British, while estimating the value of objects in the house at an incredible 1.5 million francs.[42]

The destruction of the Vendôme Column was by far the most spectacular Communard attempt at exorcism through demolition. Courbet, in particular, hated the column because it represented Napoleon's empire and thus that of his nephew. In 1860, he had suggested to the government that it be dismantled. Three years later, Napoleon III dressed his uncle at the top of the column in Roman garb. After the Franco-Prussian War, Courbet had again called for the column's toppling, arguing that its base, with bas-reliefs relating the history of the republic, could be saved and carted to the Invalides (then a hospital and retirement home for former army officers, as well as the final resting place of Napoleon). Since the proclamation of the Commune, the painter had suggested that a more artistic construction representing the glorious events of March 18 could replace the "block of molten cannons" with Napoleon standing at the top, which would simply be destroyed by its fall. Pyat had proposed the column's destruction to the Commune on April 12, and the Commune voted in favor of the proposal.[43]

Thousands of people gathered at the place Vendôme to witness the destruction firsthand on May 16. Tickets were required in principle for the event. From the first floor of the Hôtel Mirabeau on the place Vendôme, a party of Americans watched the column fall. They sang "Hail Columbia" as "some Yankee girl" pounded "violently" on a piano. A US resident paid $80 for the privilege of being last person to go up to the top.[44]

Members of the Commune were prominent in attendance, adorned with red belts and scarves. National guardsmen stood by, and musicians played songs of revolution. Cannons were readied to fire celebratory rounds. Precautions were taken so that the falling column did not crash into nearby buildings. The ceremony was scheduled to take place at 2 P.M.[45]

Cables attached to the column finally began to pull. But they snapped and had to be replaced with stronger ones. At 5:45 P.M. a "dull cracking sound" echoed. The column began to lean, then snapped into two huge pieces, which crashed down, shattering Napoleon; the globe that he carried rolled briefly on the ground below. Several people managed to get by guards and carry off pieces as souvenirs.[46] Brief, triumphant speeches followed, and then people began to drift away through the thick dust.

Although some photographs of the famous toppling show Courbet and other Communards of note, most of the people who attended were ordinary, large numbers of them from the People's Paris. Before the Commune, the vast majority would have had no reason to go to the place Vendôme, unless they worked for fancy folk living in the vicinity. They risked being stopped and questioned by the police about why they had come into a neighborhood where their appearance and diction were so out of place. Now some of these people had appropriated the *beaux quartiers*. After the column fell, they were photographed in silent triumph, or at least hope. In the early days of the medium, individual and family photographic portraits had been reserved for the bourgeoisie. But now many photographs showed ordinary Communards standing heroically before barricades.[47]

BY MAY 17, the Army of Versailles had moved even closer to the walls of Paris. Three days later, line troops forced Communard fighters out of Auteuil and back within the walls. On May 20, the peace treaty between France and the newly unified German Empire, proclaimed in triumph in the Château de Versailles on January 18, was finalized. By that evening, Versaillais troops had taken over remaining Communard posts in the villages of Issy, Vanves, and Malakoff. The next day, the Committee of Public Safety met to consider accusations of treason against Cluseret and acquitted him by a vote of 28–7—he had done absolutely nothing except oppose the creation of the committee and failed to beat the odds and improve the Commune's increasingly impossible military situation. Believing that the end was near, Cluseret and Pyat disappeared from the scene.[48]

Remains of the statue of Napoleon on Place Vendôme, toppled by the Commune before an enthusiastic crowd on May 16, 1871. (CORBIS)

Many in the Commune still held out hope that help would arrive from Lyon, Marseille, or other militantly republican cities in which movements for local communes had arisen. No such help came.

AT 5:45 P.M. on May 17 a frightening explosion shook all of Paris: the munitions factory on the avenue Rapp blew up, killing dozens of workers, mostly women. Parisians mistakenly believed it to be a Versaillais attack. Protestant minister Élie Reclus noted that the "exasperated population" shouted for vengeance—"one or two more of such days and a return to the September Massacres [of 1792] could become possible."[49]

Three days later, Reclus observed that the hostage situation now took "center stage with an imposing clarity and a dreadful urgency." At the meeting of the Committee of Public Safety that day, Citizen Urbain demanded that five hostages be shot immediately in reprisal for the shooting of a *cantinière* by the Versaillais. For its part, *Père Duchêne* denounced Darboy as "good for nothing [*jean-foutre*] number one who is raking it in . . . [and] who exercises the wonderful profession of arch-bishop of Paris and spy for Bismarck."[50]

Lawyer Étienne Plou tried to convince Rigault to call a grand jury (*jury d'accusation*) and to grant the hostages the right to legal represen-tation. On May 18, Plou requested that another lawyer defend Darboy, but on the following day the archbishop said that he would defend himself. The next day, Rigault announced the convocation of the grand jury, separating the hostages into two groups, the first consisting of Darboy and the other priests, the second including *sergents-de-ville* (municipal policemen). The jury first considered the cases of the latter, who were returned to prison not knowing if they were to be executed. Darboy and the other ecclesiastics were told that their cases would be heard the following week.[51]

The prisoners at Mazas could see each other briefly every day. Abbé Laurent Amodru joined Archbishop Darboy, Abbé Gaspard Deguerry, and Louis Bonjean following his arrest on May 17, after "the impious" searched Notre-Dame-des-Victoires. When Amodru spoke with Dar-boy, he said they should speak in Latin, as "Monseigneur, here the walls have ears and eyes."[52]

Ambassador Washburne visited Darboy on May 19, finding him "very feeble" and quite ill with "a kind of pleurisy." Yet the archbishop seemed "cheerful, and apparently resigned to any fate that may await him." Plou found him lying down, "dressed in an old cassock . . . his features changed, his skin very pale," as he repeated, "I am sick, very sick." Guards now brought him brioches and some chocolate. He said he was in no shape to appear before the tribunal of the Commune; if they wanted to shoot him, let it be right there.[53]

ON SATURDAY MAY 20, with the hostage situation unchanged, Reclus reflected on the state of the Commune, now clearly divided "into two camps." Tensions between the Central Committee of the Na-tional Guard and the government of the Commune persisted. Re-clus described the fundamental contraction in trying to organize the defense of Paris, now caught between the dictatorial authority of a Committee of Public Safety and "the ideal aspirations toward a model Republic." For the latter to exist, the Commune would have to sur-vive. Although the Versaillais were still beyond the ramparts, he wor-ried that if the Communard forces could not fight off "the invading hordes . . . the city [would be] massacred, the revolution . . . lost and everyone subject to the horrors of reprisals that could be without end." He was right to worry.[54]

That night national guardsman Émile Maury awoke at 2 A.M. to the sound of drums calling him to guard service near the ramparts. No more than two hundred of his battalion showed up, though for once Maury did. He moved with the small column along the exterior boulevards. Four "determined *ambulancières*" led the way, followed by a drummer and an officer on horseback. A red flag bobbed among them. At the place d'Italie, they stopped and stacked their rifles. The other battalions supposed to meet them there never arrived. Maury and a friend went into a wine shop and decided to return to their homes in Paris, an occurrence that may have become increasingly common. When the small column moved on to Gentilly, near Fort Bicêtre, they were not missed.[55]

Maury's battalion was not the only one with depleted numbers— and not due just to absenteeism like Maury's. As of May 21, the Versaillais move against Paris had killed at least 4,000 men, as well as a good number of women and children, and 3,500 Communard prisoners had been taken.[56] On that same day, Dombrowski noted that from Point-du-Jour to Porte d'Auteuil, the situation was "bad." He had only 4,000 fighters in the sector of La Muette, 2,000 at Neuilly, and a mere 200 at Asnières and Saint-Ouen. Troops could not stay on the ramparts, where they were fully exposed to cannon fire from Issy and Moulin-eaux.[57] Versaillais shelling remained unrelenting.

Still, on the warm and sunny Sunday of May 21, it was as if nothing were amiss. Somewhere between 10,000 and 15,000 people turned out for a concert held in the gardens of the Tuileries. The American W. Pembroke Fetridge found there "a hot stream of people who belonged to every nationality and rank of life. . . . [T]here were shop-keepers and their wives . . . gentlemen whose National Guard trousers were rendered respectable by the gray jacket or blouse of a citizen; humdrum housewives who approved everything, and gaped their admiration of so much gorgeous wall-coloring in the Tuileries Palace."[58] Maxime Vuillaume observed an officer wearing medals and polished boots, with a sword at his side and his kepi in hand, chatting amiably with a rather large bourgeois lady who fanned herself with a handker-chief. National guardsmen sang "La Marsaillaise," "Les Girondins," "Le chant du départ," and other classics from the French Revolution. The café-concert singer Madame Bordas, wearing a "flowing robe, draped with a scarlet sash . . . [standing] like a warlike apparition . . . a goddess of Liberty from the popular *quartiers*," belted out, "As for the rabble! Well, there. . . . That's me!" At the end of the final refrain, she wrapped "herself in a red flag, pointing with outstretched arm to the invisible enemy, urging [her listeners] to pursue him with [their] hatred and crush him mercilessly. The crowd [was] in raptures." Two women passed the hat for orphans of the Commune.

Even as the concert went on, the Versaillais cannons were now firing from within the walls of Paris. Their shells landed on the Champs-Élysées; one crashed down at the nearby place de la Concorde. At 4:30 P.M., the concert ended, but not before a lieutenant colonel jumped up on the stage and announced, "Citizens, Monsieur Thiers promised to enter Paris yesterday. But he is not here." He invited everybody back for another concert in a week's time. Posters announced a performance at the Opera the next day. Those attending a club meeting that evening heard about a Versaillais attack repelled with the loss of at least 4,000 line troops—which clearly had not happened—with the assurance that the enemy would face more of the same if he dared attack again. Paris seemed calm.[59]

Monsieur Thiers was not in Paris, but his troops were, and for the moment no one in the Tuileries Gardens knew it. A full-fledged assault on Paris had been planned for May 22 or 23. But at about 3 P.M. on May 21, Jules Ducatel, an employee of Ponts-et-Chaussées, had signaled from the ramparts at the Point-du-Jour to Versailles forces camped not far away that Communard forces had left bastions 65 and 66 undefended. Porte Saint-Cloud was also vulnerable. A Versaillais naval officer entered cautiously, looking left and right, and then went into several nearby houses to make sure it was not a trap. Returning to his trench, he telegraphed generals with the astonishing news. Within an hour, line troops commanded by General Félix Douay had entered the capital. Porte Saint-Cloud and then Porte d'Auteuil fell without resistance, and Versaillais troops soon snared one hundred prisoners at a munitions storage area on the rue Beethoven.

The Committee of Public Safety learned from a message sent by Dombrowski that Versaillais forces were inside Paris, advancing through Passy. Several men sent to La Muette to confirm this report somehow returned "with the most reassuring news" that all was well. Delescluze, incredibly enough, refused to allow the ringing of the tocsin and simply denied that the Versaillais had penetrated the walls of Paris.[60]

After deserting his battalion early that morning, Émile Maury could hear gunfire far away as he walked with his father along deserted boulevards. Everything "seemed to suggest that something awful was going to happen." The tocsin, which by now was ringing its call of great alarm, and the roll of drums followed them home, while the gunfire in the distance appeared as a "shroud of death and of mourning over the great city." Maury believed that the Commune could not win, and he did not want to die in a revolution that he did not really understand.[61]

That day Archibald Forbes, a British journalist, wanted to interview General Dombrowski, who was overseeing the defense of Paris from the Château de la Muette. At the Ministry of War on the Left Bank, the British journalist found astonishing "the utter absence of red tape and bureaucracy there . . . a shock to the system of the Briton." He received a pass allowing him "to witness the military operations in the capacity of a correspondent," both in- and outside Paris. His request for both types of access had met with a "simple 'fine.'"

The Commune had requisitioned his horse, however. Forbes hired a carriage. As they passed pont de Jéna, the battery at Trocadéro opened up. The Versaillais cannons on Mont-Valérien replied. Telling Forbes he had children and would take him no further, the driver deposited the journalist right there on the grande rue de Passy. Nearby houses were virtually empty, "but a large colony of shell-holes" could be seen. Forbes saw Communard soldiers and even some sailors lounging "idly about the pavements." No one seemed at all afraid, although Versaillais shells were landing "pretty freely."

General Dombrowski greeted Forbes cordially, even with enthusiasm: "'We are in a deplorably comic situation here,' he said, with a smile and a shrug, 'for the fire is both hot and continuous.'" The likable "neat, dapper little fellow . . . with very little gold lace" spoke no English but, apparently like Forbes, was fluent in German. His staff of eight to ten young men "seemed thoroughly up to their work." Dombrowski chatted as he read dispatches and ate, asking Forbes if he knew anything about possible German intervention. A battalion commander came to report that the Versaillais forces were pouring through the gate of Billancourt. A shell hit the chateau, but the general did not seem worried. An adjutant took Forbes up to the roof, where they could see puffs of smoke as Versaillais sharpshooters tried to pick off *fédérés* on the ramparts. Dombrowski admitted that he would have to abandon the ramparts from Porte d'Auteuil to the Seine. He counted on the second line of defense and believed that the Army of Versailles would have to fall back. The Polish commander insisted, "There is plenty of fight still in our fellows, especially when I am leading them."

Dombrowski asked Forbes to follow him as he left to observe for himself the progress Versaillais troops were making. They scurried down the rue Mozart with Versaillais guns "in full roar." As they came upon reinforcements waiting for Dombrowski on the quai d'Auteuil, they learned that the Versaillais also had taken Porte Saint-Cloud. Communard forces had begun to fall back right and left, and brief counterattacks had failed. Forbes lost sight of Dombrowski and never saw him again.[62]

Forbes himself retreated to the second line of Communard defense, which stiffened behind the railway line. By 11 P.M., all was quiet. Forbes made it to the rue de Rome and then Trocadéro in a dense fog.

As DOMBROWSKI orchestrated the city's defense, even more line troops marched through the gates of Auteuil, Passy, Sèvres, Saint-Cloud, and Versailles, readying for a massive assault at dawn.

Arthur de Grandeffe entered Paris on May 21 along with the Volunteers of the Seine. The residents of Passy, a relatively prosperous neighborhood, treated them as long lost friends, telling them stories of Communards smashing crucifixes. A lady offered Grandeffe and others soup that she had prepared for them. Beyond, they came upon dead insurgents. One, still alive, sat on the ground, propped up against a wall. No one left the ranks of the Volunteers to help him. Grandeffe considered the prisoners he saw "the scum of Paris," the attitude their superiors had told the Versaillais to take. One could not reason with them. In his view, they had to be dealt with harshly. Otherwise, French society risked falling back into "barbarism."[63]

After camping in the park of Malmaison, Albert Hans and his battalion of the Volunteers of the Seine moved to Rueil, where they awaited orders to return to Asnières. In the evening, a rumor spread that line troops had passed through the ramparts at Point-du-Jour, easily taking Auteuil, and commanded by Justin Clinchant were moving rapidly toward Trocadéro. The "joyous" Volunteers of the Seine soon followed, crossing a wooden bridge, the horses and wagons generating a rumble that sounded like distant gunfire.[64]

From the moment the first Versaillais troops entered Paris, it became clear that Communards could expect little in the way of mercy from them. Some of the first summary executions carried out by the Versaillais took place in Passy and Auteuil, where there had been virtually no fighting. A reporter for *Le Gaulois* came upon about thirty bodies and asked around. Troops had lined victims up along a ditch and dispatched them with a *mitrailleuse*. A merchant confirmed that the first killings had involved two men put up against the door of a tobacco shop.[65]

Eager to finish with the "bandits," the Volunteers of the Seine reached Porte d'Auteuil. They passed overturned cannons with shattered carriages, a burned-out railway station, and houses that had been blown apart. The Volunteers came upon the bodies of *fédérés* whom even Albert Hans had to admit had shown courage by remaining at their position as shells rained down from the Bois-de-Boulogne. One man was still breathing and, after some Volunteers threatened to shoot him, was finally given a drink of eau-de-vie, then left on the side of the road with a blanket thrown over him, until a priest or someone from the neighborhood arrived with a stretcher.

Coming upon a half-destroyed fort along the ramparts, Hans and the others encountered more bodies and the first group of prisoners they had seen. Kepis, military sacs, and even guardsmen's pants, whose occupants had hurriedly discarded them for fear of arrest, littered the boulevard Beauséjour. At the Château de la Muette, where Archibald Forbes had interviewed Dombrowski earlier, the troops found several dozen Communards hiding in woods and gardens. A concierge had hidden about a dozen Communard volunteers, young men and boys aged twelve to seventeen. They let the boys go.

In a charitable establishment for young women, which Communards had converted into a small barracks, Hans was outraged to find graffiti and obscene drawings scrawled on the walls and empty bottles and garbage strewn here and there. Finally Hans reached the Arc de Triomphe and the *beaux quartiers* of western Paris. Here, as in Passy, residents saluted them with great enthusiasm. A woman came down from her apartment, dutifully followed by several servants, who distributed cigars, wine, bread, and other food to the soldiers. She insisted that the troops return to her residence to rest up briefly.

Moving past the Church of Saint-Augustin, Hans reached the parc Monceau. Troops had just executed a dozen "deserters"—that is, soldiers still considered to be in the French army who had fought for the Commune. The scene smelled of fresh blood, in sharp contrast to the spring scents emitted by the surrounding greenery.

After camping at the place Wagram, the Volunteers took their first prisoners. Several claimed not to have fought; yet their rifles, which they had not had time to clean, revealed otherwise. One admitted that he had participated in a recent encounter at Levallois but claimed to have joined the National Guard because he had no work. "This poor devil" had had to choose between being "mistreated" by the Communards if he did not fight and being taken by the Versaillais if he did.

At the rue Cardinet, some *fédérés* called out from behind a barricade that they would surrender, wanting assurance that if they laid down their arms, no harm would come to them. When they hesitated, a couple of the Volunteers, including Hans, went forward and convinced three of them to give up. One kept repeating, "I did as the others. I could not do anything other than they did." Believing the man to be clueless rather than a scoundrel, Hans told him to remain quiet, fearing that he could well end up like the Communards they passed in the parc Monceau. Hans spoke with another *fédéré*, whom he believed to be drunk, when shots came from the Communard barricade. The Versaillais responded with fire, and Hans took refuge in a shop. Eventually the remaining *fédérés* abandoned their barricade and fled.

Hans and the other Volunteers received orders to take the prisoners to a post for transfer to a court-martial. Hans worried about the guardsman he had taken prisoner, fearing that he would be shot, particularly as he was technically a deserter from the army. Moreover, the prisoner's *livret* recounted only several punishments for insignificant lapses. The captive asked Hans if he thought he would be shot. Hans told him simply to deny his name and gave him a story to relate in the hope that he would be sent back to the mass of prisoners. When asked to repeat the story, the man was incapable of doing so. Hans then turned him over to someone he knew to be of good heart. By chance, the plan worked, and Albert Hans saved the man's life.

Moving past the remains of Communard barricades at the place Pereire, Hans and other Volunteers of the Seine came upon some very sad-looking prisoners. Then, when a shot rang from a nearby house, soldiers poured into it, finding a Communard sergeant. The commander grabbed him and ordered his immediate execution. The sergeant begged for mercy, then suddenly bolted from the wall against which he had been placed and managed to flee, reaching a door, aided by shots arriving from elsewhere. The Volunteers fired, but he made good his escape.

As the Volunteers of the Seine passed along the avenue de Saint-Ouen on the northern edge of Paris, residents expressed anything but warm feelings, particularly the women, "strong in their weakness," as Hans liked to say. One informed them with pride that her husband was fighting with the *fédérés* not far away and would break their heads. Hans had to admit that some of the Volunteers arrested people in the *quartier* for no particular reason, angered by such defiance.[66]

EDMOND GONCOURT spent Sunday "in fear of a setback for the Versailles troops." From his window, he could hear in the distance "the regular tramp of marching men who are going to replace others, as happens every night. Come now! It is the effect of my imagination. I go back to bed, but this time it really is the drums, it really is the bugles! I hurry back to the window. . . . Above the shouts of 'To Arms!' rise in great waves the tragically sonorous notes of the tocsin, which has begun to ring in all the churches—a sinister sound which fills me with joy and marks the beginning of the end of hateful tyranny for Paris."[67]

That morning, Élie Reclus awoke to the news that Versaillais troops were moving rapidly inside the walls of Paris. As he walked down the rue Saint-Pères on the Left Bank, a bullet whizzed by his head. He suspected it to be the work of "some good bourgeois, attached to 'order.'" In the Seventh Arrondissement, it was not difficult to see the "secret jubilation of all the concierges, shop owners, merchants of holy articles, and the religious men and women who make up the base of the population there. Their eyes follow you so that they can denounce you as soon as possible to the first gendarme or policeman" who represents their cause. Reclus could see that Communard resistance lacked a well-developed plan to defend the Left Bank. Moreover, around the École Militaire and the Invalides, Bonapartists abounded, and the noble faubourg Saint-Germain still had its niche of Legitimists, with the residence of the Jesuits and other religious congregations not far away at Saint-Sulpice. Medical students also marched under the clerical banner. Enthusiastic calls for heroic resistance, the stirring sound of the tocsin signaling grave danger, the roll of drums, and the alarmed cry of trumpets were one thing; effective organization was another.[68]

National guardsmen were now rushing about preparing to fight, although Delescluze still denied that the Versaillais had breeched the city walls. British subject John Leighton asked a guardsman if the news was true. Yes, the guardsman replied, "we are betrayed." The red trousers of line troops had been seen in the distance. Leighton heard the heavy sound of rolling wheels and beheld a "strange sight": a "mass of women in rags, livid, horrible, and yet grand, with the Phrygian cap [of the French Revolution] on their heads, and the skirts of their robes tied round their waists, were harnessed to a *mitrailleuse*, which they dragged along at full speed; other women pushing vigorously behind." He followed along, to the point where a barricade was under hurried construction, when a boy confronted him: "Don't you be acting the spy here, or I will break your head open as if you were a Versaillais." An old man with a long beard told the boy that that would be a waste of needed ammunition, then turned to Leighton and politely asked, "Will you be so kind as to go and fetch those stones from the corner here?" Leighton complied, and when the barricade was completed, the guardsman told him, "You had better be off, if you care for your life."[69]

A Parisian living near Porte Saint-Denis awoke at 6 A.M. on May 21 to hear newspaper vendors announcing, "Great Victory of Dombrowski at Neuilly." He stayed in his room all day, smoking his pipe and reading Communard newspapers. After going to bed, he awoke about midnight to the tocsin sounding from the bells of the churches of Paris. Below, national guardsmen moved along the boulevards. He did not think much of it. The next morning, the same newspaper vendors were out early, shouting the same news as the day before. Sent out to buy more papers, the concierge returned with the news that Versaillais troops had entered Paris. Parisians on the boulevard below seemed "worried and stupefied."[70]

A sizable barricade went up at the base of the rue Saint-Denis. The Parisians living near Porte Saint-Denis at the other end of the street watched as Communard fighters who had been fighting at the Church of the Madeleine and the place Vendôme returned to their neighborhoods, some wounded. In the evening a delegate of the Commune for the arrondissement, a large man of about fifty or sixty, turned up. Looking around, he ordered the construction of several barricades, instructing people standing nearby to help. A paver oversaw the work, and about a dozen children joined in. Soon a National Guard platoon of about twelve men showed up. They parked their rifles and slept on the sidewalk. By now shells had begun to scream above the building at Porte Saint-Denis. One witness wondered if the barricades below would keep him and his neighbors from getting out if the shooting drew nearer. Yet he went out to dine. Returning home, he heard shouted orders to turn off the lights and close the windows. Then all fell still.[71]

FIFTY THOUSAND line troops were soon in Paris, and within seventeen hours of the first breech of the ramparts, 130,000 Versaillais soldiers, along with artillery, had entered the city.[72] Soldiers moved easily down the avenue de Versailles and then along the quay, sweeping aside a single barricade that stood between them and Trocadéro. No Communard cannon fire greeted them, demonstrating the ultimate lack of coordination and inadequacy of the Commune's military defense. Versaillais line troops reached Trocadéro before daybreak on May 22. The marquis de Compiègne stood at Trocadéro: "Paris stretched out beneath our feet. Joy took over all our faces." The Versaillais had taken the barely defended Trocadéro along with 1,500 prisoners. The fall of Trocadéro shattered the illusion for many Communards that they could hold off the Versaillais.[73]

There were more signs during the assault of the violence to come. Near Trocadéro, a Versaillais officer called Filippi came across a wounded National Guard officer lying on a stretcher. He ordered four soldiers of the 79th regiment to carry him to an improvised care facility. When they grumbled, Filippi reminded them that a wounded combatant was "sacred" and told them to carry out the order. He had just begun to walk away when shots told him that "the unfortunate wounded man had been finished off."[74]

Versaillais forces moved toward the Champs-Élysées. They took the vast Palace of Industry, used by the Communards as a warehouse for supplies and a hospital; Thiers's forces transformed it into a prison. The seizure of 30,000 rations reduced the food available to the *fédérés*. Early that morning, the tricolor flag fluttered above the Arc de Triomphe. Hundreds of Communards had simply abandoned their posts in western Paris, so the Versaillais faced little to no resistance. A large column moved along boulevards toward Porte de Clichy, preparing for an ultimate attack on Montmartre.

It quickly became apparent—to Versaillais forces and Parisians alike—just how unprepared the Commune was. At daybreak on Monday, Archibald Forbes could easily see Versaillais forces advancing. Heading toward the Champs-Élysées he came upon newly arrived line troops with their red pants. The Versaillais faced no cannon fire, just rifle shots, and they now held the boulevards Haussmann and Malesherbes, as well as the entry to the rue Royale. Beyond stood imposing Communard barricades, the only defenses that slowed the Versaillais down. Built of furniture, omnibuses, carriages, and mattresses, as well as stones and sandbags, one blocked the rue Rivoli and the other the rue Saint-Honoré. Communards forced Forbes at bayonet point to add chunks of pavement to the barricade, despite his insistence that he was British. His immediate goal was to reach his hotel in Chaussée d'Antin and have breakfast. Back in his room, he found a bullet hole in his tobacco pouch.[75]

On the Left Bank, a force commanded by Joseph Vinoy moved along the quays, nearing the Seventh Arrondissement, while another under General Ernest de Cissey duplicated the strategy on the Right Bank by moving along the exterior arteries toward Porte de Vanves. Both were protected by Versaillais guns now pounding away from Trocadéro, where Marshal Patrice de MacMahon had set up his headquarters. Already 1,500 national guardsmen had been taken prisoner.[76]

Communard generals and civilian leaders, meanwhile, provided little or no direction to those defending Paris. Dombrowski sent Louise Michel and a few others to warn the Montmartre vigilance committee that the Versaillais army had entered Paris. "I didn't know what time it was. The night was calm and beautiful. What did the time matter? What mattered now was that the revolution not be defeated, even in death." The cannons on Montmartre were still. In any case, several weeks of neglect had left them in poor shape. By the time they began firing, at about 9 P.M., the Versaillais were already well ensconced.[77]

IN LITTLE MORE THAN twenty-four hours, the Versaillais troops had wrested control of about a third of Paris. They now paused so that their reserves could catch up. They had encountered very little resistance from the remaining residents of the fancier neighborhoods of the western arrondissements. They now held all of the Fifteenth and Sixteenth Arrondissements, most of the Seventh (including the Invalides, École Militaire, and the Quai d'Orsay) and Eighth, and some of the Seventeenth. Much of the Commune's gunpowder had gone up in the explosion on the avenue Rapp. Some unrealistic optimism remained. A National Guard officer related to Leighton in a café that although a good chunk of the Left Bank had fallen to the Versaillais, he remained confident: "Street fighting is our affair, you see," he insisted. "In such battles as that, the merest *gamin* from Belleville knows more about it than MacMahon."[78] But the Commune at this point stood very little chance of surviving, and some Communard fighters must have started to wonder if they could only hope not to be massacred. There was already quite a bit of evidence that they would be.

Versaillais troops continued to gun down captured Communards. They marched sixteen national guardsmen to the Babylon barracks on the rue du Bac and shot them dead. Soldier Julien Poirier witnessed soldiers tearing into a building they had seen a woman enter carrying a red flag. They found her in the attic, with weapons. They hauled her down the stairs, but she never reached the bottom. They killed her on the way.[79]

An American family on the avenue Friedland welcomed the Versaillais troops as saviors. Several Communard barricades had been hastily constructed nearby, and a few shots were exchanged, but that was about it. They watched as Communards pushed cannons down the avenue as fast as they could. A short time later, line troops arrived. The mother of the family ordered the servants to distribute wine and cigarettes to the soldiers, and her young daughter chatted with them. The woman heard one of them bragging that he had run through five "Communists" that morning with his bayonet, which was bent and caked with blood.

Soon, as the young girl was jumping rope in front of their door, she saw a Versaillais officer and several soldiers dragging a man who was begging for his life. The scene made the girl's "blood run cold": "My heart stop beating, to see that poor wretch on his knees, screaming to be spared, and the officer holding a pistol at his head." The soldiers kicked him to make him get up. Some people watching from a window above called out to the officer not to shoot the man in front of women and children, "so they pushed and kicked him till they came to the end of our street," where they shot him dead. A daughter of the girl's family's concierge later told her that she had wanted to see him killed and had been disappointed because she had reached the corner a bit late. The girl had seen a lot in a very short time, more than enough for a lifetime.[80]

SUMMARY EXECUTIONS had become routine, even organized. French commanders, humiliated by their defeat at the hands of Prussia and its allies seven months earlier, appeared to be taking revenge on ordinary Parisians. The marquis de Compiègne recalled, "The orders to shoot anyone taken prisoner were formal, and the soldiers were exasperated by the fires in Paris" and by the resistance, "without hope and without goal," that they encountered.[81] The Versaillais troops—many, if not most, of them of rural origin—had been told that the Communards were lawless insurgents and criminals. As a result, many soldiers believed that they could kill captured Communards with the blessing of their officers, who would at least turn a blind eye to the killings. Would the killings become a massacre?

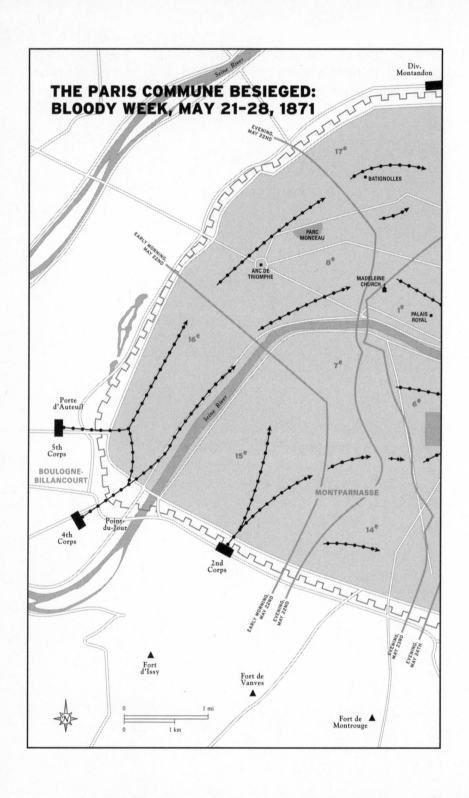

THE PARIS COMMUNE BESIEGED:
BLOODY WEEK, MAY 21-28, 1871

Seine River

Div.
Montandon

EVENING,
MAY 22ND

17ᵉ

BATIGNOLLES

EARLY MORNING
MAY 22ND

PARC
MONCEAU

ARC DE
TRIOMPHE

8ᵉ

MADELEINE
CHURCH

1ᵉ

PALAIS
ROYAL

16ᵉ

7ᵉ

6ᵉ

Seine River

Porte
d'Auteuil

5th
Corps

BOULOGNE-
BILLANCOURT

15ᵉ

MONTPARNASSE

14ᵉ

Point-
du-Jour

4th
Corps

2nd
Corps

EARLY MORNING
MAY 22ND

EVENING,
MAY 22ND

EVENING,
MAY 23RD

EVENING,
MAY 24TH

Fort
d'Issy

Fort de
Vanves

Fort de
Montrouge

N

0   1 mi

0   1 km

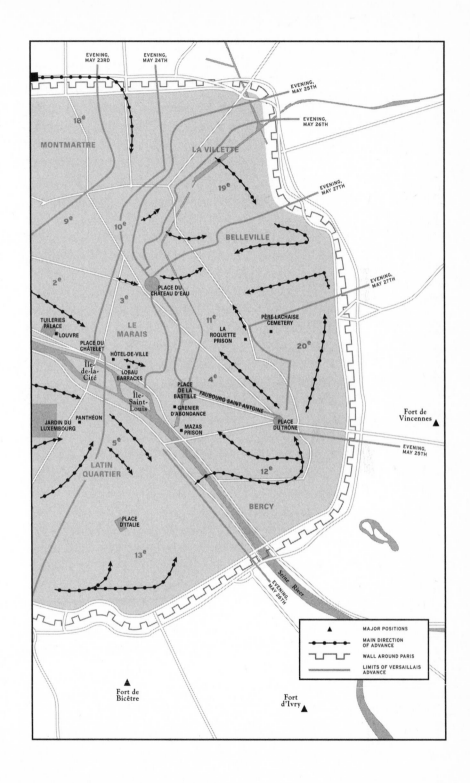

EVENING,
MAY 23RD

EVENING,
MAY 24TH

EVENING,
MAY 25TH

EVENING,
MAY 26TH

EVENING,
MAY 27TH

EVENING,
MAY 27TH

EVENING,
MAY 25TH

EVENING,
MAY 26TH

18e

MONTMARTRE

LA VILLETTE

9e

10e

19e

BELLEVILLE

2e

3e

PLACE DU
CHÂTEAU D'EAU

TUILERIES
PALACE

LE
MARAIS

11e

LA
ROQUETTE
PRISON

PÈRE-LACHAISE
CEMETERY

20e

LOUVRE

PLACE DU
CHÂTELET

HÔTEL-DE-VILLE

Île-
de-la-
Cité

LOBAU
BARRACKS

Île-
Saint-
Louis

4e

FAUBOURG SAINT ANTOINE

PLACE DE LA
BASTILLE

Fort de
Vincennes

JARDIN DU
LUXEMBOURG

PANTHÉON

GRENIER
D'ABONDANCE

MAZAS
PRISON

PLACE
DU TRÔNE

5e

LATIN
QUARTIER

PLACE
D'ITALIE

12e

BERCY

13e

Seine River

MAJOR POSITIONS

MAIN DIRECTION
OF ADVANCE

WALL AROUND PARIS

LIMITS OF VERSAILLAIS
ADVANCE

Fort de
Bicêtre

Fort
d'Ivry

*An enormous Communard barricade blocks the
rue de Castiglione* (CORBIS)

CHAPTER 6

BLOODY WEEK BEGINS

W ITH VERSAILLAIS TROOPS pouring into Paris through the western gates and with much of western Paris having fallen, the next three days—the harrowing of hell—would be crucial, determining the fate of the Paris Commune and thousands of people who backed it. Barricades constructed across narrow streets and in places blocking major squares and wide boulevards were insufficient to hold off the Versaillais for long. Communard defenses on the heights of Montmartre, where the Commune had begun sixty-two days earlier, presented the greatest challenge for the Army of Versailles, particularly as Communard fighters increasingly fell back to their own neighborhood strongholds, abandoning the rest of Paris to the mercy of the invading troops.

ON MONDAY, MAY 22, at about 2 P.M., Raoul Rigault ordered the transfer of Archbishop Georges Darboy, Abbé Gaspard Deguerry, Louis Bonjean, and thirty-five other hostages from Mazas to the nearby prison of La Roquette, located even deeper in the heart of the People's Paris. Gaston Da Costa, Rigault's faithful assistant, requisitioned two wagons for the journey. The prisoners assembled on the ground floor of Mazas, some seeing each other for the first time in six weeks. Darboy, wrapped in an old raincoat, alluded to the approaching end "at last" as prisoners and guards waited an hour for a wagon to arrive. The move to La Roquette did not auger well. A hostile, threatening crowd of men and women, some wearing work clothes, surrounded the wagon. Da Costa remembered being unnerved by "the shrieks of the delirious mob" in the faubourg Saint-Antoine. Paul Perny, a missionary priest, recalled that the crowd was "exasperated, shouting ferociously against the 'papists'!" Under his breath, he said to Darboy, "So there are your people!" calling for the "priests of Bonaparte" to be thrown into the Seine. Perny recounted that he had spent twenty years living "among savages" as a missionary and had never seen anything "so horrible" as the faces of the men, women, and children who "raved" at them during the painful journey from Mazas to La Roquette. Deguerry, who as curé of the Church of the Madeleine, had never visited these neighborhoods, asked on several occasions, "Where are we?"[1]

The fates of Darboy and the other hostages would be tied to the rising swell of anticlericalism that gripped Paris. Da Costa described the mood as one of "legitimate exasperation" that had increased with military reverses. Gustave Courbet recalled the hardening tone of the Communards: "There was nothing left to do. Despair had taken over and with it despairing methods. The drunkenness of carnage and of destruction had taken over this people ordinarily so mild, but so fearsome when pushed to the brink. . . . We will die if we must, shouted men, women, and children, but we will not be sent to Cayenne."[2]

When the prisoners arrived at La Roquette, the clerk went through the formalities of their incarceration. Seeing that they were to be kept in holding cells, the hostages had reason to fear that their stay at La Roquette would be short indeed. Outside the gate, members of the neighborhood's 180th and 206th National Guard battalions stood watch. The thirty-four-year-old director of La Roquette, Citizen Jean-Baptiste François, was decked out in Communard red—belt, tie, scarf, and pants. Small, thin, and pale, he was a hard-drinking worker who had been in debt before being hired by the Commune. He had spent four months in prison for a speech given at a public meeting in 1870. He lived with a woman on the rue de Charonne. François, who hated the clergy, signed a paper: "Received, four priests and magistrates." When a guard referred to Darboy as "Monseigneur," a young national guardsman snapped, "There are no seigneurs here, only citizens."[3]

La Roquette consisted of three large buildings. The one on the street housed its offices and a chapel that had seen no use of late. About forty guards were always present. Darboy and the others from Mazas were held in the fourth section, the archbishop in cell number one. Other hostages were held on the third floor in the opposite building, close to the Père Lachaise Cemetery, a proximity they could not have overlooked. Extremely small and dirty, without a table or a chair, the cells were even more spartan than those of Mazas. Insects abounded. An open but barred space linked the cells; thus inmates could talk easily.[4]

From their cells prisoners heard the sounds of explosions. As cannon fire moved closer, one priest cried out, "In two days, we will all be saved!" Someone had earlier managed to sneak in Communion hosts hidden in an empty container of milk, providing the priests with some consolation. The bell awakened them at 6 A.M. At 3 P.M., the hostages were allowed to walk in the prison courtyard. The prison doctor treated Darboy, who felt nauseous. At 4 P.M. the hostages returned to their cells, where they awaited food brought by young prisoners, not knowing what the Commune planned to do with them and fearing the worst.[5]

VERSAILLAIS TROOPS MOVED swiftly through western Paris. Ernest Vizetelly watched a gendarme carrying a dispatch bag riding down the street from Saint-Philippe-du-Roule. As he approached, "a gun-barrel gleamed between the slightly-opened shutters across the street." A shot rang out. The gendarme threw up his arms and fell from his horse, dead or dying. Several Versaillais soldiers ran up to help him, and others raced to the house from which the shot had originated—a trace of smoke gave away the location—battering down the door. In a few minutes, the soldiers emerged from the building with "a grey-haired disheveled woman, whose scanty clothing was badly torn." They pushed her quickly up against a wall, "but she gave no sign of fear. She drew herself up, and answered tauntingly: 'Well done! Well done! You killed my son this morning, and now I have killed one of you. You bunch of cowards!" Her cry, "Long live the Commune!" expired in her throat as she was shot and fell face-first to the pavement.[6]

In retreat, Communard soldiers returned to central Paris from the fighting in the western neighborhoods. On the rue Montmartre, one of them shouted, practically in tears, "Betrayed! Betrayed! They came in where we did not expect them!" Nearby shops closed or simply did not open. A newspaper vendor on Tuesday shouted, "Get one today! You will no longer have one tomorrow!" At the place d'Italie, a Communard stronghold in the Thirteenth Arrondissement, some national guardsmen hurriedly disposed of their rifles, muttering, "It is the end!"[7]

On the morning of Monday, May 22, while the hostages awaited their fate, Commune leaders met at the Hôtel-de-Ville. Félix Pyat was among them, but not for long; he soon slunk out of Paris and managed to reach London. Soon after the meeting, a proclamation signed by Charles Delescluze appeared on the walls of Paris: "Citizens, enough of militarism, no more fancy officers sporting decorations on their uniforms. Give way to the people, to bare-knuckle fighters! The hour of revolutionary war has arrived!"

As during the French Revolution, the *levée en masse* had been proclaimed. The Commune began to organize defenses in the arrondissements not yet occupied by Versaillais, hoping to use to advantage the narrow streets of the People's Paris. Communard defenders assumed that Adolphe Thiers's army would launch frontal assaults on barricades. A swarm of men, women, and children reinforced barricades that already existed or put together new ones. The role of women rose to even greater significance in the defense of the Commune because barricades took on such enormous importance. The American W. Pembroke Fetridge watched about thirty women demand a *mitrailleuse* to protect the barricade defending the place du Palais-Royal: "They all wore a band of crepe round the left arm; each one had lost a husband, a lover, a son, or a brother, whom she had sworn to avenge. Horses being at this time scarce in the service of the Commune, they harnessed themselves, and dragged [the *mitrailleuse*] off, fastening their skirts round their waists lest they should prove an impediment to their march. Others followed, bearing the caissons filled with munitions. The last carried the flag."[8] These were ordinary women catapulted into an exceptional situation, one that had begun with their role in defending the cannons of Montmartre on March 18.

At the faubourg Saint-Antoine, women, children, and workers in smocks built barricades, calling on passersby to lend a hand: "Let's go, citizen, a helping-hand for the Republic!"[9] Despite the rapid Versaillais advances, Delescluze remained convinced that the Commune could hold Paris by defending it *quartier* by *quartier*, street by street. But the stirring sound of the tocsin and calls for a "revolutionary war" could not compensate for numerical inferiority and chaotic organization.

It was more difficult to barricade boulevards then narrow streets in workers' *quartiers*, as Baron Georges Haussmann had fully understood. The Army of Versailles could blast away at barricades blocking these major arteries while outflanking the defensive impediments. However, for the most part, troops did not attack barricades head-on, to the surprise of Communard defenders. The Versaillais circumvented major defenses by sweeping through adjoining streets, entering nearby buildings, and firing down on barricades. Wickham Hoffman watched line soldiers entering "adjoining houses, passing from roof to roof, and occupying the upper windows, till finally they commanded the barricade, and fired down upon its defenders." At Porte Saint-Denis, the Fifth

Corps overcame twelve barricades without attacking any of them from the front. It soon became clear that the Communards' chances of holding a barricade depended on their ability to hold adjacent buildings.[10]

British subject John Leighton, no friend of the Commune, noted that in some places people seemed to greet these dangerous events with "silence and apathy." Strangely, life seemed to go on as usual on some major streets: "Some ribbons here and there brighten up the shop-windows; bare-headed shopgirls pass by with a smile on their lips; men look after them as they trip along." Yet, at this point, only old men dared appear without a National Guard uniform. Overall, "solitude has something terrible about it just now. . . . Quite a crowd collects round a little barefoot girl, who is singing at the corner of a street." The theaters were virtually empty. Laughter seemed out of place. Death was in the air.

A sergeant stopped Leighton while he was walking and asked why he was not in uniform. The man was a Spaniard, to whom the Englishman had given some cigars during the Prussian siege. Leighton replied that it was not his turn, and the Spanish sergeant answered sarcastically, "No, of course it's not, it never is. You have been taking your ease this long time, while others have been getting killed." Seeming to forget about the cigars, he escorted Leighton to Notre-Dame-de-Lorette, where about fifty men who had avoided National Guard service were being held. All ended well for the moment, as Leighton pulled off an improbable bluff, telling the officer who questioned him that he was a prizefighter, then entreating his stunned interrogator, "Be kind enough to allow me to depart instantly."[11]

Élie Reclus walked down the rue des Saint-Pères in the Sixth Arrondissement, but his trek ended when a nervous guardsman told him that he could proceed no further, while "worried, somber, concerned figures" built barricades, preparing for the onslaught. Concierges immediately began relating their narrow escapes to attentive listeners, describing how they had absorbed Communard bullets with mattresses placed in windows and searching out fleeing Communards hiding in their houses. One proudly related, "I found three of them in my court; I told a lieutenant they were there, and he had them shot. But I wish they would take them away; I cannot keep dead bodies in the house." "Citizen" quickly disappeared as a greeting, "under pain of being suspect," replaced by "the undemocratic Monsieur."[12]

Communard resistance stiffened briefly on Monday at the place de la Concorde, where Napoleon Gaillard's massive barricade, the "chateau," stood. A young woman climbed on top and waved a red flag. Versaillais troops shot her dead as an American family looked down from an elegant apartment above. They also watched as soldiers put an elderly female resister face-first up against a wall. Before they gunned her down, she turned and offered her killers a gesture of defiance, amid bodies and shattered poles that had proudly held the gaslights of the enormous *place*.[13] There, too, Communards had hoped for a frontal attack by the Versaillais, but the line troops simply went around, taking nearby buildings and firing down on Gaillard's giant barricade. When wealthy Parisians still occupied buildings looming above barricades, this became even easier. The fall of the place de la Concorde opened central Paris to the Versaillais troops.

Nearby, on the rue Royale, at the corner of the rue Saint-Honoré, Communards hung a dead rat from a miniature gallows on a barricade with a sign indicating that the same fate awaited Thiers and Marshal Patrice de MacMahon, "who have so long devoured the people." However, Parisians looking from the upper reaches of their buildings toward the west could now see soldiers in the distance wearing red pants. Closer, they could also spot units of *fédérés* moving about in disarray.[14]

Against the reconstituted and, at 130,000 strong, relatively enormous forces of Versailles, the Commune could muster only about 20,000 fighters, if that, in what increasingly became a mismatch, despite the resolute courage of so many Parisians. The Committee of Public Safety met at the Hôtel-de-Ville, amid the chaos of the arrival of messengers carrying increasingly bad news. Conflicting orders, for example, coming from the Commune's War Delegation and from the Central Committee of the National Guard and individual officers, reflected the absence of effective military leadership. Above all, they reflected the virtual impossibility of centralizing authority over the defense of Paris and, in particular, over the National Guard, on which the Commune would depend for its survival.[15]

On the Left Bank, General Ernest de Cissey's army moved easily toward the Champs-de-Mars, Invalides, École Militaire, and Quai d'Orsay, which it took by Monday evening. *Fédérés* were running for their lives, crossing the Seine in the direction of the Tuileries, where thousands of Parisians had enjoyed a concert the day before. After taking a barricade on the rue Bellechasse, Versaillais soldiers overran a telegraph office, killing everyone there, including a canteen woman. Conservatory composer and director Daniel Salvador fought with the Communards on the rue de l'Université. When the Versaillais advanced, he took refuge in a nearby house, but troops found him. They gave him a moment to straighten his necktie, then shot him and tossed his body into a common grave.[16]

Later that day, Cissey's army reached the Gare Montparnasse on the Left Bank, an important point defended by only twenty-six men. Troops moved through the outer districts of the Fifteenth, Fourteenth, and even the Thirteenth Arrondissements, beginning to encircle the central Left Bank. Justin Clinchant's army pursued a similar strategy on the Right Bank, moving along the ramparts. By nightfall, the Versaillais had retaken half the city, including all or most of ten arrondissements. They held a line that stretched from below Montmartre to the rue de la Paix and the Opera on the Right Bank and much of the Sixth Arrondissement on the Left Bank.

The battle drew closer and closer to Edmond de Goncourt's apartment. Workmen arrived with orders to block the boulevard at the rue Vivienne and began to construct a barricade right under his windows. But they worked slowly, not putting "much heart into it. Some move two or three paving stones; others, to satisfy their consciences, give two or three blows at the asphalt with their picks." When shots rang out, they quickly left, replaced by national guardsmen who were soon carrying bodies away. In a few minutes only a few boys remained to defend the barricade, as "bullets [made] the leaves of a little tree spreading over their heads rain on them." A guardsman bravely ventured out to retrieve the body of a woman killed in the fighting but was hit as he insulted the line troops firing at him. A second guardsman also tried, and he too was shot, falling on the woman. It was now nightfall, and someone in an adjacent building foolishly lit a pipe, drawing fire from the Versaillais. Goncourt could barely see from his windows in a "dark Paris night without a glimmer of gas."[17]

With the Versaillais in complete control of the western neighborhoods, wealthy residents who had taken refuge in Versailles began to return. Paul Martine commented that they followed safely behind the columns of troops "as in Africa . . . the hyena and the jackal follow the caravans." One returned denizen bragged about the unlikely exploit of having killed fourteen people who were not his renters whom he found in his building.[18]

Gustave des E. had remained in Paris and was relieved when his servant told him that a tricolor flag had replaced the red flag flying on the Arc de Triomphe. The Communards still managed to annoy him, however, interrupting his sleep and confining him to his apartment.

Soon Versaillais troops could be seen on the roof of a house at the corner of the boulevard Haussmann and the rue Auber, across the street from the Printemps department store. National guardsmen were firing at that building, and Communards were hurriedly putting up a barricade across Gustave's very street at night while he tried to sleep. Gustave could not leave his apartment to go to his club. For safety's sake, he slept on the floor. After lunching on a cutlet, ham, and potatoes, he took a nap, at least until a shell struck the roof of his building. He sent his servant up to fetch a piece to show him. The nearby barricade on the rue Auber fell, and sixty Communards were executed on the spot. A Versaillais lieutenant was killed, and so were eight national guardsmen, whom Gustave had seen below the previous evening. Gustave was never in any danger, despite all the noise. He even dared open the windows to look outside.[19]

Speaking from a window at the Hôtel-de-Ville on Monday, Jules Vallès's attempt to whip up the defensive effort met with confident applause. Down below, women dressed in black with black crepe tied around their arms and red cockades in their hats went off to help the wounded. Children filled cloth sacks with dirt for barricades and loaded rifles. National guard officers dashed here and there, and men suddenly left café tables to head toward the battle. A woman rushed up to and berated a youth who lagged behind: "Well, and you, are you not going to get yourself killed with the others?"[20] By now the Communards had fallen back to the Church of the Madeleine. In the western districts, which the Versaillais had taken, tricolor flags went up.

Versaillais troops now moved along the inside circumference of northwestern Paris, as well as beyond the ramparts, preparing an attack on Montmartre. Already well ensconced on the Champs-Élysées and in the faubourg Saint-Honoré, they moved rapidly to seize strategic locations and take prisoners on their way to Montmartre. Versaillais troops took the Palais-Royal, which Communards had set on fire to slow the enemy's advance, the place Vendôme, the rue de Richelieu, and the Bourse. Line troops seized the Bank of France. The Church of Saint-Augustin and the Gare Saint-Lazare fell, along with the place Saint-Georges, the site of the ruins of Thiers's house. On the rue Richelieu next to the Théâtre Français, the corpses of Communard defenders filled two ditches. Versaillais troops surrounded the Church of Saint-Eustache, forcing five hundred *fédérés* inside to surrender. The troops did not bother to take prisoners and instead executed them en masse.[21]

On a narrow street behind the Louvre, Englishman Denis Arthur Bingham saw a young man shot by "some infuriated soldiers, who had evidently been drinking deeply." They then stopped a student, accusing him of arson and also of trying to poison soldiers. The young man protested his innocence; he was twice put up against a wall and twice wriggled away, "only to be seized and pulled back again. It was a terrible struggle to witness." He was finally taken away to a court-martial and probable death. In the barracks on the rue de la Pepinière, near the Gare Saint-Lazare, the Versaillais shot men imprisoned by the Commune for refusing to fight, assuming them to be deserters. "What struck me as deplorable in these days," Bingham remembered, "was the conduct of the population, which, after having shown the most abject submission to the Commune, now clamored for blood. No sooner was an arrest made than the cry, '*À mort! À mort!*' was raised" by anti-Communards. Bingham, who, unable to return to his home near the Arc de Triomphe with bullets flying in every direction, had taken a room on the rue Saint-Lazare, finally found his wife, who had assumed he had been killed.[22]

AS THE VERSAILLAIS TROOPS pushed forward, the *fédérés* took to setting fire to buildings to slow the attack. In some cases Versaillais shells started the fires, but regardless of the cause, houses went up in flames, leaving residents scrambling for safety. The Cerfbeer family huddled in their apartment on the rue Saint-Honoré in great anxiety. Neither news nor provisions were generally to be had, although the family cook had been able to purchase bread. They could not leave, for the *fédérés* were organizing resistance right outside their door. Soldiers ordered doors and windows shut and rudely sent some residents who went out into the street back inside. When an imposing cannon placed below residents' windows fired from time to time, the entire building shook.

On Monday night, an officer knocked on the door of the concierge of the Cerfbeer family's building, located in a neighborhood that formed a secondary line of defense between the place de la Concorde and the Champs-Élysées. The concierge and his family were Alsatians, their strong German accents noticeable to any Parisian. They had two sons. The Communard told them to evacuate the building immediately because it was to be set on fire: "No comments. Get out right now!" He gave everybody ten minutes to leave, saying that houses nearby were burning.

Twelve-year-old Gaston Cerfbeer's father told him that the family must leave their home immediately, saying that he would follow once he had gathered up some important papers. Gaston left with the Alsatian concierge, his wife, and their two young sons, twelve and fourteen years old. Disoriented people poured into the street. The boy found the faubourg Saint-Honoré "completely covered by a wall of flames, because its old houses burned like straw—the scene was terrifying, but strangely beautiful." Gaston and his mother and the concierge's family plunged into the night. A half-destroyed barricade blocked their way, but they managed to get through the corner of the rue Richepance, with Gaston pulling one of the concierge's sons, Fritz, by the hand as they scaled stacked paving stones. Then they heard shots, and Fritz let go of Gaston's hand and slid to the ground, bleeding from the head. His mother cried out as she reached him, but her husband, seeing that nothing could be done, pulled his wife toward the presumed safety of the place Vendôme. Their son was dead.

Further down the rue Saint-Honoré, shots came from the rue de Castiglione, where Versaillais troops had just appeared. Seeing a shadow move, they quickly blasted away in its general direction. Gaston froze. At some risk to herself, a domestic servant waved to him from a balcony, indicating that he, his mother, and the rest of the concierge's family should enter the building, the door of which was half open. They entered the total darkness of the stairway, the only sound the concierge's lament at his son's death: "Mein Fritz! Mein lieber Fritz!" As the shooting had stopped someone in the building gave them a candle. A young girl told them that more fires had been set nearby. Gaston wanted to see for himself, and the two went up to the sixth floor. From the roof they could see "an immense red inferno, with columns of smoke filling the air with burned paper." As the Ministry of Finances burned—set ablaze by Versaillais shells—they could see "a swarm of black things fleeing rapidly": rats from the ministry taking refuge in nearby houses.

The next day uniformed line soldiers dressed in blue and red opened the door and told them it was now safe to leave. Gaston and his family, as well as the concierge and what remained of his family, walked quickly toward the rue Royale, asking soldiers news of their home. The responses varied. Number 414? Yes, it is burning—no wait, rather 410 and 414 are ablaze. As people could see houses of the faubourg Saint-Honoré burning, "a frenzied, irresistible panic took over everyone." Rumors arrived that the *quartier* had been mined and was to be blown up. Luckily, Gaston and his mother found their building intact. His very worried father was waiting for them.

Years later, Gaston could still see the scene, "the deep rumble of houses collapsing in the middle of cries, falling on unfortunate residents later found burned or asphyxiated in cellars." At the place de la Concorde, a shell had decapitated the female statue representing the city of Lille. Far more terrifying were real corpses; a pile of them stood in a corner of the courtyard of the Assumption Church, and there was an even bigger pile at the Tuileries Palace, where squads of soldiers were busy killing Communard resisters. A tarp covered the stack of bodies there, as a veritable sea of blood formed around the pile of death. Gaston watched the sad parade of prisoners heading along the rue de Rivoli and up the boulevards toward the horrors of incarceration at Satory, a prison camp set up on a plateau near Versailles.[23]

Gaston's experience was by no means unique. Monday had brought the first indication that the Communards might use fire as a means of defense. On the rue de Lille in the Seventh Arrondissement, Communards told residents to leave their buildings, saying that they planned to set fires with petrol. One *fédéré* surmised that fire could provide a means of slowing the advance of Thiers's troops; another retorted that Versaillais shells must have caused the fires that had burst forth.[24] Both were reasonable explanations.

On Tuesday, Delescluze and Alfred-Édouard Billioray, a painter and member of the Commune, signed an order stating, "Blow up or set fire to the houses which may interfere with your system of defense. The barricades should not be liable to attack from the houses." The Commune threatened to burn any house from which Versailles allies fired shots against them. When about to be overrun, Communard resisters tried to create space between themselves and their attackers by setting strategically positioned houses ablaze. They also set fires out of vengeance to punish traitors. Those setting fires warned residents in advance. Other conflagrations served as a means of appropriating and purifying contested space. A commander of the National Guard wanted to torch the Imprimerie Nationale: "Here is the house of Badinguett [a contemptuous nickname for Napoleon III]: we have orders to burn it down."[25]

Versaillais soon believed that the journalist and deputy Jean-Baptiste Millière commanded a force of 150 tasked with setting fire to houses and monuments on the Left Bank. This was absolutely false. Pierre Vésinier, a member of both the International and the Commune, supposedly organized a band of fifty incendiaries assigned to burn houses on the boulevards from the Church of the Madeleine to the place de la Bastille. A rumor circulated that Communards had shot people on the rue de Lille who attempted to put out the fires. Panic spread in the *beaux quartiers* as buildings went up in flames—the burning of one on the rue Saint-Honoré may have killed seven residents—and rumors of an organized plot by female incendiaries (*pétroleuses*) swept the city. *La Patrie* reported that Versaillais soldiers found the charred remains of a woman in the chic faubourg Saint-Germain, (somehow) with the remains of a pipe in her mouth and pieces of clothing doused with pet- rol. To those seeking confirmation of a Communard plot to burn Paris, this suggested that the pipe had been used to light the gasoline.[26]

DURING THE BATTLES ON MAY 22 AND 23, Joséphine Marchais, a washerwoman originally from Blois, picked up a gun, donned a Tyrolean hat, and shouted, "You cowardly crew! Go and fight! If I'm killed it will be because I've done some killing first!" She was arrested as an incendiary. In fact she had worked as a *vivandière* with the Enfants Perdus battalion. Joséphine had carried laundry that guardsman gave her to wash, and she had carried away the body of her lover, a butcher's apprentice called Jean Guy, after he was killed, but no one had seen her with any petrol.[27]

The *Paris-Journal* reported that line soldiers took to the military post at the place Vendôme thirteen women, most of them young, who had allegedly thrown petrol into basements. Several seconds later, "a lugubrious detonation indicated that justice had been done." A woman may have been gunned down because she was seen too close to the Opéra-Comique, which was not burned. Another newspaper an- nounced to eager Versaillais readers that a woman had been arrested with 134 meters of fuse line in her pocket. She must have had an enor- mous pocket! Marie-Jeanne Moussu, a laundress from Haute-Marne married to a man called Gourier, seemed to the Versaillais "the most perfect example imaginable of these vile creatures of the faubourgs, who provide the Commune with powerful auxiliaries to burn down Paris." She had indeed set a fire, but she was trying to burn out her for- mer lover—her act had nothing to do with the Commune.[28]

Leighton believed a rumor that *pétroleuses* received ten francs for every house they sent up in flames. According to him, the *pétroleuse* "walks with a rapid step, near the shadow of the wall; she is poorly dressed; her age is between forty and fifty; her forehead is bound with a red checkered handkerchief, from which hang meshes of uncombed hair. The face is red and the eyes blurred. . . . Her right hand is in her

An accused pétroleuse *is shot by Versaillais* (THE GRAPHIC)

pocket, or in the bosom of her half-unbuttoned dress; in the other hand she holds one of the high, narrow tin cans in which milk is carried in Paris, but which now . . . contains the dreadful petroleum liquid." He heard that one had been caught in the act in the rue Truffault and fired six shots with a pistol at Versaillais before being killed; "Another was seen falling in a doorway of a house in the rue de Boulogne . . . a young girl; a bottle filled with petroleum fell from her hand as she dropped."

US Ambassador Elihu B. Washburne believed the rumors too and gave the astonishing figure of 8,000 incendiaries at work in Paris, adding that "of all this army of burners, the women were the worst." Children, it seemed, were equally culpable. He related that an employee of his legation had counted the bodies of eight children, the oldest younger than fourteen, shot after being caught with petroleum.[29]

One rumor claimed a household search on the rue des Vinaigri-
ers had turned up thirty small containers (*oeufs à pétrole*) filled with
nitroglycerine. Woe—and thus death—to women found carrying bottles with anything suspicious, including even oil for heating. *Le Siècle* reported that on May 31 a woman "was practically cut into pieces"
because she had purchased olive oil. Among accused *pétroleuses* was a
twenty-year-old woman carrying her baby. An officer ordered her shot
on the spot. Asked what to do with the baby, he supposedly barked,
"Shoot it too, so that the very seed disappears!" Denunciations for in-
cendiarism flowed more freely than water to put out the fires.[30]

Without question Communards set some of the fires. Like barricades, the flames both served as a means of defense and represented an
appropriation of space on behalf of the Commune. There is clear evidence that Communards started fires in houses on the rue Royale and
in the faubourg Saint-Honoré, trying to create a "barrier of flames" that
would slow the onslaught and prevent Versaillais troops from climbing to the upper reaches of the buildings and firing down on barricade
defenders.[31]

As the Versaillais advanced and killed, Communard leaders ordered
the burning of a number of monumental Parisian buildings, all in the
fancy parts of town. Émile Eudes ordered the burning of the Palace of
the Conseil d'État, and the Committee of Public Safety condemned
the Palais-Royal. Théophile Ferré signed the order (subsequently found
in the pocket of a Communard who fought at a barricade on the rue
Royale, dated 4 prairial '79) to burn the Ministry of Finance. Courbet
remained at the Louvre to protect its invaluable collections, but fire
broke out or was set on a roof. Paintings and sculptures still in the great
museum were saved when passersby extinguished the conflagration.
General Paul-Antoine Brunel ordered fire set to the Naval Ministry
next to Gaillard's giant barricade on the place de la Concorde to prevent Versaillais troops from taking it and shooting down on defenders,
but the fire did not catch.[32]

Could Communards in defeat actually intend to burn down their
city? The Versaillais siege had pushed the Communards toward despair
and intense anger. Some among them could imagine the entire destruction of Paris—anything was better than ceding it to Thiers. Prosper-
Olivier Lissagaray insisted that it was better to burn down "our houses
rather than to turn them over to the enemy." And Louise Michel had
warned, "Paris will be ours or cease to exist." However, she had gone
no further than insisting that Communards defend Paris "until death."

After finishing his meal on the terrace of the Louvre on Tuesday, Communard general Jean Bergeret ordered the Tuileries Palace set ablaze. Watching the conflagration consume the palace where Napoleon III and his entourage had romped, Gustave Lefrançais admitted to feeling "shudders of joy seeing that sinister palace go up in flames." Two days later, seeing fires in the distance, a Montmartre woman asked Nathalie Le Mel what was burning; Le Mel replied, "It's nothing at all," only the Palais-Royal and the Tuileries, "because we do not want a king any more."

The fires that raged throughout Paris stoked anti-Communard hatred. The burning of the Tuileries, a symbol of the Second Empire, particularly intensified anti-Communard demands that prisoners be shot immediately and shouts of "*Pas de quartier!* [No quarter!] Death to the burners!"[33] The writer Louis Énault accused the Communards of striving to burn Paris to the ground. They began, in his view, with several *beaux quartiers*, such as the rue de Lille, "a sumptuous and aristocratic residence," with the same cachet as the nearby boulevard Saint-Germain. From a faraway window, Énault marveled at the horror of it all, as the evening wind pushed the fires. As the flames gathered force "with a violent speed," he wrote, "the fire took on . . . fantastic tones . . . blue, greenish, violet, deep red." As some Parisians watched the fires spreading in the distance, they wondered which *quartier*, which monuments, which buildings were burning. Théophile Gautier believed he was witnessing a modern Pompeii. It was as if the destruction begun under Haussmann had continued. The explosion of an occasional shell launched by the Communards from Montmartre added to the fear.[34]

WALKING FROM THE CHURCH of the Madeleine to the place du Château-d'Eau (now de la République), Reclus encountered so few people that it might have been 2 or 3 A.M. and not the middle of the day. Yet, at Porte Saint-Martin, ordinary people formed a human chain to move paving stones to a barricade, while others stopped passersby with "*Citoyen, Citoyenne*, to work!" Children of all ages were actively involved in building the barriers, two or three struggling together to carry heavy blocks of stone. Reclus had to show his *laissez-passer* at each barricade. Even after he had carried stones—despite his handicapped right hand (mangled in a fall when he was a child)—a national guardsman stopped him briefly on the rue Lafayette and accused him of covering up his spying activities for the Versailles by helping out. Reclus remained calm, and a police official ordered him freed.[35]

Reclus did not return home that night, fearing capture. He stayed with friends who lived in the faubourg du Temple. "We are," he assessed, "like sailors whose ship is taking on water during a storm and which every quarter of an hour sinks a bit further down. Leaning against the front of the ship, we can see against the horizon vast waves pounding toward us, howling and frothing in rage." Would the first big wave carry them away, or would the second or perhaps the fourth "in this stormy sea that is Paris"? Perhaps that very day they "would die . . . perhaps tomorrow . . . or perhaps the day after that. . . . No matter, it will not have been in vain!"[36]

From Versailles Thiers proclaimed, "We are *honnêtes gens*. . . . The punishment will be exemplary, but it will take place within the law, in the name of the law." This was clearly not the case, as Versaillais troops were already gunning down Communards right and left. The term *honnêtes gens* was loaded with class connotations that had turned murderous. Many among the *honnêtes gens* were delighted to see Paris purged of lower-class insurgents intent on overturning social hierarchy and privilege.[37]

As Versaillais troops moved through Paris, they shot down the Communards they had been taught to despise. Moreover, in a civil war, almost anyone, anywhere, could be an enemy. The summary executions probably stiffened resistance in some cases, but over the next days they also demoralized resisters. Few could have any doubt at this point about what was occurring in the streets of Paris and what the eventual outcome of the struggle would be.

When Versaillais encountered resistance in narrow streets, being fired upon from the windows of houses, they conducted brutal searches and executions. Always on alert, line troops constantly scanned upper-floor windows for Communard snipers. With fighting nearby, a woman living on the elegant faubourg Saint-Honoré had a chimney sweep come to work. When he left the building, troops seized him, taking the soot covering his hands and face to be gunpowder, and immediately shot him as the woman looked from her window above. The soldiers did not bother to consider his perfectly plausible alternate explanation.[38]

Probably made more ruthless by fear, the Versaillais often killed Communard insurgents they discovered, regardless of whether the fighters put up resistance. On the rue Saint-Honoré, line troops found thirty national guardsmen hiding in a printing shop. They had thrown away their weapons and hurriedly put on work clothes, but that would not save them. The soldiers took them to the rue Saint-Florentin and shot them in the enormous ditch in front of what remained of the barricade. Nearby, on the rue Royal, troops came upon six men and a young woman in National Guard uniforms hiding in barrels. They were thrown into a ditch and killed. Volunteers of the Seine shot fifteen men and a woman at the parc Monceau.[39] When line troops reached the place Vendôme, the fallen column elicited further reprisals against Communards who had surrendered or been captured; Versaillais shot at least thirty people there.[40]

Édouard Manet's lithograph *Civil War* evokes the horror of the slaughter at the Church of the Madeleine, where the Versaillais gunned down about three hundred Communards who had taken refuge there. No insurgent escaped. At first glance, one might think that Manet was depicting in the image the tragedy of civil war in a general, neutral way. However, the dead man, clearly wearing a National Guard uniform, clutches a piece of white cloth, suggesting that he and the others had tried to surrender; the Madeleine appears unmistakably in the background. Manet's *The Barricade*, another gripping indictment of the repression during Bloody Week, depicts a firing squad killing Communards.[41]

The killing went on, supported in no small part by Parisians who welcomed Versaillais troops. Archibald Forbes, for one, was appalled by the "Communard hunting" of Versaillais soldiers, aided by some people whom he suspected had earlier shouted for the Commune and now denounced *fédérés*. Concierges eagerly informed soldiers where Communards might be hiding: "They knew the rat-holes into which the poor creatures had squeezed themselves, and they guided the Versaillist soldiers to the spot with a fiendish glee."

Versaillais troops seized on any evidence they could find of insurgency. Soldiers gunned down three women after coming across several pairs of national guardsman's pants in their apartment. A furrier on the rue des Martyrs was allegedly executed because he had invited Pyat to his apartment six months earlier. When the man's wife protested, she was also killed. Investigating a light spotted in an upper apartment on the place du Trône (now de la Nation), soldiers found two elderly men drinking tea and shot them for no reason, despite the pleas of their concierge that they had had nothing to do with the *fédérés*. Social class did them in. Versaillais paid no mind to the fact that some of the Communards they killed had a few months earlier fought for France against the Prussians and their German allies.[42]

THE COMMUNARDS frantically began to organize resistance in the Sixth Arrondissement. On Tuesday, Jean Allemane helped organize the defense of the rues Vavin and Bréa just below the boulevard Montparnasse, thus joining defenses at the place de l'Observatoire, protecting the Luxembourg Gardens. Not far away, Eugène Varlin readied defenders at the small carrefour de la du Croix-Rouge. The task was imposing, with Cissey's huge army of three divisions attacking only three battalions of national guardsmen. When orders came from Commune leaders that they should fall back to defend their own *quartiers*, the defense of the Left Bank became impossible. Two battalions of national guardsmen from the Eleventh and Twelfth Arrondissements refused to obey Allemane and crossed the Seine to their own neighborhoods, saying that if they were going to die fighting, they preferred to do so in their own *quartiers*.[43]

Communards continued to fall. An English doctor helping wounded insurgents recalled, "We took in only the worst cases on 21, 22, 23 May. Our garden, court, corridors, and floor were crowded with wounded brought in fresh from the fight. . . . Many did not make it."[44]

Many of the barricades on the Left Bank had been built within a day, after the first line troops had entered Paris. They did not survive Versaillais attacks on Tuesday. A barricade on the rue de Rennes, below the Gare Montparnasse, was the largest, but no more than thirty men defended it. Yet Communard cannons firing behind sizable barricades still inflicted casualties on the attackers. Barricades fell at the carrefour de la Croix-Rouge and the rue du Dragon. The *quartier* was ablaze, and the barricades at the rue de Rennes fell on Tuesday, with their defenders, including the Enfants du Père Duchêne, falling back along the boulevard Saint-Germain. A Versaillais officer believed they were executing more men than had fought behind barricades.[45]

Allemane and others sought to impose some order on the defenses at the rue Notre-Dame-des-Champs and the boulevard Saint-Michel, but it did no good. Now that the fight seemed all but lost, guardsmen cared only about protecting their own neighborhoods. Versaillais troops surrounded remaining barricades and fired down on them from adjacent buildings. Calls for reinforcements brought no relief. Smoke rising from the Hôtel-de-Ville and other important buildings further demoralized remaining Communard fighters.[46]

At this point, forced to acknowledge that there was little hope of victory, most Communards began to prepare themselves for the end.

As the battle drew nearer to the Latin Quarter, Maxime Vuillaume went to his apartment on the rue du Sommerard to burn papers that, if seized by the Versaillais, would surely mean big trouble. He had copies of the letters Archbishop Darboy had written to Thiers and Vicar Ernest Lagarde on April 12; he gave them to Benjamin Flotte, who lived nearby. They went together to have a drink at the *brasserie* Chez Glaser, which they found totally empty. After that brief meeting, Vuillaume never saw Flotte again.[47]

Jean Allemane, like so many other Communards, now also had few illusions about what lay ahead. He pulled everything out of his pockets: a pocketknife, sixty centimes, some papers, and a card indicating that he worked for the *Journal Officiel.* He began to imagine how he would die. Walking toward the boulevard Saint-Germain, he ran into a friend, Treilhard, who was going home to put the Assistance Publique (Welfare Assistance) accounts in order, as he had promised. Allemane advised Treilhard to come with him to the Eleventh Arrondissement, where the remaining Communards intended to hold their ground; if he did not, he risked being captured and shot. Treilhard declined and was soon arrested, put up against a wall, and gunned down.

Allemane managed to get down the boulevard Saint-Germain, where various undercover Versaillais policemen were making arrests; one stopped him on the quay and asked what he was doing out at 1 A.M. He replied that he was going to the boulevard de l'Hôpital to check on his aged parents. He got through but passed soldiers marching along a young boy, Georges Arnaud, whom he knew from the neighborhood. The boy did not give him away by nodding, which could well have cost him his life. When a neighbor who ran the bistro Au Chinois told a Versaillais officer that he knew the boy very well and that he did not fight, the boy was released (only to die at twenty-four of tuberculosis). Georges's parents took Allemane in. From their apartment they could hear line troops searching the building. Allemane barricaded the door of the room where he was hiding, preparing to defend himself, but the soldiers were looking for someone else. He then resolved to leave and take his chances so as not to endanger his rescuers.

After a quick dinner, Allemane headed for the apartment of his brother, who lived in the Twentieth Arrondissement. Not long after he arrived in the rue Levert, police and troops surrounded the building and arrested him. He had no money and no papers that could get him out of Paris. Moreover, "denunciations rained down on Paris . . . where the police spy was king." After giving his name as Monsieur Roger, he admitted the next day that he was Jean Allemane. There had been little chance of escaping arrest. He was soon a prisoner in Versailles.[48]

THE ARMY OF VERSAILLES and the Volunteers of the Seine had, in little more than two days, taken well over half of Paris. The only hope increasingly seemed to be for Communard fighters to fall back to their neighborhoods in eastern Paris and organize the defense of *quartiers populaires*.[49] A sergeant in the National Guard, who could have gotten out, related, "I can't leave, because what would my comrades from the *quartier* say?"[50] For the Communards, neighborhood solidarities became even more essential to survival. The defense of Paris withered into the defense of quartiers. The role of women grew even more important. One strange thing about the conflict was that in the street fighting, "you were sometimes certainly surprised to come upon a childhood friend" fighting for the Versaillais.[51]

Montmartre, where the Commune had begun little more than two months earlier, remained potentially the strongest point of defense. The Commune sent General Napoleon La Cécilia there. Of "sad and solemn appearance, without charm, with a cold and proper air," he had difficulty communicating because he was Corsican and did not speak French well. La Cécilia's abilities were also far below what the daunting task before him required. He found defenses on Montmartre disorganized and National Guard battalions demoralized. Communard fighters instinctively resisted his authority because he was virtually unknown in the Eighteenth Arrondissement. More importantly, it was too late for anyone, even the savviest general, to make any difference. Some of the barricades erected on March 18 remained, but although they could provide some resistance to attacks from the south, they could not help if the Versaillais attacked from other directions. By 5 A.M. on May 23, line troops had reached Porte de Clignancourt to the north beyond the butte, a distance of about three kilometers from Batignolles in the Seventeenth Arrondissement.[52]

Louis Barron agonized over the state of the defenses in Montmartre: "so poorly defended! Spies of Monsieur Thiers, your task will be easy. . . . [There are] no moats, no trenches, no dry walls at the approaches to this position, whose strength has been exaggerated, because indeed it could have been made formidable." Barron had a premonition of "the coming horrible carnage, furious massacres, uncontrolled shooting; I smell the insipid, nauseating odor of streams of blood, saturating the pavement, flowing in the streets." Yet somehow—at least in the People's Paris—the illusion of the invincibility of the popular will persisted.[53]

La Cécilia wanted to know why cannons on Montmartre were silent. He found eighty-five cannons and about twenty *mitrailleuses* just sitting there, unattended and unused for two months. Finally, under La Cécilia's direction, the cannons fired several shells. Some of the guns then slid back into the mud and became unusable. Reclus reflected on the irony that when Communard shells were finally launched from the heights of Montmartre, Belleville, and Ménilmontant, they fell on "the rich and commercial neighborhoods" of western Paris, where nonetheless many good republicans were still to be found, neighborhoods that had already suffered Versaillais shelling.[54]

Knowing that line troops had swept so easily through Batignolles, and having insufficient numbers of national guardsmen to organize a stout defense, Polish general Jaroslaw Dombrowski now realized that there was no hope. He tried to get out of Paris, but *fédérés* stopped him at Porte Saint-Ouen, then took him to the Hôtel-de-Ville, where the Committee of Public Safety expressed confidence in him and refused to accept his resignation. Still loyal to the Commune and with nowhere to go, Dombrowski returned to service, just like that. Despite the increasingly desperate situation, on May 23, 1871, Pyat's *Le Vengeur* reassured readers that all was well, although *Père Duchêne* published its last issue that day, carrying the date "3 prairial, year 79."[55]

Early that day, the Army of Versailles launched its assault on Montmartre. Armies attacked from three directions. The army commanded by Clinchant had easily moved through Batignolles, left virtually undefended despite the best efforts of Benoît Malon. Troops killed indiscriminately along the way. A Versaillais officer apparently ordered a soldier who refused to gun down women and children shot. Not far away, troops allegedly killed a man who had done absolutely nothing, then shot his wife and child when they hugged him too long, and finally finished off, for good measure, a doctor who tried to help the child.[56]

With rifle fire from the butte passing well over their heads, no cannon fire to fear, and only a single *mitrailleuse* to avoid, the Volunteers of the Seine reached Montmartre. They encountered a defended barricade on the rue Marcadet on the far side of the butte, but the curve of the street protected them. Soldiers entered houses on both sides of the street to fire down on the defenders. Two cannons were brought up. The fire of the *fédérés* soon weakened, and then the Communards abandoned the barricade. Albert Hans was amazed to find Montmartre, a traditional hotbed of radicalism, defended with so little organization, personnel, or energy. The Volunteers of the Seine reached two barricades at the rue des Abbesses and took both quickly, along with six hundred prisoners.

Another Communard barricade awaited the Volunteers of the Seine, also on the rue Marcadet. They first occupied houses on both sides of the street, mounted the stairs, and from windows above fired down on the defenders. Soon only four *fédérés* remained at the barricade, and they fell almost immediately. Commander Gustave Durieu—a man, as Hans wrote admiringly, of "savage energy," "cruel expressions," and a "truly strange and fearsome look," personally killed ten men found in nearby buildings. The Volunteers began searching houses before regular troops arrived and shot dead anyone wearing a National Guard uniform and carrying a rifle or with traces of powder on the palm of a hand. Later the same day, gravely wounded on the butte of Montmartre, Durieu was carried to the house on the rue Rosiers next to where Generals Claude Lecomte and Clément Thomas had been put up against a wall on March 18. He died the next day. The officer who replaced him ordered more killings. Leighton remembered that on that hot day, "all the young men who were found in the streets were provisionally put under arrest, for [the Versaillais] feared everyone, even children, and horrible vengeance and thirst for blood had seized upon all. Suddenly an isolated shot would be heard, followed a minute or two after by five or six others. One knew reprisal had been done."[57]

In the courtyard of a building, the marquis de Compiègne of the Volunteers came upon a horse, which he believed must belong to an insurgent. As he considered how to find its owner, he suddenly found himself assailed by several angry women, young and old, crying and shouting, "My father!" "My son!" Several Volunteers appeared, carrying a young man about seventeen years old wearing a National Guard uniform, "more dead than alive": "He gave the appearance of a sheep with such a stupid aspect that it seemed impossible to believe that he could commit any malicious act." The marquis took pity, pushing him into a small room. Each time a soldier came in, the marquis told him that he had already searched the room and found nothing suspect. Presumably the young man survived. Others were not so lucky. The marquis took to his commanding officer, Escolan de Grandpré, a prisoner wearing a sailor's uniform. Grandpré told the captured man that he had dishonored his uniform and blew his brains out on the spot. On the rue Marcadet, the marquis remembered, "the streams . . . ran with blood as in a street next to the slaughterhouses."[58]

On the western side of Montmartre, General Clinchant attacked via the avenues Clichy and Saint-Ouen and the cemetery. General Paul de Ladmirault's troops moved along the rues Blanche and Pigalle, southwest of the butte. The attack from the north faced little resistance, as the Versaillais commanders had anticipated, thanks to their spies.[59] The Versaillais took the massive barricade at the place Clichy on that Tuesday and would control all of Montmartre by the end of the day.[60]

In the meantime, Nathalie Le Mel planted a red flag on the barricade at the place Blanche beneath the butte. She and perhaps as many as 120 other Communard women, as well as male defenders, offered stiff resistance. In the fighting in Montmartre, those defending barricades had little in the way of reinforcements, munitions, or food. The barricade at the place Blanche fell to General Paul de Ladmirault's troops before noon. Some defenders who had survived the fighting were immediately shot. Others managed to retreat to the barricade at the place Pigalle. Sébastien Commissaire saw a company of women hurry into combat. As they approached the place Pigalle, "all of those who were part of this little troop were killed or taken prisoner. From my window, I saw several of the women, whom I had seen go down the street with their arms a few moments earlier, marched back up it, disarmed and surrounded by soldiers." Line troops took a Communard to a Versaillais officer, who asked the man his identity; he replied, "Lévêque, mason, member of the Central Committee!" The officer shot him point-blank in the face with his pistol.[61] The barricades at the place Pigalle held on for three hours of brutal combat, but no more. A few other Communard fighters managed to get to the boulevard Magenta. Others fell back on Belleville.

Well known in Montmartre because of her work with the consumer cooperative La Marmite, Nathalie Le Mel was older than the group of young women, wearing the armbands of *ambulancières* and red scarves and carrying rifles, who followed her. When a Communard artilleryman was wounded, Le Mel and two other women forced open the door of a pharmacy on the boulevard de Clichy. She went to a concierge in a nearby building to ask for oil to care for a wounded woman, but none was to be found. She tried to restore morale, saying, "We are beaten, but not conquered!" as Montmartre had not yet been taken, although Versaillais troops were overrunning it.[62]

Louise Michel, who had helped care for the wounded, had gone from the Montmartre cemetery, where Communards were being killed, to the *mairie* to try to find fifty more men for the struggle. Upon her return to one of the barricades, only fifteen were still there fighting. General Dombrowski came up on horseback, telling Michel, "We're lost." She exclaimed, "No!" They shook hands, before Dombrowski departed. Within hours, he was killed at the barricade on the rue Myrha. Dombrowski's last words were, "I am no traitor." He was buried in his Polish army uniform.[63]

MARIE HOLLAND, wife of Protestant pastor Eugène Bersier, remembered Tuesday, May 23: "What a night of hell we spent, with cannons and machine guns all around us." They awaited their "saviors" and early that morning heard a shout from outside that the tricolor now graced a barricade further up the street. Bullets whizzed about. Not long thereafter, the religious couple could exclaim, "God be blessed! Montmartre is taken!" Returning to their house, which Communards had occupied, they found all in order and a note: "Dear Pastor, may God protect your house, where we were!" All signs indicated that the temporary occupants had left quickly. The pastor and his wife wondered where they had gone, if they were fighting somewhere or perhaps already dead. The next day, Pastor Bersier came upon more than sixty bodies of national guardsmen. He wanted to copy down their names so that he could attempt to notify their families, but line troops would not have it. He became angry when he saw a man yelling at troops escorting prisoners, "Kill them, saber them, without pity, my boys!"[64]

THE YOUNG MONTMARTRE resident Sutter-Laumann, who had gone to work at the *mairie* of the Eighteenth Arrondissement the day before, was among those drawing fire near the place Clichy. He quickly noticed that a good many guardsmen had exchanged their uniforms for civilian clothes in a last-ditch effort to avoid capture and certain death. A barricade at the rue Lepic had only about a dozen defenders, and another further up the street had only five or six. Resisters seemed either old or very young, with few in between. Twenty women marched toward the rue Lepic behind a red flag. However, the guns at Moulin de la Galette were again quiet, offering Communard fighters no encouragement. After an exchange of gunfire between the defenders of the larger barricade further down the rue Lepic, the Versaillais swept into nearby buildings and fired from above. Within a few minutes, about half the guardsmen and women lay dead or wounded.

Sutter-Laumann managed to escape the Versaillais attack, moving quickly from the place Clichy; via the rue Véron he reached a barricade further up the rue Lepic. The Communard cannons there had no shells. Five or six *fédérés* were still in position, but they soon retreated. The young Communard went to the place Saint-Pierre, where Versaillais shells were falling. He learned that line troops had taken the boulevard Ornano and that the place du Château-d'Eau was completely surrounded, ravaged by a "cyclone" of shells. From the rue Tholozé Sutter-Laumann could see line troops in red pants below at Moulin de la Galette. Shouts here and there of "Long live the Commune!" and "The Versaillais are cowards!" would not be enough. It was time to think about getting out. At the home of a friend, he carefully cleaned his National Guard uniform and waxed his shoes, attempting to eliminate any trace of combat.[65]

Suddenly shots resounded outside. Hoping against hope, the father of Sutter-Laumann's friend assumed that *fédérés* had fired them. They had not. Almost immediately, Versaillais officers ordered from the street that all widows be shut and demanded to know if any guardsmen were inside. There were eleven in the cellar, including Sutter-Laumann and his friend. When they emerged from the basement, they soon faced the line troops' rifles. An officer barked, "Did you serve the Commune?"

"No, my lieutenant."

"Then why are you wearing a National Guard uniform?"

Sutter-Laumann's response came quickly: if he had gone out without a uniform that morning, he would have risked arrest. When the officer asked why he had not gone to Versailles, he answered that he was only nineteen years old and lived with his parents, who had not been able to get out of Paris. The interrogator said that he had managed to get to Versailles. Desperate, Sutter-Laumann asked how he could live there with no resources. When the Versaillais replied that his expenses would have been paid, Sutter-Laumann asked hopefully how he could have known that.

Sutter-Laumann made a point of answering the Versaillais officer "in good French, without the accent of the faubourg," which could have got him shot immediately. Suddenly, nearby volleys sounded: "Those are your comrades whom we are shooting." The young man repressed a shudder. The Versaillais asked what grade of officer he had been. "None," came the reply. When asked the same question, his friend Alcide admitted that he had been a sergeant. The officer told them to fetch their guns, which luckily bore no traces of having been fired. When the officer told them to change their clothes, they replied that they had no others. The officer brought his loaded pistol up to Sutter-Laumann's head. The latter sputtered that they had sold their clothes during the siege.

Sutter-Laumann and his pal Alcide were incredibly lucky. Many others were not. The officer of the Volunteers of the Seine knew that often the Versaillais were not taking prisoners. Summary executions were becoming routine. He rather liked the two young men and suddenly confided that he had lived in the same *quartier* for a long time. He advised them to go home, stay there, and get rid of their uniforms and anything else—buttons, military decorations of any kind—that suggested a connection with the Commune. The officer assured them that the soldiers behind them would not be as lenient. The two young men hurried to the apartment. The other national guardsmen finally emerged from the cellar, as had Sutter-Laumann and Alcide a few moments earlier, having been fortunate that no search of the building had been undertaken. They too quickly transformed themselves into civilians and may have survived.

Now where to go? Women from the neighborhood had just found thirty-seven corpses on the rue Lepic. Sutter-Laumann, Alcide, and his family amounted to ten people in the small apartment. Versaillais troops arrived. They took a look at Sutter-Laumann and the others and moved on. Then another more determined group came, demanding that all weapons in the building be brought down. They too moved on. Then more soldiers came, searching each apartment. They uncovered one line uniform but could not find its owner, and they too departed. How much longer could this good fortune last?

The next group of Versaillais line soldiers to enter the courtyard below were drunk, some barely able to stand for all the wine and eau-de-vie they had knocked back. They smashed empty bottles on the ground. Their officers were also drunk—"a redoubtable drunkenness—drunk with blood. Their movements are jerky, nervous. They express themselves violently," Sutter-Laumann recalled. Occasionally a woman's scream pierced the air outside, as someone else was arrested. Dark came. Alcide's dog barked during the long night, to the point that Sutter-Laumann tried—and failed—to strangle it, fearing that Versaillais troops might come calling. Putting the animal under a blanket finally silenced it.

Early the next morning, Sutter-Laumann persuaded a young woman to go out with what money he had to buy him some more convincing civilian clothes. She was horrified to find bodies strewn about almost everywhere. Sounds of fighting were still audible but now further away. The woman returned with a small melon-shaped hat and sewed buttons onto his clothes, eliminating all traces of red trim. He was no longer a national guardsman. Early in the afternoon, a small boy knocked on the door with a message from Sutter-Laumann's father, telling him that at this point hiding was more dangerous than venturing into the street. His father had also been very lucky. After his wife dissuaded him from fighting at a barricade, a Versaillais accosted him, and he tried to play himself off as a wine merchant's employee. From his responses, the soldier took him to be "worthy man" and overlooked the fact that he had inadvertently worn his military boots to his job at the *mairie* of the Eighteenth Arrondissement.

Extremely fortunate to have survived, Sutter-Laumann went to work at the *mairie*, taking a seat at his usual desk. As always, women seeking certificates authorizing them to receive additional bread filled the room in which he worked—"destitution does not take time off." He could not help but notice men he had never seen before observing everything very carefully. They were police spies, looking for Communards.

As father and son left the *mairie*, their boss ran up to them and told him of a purported plan to shoot all the municipal employees there. "My poor son," Sutter-Laumann's father stuttered, "I have thrown you into the mouth of the wolf." A civil delegate of the Versailles government had arrested a worker who slipped into old habits and called him "citizen"; now the Versaillais delegate wanted them all shot. Terrified, Sutter-Laumann and his father resolved to get to work at 7 A.M. to demonstrate their eagerness. They shook hands with those wearing Versaillais uniforms. Each evening for eight days, an armed soldier escorted employees home, more to keep them from being arrested and perhaps shot than to prevent escape. Sutter-Laumann managed to get rid of compromising cartridges in his apartment by burning some of the powder and tossing the remainder into a fountain.[66]

IN THE FIGHTING, confusion was inevitable. A laundress kindly provided onion soup to some Versaillais troops, not realizing that her "guests" were not Communard national guardsmen. Uniforms contributed to such errors. On one occasion Hans and other Volunteers of the

Seine entered a house from which they believed a shot had been fired and came upon a Communard in the process of changing out of a cavalryman's uniform into a workman's clothes. Assuming that his visitors were national guardsmen, he explained that he was disguising himself in order to get closer to fire at the soldiers of Versailles. The Volunteers shot him as a deserter. A woman in Montmartre heard someone pounding on her door. Several uniformed men in the hallway asked where they could find her husband. She replied that he was sleeping, having just returned from fighting all night on the barricades. Unfortunately, the armed men were not national guardsmen but Volunteers of the Seine. They hauled her husband away to an uncertain fate.[67]

THE FALL OF MONTMARTRE, with its reputation for being impregnable, dealt an enormous blow to Communard morale. The Versaillais were now within range of the *quartiers* below, which the cannons on Montmartre could perhaps have protected. Resisters abandoned these central *quartiers*, falling back to the northeastern neighborhoods. The way was now open for the Versaillais forces to storm Belleville, where the Communards retained artillery and munitions. But their artillerymen were nowhere to be found. Line troops and Volunteers of the Seine had taken 2,000 prisoners during the fighting and then the systematic house-to-house searches. For his part, the marquis de Compiègne would happily watch Versaillais gun down "all those who were leaders of the insurrection," which they had so carefully prepared "with the only goal of satisfying their ambition and their vengeance." However, the Pyats, Rocheforts, and Courbets were not to be found at the barricades. Many Communard leaders had simply disappeared into the night.[68]

Raoul Rigaul was still in Paris, determined to fight to the end. On Wednesday, he rode to the prison of Sainte-Pélagie to settle a personal score. He went to the cell of Gustave Chaudey, whom he had ordered arrested on April 13, to tell him that he would be shot immediately. Rigault had never forgiven Chaudey, once his friend, for having ordered guardsmen to fire on demonstrators at the Hôtel-de-Ville, killing Théophile Sapia, another of Rigault's friends. A firing squad of eight men, commanded by Rigault, shot Chaudey, then gunned down three gendarmes for good measure.[69] Then Rigault met with other Blanquists at the prefecture of police, where he had always felt at home. He proposed blowing up the bridges and organizing the final resistance on the Ile-de-la-Cité, where the hostages would be taken. He now believed defeat inevitable and that the Commune should end in a way that would encourage its successors in further revolutions. Rigault began piling police documents into boxes.

The remaining Communard leadership, now consisting of only about twenty men (and without Rigault present), met at the Hôtel-de-Ville that evening of May 23. They knew that Montmartre had fallen and that hope for the Commune's survival was fading with every hour. Charles Delescluze had been there all day, signing proclamations with a shaking hand while hearing nothing but bad news. He had not slept for three days and could hardly talk due to laryngitis. The next day, Commune member Charles Beslay asked if they should not evacuate women and children from Paris. Delescluze replied that with the streets blocked by barricades and Versaillais troops guarding the western gates, he did not see how they could. Even though all was lost, the final issue of *Le Cri du Peuple* that day bravely proclaimed, "One last effort and victory is ours."[70]

Sturdy Communard defenses did remain in the Thirteenth Arrondissement and on the Right Bank at the places de la Bastille and du Château-d'Eau and in the Eleventh Arrondissement, as well as in Belleville and much of the proletarian Twentieth Arrondissement. Thiers's forces advanced rapidly on all fronts, slaughtering as they went.

IF DOWN BELOW in Paris Communards were bitterly discouraged, up in Belleville, they still held out hope. Reclus walked into Belleville's neo-Gothic church at about 10 A.M. that Tuesday morning. A young vicar was teaching the catechism to boys and girls. He reminded them that hell awaited "the ungodly and revolutionaries" and related that in the two preceding months of anarchy, the Commune had inflicted on the Church unprecedented persecution. Even in Belleville, churchmen continued to oppose the Commune, as the fighting drew ever closer.

Looking down on Paris from Belleville, Reclus was reminded of the view of Geneva. In glorious sunshine, the city stretched out far beneath his feet, "a vast rocky plain, rather an immense beehive, in which straw and twigs had replaced bell towers, columns, and arcs of triumph." Below, the "Party of Order" was at work with cannons, rifles, and bayonets.[71]

In the Eighteenth Arrondissement, executions continued into Wednesday, even after Montmartre had been taken. On the rue Myrha, two Versaillais soldiers followed a man into a house, where he tried to hide. They shot him on the spot. The concierge asked them as they were leaving if they were simply going to leave the body there. When they answered yes, he paid them to cart it away. Each took one of the man's legs, leaving his head to bounce on the ground as they dragged the corpse to a garbage heap. Onlookers applauded. On the rue Montmartre, soldiers sought a Communard captain. Finding only his twelve-year-old son at home, they killed him; when a young man reproached them for the act, they shot him as well.[72]

The Versaillais set up a court-martial in Montmartre that same day at 6, rue de Rosiers, where a crowd had killed Generals Thomas and Lecomte on March 18. Forty-two men, three women, and four children were shot there, some forced to kneel in front of the wall before being executed.[73]

One Versaillais supporter living near Porte Saint-Denis watched from his window as guardsmen hurriedly reinforced the barricade below and hauled a cannon toward the Church of the Madeleine; they too seemed determined to keep up the defense. Early in the afternoon on Wednesday, a National Guard company appeared. Sentinels at the intersection of the boulevard Saint-Denis forced passersby to add a paving stone to the barricade. More *fédérés* appeared, threatening to "blow the brains out" of anyone who fled. After sleeping badly, the resident went down the next morning to get a closer look. He strolled about, as on an ordinary day, seemingly oblivious to the danger, and calmly asked his neighbor, "And so! Things are heating up?" He must not have noticed the *fédéré* riding by, his horse carrying the body of a fallen Communard.[74]

Edgar Monteil, a journalist for *Le Rappel* and a national guardsman, survived the battle and executions but witnessed firsthand the hatred that enabled the Versaillais to kill so many Communards—men, women, and children alike—en masse. He and a colleague called Lemay returned to their office to sleep. Soldiers broke through the office door. The Versaillais searched the office, finding only a gun that had not been in service since the Prussian siege. Copies of *Le Rappel* were enough to ensure arrest. When a commander asked about these new prisoners and learned, "They are from *Le Rappel*," he turned toward the journalists and said, "You are the ones who lit the fires of this civil war!" But for the moment no rifles clicked into readiness. Monteil and Lamay were locked in an old guard post, hungry and thirsty. While hiding compromising documents, Monteil had thought to take along some money. They pounded on the door, asking a guard outside for bread and water. He asked if they had money, and Monteil gave him ten francs. They never saw the bread or water, the guard, or the money.

Monteil and Lemay were taken to Versailles as part of a convoy of five hundred prisoners. An officer told them as they passed near the ramparts that Versaillais were killing Communards there, but not all of them: "We will make a choice, that's for sure." Monteil realized that he had never detested the Versaillais as much as the anti-Communards hated them. In contrast to the Parisian middle classes, the inhabitants of outlying villages seemed sympathetic to the prisoners' plight. But at the gates of Versailles, the abuse started up again: "Dirty Parisians!" yelled a captain. "Heap of rabble. You are going to enter the capital of the good, worthy, and honest rural people! Take off your hats, vermin, hats off!" He hit those who refused with the flat of his sword. At the place des Armes, the well dressed hurled mud at the ragged prisoners, and a lady struck at them with her cane. Another captain ordered them to salute the palace of kings, raising his sword in warning. When they reached the prison camp of Satory at Versailles, line troops shouted, "Don't you see the pepper-mill [*la mitrailleuse*]? . . . Nothing to fear!"[75]

CHAPTER 7

DEATH COMES FOR
THE ARCHBISHOP

WEDNESDAY, MAY 24, would be another critical day because Montmartre, the great stronghold of the Commune standing tall above Paris, had fallen the day before. The task of Thiers's soldiers now seemed easier. The Committee of Public Safety—a couple of members had already fled the city—now met in permanence in the Hôtel-de-Ville. The Commune on Wednesday issued a proclamation to the Versaillais troops: "Do not abandon the cause of the workers! Do as your brothers did on March 18!" The Committee of Public Safety followed with its own message, hoping against hope that the Commune might survive: "Like us, you are proletarians. . . . Join us, our brothers!"[1]

The Versaillais did not slow down. There would be no repeat of March 18. Communard fighters readied their weapons. Paris awoke to skies stained red and black by smoke rising from the Palace of the Legion of Honor, the Palais-Royal, and houses on the rue Royale, where the clock had stopped at 1:10 P.M. the previous afternoon.[2] In the Hôtel-de-Ville, national guardsmen slept where they could, among wounded men lying on bloody mattresses. Two men arrived carrying an officer who had lost most of his face and jaw to a Versaillais shell. Barely audible and clutching the remnants of a red flag, he encouraged his compatriots to keep fighting. Gabriel Ranvier, a Commune member from the Twentieth Arrondissement, ordered two men to return to their arrondissements and lead the fight, threatening to have them shot if they failed to do so.

In another upper room, members of the Commune and various military officers, some in civilian clothes, sat around a large table, solemnly discussing the worsening situation. They had been meeting all night and must have been exhausted. During the course of their deliberations, they ordered the execution of a Versaillais spy, whose body was tossed into the Seine. As Prosper-Olivier Lissagaray observed, hope was gone, but courage remained. Charles Delescluze was there, determined, but he gave the impression of a defeated man, going through the motions as he awaited the final act. In a room near the entrance to the Hôtel-de-Ville lay the body of the Polish general Jaroslaw Dombrowski. The murderous thunder of cannons filtered in from outside.[3]

A proclamation of the Committee of Public Safety tried to reassure the population. Despite the fact that, thanks to "treachery," Versaillais forces had occupied some of Paris, such setbacks should not "dishearten you but rather spur you to action." Parisians should build more barricades to make Paris "impregnable." But it was certainly too late. The absence of centralized planning for the defense of the capital had become even more sadly apparent. The Central Committee appealed also to the soldiers of Versailles, urging them not to fight for "military despotism," to make disobedience "a duty," and to "fraternize" with the people.[4]

That same day, Adolphe Thiers, fearing a hostile reaction from other parts of France to the summary executions, sent a telegram to the prefectures of the provinces announcing that Marshal Patrice de MacMahon had warned the Communards to surrender or risk being shot. In fact, no such notice to Paris had gone out. Thiers and his government hoped to execute as many insurgent Parisians as possible. The president of the provisional government assured the National Assembly, "Our valiant soldiers conduct themselves in such a manner as to inspire foreign countries with the highest esteem and admiration."[5] The members of the National Assembly may not have understood the extent of the summary executions, but most of them certainly did not care.

At 9 A.M. the Commune's War Delegation issued an order, dated "4 prairial an 79," for the destruction of any house from which anti-Communards fired on national guardsmen and the execution of everyone in the building if they did not immediately hand over the "authors of the crime." As the Versaillais advanced even deeper into the city, the National Guard insisted that windows be closed because some Communard soldiers had "treacherously" been shot from such places.[6]

Even though Montmartre had fallen, the fighting continued and casualties mounted. Early that morning, May 24, Albert Hans's battalion went down the hill from Montmartre toward Porte Cligancourt, where barricades had also fallen the day before. Turning in the direction of the Gare du Nord on the chaussée Cligancourt, the soldiers came upon the bodies of a dozen Versaillais troops. They also passed weapons hastily abandoned by Parisians, including some of the cannons seized by the population at the place Wagram on March 18, a seeming eternity ago. A tricolor floated above the Moulin de la Galette. At the rue Rochechouart, bullets still flew from behind the barricades at the corner of the rue du faubourg Poissonnière and the boulevards d'Ornano and Magenta. These positions, too, soon fell. In the confusion, regular Versaillais troops fired on Hans and other Volunteers of the Seine before they could identify themselves.[7]

In the apartment where Élie Reclus was staying, a guardsman came to the door asking the friend hosting him to "take a position at the barricade being constructed nearby." The man remarked that he was over forty and therefore exonerated from National Guard service. The guardsman replied that this was fine and returned to the barricade below. He had not addressed a word to Reclus, who was in the next room with the door open. Suddenly, an explosion like thunder, all too close, enveloped everything in a cloud of white smoke. Communard fighters had blown up the munitions storage facility in the Luxembourg Gardens in order to slow the Versaillais advance. From the window Reclus and his friend could see fires burning in the distance. Soon after, line troops swept through nearby barricades, leaving nothing but rubble. Reclus would not forget the scene: "Victorious, the tricolor flag was hoisted above a pile of cadavers, in a sea of blood."[8]

Reclus reflected on the hopelessness of the situation. Paris was powerless before an army of 130,000 men with five hundred cannons, a giant "horde of Bonapartists, clergy, Orleanists, and conservatives" intent on destroying the democratic and social republic. Poorly organized and without effective leaders, the Communards were "floating like the unfortunate jellyfish left aground by the ravages of a storm." Reclus lamented, "Our willpower is useless, our efforts in vain, our hope has become ridiculous. . . . [O]ur little lives are engulfed by these incredible events." All night one could hear the "horrifying clamor of the painful tocsin rung in Belleville and Ménilmontant, falling still, and then taking up again, followed by the desperate roll of the drums calling everyone to combat."[9]

Not all Parisians noticed the bloodshed. While the fighting moved eastward through Paris, Gustave des E. slept. He bravely ventured out, "after a nice lunch" of course, to his club, avoiding the smoldering rue Royale, where, according to Théophile Gautier, flames had "continued the work of the cannon fire and shells. Gutted houses reveal their insides like gutted bodies." Twelve members had somehow managed to get to the club, so Gustave did not have to dine alone.[10]

Georges Jeanneret watched the Versaillais tide sweep through Communard defenses: "While the battle continues in Paris and its faubourgs, bourgeois Paris celebrates its triumph in its sumptuous neighborhoods." It was impossible to ignore that this was very much a class war. The weather was beautiful. Well-dressed ladies, some carrying parasols "in order to protect their complexions from the bright sunshine . . . approach the corpses . . . lying about, and with the tips of their parasols deliberately remove the caps or clothing placed over the faces of the dead." A woman stepped up and chided one of them: "Madame, death should be respected."[11]

Maxime Vuillaume knew full well that the end was near and that he needed to destroy any evidence tying him to the Communards. He tore up a ticket to the toppling of the Vendôme Column and, even more compromising, an identity card issued by the Commune stating his name, address, and profession—journalist. He had no illusions: from the rue Lacépède in the Fifth Arrondissement, he could hear the volleys of executions in the Jardin des Plantes. As he crossed the place Saint-Michel, a young woman demanded, "Let's go, citizen, your cobblestone!" Vuillaume obliged, putting a large stone on the barricade intended to block the entry to the quay and the pont au Change. At 11:30 A.M., the barricade was more or less ready, but where were the guardsmen to defend it? Hoping to get both lunch and news, Vuillaume headed to the restaurant Chez Lapeyrouse along the Seine, where Raoul Rigault often dined with his Communard colleagues from the prefecture of police. Five or six tables were taken. Vuillaume lunched with friends. With the bill came the news that the Versaillais were near.

Returning to the place Saint-Michel, Vuillaume ran into Rigault, who suggested a drink at the Café d'Harcourt. Rigault told him about having his old friend Gustave Chaudey shot the previous evening. Before Vuillaume, shaken by the news, could reply, Rigault was off, saying, "See you in a minute. At the Panthéon!" Vuillaume walked up the boulevard Saint-Michel, came upon an *ambulance* next to the gardens, and shook hands with people he knew. No one said a word. On the rue Royer-Collard, he ran into Rigolette, who ran the café Cochon Fidèle on the corner of the rue des Cordiers. There two Communards stood ready to fight behind a barricade in front of the house of one of Vuillaume's former teachers, Joseph Moutier, who had taught Rigault physics. Death was in the air, intensified by the seeming normalcy of walking by the house of someone the two Communards had known and admired.[12]

Having slept the previous night with troops on the sidewalk outside the Invalides, Julien Poirier's Versaillais infantry unit took fifty prisoners without firing a shot. As they neared the Luxembourg Gardens, they faced cannon fire, which killed several Versaillais troops. As they made progress, Poirier saw a woman carrying a red flag enter a building and informed his captain, who sent men in after her. At the top of the stairs, they found her in the attic, "armed to the teeth." Pushing her into the middle of the room, they took turns beating her with the butts of their rifles. Poirier and some of the others then forced her down the stairs, killing her before they reached the ground floor.

Once outside again, they noticed that no more Communard shells were falling. As the powder magazine at the Luxembourg Gardens exploded, the troops continued to advance, eying the buildings on either side, fearing snipers. Arriving at the boulevard Saint-Michel, they faced determined opposition and for the moment could not cross one of Paris's main arteries.[13] Although Baron Georges Haussmann's boulevards helped the Versaillais by allowing them to move quickly into central Paris, they also gave Communard fighters the chance to defend themselves with cannon fire, slowing the onslaught.

According to Edmond de Goncourt the dark smoke hanging aggressively above his city created the impression of "a day of an eclipse." The acrid smell of gasoline permeated the air. Paris had become apocalyptic. As clouds of smoke streamed into the air, wild stories spread that new and terrible means of destruction were imminent. Baron de Montaut, a Thiers agent working inside Paris, insisted that Communards had mined the sewers of Paris, which was not true.[14]

Versaillais troops encountered pockets of Communard resistance in the Sixth Arrondissement that Wednesday. Line troops overwhelmed the barricade at the Carrefour de l'Observatoire above the Luxembourg Gardens and soon besieged the neighborhoods around the boulevard, Saint-Michel, and the Panthéon. A Communard posting warned that in the interest of defending Paris, *fédérés* would blow up the Panthéon in two hours and asked those living in the *quartier* to "move away a reasonable distance from the area of the explosion." The *quartiers* around the Panthéon became a battlefield. Versaillais soldiers drove the Communards out of the Luxembourg Gardens, attacking the barricade defending the rue Soufflot, beneath the Panthéon and the Sorbonne. Communard defenders retreated toward the Seine, abandoning barricades on the rues Royer-Collard and Gay-Lussac, which fell when the Versaillais outflanked the resistance by taking side streets. Troops commanded by Ernest de Cissey moved toward the Panthéon but were stalled when Maxime Lisbonne ordered the munitions storage facility in the gardens blown up.

Still, the Versaillais had utterly destroyed what little Communard resistance remained. That day they shot about seven hundred Communards in the vicinity of the Panthéon, including forty on the rue Saint-Jacques. Local Communard officers met for the last time in the *mairie* at the place du Panthéon.[15] They rejected a suggestion to surrender, but surviving Communards headed down the hill and over the Seine to the Eleventh Arrondissement.

Alexander Thompson, a young Englishman, lived with his parents on the boulevard Saint-Michel across from the Luxembourg Gardens, so he witnessed the fighting there firsthand. Two barricades stood before his family's house, "under the command of a pretty Amazon whose beauty, charming way, and always ready revolver convinced each passerby to lend a hand." Several hours later, he saw the woman, clutching a rifle, lying dead on the barricade of the rue Soufflot. A soldier tore open her clothes with his sword for the amusement of the other troops.[16]

Reclus watched the sunset from the pont de Bercy behind the Gare de Lyon, "the green waters flowing slowly and quietly: the beacons, their masts, and the arches of the bridges are clearly reflected in their peaceful mirror." In the distance he could see "a golden and silver rain of opaline, iridescent pearls, an orange dust, [as] the monuments stand profiled in lightly violet fumes." A red flag still flew from the top of the Panthéon, soon to be replaced by the tricolor. He could hear "the distant sounds that float in the luminous sky, the song of the trumpet, the whistling of bullets and the crackle of machine guns."[17]

Unfortunately for Raoul Rigault, he was near the Panthéon just before it fell. Earlier that day, he had gone to his beloved prefecture of police with the ever-faithful Théophile Ferré. Rigault freed the few political suspects and several common criminals still in custody, shouting, "Let's go, bandits, we are going to burn this place down! We don't want to roast you!" A man called Veysset, arrested ten days earlier as a presumed Versailles spy and accused of trying to bribe General Jaroslaw Dombrowski, was also in a cell there. Seeing him, Rigault turned the man over to Ferré and Georges Pilotell, a mediocre artist and Communard policeman, who took him with soldiers from the Vengeurs de

Flourens to the statue of Henri IV on the western tip of the Ile-de-la-Cité. There they shot him.[18]

Rigault, wearing his uniform as a commander of the 114th National Guard battalion, went to the Panthéon, in his old *quartier*, to encourage resistance. A friend reminded him that wearing this uniform was perhaps not a good idea, should he be captured. "*Mon vieux,*" he replied, "better to die like this! This will be useful for the next time!" After the barricade on the rue Soufflot fell, Rigault entered a hotel on the rue Royer-Collard. He had rented a room there under the name Auguste Varenne. Perhaps he wanted to rest and await his fate. Several nearby line troops, including a corporal who had seen a guardsman open the door and enter, stormed the hotel and accosted the owner, a Monsieur Chrétien.[19]

Rigault, hearing the commotion, ran up the stairs to the sixth floor. The soldiers ordered the hotel owner to go after his guest and plead that the soldiers would shoot him—Monsieur Chrétien—if he did not come down. The Versaillais did not know the man they hoped to capture was Raoul Rigault, who proposed to the hotelier that the two of them escape by a perilous journey across rooftops. When the owner refused, Rigault replied, "I am neither an idiot nor a coward. I will go down." The soldiers, waiting for him on the second floor, took him in the direction of the Luxembourg Gardens, where execution squads were at work. Rigault announced to his captors, "Here I am! It's me!" (*Me voilà!*), as he surrendered his pistol. Unsure whom they had captured, they found an officer, who asked the prisoner his identity. Rigault, a prize catch, gave them his name. When he shouted, "Long live the Commune! Down with the murderers!" the soldiers put him up against a wall and shot him dead.

Rigault's body lay on the ground. The so-called men of order who had shot him poked at it with their umbrellas and canes. Georges Pillotel, who admired him, came upon the corpse and sketched it. Finally, Rigolette brought down an old blanket and covered up Rigault's bloody head.[20]

HENRI DABOT WAS A BOURGEOIS, a moderate republican, and a fervent Catholic. Fighting now swirled around his neighborhood. Communards were killed at the barricade at the rue Cujas above the rue Saint-Jacques. Dabot's cook Marie tried to hide a boy of about fourteen or fifteen whom soldiers were chasing, believing that he had fired a shot at a captain after the barricade at the corner of the rues Saint-Jacques and des Écoles fell. The boy, who lived near the Church of Saint-Éti-enne-du-Mont next to the Panthéon, was small enough to hide under the cook's skirts. The soldiers found him, however, marched him to the Cluny Museum, and shot him in front of it. The boy's friends came upon his body.

Now that the barricades on the rues Saint-Jacques and Cujas had fallen, Communards began to retreat from the Fifth Arrondissement. A *fédéré* went from house to house, telling people to run for their lives. On the rue Clovis, a mother replied, "Run! Run where? A hail of bullets everywhere! Leaving here would be the most certain way of finding death." She held her two young sons in her arms, saying, "At least we can die together," and praying to Sainte Geneviève for protection.[21]

The fighting moved down the boulevard Saint-Michel and then the rue Saint-Jacques to the rue des Écoles and the boulevard Saint-Germain. The barricade at the rue de la Montagne-Sainte-Geneviève fell, followed by others on the rues Ulm, Lacépède, and Monge. Jean Alle-mane believed only about two hundred Communards still fought in the Fifth Arrondissement, some of them no more than fifteen years old. After two days of bitter battle, on Wednesday evening the last Commu-nard defenses in the Fifth Arrondissement in the Latin Quarter fell to the Versaillais on the rue Monge, next to the Roman wall of the amphi-theater, dating to the origins of Paris itself.[22]

When the fighting ended in the Latin Quarter, twenty bodies lay on the rue Sommerard; more were scattered above at the intersection with the boulevard Saint-Michel. On the rue Cardinal Lemoine, sol-diers roused from bed Eugène André, a mathematician and professor known for his opposition to the empire. He had not served in the Commune and refused a position in education when offered. André, who had ignored advice to hide, was shot immediately, leaving behind his carefully calculated mathematical tables—not the kind of thing that would interest Adolphe Thiers.

THE VERSAILLAIS NEWSPAPER *La Petite-Presse* informed readers in Ver-sailles and the provinces that the soldiers refused to take more prison-ers. The news almost certainly pleased many readers. A Communard remembered that in the Latin Quarter, one could hear only the "sounds of execution squads . . . at every step, bodies, every second, the sound of shots killing ordinary people." This spelled the end for an eighty-year-old man on the rue du Dragon, arrested for wearing the cap of a national guardsman.[23] Thousands of other Parisians met the same fate.

Rumor now had the Communards preparing to win back lost territory by sending National Guard battalions beyond the ramparts around northern Paris and then back into the western districts of the capital—no longer a feasible tactic by this point. Most national guardsmen would not have left their neighborhoods to participate in such a maneuver. The Versaillais, who had advanced on Tuesday morning as far as the Church of the Trinity on the Right Bank, seemed to hold back, for the moment not pressing the enormous advantage they now held. Many Communards battled courageously, as on the rue de la Ferme des Mathurins, where guardsmen constructed a barricade while under fire from Versaillais troops. However, their only advantage—beyond, for many, their passion—was that they now defended their own neighborhoods.

The Versaillais did not hold back for very long. Thousands of Versaillais troops attacked the barricade of the rue Thévenot, which *fédérés* had defended well near the rue Saint-Denis. Once the barricade fell, the latter street was overrun, opening the way to the quartier du Temple, a center of Communard support and gateway to the Nineteenth and Twentieth Arrondissements. Few barricades now obstructed the Versaillais' path, and fighters quickly abandoned those on small connecting streets.

NOW THAT MONTMARTRE and much of the Left Bank had fallen, the Versaillais were making their way through the Right Bank, getting closer and closer to La Roquette prison. The Commune would have to decide the fate of the hostages—and soon. The prison pharmacist recommended that Georges Darboy be transferred to the infirmary, but the archbishop refused to be separated from the others. Enormous tension hung over the *quartier*—and the prison in particular—as the Versailles troops drew nearer. Cannon fire launched against the Versaillais from the heights of the Père Lachaise Cemetery alarmed the hostages, who greeted the slightest noise in the corridor with gnawing apprehension. The angry members of the Vengeurs de Flourens were omnipresent in the neighboring streets.

An event nearby reflected popular anger at the impending catastrophe in the neighborhoods near La Roquette. Fear and outrage swirled around the prison in which the hostages awaited their fate. Charles de Beaufort served as captain in the 66th battalion, assigned, before the Versaillais entered Paris, to guard the Ministry of War in the Seventh Arrondissement. When Beaufort tried to enter the ministry on

Saturday, May 20, a guardsman barred his way, and the captain announced drunkenly that he could go where he wanted. He threatened to "blow out the brains" of the guard and bragged that he would purge the battalion. His behavior won him no friends in the neighborhood of the guardsmen.

Now, with Versaillais guns drawing closer and nothing but bad news arriving from other *quartiers*, Beaufort turned up to help defend the boulevard Voltaire. People in the neighborhood, increasingly anxious about their own fates, quickly directed their ire toward this unwelcome officer. Marguerite Lachaise, who ran a small business with her husband and belonged to the International, recognized Beaufort and denounced him as the officer who had sent insurgent fighters into a hopeless situation in which many men from the *quartier* had died. She and soon others, mostly women, began shouting for his execution.[24] Some accused Beaufort of working secretly for Versailles. It did not help that, at the same time, stretchers were carrying back more badly wounded men from the barricades, the same guardsmen Beaufort had sent into battle. Several people went to find Gustave Genton, recently appointed *juge d'instruction* (examining magistrate).

A forty-five-year-old woodworker and the son of an unknown father, Genton was in some ways typical of many working-class Communards. He and his wife had one child and lived at 27, rue Basfroi, not far from where Genton had been born. He had spent six months in prison in 1866 for participating in the "illegal" gathering at the Café de la Renaissance that had involved Rigault. A Blanquist and member of the Commune, he served as lieutenant and flag bearer in the 66th National Guard battalion but resigned after becoming ill. His friend Ferré then nominated him to the position of *juge d'instruction*.[25]

Genton now set up a court-martial to placate the crowd. It quickly found Beaufort guilty and stripped him of his rank. Delescluze was there and tried to calm things down, as did Marguerite Lachaise, although she had just called for his execution. The crowd paid them no mind and continued to shout for Beaufort's death. Three men in navy uniforms grabbed him and hauled him to a vacant lot just off the place Voltaire, where they killed him.[26]

At about 3 P.M., apparently to sooth popular agitation, Communard leaders organized another improvised court-martial over which Genton presided, this time at the *mairie* of the Eleventh Arrondissement. On trial at this court-martial were the hostages held at La Roquette, including Darboy. The court-martial condemned six of the hostages to death, apparently in retaliation for the summary executions of *fédérés* captured at the barricade of the rue Caumartin near the Church of the Madeleine. In principle the execution of these high-profile hostages required the signature of a justice of the peace. Ferré signed the order, adding as an authorizing signature the name of Raoul Rigault—killed a few hours earlier although this news may not yet have crossed the Seine—along with a third, illegible name. Genton and his secretary, Émile Fortin, arrived at La Roquette with an execution squad of about thirty or forty men and an order instructing prison director Jean-Baptiste François to turn over, "without any explanation," Archbishop Darboy and Louis Bonjean (the former imperial senator), in addition to "two or three others to be chosen."[27]

François insisted that he required more specific instructions listing the names of all those to be executed, along with a copy of the official judgment. Genton returned to the *mairie* of the Eleventh Arrondissement to clarify the matter, leaving the execution squad at La Roquette, rifles readied. The *juge d'instruction* returned at about 7 P.M. with an order that François again did not find explicit enough. It was virtually the same order for the execution of six hostages, signed by Ferré, who now added, "And notably the archbishop," the most prominent hostage of all. Fortin and Genton came up with the list of the others to be shot, in addition to Darboy. At the bottom of the document were three stamps of the Commune. Genton scratched out the name of Swiss-born Bonapartist banker Jean-Baptiste Jecker, replacing him with Deguerry, the *curé* of the Church of the Madeleine.

Finally accepting the order, François sent a guard to get the six men The guard had no idea why he was to bring down these hostages until he came upon the execution squad, commanded by a certain Captain Vérig who had selected its members from men of the neighborhood. They were for the most part young volunteers (some eighteen years old) out to avenge the deaths of relatives at the hands of the Versailles forces. Two-thirds were from the 66th battalion; others probably came from the Vengeurs de Flourens or were simple defenders of the republic.[28]

Ferdinand Évrard, who described himself as "only a Parisian bourgeois," was in the cell next to Darboy's. An army officer arrested on April 6 after being taken off a train as he attempted to get to Versailles, he heard the "chief of these wretches" shout, "I need six!" Some prisoners saw an officer enter the prison courtyard and heard him bark, "Are the soldiers ready?" Vérig went to cell number 23, to which the archbishop had been transferred the day before, and asked, "Citizen

Darboy?" "Present," came the reply. Bonjean, in the next cell, did not hear his name called, but his other neighbor, Abbé Auguste-Alexis Surat, told him they wanted him. He started out and then turned back to get his overcoat. "It is useless," said the guard Antoine Ramain. "You are very well as you are!" Ramain told another who had to go to bathroom, "It's not worth it!" Two of the priests swallowed the last two Communion hosts before the six hostages—Darboy, Bonjean, Deguerry, Michel Allard (a missionary priest who had been a frequent presence in the *quartier* of Saint-Sulpice), Léon Ducoudray (a Jesuit and director of the school of Sainte-Geneviève), and Alexis Clerc (another Jesuit priest)—were marched out.[29]

A Polish guard from La Roquette's infirmary heard someone say to the hostages, "You are going to die. You have done nothing for the Commune. You have always been hostile to it. You are going to die!" A guard who saw the execution squad remembered that many of them showed sangfroid, and none were drunk. When the gate was opened and the hostages taken out, he heard other prisoners shout obscenities at them and denounce them as "papists" and "traitors."[30]

Obviously poorly prepared for the task, the execution squad discussed, in the presence of the hostages, the best place to shoot them. The first plan was to shoot them in the small exercise yard, but this could be seen from the infirmary windows, which would be bad for morale. In the end, they decided to execute the hostages at the "Gate of Death," the *chemin de ronde* leading to the guillotine.

The hostages passed through two lines of executioners. While waiting ten awful minutes for guards to locate the keys to the gate, Darboy asked if there were many barricades in Paris. "Ah! If I could only go and die like my predecessor! I envy the fate of Archbishop Affre." When a guard asked Darboy why he had done nothing for the Commune, the archbishop noted that he had been arrested after the first real fighting. "In God's name, at least spare us such insults." One young *fédéré* asked Darboy which party he adhered to. The archbishop replied that he was of the "party of liberty," adding that he and the others would die for freedom and for their faith. The response: "Enough sermons!" An officer intervened, telling the executioners in no uncertain terms to shut up: "You are here to carry out justice, not to insult the prisoners!"[31]

Following Ramain, Allard led the prisoners, singing prayers in a low voice. Darboy followed. They passed along the wall of the infirmary, until the gate of the *chemin de ronde*. Darboy could barely walk, and a guardsman pushed him along. Bonjean offered his arm for support.

Another guard discretely held out his hand to the hostages as if to say good-bye. Ramain stopped at the corner of the wall along the rues de la Folie-Regnault and Vacquerie. From his cell, *Père* Perny could see Darboy below, raising his arms to the heavens as he called out, "My God! My God!" The archbishop and the others knelt down and said a short prayer. Darboy then stood with the others and blessed them, amid shouts from the Communards of "Enough prayers."

Ramain arranged them in front of the wall, with Allard first, followed by Darboy. The names of the hostages were read out loud. Deguerry opened up his shirt to expose his chest to the rifles. Several minutes later, Vérig raised his sabre and commanded the squad to fire. Two quick volleys followed. Darboy fell. One of the executioners reportedly said, "This old bastard Darboy did not want to die. Three times he got up, and I began to be afraid of him!" Vérig, whom Fortin had loaned Ferré's sword to command the execution, later claimed to have given the archbishop the coup de grâce. He proudly showed a prison warden his pistol, still hot from firing. From his cell above, Abbé Laurent Amodru could hear "first a long volley, then a pause, and then several single shots, and finally a last salvo."[32]

The execution of Archbishop Georges Darboy and five other hostages on May 24, 1871 (ADOC-PHOTOS/CORBIS)

With silence engulfing the inside of the prison, the bodies lay where they had fallen for six hours, until 2 A.M., when they were taken to the Père Lachaise Cemetery and dumped in a ditch. Darboy's sapphire ring, cross, and even the silver buckles of his shoes had disappeared from his body. In their cells, Pères Perny and Amodru and the other hostages assumed that they would soon hear the steps of guards coming down the corridor for them, even as the forces of Versailles drew nearer and nearer.[33]

Since April 4 the prisoners' fate had hung in the air. The communards' ploy to take Archbishop Darboy and other clerics hostage to discourage the Versailles government from carrying out further summary executions had backfired. Now, the shooting of Darboy and the others gave Thiers an excuse to escalate the killing, both during ongoing fighting in the streets of Paris and in hastily organized courts or tribunals dispensing Versaillais "justice" in the name of the upper classes.

WITH VERSAILLAIS TROOPS moving up the rue de Rivoli that Wednesday, the Hôtel-de-Ville itself was no longer secure. Remaining members of the Commune decided to move to the *mairie* of the Eleventh Arrondissement, at the intersection of the boulevard Voltaire and the rue de la Roquette. Théophile Ferré ordered the building set on fire, and it was in flames by 9 P.M. At Ferré's order the prefecture of police was also set ablaze. That same evening the Palace of Justice burned. Ferré hoped to slow the advance of the Army of Versailles and to ensure that if they captured the palace, there would be nothing left for them to celebrate. He certainly also intended to burn compromising documents.

One Communard believed that the Versaillais gained two days because the destruction of Hôtel-de-Ville, as symbolic as it was strategic, and the fall of barricades blocking the rue de Rivoli and the avenue Victoria had compromised defenses across the Seine and the forts beyond the southern ramparts. Thus the Commune lost a line of defense that had stretched across to the Latin Quarter. Communard resisters continued to retreat to their neighborhoods in the Nineteenth and Twentieth Arrondissements, leaving no one to defend central Paris against the Versaillais troops.[34]

Chaos reigned with death. Many Communards still believed they could hold out. Edgar Monteil and Ferré were among the few Communard officials still giving orders. In one case, they signed a *laissez-passer* for Edmond Mégy, authorizing him to move about Paris and around "all barricades." The *laissez-passer* did not likely do him any good. Some

The Hôtel-de-Ville after the fire and the fall of the Commune
(HULTON-DEUTSCH COLLECTION/CORBIS)

Communard leaders had disappeared into the night, every man for himself. In the *mairie* of the Eleventh Arrondissement, leaders who remained began to debate whether to move up to Belleville and make a last-ditch stand from its heights.[35]

Élisabeth Dmitrieff was still fighting at barricades in eastern Paris, "encouraging the federals in their resistance, distributing ammunition, and firing." She said she was prepared "to die on the barricades in the next few days." Her final written communication, dated May 23, to Communard leaders at the *mairie* of the Eleventh Arrondissement read, "Gather all the women . . . and come immediately to the barricades."[36]

CHAPTER 8

THE COURTS-MARTIAL
AT WORK

T HE VERSAILLAIS KILLING MACHINE was now fully at work. By May 22, some twenty military courts were in operation, with bloody consequences. A decree of the Government of National Defense issued on October 2, 1870, during the war and Prussian siege, permitted courts-martial during times of war and granted them the power to condemn to death both soldiers and civilians. Thiers took advantage of this decree after his forces had overrun Paris, using it to insist that Versaillais military courts indeed fell within the law. It helped, too, that Thiers and the Versaillais continued to assert that the Communards were not political opponents, refugees, or legitimate belligerents but rather ordinary criminals. As such, he considered them to be under his jurisdiction and deserving of no special treatment.[1] The senior Versaillais commanders were not interested in legal precedents for the martial law tribunals they set up or, in a few cases, presided over, which failed to act within the law. The right to appeal convictions was systematically ignored.[2]

The Lobau barracks became the most infamous Versaillais slaughter house. The prevotal court, or court-martial, set up at Châtelet on Wednesday, May 24, operated day and night for seven straight days. Following rapid and sometime instantaneous judgments, prisoners were divided into "travelers to Lobau and travelers to Satory." Those headed for Satory might live, but travelers to Lobau faced almost certain execution. A British journalist estimated that between 900 and 1,200 were killed at Lobau in twenty-four hours under the supervision of Colonel Louis Vabre of the Volunteers of the Seine, a murderous friend of Thiers. The massacre was carried out ruthlessly and efficiently.

As Victor Hugo wrote in "Les fusillés," "A lugubrious sound permeates the Lobau barracks: it is thunder opening and closing the tomb." Thus, at Châtelet, "it was by batches [*fournées*] that the victims were sent to the slaughterhouse." On May 25, at the Lobau barracks, after troops marched victims past the smoldering ruins of the Hôtel-de-Ville, execution squads did not bother to line the condemned up, gunning them down in groups of about twenty, sometimes with machine guns, after forcing them through the door.[3]

The *Standard*, a conservative British newspaper, reported matter-of-factly that Versaillais were killing groups of fifty to a hundred "insurgents." The army would subsequently claim that officers could not find the names of those executed. Crowds of anti-Communards, now confident enough to pour into the streets of relatively fancy neighborhoods, shouted for more deaths, and *La Patrie* reported that soldiers had a tough time keeping onlookers from assaulting *ces misérables*. Abbé Antoine-Auguste Vidieu of Saint-Roch watched the prisoners "as one would look at the ferocious animals at the Jardin des Plantes." He saw wounded men arriving at Châtelet, their injuries their only crime.[4]

On May 25, by which date the Versaillais held well more than half of Paris, anyone living near the Luxembourg Gardens heard the work of execution squads. Lawyer Henri Dabot was pleased to relate that many of the condemned accepted the consolation of priests willingly, but others refused obstinately to kiss a crucifix or say a prayer. A priest named Hello served as chaplain for "those to be shot." Abbé Riche carried out the same lugubrious duties, "more moved than any other by his awful task."[5]

As Versaillais execution squads were at work killing prisoners, the fighting in Paris continued, resulting in even more Communard deaths. National guardsmen still held part of the Thirteenth Arrondissement, but increasingly those who had been defending the Left Bank had retreated back into the Eleventh, Twelfth, Nineteenth, and Twentieth Arrondissements, the heart of the People's Paris on the periphery of the capital. Against all odds, they kept up the resistance.

Parisians loyal to Thiers eagerly greeted the Versaillais troops who cleared their neighborhoods of guardsmen. Gustave des E. watched a convoy of prisoners taken at La Villette pass on the way to Versailles. Now that a Versaillais victory seemed assured, Gustave's portly neighbor from across the street returned to his apartment, installing his mistress in his Parisian abode (he had left his wife and children in the provinces). Gustave and his friends eagerly told each other their horror stories. A well-heeled man with whom Gustave dined at the club related a story about being asked by Versaillais troops to assist in taking down a barricade. He had enthusiastically joined them, as "reactionary number 1"—that is, until his kidneys began to ache, and he was forced to excuse himself. Another club member with whom Gustave dined related at least seventeen times that a shell had fallen above a room in which his maid—but not he—had been standing several hours before.[6]

AT PORTE SAINT-DENIS, residents of a nearby building who, for whatever reason, had not left Paris experienced the terrors of civilian life in a war zone as cannon, rifle, and machine-gun fire in the streets kept them inside. Guardsmen entered and demanded that the windows be closed. Then another Communard fighter entered and asked how to get to the attic so that he could shoot from there, using mattresses for protection against return fire. Madame Théo, who owned the building, did not want them firing from her windows and offered them cognac and rum in exchange. By now the residents had gathered in two rooms as bullets tore into the building, breaking windows and shredding curtains. Another Communard fighter appeared and began to fire from an upper window. When Madame Théo asked him to do as little damage as possible, he took her hands, called her *citoyenne,* and reassured her that she had nothing to fear. The Communard would fight until the death but nothing in the house would be destroyed. It turned out that this sniper was actually a woman with short hair and *"une belle paire de Tétons* [a nice pair of tits]." Her husband, a wine merchant, had left Paris after March 18 when the Communards of their neighborhood had come looking for him. She had taken his place, perhaps out of shame, and had been accepted by a battalion. The female insurgent then returned to the street, yelling, "Long live the Commune! Fire, citizens!" Communard fighters followed "their officer."

The residents moved up the steps to the third floor. One neighbor was not doing very well; she had to be sponged off by her husband with a wet cloth and revived with smelling salts. The others seemed calm. There was no way out of the building, as the front door led directly to the barricade. No ladder—not even a rope—could be found to climb out a back window. A small door leading to the house next door only opened from the other side, and the owner, a nasty character, had left it locked. He opened it only after a national guardsman threatened to burn down his "shack" in five minutes if the door remained closed. The door opened. His neighbors found relative safety, at least momentarily, in his cellar.

Soon shells and gunfire came dangerously close, forcing guardsmen to retreat to the barricade at nearby Porte Saint-Martin. A guardsman put a remaining cannon out of service so that the Versaillais could not use it when it ultimately fell into their hands. One officer stayed behind, seemingly awaiting death. A bullet struck him, and he staggered a few steps toward the faubourg Saint-Denis, then fell. The fighting moved away but not the danger, as a fire broke out several doors away. A woman who had taken refuge in the building drew suspicion. She claimed that Versaillais troops would not allow her to climb over the barricade in order to return home. The residents thought her an incendiary. It turned out that she did indeed live nearby on the boulevard Bonne Nouvelle. The residents of the neighborhood, at least those who opposed the Commune or now pretended to, feted the line soldiers who had taken the barricade with ham and sausages.[7]

That same day, Élie Reclus took refuge in the basement of a house. He found himself sharing space with about thirty-five other people of all ages and social classes. "In normal times, these wild beasts would chase and devour each other," but now, in a time of enormous peril, they found themselves sharing space and an unspoken truce. Given the circumstances, any affirmation of political views, direct or indirect, was carefully avoided. Gazing upon pale, bourgeois faces, Reclus reflected on what he dared not say: "So, it's you, bourgeois. Now it's those like you whose cowardly ignorance and cruel egotism have brought these horrors, past horrors, and those in the future which you will inflict on us!" He could imagine what was going through the mind of the bourgeois as well: "It's you, revolutionary of all evil, with your brothers and accomplices, through your criminal stubbornness, force the Friends of Order to shoot you, and this I do not at all regret."

Lost in such thoughts, everyone suddenly heard the unmistakable sound of heavy boots on the stairs. "Property, Order, and Religion" appeared in the person of three line troops, their faces drenched with sweat and twisted with anger. Their bloody bayonets leading the way, they demanded, "Where is this rabble, where are these cowards? We are going to take care of them!" The bourgeois of the group eagerly arose and moved beaming toward the red pants: "Oh, there you are! We are friends of Versailles!" The soldiers inspected the others up and down, one of them proudly showing his pistol, still hot after gunning down a

Communard. The Versaillais soldier quickly added, "Yes, we captured two hundred of them and we shot them."[8]

Elsewhere in Paris, Alix Payen, caring for wounded Communards, seemed surprised to still be alive. "Our building was shaking as in an earthquake, doors and windows blown out in splinters." It was impossible to flee; the boulevard on which she lived was engulfed in fighting. In any case, there was nowhere to go. Alix had no news of her husband, Henri, who lay gravely wounded elsewhere.[9]

Julien Poirier, fighting for the Versaillais, remembered May 25 as "a real massacre," with women with infants and small children in their arms gunned down by Versaillais *mitrailleuses*. Poirier fought all day, as thunder, lightning, and rain swept Paris. His unit battled near the Panthéon and down toward Gobelins, searching houses as they went. At about noon, they came upon two Communards loading guns and shot both in the chest. This only wounded them badly, so they threw them out of the third-floor window. In another room, they came upon two young men sharing a bed, pretending to be asleep. A lieutenant stuck them in the side with his sword. One of them suddenly leapt out of bed and jumped one of the soldiers, trying to get his pistol; in the subsequent melee, he escaped down a flight of stairs. In a basement, Poirier, his captain, and some other soldiers found a young woman hiding who offered them some of her wine. Given rumors that women were offering poisoned drinks to Versaillais soldiers, the captain advised his men not to accept. Nonetheless Poirier downed two bottles, and the captain, reassured, polished off another. Then looking around, Poirier saw a young man, the woman's husband, hiding under a mattress. They put him with other prisoners, and their colonel told the captain in no uncertain terms to take him to Luxembourg for execution. When one of fifty or so prisoners tried to escape, they beat him and ordered him to march to his death into a nearby garden. The man refused, so they shot him right there, taking the ten francs in his pocket for their time.[10]

The American Wickham Hoffman despised the "Communists" but was nonetheless appalled by the reprisals: "There is no excuse for the wholesale butcheries committed by the troops." One of his friends saw soldiers enter a house on the boulevard Malesherbes and demand of the concierge whether any "Communists" were hiding there. She told them no, but the troops rushed in all the same. They discovered a man, took him out, shot him, and killed the concierge for good measure.

No sympathy for the Communards was acceptable. When another American witnessed the burial of a Communard, he remarked, "Why, he hasn't a bad face after all!" An officer advised him "not to express any such sentiments again." House-by-house searches brought thousands of arrests. Line troops even went down into the sewers and catacombs of Paris looking for hiding Communards.

Even after the Left Bank's last defenses fell on Wednesday, Communard resistance remained organized, determined, and somewhat effective in the Thirteenth Arrondissement, near the place d'Italie and Porte de Choisy, and at Gobelins. Polish general Walery Wroblewski oversaw a line of defense that ran from the Butte-aux-Cailles near the place d'Italie to the fortified wall and Fort Bicêtre. After four attempts, that afternoon the Versaillais troops of General Ernest de Cissey took the Butte-aux-Cailles, a neighborhood of ragpickers and the last Communard bastion on the Left Bank. The resistance had been stiff, but reinforcements poured in on the Versailles side. National guardsmen abandoned Fort Bicêtre to return to defend their own *quartiers*. At the end of the day, by attacking from three directions, with the goal of isolating the arrondissement and taking control of the Paris-Orléans rail line, the Versaillais killed and captured many demoralized Communard fighters. When the fighting ended, four hundred bodies littered the ground. Wroblewski made it across the Seine to fight another day.[11]

However, not only Communards died on May 25. Members of the Dominican order housed in Arcueil just south of Paris also perished. Léon Meilliet, Communard commander of Fort Bicêtre, accused them of passing information on military strategy and Communard forces to the Versaillais. Backed by some evidence, these were not just random allegations. Local opinion also held that priests in cahoots with Versaillais were responsible for a fire that broke out inside a chateau near the Dominican school on May 17, although this was highly unlikely.

A number of Sisters of Charity were taken into Paris and held in Saint-Lazare prison. On Thursday, May 25, national guardsmen took about forty people, including Dominican priests and several employees, to Fort Bicêtre, where Communard resisters still held out. Two of the priests demanded to be interrogated, hoping to be freed. They were taken to a judge, Louis Lucipia, who had been an attorney's clerk and journalist. Although Lucipia concluded that the prisoners were not guilty, he told them they were being held as material witnesses to the chateau fire.

National guard commander Marie Jean-Baptiste Sérizier, a leather worker, member of the International, and militant in the Thirteenth Arrondissement, that day ordered the twenty-three remaining prisoners (several had been released, and a few had managed to escape) taken from their temporary prison at Fort Bicêtre. They were told that they were being moved into central Paris, where they would be safer—Versaillais troops were advancing rapidly. Once out in the street, the prisoners faced insults hurled by passersby. As they moved past the cemetery of the Champs-des-Navets, bullets from nearby fighting began to whiz past. A priest wearing civilian clothes managed to escape. After entering Paris through Porte de Choisy, they reached the *mairie* of the Thirteenth Arrondissement. Shells exploding nearby made clear that they would have to move on immediately.

The prisoners were taken at about 10 A.M. to a building converted into a disciplinary prison at 38, avenue d'Italie in the Thirteenth Arrondissement. Barricades covered the district, many built of materials from nearby construction sites. At about 1 P.M., Sérizier demanded that the prisoners, including the priests, be taken to help defend nearby barricades, along with fourteen national guardsmen who had been incarcerated for disobedience. One of the guards protested against the inclusion of the priests, demanding a written order, but an officer ignored him, shouting out, "Let's go, you there in the cassocks! Get out! To the barricade!" The prisoners gathered in the courtyard of the prison and were moved toward the gate. When they left the confines of the prison, shots were fired at them, some perhaps by their guards, others by people on the avenue d'Italie. In the end, thirteen bodies lay on the street, including those of five Dominican clergy, a professor, three domestics, a nurse, a clerk, and two guards.[12] This unplanned massacre occurred spontaneously in the incredibly charged atmosphere of the struggle for Paris.

POIRIER AND THE other Versaillais troops arrived at the place d'Italie soon after the shooting of the prisoners. They estimated—exaggerating—about 5,000 or 6,000 Communard dead. By now Poirier's unit had captured fifty-five Communards, whom they made stand on the piles of bodies as soldiers pumped bullets into them. Poirier thought one man "wasn't so bad." No matter. A sergeant killed him with a rifle shot to the head. Then Poirier's company left to join the remainder of their regiment on a boulevard about five hundred meters away, their *mitrailleuses* still hot from so much firing. The Versaillais then attacked a remaining barricade, with bayonets fixed. A Communard stabbed at Poirier with his own bayonet, grazing his coat. Poirier stepped back and shot him in the chest, finishing him off with his bayonet as the man struggled to get up. Eight men and three women, all of whom now dead, had defended the barricade. All told the Versaillais may have lined up and shot several thousand prisoners at the place d'Italie, which Poirier assures us became "a veritable slaughterhouse."[13]

WITH THE FALL of the place d'Italie that morning, line troops held the entire Left Bank. That same day, national guardsmen abandoned the southern forts of Montrouge, Bicêtre, and Ivry, falling back in the Right Bank, protected—for the moment—by the ramparts, the Seine, and the canal Saint-Martin.[14]

The Prussians had assisted the Versaillais by abandoning the zone immediately beyond the northern walls, an area that was supposed to remain neutral. However, since Germany and the French government signed the Treaty of Frankfurt on May 10, the Germans had been increasingly helpful to Versailles.[15] Line troops occupied territory north of Paris once German troops withdrew a little further out. And on May 26, the Prussians readied troops to help prevent Communards from escaping out of Paris to the east.[16]

The Communard commanders' failure to protect Montmartre's flanks within the city of Paris was catastrophic. Soldiers gunned down defenders right and left, as Camille Pelletan, a Communard participant, related. "As many people defending the barricades, the same number of bodies. Slaughter on rue Lepic, across from rue Tholozé. In front of the house at number 48, twenty bodies lie along the sidewalk. Massacre place de la Mairie. *Fédérés* there were cut up by bayonets. Carnage Moulin de la Galette." At Château-Rouge, witnesses counted fifty-seven bodies carted into the courtyard of a school. These included an elderly man, gunned down with his devoted dog at his side.[17]

A story about the shooting of a beautiful *fédérée* when a barricade fell quickly made the rounds. Arrested, she had pressed against her chest a red flag carrying the words, "Don't touch it!" Because of her determination, and probably also her stunning appearance, at first none of the soldiers wanted to be the one to kill her. They got over their hesitation, however, and gunned her down with many others. Augustine Blanchecotte came upon the bodies of three boys who had been shot on the boulevard d'Italie: one was a portly worker in a blue smock. He may have had a toothache, as a bandana enveloped a cheek as he lay with his head on the ground, a hand to an eye, as though sleeping. The other hand held a revolver. Little was left of another boy's head, and an arm extended, rigid in death, recalled his last defiant gesture.

A Versaillais had at least had the decency to place a handkerchief over what was left of his head. As the fighting moved on, women slowly emerged from nearby buildings, looking for their men. Wagons rolled by, their drivers asking if there were more bodies to cart away.[18]

Defeated Montmartre had been "pacified." Once the shells and bullets no longer crashed and crackled, the neighborhoods of the butte appeared deserted, as if all the residents were dead—and a good many were. But others had taken refuge. Rifles lay in the streets, tossed aside in haste by the Communard fighters they might otherwise have compromised.

The army rubbed the Parisians' faces in their defeat: "Parisian rabble, slackers, good-for-nothings, you won't be bellowing any more. If you move, to Cayenne! And it will be your turn to see what misery really is!" They would show those Parisians. Montmartre's reputation as a center of left-wing activism determined the fate of many prisoners taken by the army—they were more likely to be killed because of the location of their capture.[19]

Yet Albert Hans had to admit that on Montmartre, "errors" were committed in house-to-house searches and subsequent arrests. Indeed, line troops arrested one of Hans's colleagues, taking him for a Communard officer because of his uniform. As they were escorting their own comrade to a very uncertain future, the soldiers came upon others from the prisoner's battalion who vouched for him.

Then Hans found himself under arrest for intervening when two soldiers and a Volunteer of the Seine seized a man they accused of shooting at them from a house near the place Pigalle; when they apprehended him, they found a recently fired rifle nearby. The man claimed that it was not his weapon. Hans convinced the testy captors to take him to his house and ask his neighbors about him, but they did not have much good to say about him. The Volunteers of the Seine then turned on Hans, accusing him of being a Communard and trying to protect a guilty man. A junior army officer shouted to put him up against the wall, but, fortunately for Hans, a captain came by and ordered him taken to a commander. The captain, too, wanted to have Hans shot, but luckily, the more senior officer was willing to send him to his nearby apartment so that his personal papers could be inspected. Hans was ultimately freed.

Having returned to the Volunteers of the Seine, Hans came upon a woman taken prisoner at the barricade at the place Blanche—the barricade defended ably, at least in legend, by Nathalie Le Mel and the

Amazons of the Seine until they were finally overwhelmed. A corporal and two line soldiers escorted the prisoner, who wore the pants of a national guardsman, a small Tyrolean hat low on her head, and walked as quickly as her captors, her face fixed as she stared straight ahead. A small, hostile entourage followed, yelling insults and shouting for her immediate death. A bourgeois strode up and knocked off her hat. Another Volunteer picked it up and handed it back to her. Her fate is unknown. For his part, even Hans was shocked: "How the spirit of the Parisian bourgeoisie was completely demonstrated in this act of cowardly and useless brutality!"

Near the Church of Saint-Vincent-de-Paul in the Tenth Arrondissement, most residents seemed favorable to the Versaillais. Yet, even in a relatively conservative neighborhood, house-by-house searches turned up copies of Communard newspapers like Félix Pyat's *Le Vengeur*—in Hans's words, preaching "pillage"—as well as a decree signed by Charles Delescluze authorizing requisitions to assist in the defense of Paris. These small discoveries confirm how widespread allegiance—and in many cases devotion—to the Commune had been. Hans and the others then reached the Gare du Nord, where several prisoners were killed on a nearby lot, among them a delegate of the *quartier* "who died with dignity."

Ordered the next morning to proceed to the northern fortifications, Hans and his colleagues came upon the remains of a barricade taken the previous evening. They paused to toss into a ditch the badly mutilated corpses of twelve *fédérés*, barely recognizable as humans for all the mud and blood that covered them. From Porte de Pantin, Communard troops could be seen in the distance firing from Belleville. Beyond the northern ramparts were Prussian troops, easily identified by their hats. They made their allegiances clear, turning in guardsmen who had tried to save themselves by passing through Prussian lines. The Volunteers of the Seine encountered some of their own escorting captured members of the group Vengeurs de la Commune, dressed in blue-gray pants. These men "tremble[d] with fear," and with reason.

With the Left Bank subdued and Montmartre defeated, Hans's unit, along with other Versaillais troops, headed to the last stronghold of Communard resistance. They moved from Montmartre to Belleville and the Twentieth Arrondissement as shots ricocheted off the buildings. The Carrières (Quarries) de l'Amérique, where many *fédérés* were hiding, stood to the right. Straight ahead Communards fired from behind more barricades and houses, trying to knock out a *mitrailleuse*.

Reaching the rue des Lilas with two companies of line troops, Hans's unit arrived at the heights of Belleville. As the unit approached a barricade, a civilian informed them that an out-of-service cannon stood behind it. Hans and other Versaillais entered nearby houses from which they could fire on the barricade below. A shopkeeper let them in—he had no choice—asking them with a nervous smile what they might want to purchase. He quickly added that he was of no political party, adding that Versaillais had shot the concierge of his building, having surprised him wearing his National Guard uniform. The shopkeeper and his wife shook with fear; the soldiers reassured them, adding that they would indeed purchase some food. Nearby, two *fédérés*, believed to have fired at a house the Versaillais had occupied, were captured, surrendering when a soldier promised they would be spared. A colonel ordered their immediate execution, relenting grudgingly when the captor disclosed his promise to them.

Hans imagined at the place des Fêtes what it would be like to fall into the hands of the *fédérés*. He would be insulted, mistreated, and probably killed, like Generals Claude Lecomte and Clément Thomas on March 18. Versaillais could expect that the Communards would "cut us up into pieces or burn us alive," officers unable to restrain their frenzied underlings. He was sure that any number of line troops had perished like that. But he assumed that Communards captured by the Versaillais had nothing to fear: "Our discipline holds in check any malicious instincts, the cruelty and ferocity that sometimes can spring up in certain circumstances from the heart of the mildest man." Officers would of course protect prisoners. Ironically, he follows these ruminations with a description of taking another barricade—"several *fédérés*, drunk or desperate, still refused to give up: we had to kill them!"

Hans's pride in Versaillais discipline and moral superiority did not extend to all of his fellow soldiers. More often than not, the Versaillais were ready to shoot anyone they captured, with some soldiers seeking vengeance for a few of their own killed in the fighting. Several hauled along two Communards, ready to shoot them, insisting that as the men were their prisoners, they could do what they pleased with them. Hans and a few others protested and made their case to a cavalry officer, who agreed with them. When the most adamant of his soldiers protested, the officer broke his shoulder with several blows of his cane.

They came upon another prisoner, a Communard naval officer— the fleet was small and obviously limited to the Seine within the city—proud and resplendent in a fine uniform that sported several medals. Hans mocked the rapid promotion of this "officer," but the latter's courage impressed him: the prisoner asked only time to write a final message to his daughter. Overcoming the objections of an eager colleague who wanted to shoot the Communard immediately, Hans provided a pencil and paper, and the *fédéré* quickly penned his final message, as a line soldier barked, "Don't be sentimental. This is no longer the time for it. Shoot him!" The prisoner stepped down into the trench and was gunned down. Several minutes later, another captured Communard, a deserter from the Versailles army, joined him in the trench, defiantly shouting, "Go ahead, shoot me, scoundrels, bandits, murderers! Yes, I am a deserter. You will see how I am going to die! Long live the Commune!"

Hans could never forget another elderly Communard prisoner in a ragged uniform, hauled by two cavalrymen walking faster than the old man could manage. His face was thin, drawn, and yellowed; he wore glasses and had "misery," Hans remembered, written all over him. He was without doubt "honest," a "Don Quixote of socialism, a madman, an old marabout of the clubs." At each insult he endured from the Volunteers of the Seine, he politely removed his National Guard cap, revealing sparse white hair. Hans spoke favorably of him to their lieutenant, who ensured that the old man remained with the Volunteers rather than going with regular troops. This probably saved his life.[20]

Many others were not so lucky. In a fancy western neighborhood, Marie Holland knew well what was going on not far away. Her husband, Protestant minister Eugène Bersier, coming upon sixty Communard corpses, asked soldiers if he could take down their names so as to notify their families. The answer came quickly: no. Women were being shot, too, and they got no sympathy from onlookers, who shouted, "Kill them! Cut them down without pity!" If her husband would not be permitted to record the names of murdered or dying Communards, Marie would do her best to do so where she could. She spent that afternoon working in an American medical facility, writing down the names of the dying so that she could notify their relatives.[21]

More and more increasingly horrifying stories of the cruelty of the Versaillais now circulated among Parisians. A soldier allegedly raped a young girl, then finished her off with his bayonet. Prisoners being escorted to Versailles, including a woman, never made it past Saint-Augustin; for no apparent reason, troops suddenly killed a group of them, with one soldier dispatching some with his sword. At Porte Dauphine, dead and wounded prisoners were thrown into mass graves.

Near Tour Saint-Jacques, soldiers supposedly laughed and took turns throwing stones at a small arm moving in a pile of bodies until it was still. A merchant did the best he could caring for two wounded Communards, but no surgeon was to be found. An officer told him that those under his command would take the men to a hospital to receive care, but the soldiers killed them.[22]

An awful story quickly circulated: a woman asked to see her captured husband, the father of their four children. A general replied with a smile, "Worthy woman, we are going to take you to him." She expressed her thanks, and then several young soldiers escorted her no further than a wall, where they shot her. The Army of Versailles had given new meaning to the notion of reuniting a woman with her husband.[23]

John Leighton had little good to say about the Commune, which he insisted consisted of "robbers, incendiaries, assassins." But he also had to admit, "They are fearless of death. They have only that one good quality. They smile and they die. . . . [T]he wounded men drink with their comrades, and throw wine on their wounds, saying, 'Let us drink to the last.'"[24]

Communards were particularly fearless in the Eleventh Arrondissement, where they kept up the defense of Belleville, even though much of the rest of Paris was occupied. They built new barricades on the boulevard Voltaire, particularly at the intersection with the place du Château-d'Eau. Joseph Vinoy's reserve army had difficulty overcoming resistance there: that arrondissement had more effective military organization than any other,[25] but barricades at this point were utterly inadequate, and the two cannons that protected them were hardly enough to hold off the Versaillais onslaught. Beyond the occasional hand-delivered message, there was now no reliable way for *fédérés* to know what was transpiring elsewhere in Paris. The silence above in Montmartre was a terrible sign. Down below, the defenses at Porte Saint-Denis and Porte Saint-Martin were no more. The Communards still had weapons, however, and they were prepared to use every last one against the Versaillais. The Church of Saint-Ambroise had become an arsenal. Bigger batteries had been moved above to the Père Lachaise Cemetery, from which shells were launched into now occupied central Paris, whizzing over the heads of the Communards on the boulevard Voltaire.

At the parc Monceau, Châtelet, École Militaire, and Luxembourg, courts-martial dispatched hundreds of Communards, men and women alike, after interrogations that sometimes lasted no more than ten seconds. Augustine Blanchecotte remembered, "The noise of shells, which

I believed unrivaled, are only innocent music when compared to these latest sounds. The most troubling and the most unforgettable was between the Panthéon and Luxembourg—the nightly sounds through an entire week of the incessant shots of execution squads, following the rapid decisions of human justice." At Châtelet, soldiers killed a woman simply for wearing a red belt. Like other female victims, she had managed to survive the Prussian siege without complaint only to be shot by a French firing squad.[26]

News of the courts-martial reached the *mairie* of the Eleventh Arrondissement, which now served as the headquarters of what remained of the Commune's administration. Leaders spoke gravely to one another, while one of them dispensed written orders. Bitter disputes and recriminations echoed through the building. Surprisingly, there was little palpable sense of panic; instead, leaders became increasingly enraged as more and more reports related the summary executions of prisoners by the Versaillais troops. Wagons full of munitions and cartridges stood in the courtyard. The dead and wounded lay here and there amid general confusion. All night long, messages arrived from the remaining points of defense asking for men and cannons, without which fighters would have to abandon their positions. The Commune could offer neither.

Tricolor flags floated above the boulevard Saint-Michel. The quays had been taken. At the place Saint-Michel, the Fountain of the Médicis was full of corpses, their eyes still open. Although they could not doubt the final outcome of the struggle, some national guardsmen continued to fight, despite the lack of effective or even apparent leadership. Reclus admired that "they don't give ground little by little. They hold on to it as long as they are living; they still occupy it with their bodies."[27]

CHAPTER 9

MASSACRE

O N Bloody Thursday, May 25, Élie Reclus reflected on what he saw around him. Paris had been transformed into "a workshop, an immense workshop . . . but a workshop in which machine guns are at work, a workshop in which the work of destruction is accomplished on such a great scale. . . . It is a horrible cacophony, this infernal charivari of hatred and passion."[1]

That evening Communards mounted a sturdy defense at the pont d'Austerlitz, with a half-circular barricade stretching between the quay on the Left Bank and the boulevard de l'Hôpital. In an artillery battle, the Commune lost twenty-six people and had to abandon the first barricade. Soon the Versaillais had crossed the bridge, taking the quai de la Râpée and then Bercy. Losing ground, Communards set fire to the Grenier d'Abondance near that Place de la Bastille, a measure to prevent the Versaillais from going around the sturdy defenses of that Place de la Bastille and firing down on *fédérés* from the imposing structure. Its smoke filled the skyline, giving off the awful smell of burning oil and codfish.[2]

Not far away, Émile Maury ditched his weapon and National Guard uniform. He walked down the boulevard Mazas (now Diderot) toward the Seine. A few barricades were still going up, including one in front of his apartment building. An enormous barricade still stood on the rue de Charonne. But not many people were left to defend these improvised structures. Maury saw what was coming: "The noose is getting *tighter.* . . . [T]he Commune begins its agony."[3]

And although randomness and serendipity still marked the killings, the violent repression was increasingly organized, especially in and around northeastern Paris, where the fighting continued. The army had become "a vast execution squad" as it moved toward the last bastions of Communard resistance in northern and eastern Paris. There Communards had had more time to prepare their defense.[4]

ALL COMMUNARD DISCIPLINE had evaporated. Improbable suggestions surfaced in the *mairie* of the Eleventh Arrondissement: to form an entire column of remaining *fédérés* and recapture Montmartre or to march in and retake the center of Paris. Charles Delescluze was prepared to die. After an unsuccessful trek to Porte de Vincennes to convince the Prussians to intervene to save lives by arranging a truce,[5] he now sat quietly at a small table in the *mairie* on the boulevard Voltaire. His continued insistence that all was not lost belied what he knew. He calmly wrote out a few orders. At one point he held his head in his hands, repeating, "What a war! What a war!" He only hoped to die without shame—that "we also . . . will know how to die." His *mot d'ordre* remained duty. Delescluze said simply, "I don't want any more. No, everything is finished for me." He wrote a friend to say that he would await the judgment of history on the Commune and to his sister to say good-bye, confiding the letters to a friend.

Wearing, as always, a frock coat, patent leather boots, a silk hat, and a red sash around his waist, he walked with Commune member François Jourde and about fifty national guardsmen toward the barricades under Versaillais attack at the place du Château-d'Eau. They passed Maxime Lisbonne, who had been badly wounded in the fighting as he led a courageous, tenacious Communard defense there, being carried by Auguste Vermorel and Victor Jaclard. At a barricade, Vermorel fell wounded. Delescluze shook his hand. As the sun set and bullets whizzed by, national guardsmen urged Delescluze to take shelter. But he kept walking, straight ahead, very slowly to a barricade. Jourde moved away after the two friends shook hands. Delescluze stood on the barricade, awaiting death. It came in a matter of seconds. Four men ran forward to get his body, and three of them were shot. Delescluze lay where he had fallen for several days, a courageous martyr to a cause whose end was approaching.[6]

Eugène Varlin replaced Delescluze as delegate for war, but his tenure would be short. Jaclard and a badly wounded Vermorel were carried to a building on the boulevard Voltaire, where they managed to avoid arrest thanks to the quick thinking of the person who had taken them in. But near the parc Monceau their luck ran out, and they were captured.[7]

The Commune's leadership was almost entirely annihilated, but still the violence persisted. Anti-Communards sporting tricolor armbands contributed to the carnage. Organized secretly before Adolphe Thiers's troops entered Paris, they had, as we have seen, prepared such armbands in advance as marks of identification. Those wearing them now took on the role of military police, organizing searches and setting themselves up in *mairies* abandoned by the Commune. They responded to the wave of denunciations that began to arrive after each neighborhood had been secured and conducted arbitrary arrests. In a typical case, a concierge indicated to a man wearing a Versaillais armband that "Monsieur B. buys lots of newspapers, perhaps he is hiding someone, perhaps a Communard."[8]

CLEARLY BLOODY WEEK provided French officers with a way to restore morale and prestige after their inglorious defeat in the Franco-Prussian War and their failure to hold onto Paris in March. The National Guard seemed the antithesis of the French army; it accepted men from all social classes, and many, including some officers, were ordinary workers. This flew in the face of the values of the professional army and its aristocratic leadership. Members of the officer corps, many of whom despised the Commune and all who stood for it, distrusted their few republican colleagues. The arrogant Ernest de Cissey hated the Commune and was eager to take revenge. Joseph Vinoy, humiliated after the surrender of France to Prussia and marked as a *capitulard* (defeatist) and also identified with the failure to seize the cannons on Montmartre, awaited the chance to settle scores. He offered no apologies for the executions of "modern barbarians." General Félix Douay played a lesser role in the mass killings, having turned operations at Châtelet over to Colonel Louis Vabre, who gleefully presided over the prevotal court. Justin Clinchant, who had moderate republican sympathies, forbade the shooting of prisoners in parts of Paris under his control, and he was one of the few officers who did anything to hinder the executions. Lesser officers followed the instructions of those who commanded them, yet with some variation, depending on their personalities, attitudes toward the Communards, and circumstances.[9]

Paul de Ladmirault was one officer who resisted the urge toward violent reprisals to which his colleagues were succumbing. He was from an old, aristocratic, Catholic military family from Touraine that had lost land during the French Revolution, against which his father had fought, and there was no doubt that Paul would fight against the

Commune eighty years later. Hearing the volleys of an execution squad, Ladmirault insisted that he did not like "summary justice" because of the potential for errors. On seeing several pale, frightened Communards about to be executed, he stopped the firing squad and asked if the Communards had fired at the soldiers or were carrying weapons. The squad members answered no, but the captives' hands were blackened, possibly by gunpowder. Ladmirault told his soldiers that the prisoners' fate was up to judges and not to them. He expressed some sympathy for ordinary Communards who had joined the National Guard in order to receive the 1.50 francs per day. At one point, Ladmirault watched a badly wounded prisoner being taken in a convoy to Versailles. Barely alive, he raised his hand and fixed his eyes on his captors. With what remained of his voice, he told them, "The insurgents are you!"[10] Ladmirault did not retaliate in anger as others might have. He was by far one of the least murderous of his fellow commanders.

The mentality of the soldiers themselves also contributed to the violence of Bloody Week. Negative images of Paris, particularly Montmartre and Belleville, abounded in Versailles and in the country at large, and the propaganda had the desired effect. For example, in late April *Le Soir* warned its readers that once the Commune had fallen, property in Paris would require fumigation. For its part, *Le Gaulois* related that residents of Belleville had taken over homes in prosperous Passy and that "all your cupboards and your wine cellar have been broken into. . . . [M]en and women lay in your beds."[11] Soldiers conscripted from rural areas, especially from regions with a relatively high degree of religious practice, such as Brittany and Normandy, particularly opposed the Commune, which in its propaganda and in reality had taken aim at the Church.

Of course, soldiers also acted on the orders of their leaders. In the view of Jules Bergeret, a Commune member from the Twentieth Arrondissement, Versaillais troops entering Paris had received instruction "to give no quarter." A municipal policeman related that he had proceeded with the execution of a Pole, referring to "the orders of [Marshal Patrice de MacMahon] and also those of the Minister of War . . . [which were] definite concerning deserters and foreigners who have served the Commune." MacMahon knew what was going on, although perhaps not the exact extent. Like Thiers, he failed to forbid or denounce the shooting of prisoners, at least those taken with weapons. General Alexandre Montaudon, for one, excused the summary executions, claiming that the soldiers took the initiative, following the orders of their officers. But he had to admit that hatred existed among soldiers for "the agents of this awful civil war," which they had fomented in "their meetings and in their [political] clubs."[12]

One woman bragged that her brother, a "distinguished" officer in the army, had ordered the shooting of four hundred "obstinate insurgents . . . at the last barricades of Belleville." She added, "The cowards! They were crying!" Another Parisian ran into a policeman who proudly claimed that he had killed more than sixty people himself and that "the cowards" had asked for mercy.[13]

Soldiers and commanders alike frequently compared Communards to colonial "barbarians." Théophile Gautier described them as "savages, a ring through their noses, tattooed in red, dancing a scalp dance on the smoking debris of society." Gaston Galliffet once contrasted the Communards with North African Arabs, whom the French army had brutalized for forty years: "The Arabs have a God and a country; Communards have neither."[14] Another general noted, "If given the choice between Arabs and these rioters, I would easily choose the Arabs as adversaries." Many of the line troops had fought in Algeria, Mexico, and even China, and in their view, the Communards no more qualified as French than the insurgents they encountered abroad. Alphonse Daudet, another anti-Communard, intoned that Paris had been "in the power of negroes."[15]

Charles de Montrevel held that of the Parisians who participated in "this immense orgy," by which he meant the Commune, most were "lower-class provincials." His view associated large-scale immigration to large urban centers with social and political turmoil, as newcomers were torn away from traditional rural roots, including family and organized religion, that might have kept them in check, resulting in collective psychosis. History would surely render this verdict and none other, Montrevel believed. So did Gustave de Molinari, for whom Paris had become "a sort of interior California" through immigration from the provinces into plebeian, peripheral neighborhoods. What was to be done to prevent government from becoming "subject to a harsh slavery" at the hands of such people?[16]

A man originally from Bordeaux living in the capital during the Commune had little good to say about the Parisians, whom he considered "artificial creatures": "The true Parisian, eternally and tiringly cheeky, [is] incapable of a serious and deep sentiment [and] laughs or is ready to laugh wherever, on any occasion: he respects nothing, believes in nothing." Thus the Parisian was incapable of making political decisions but rather quietly awaited orders from "stronger minds and free-thinkers, ornaments of common bars."[17] If they could not be political actors in their own right—as the much despised Commune made all too clear—stronger forces would have to come in and set things right, even if doing so entailed unprecedented violence.

MacMahon, the one man who might have put an end to the executions, turned a blind eye to what was happening in Paris. On May 25, Jules Ferry reported that three generals had ordered the execution of captured "insurgent leaders." MacMahon claimed to have reminded the generals of his orders to send prisoners who surrendered to the courts-martial at Versailles.[18] In the end, however, MacMahon simply allowed the slaughter to go on.[19]

Whatever MacMahon professed to Ferry, his commanders seem never to have received the order to send all prisoners to Versailles. Commanders often ordered that Communards taken prisoner with weapons be shot, although, to repeat, life and death was in the hands of individual officers. Cissey had no qualms at all—he notified General François du Barail that anyone found fighting for the Commune was to be executed. The missive reached Thiers, who knew very well about the summary shooting of prisoners and did nothing to stop it.[20]

Some generals, like Gaston Galliffet, "the star of the Tricolor Terror," took matters into their own hands and handed down instantaneous decisions about who lived and who died. Galliffet bragged that he had killed seventy Communards himself. When a woman threw herself at his feet to beg that her husband's life be spared, the general replied, "Madame, I have attended all the theaters in Paris; it serves nothing to put on this performance." Although the number of prisoners Galliffet ordered killed in the Bois-de-Boulogne will never be known, he reveled in his infamy, once bragging that he would rather be known as "a great murderer than taken for a little assassin." He announced with pride, "Above all, to the highest degree, I have disdain for the lives of others." General Galliffet yelled at a convoy of prisoners, including Louise Michel, "I am Galliffet! People of Montmartre, you think me a cruel man. You're going to find out that I am much crueler than even you imagined!"[21]

Although the executions stemmed from the murderous hatred of many Versaillais of all ranks, and although they could seem haphazard to those who witnessed them, the massacre was organized. Even before the Army of Versailles entered Paris, Thiers had organized courts-martial to be held there. He fully expected that his troops would be executing Communards in the city. Given this kind of foresight, there is no reason to believe that he intended his men to keep all prisoners alive and bring them back to Versailles. After his troops entered Paris, they had set up two of the big centers for executions by at least May 23 at the parc Monceau, where they had shot fifteen men and a woman the day before, and the École Militaire. The killings then proceeded systematically.[22]

Convinced that the massacres had been planned and that lists of people to be arrested and killed existed, Communard journalist Camille Pelletan noted right away that the fact that the Versailles troops encountered so little resistance, particularly upon their entry into Paris on May 21, made it even more difficult to excuse the mass killings. "Most [Communards], discouraged, gave up the struggle; only a handful of men, resolute, scattered, remained to defend the Commune." Pelletan had it right when he insisted that the massacre was much more than "a ferocious repression undertaken against the *fédérés*." It was directed "against all of Paris, and not just against supporters of the Commune." The capital had seen nothing like it since the Saint Bartholomew's Day Massacre in 1572, when Catholics had slaughtered Protestants. To Thiers and his entourage, Paris was the enemy and merited "a considerable, rapid massacre." Thiers boasted in a speech of May 24, "I shed torrents of [Parisian] blood."[23] Indeed he did.

Those interrogated were routinely asked, "Were you part of the Commune? You were there! It is written all over your face. Your age? Your name? Where are your identity papers? Well . . . Go!" This meant death. One victim was asked if he had participated in the insurrection. "He's a scoundrel [*coquin*]," said a soldier. The presiding officer responded, "*Classé*" (kill him).[24]

There is thus truth to Pelletan's claim that the Versaillais had in their sights all of Paris, not just the Communards. Although Thiers's troops targeted certain groups in particular, of course, some soldiers were eager to find any reason to kill those they encountered. They were by no means careful or discerning. One unlucky victim, Jean-Baptiste Millière, was arrested on Friday although he had not participated in the Commune. When a captain named Garcin asked him if his name was Millière, he answered in the affirmative but said that surely the officer knew he had been elected to the Chamber of Deputies. Garcin said that he did, but clearly this made no difference to him. General

Cissey was having a nice lunch in a nearby restaurant. When an officer interrupted his meal to relate Millière's arrest, Cissey ordered his immediate execution, between mouthfuls of "the pear and the cheese." When Millière asked why he, a deputy, was to die, Garcin related that he had read articles the deputy had written and considered him a "viper on which one should stomp." The general had ordered that he should be shot at the Panthéon, on his knees, and forced "to ask pardon of the society to which you have done evil." When the time came, Millière refused to kneel and opened his shirt to receive the bullets. Garcin had two soldiers throw him to his knees. The deputy shouted, "Long live humanity!" and started to add something more, but shots silenced him before he could finish.[25]

Social class could determine life or death. Middle-class Communards were more likely to talk their way out of encounters with Versaillais. Sutter-Laumann survived because he washed carefully, combed his hair, and spoke, as we have seen, "without a working-class accent in good French" when stopped by an officer of the Volunteers of the Seine. If those so confronted spoke the argot of the Parisian street and workplace, execution usually followed. An officer interrogated a man at a barricade on the rue Houdon:

"Who are you?"

"A mason."

"So, now it's masons who are going to command!"

He shot the man dead on the spot.[26] Social stigma led to massacre.

Captured foreigners had little chance of surviving, because their presence in Paris corresponded to one image of the Commune as partially the work of good-for-nothing Poles, Russians, Germans, and members of the International Workingmen's Association. Responding to a question from a Versaillais with a foreign accent could prove immediately fatal, as could having an "exotic" name. Men over age forty, French or foreign, were particular targets—thus the infamous story of Galliffet "reviewing" a convoy of prisoners on the way to Versailles and pulling out several for immediate execution because they had gray hair and thus had presumably fought with the insurgents in the June Days of 1848.

People were disrobed and their shoulders checked for marks left by a recoiling rifle. If any were found, the bearers were immediately shot. Men who looked "ragged," were poorly dressed, and could not instantaneously justify their time or did not work in a "proper" trade had little chance of surviving the brief audience before a prevotal court. Near the Gare de Lyon, soldiers stopped two men and demanded to see their hands. Those of one were white, thus not the hands of someone who worked or had helped to defend a barricade; he was spared. According to a witness hostile to the Commune, "his companion did not have the same fate. His hands, his rifle, everything condemned him. A shot from a chassepot finished off his account with society, and our sailors continued their searches."[27]

Men who had previously served in the regular army became targets, even those who had fought during the Franco-Prussian War, because they were assumed to have deserted. A few soldiers who had fought against the Commune were killed by mistake, including a wounded Breton who had difficulty expressing himself in French. An officer took him for a deserter and shot him with his revolver.[28]

Despite his insistence on making all decisions and overseeing every aspect of the civil war, Thiers claimed that the executions occurring in Paris were out of his control. On May 27 he told Ferry, who had expressed concern about the image of the Versailles government abroad after the British and Swiss press had started to denounce the mass executions, "During the fighting we can do nothing." Still, Thiers or Mac-Mahon likely ordered the end of such killings on May 27 or 28. Vinoy instructed a subordinate not to have any more prisoners shot "without careful examination" of each case—in other words, Versailles did not order a stop to the executions but may have called for their decrease. In districts under the authority of Cissey and Vinoy, however, Versaillais shot Communard prisoners (including an English student perhaps killed because his name was Marx) well into June both in Paris and at Vincennes just outside the city.[29]

Adolphe Clémence compared the Versaillais' hunt for anyone remotely suspected of Communard sympathies to the "hunt for [escaped] slaves" in America. Philibert Audebrand heard shouts of "Let's kill them all! So that not one survives."[30] In the Luxembourg Gardens, the carnage continued from May 24 to 28, with perhaps 3,000 men and women shot there, many as they stood against the wall in the center of the gardens. Unlike in the aftermath of the June Days of 1848, when prisoners were killed secretly, the massacres of Bloody Week took place for the most part out in the open. Smaller tribunals also functioned, under the authority of junior officers acting independently in various parts of the city with the encouragement of the major commanders. The *Paris-Journal* reported that each time the number to be shot exceeded ten, a machine gun replaced the usual execution squad.[31]

On the boulevard Saint-Martin, where many Communards had fallen, a handwritten poster said it all:

> Officers and soldiers of Versailles,
> Beaten by the Prussians,
> Victors over Paris, four to one,
> Murderers of women
> And children
> Thieving in houses by orders from above,
> You have really shown yourselves worthy of
> The papists.[32]

AT ABOUT MIDNIGHT on Thursday, Gabriel Ranvier, Varlin, and a few others abandoned the *mairie* of the Eleventh Arrondissement on the boulevard Voltaire as the Versaillais noose tightened. They moved their operations first to the *mairie* of the Twentieth Arrondissement, then to a building near the place des Fêtes, sending the remnants of the military authority to 145, rue Haxo in Belleville. Varlin, Delescluze's replacement as delegate for war, was still giving orders, but no one was paying any attention. The remaining Communard leaders decided that each would return to a barricade and do what he could. There was nowhere to go, no exit.

At 6 A.M. on Friday, the Versaillais launched an assault against the well-defended barricade at the intersection of the boulevards Voltaire and Richard-Lenoir. General Clinchant's forces moved along the canal Saint-Martin, and Ladmirault's troops overwhelmed barricades on the rues de Flandre, Kabylie, and Riquet, reaching La Villette and the canal de l'Ourcq.[33]

Line troops took the place du Trône (now de la Nation), from which their cannons could shell the place Voltaire and their forces could attack the place de la Bastille from the east. They then took the place de la Rotonde (now Place Stalingrad).[34] The well-fortified place Château-d'Eau fell that afternoon, forcing Communards to flee. The Versaillais then took the place de la Bastille. Line troops overwhelmed two enormous barricades protecting the rue Saint-Antoine. There, more than a hundred Communard resisters died. An elderly Communard being led to a pile of garbage on which he would be killed, said "I am a republican. I have fought bravely. I have earned the right not to die in shit."[35] Élisabeth Dmitrieff was injured but managed to get away. When Léo Frankel also fell wounded, she saved him. A hundred Communard corpses lay near a barricade on the nearby rue de Charenton. Communard fighters now cried, "Better death than Cayenne!"

On the boulevard du Prince Eugène and at the places du Château-d'Eau and de la Bastille, troops threw both corpses and live national guardsmen from the windows of nearby buildings where they had been killed or captured. The air was foul with the stench of death. Among the corpses, many seemed relatively old, but there were also many young men. It was not uncommon to see men fighting alongside their sons, grandfathers alongside grandsons. Reclus reflected bitterly that 200,000 "slaves" had managed to overcome 50,000 Communards. In reality, however, as only about 20,000 men and women fought for the Commune, in the final days the number was far smaller than that. The Communards were completely outmanned. Small groups of experienced, determined resisters were not nearly adequate.[36]

National guardsmen retreated up the faubourg Saint-Antoine, that traditional center of artisanal militancy, and along the boulevard Richard-Lenoir to the boulevard Voltaire in the Eleventh Arrondissement.[37] The Versaillais now launched a full-scale assault against the boulevard Voltaire, a fitting name for one of the last remaining targets of clerical reaction against the godless republic. As line troops moved rapidly into the Eleventh and Twelfth Arrondissements, *fédérés* retreated up to Ménilmontant in Belleville. Communard defenders heard only bad news. The Versaillais shot nine employees in a gas factory at La Villette, which fell in the evening. Word reached remaining Communard commanders of Thiers's announcement that the Versaillais had 25,000 prisoners in custody.[38]

THAT FRIDAY RANVIER posted a decree, the Commune's last, asking people of the Twentieth Arrondissement to resist the Versaillais in cooperation with their neighbors in the Nineteenth, again revealing the strategy, and the weaknesses, of organizing the defense by *quartier*: "If we succumb, you know what fate awaits us. . . . Don't wait until Belleville is attacked." But to no avail: no one turned up to help defend Belleville. While the last of the *fédérés* might fight to the death, they would do so in their own neighborhoods without any effective military authority coordinating their efforts. In the end, the remaining

Communard fighters fought in their districts, hoping against hope. John Leighton put it this way: "Everyone gives orders, no one obeys them."[39]

WITH ONLY A FEW *fédéré* strongholds remaining, there was almost no one to challenge the Versaillais troops executing Parisians indiscriminately. Generals, unchecked by Thiers and MacMahon, certainly did nothing to stop the carnage.

Versaillais arrested Melchior Arnold Tribels and his wife on Friday as they walked on the rue de Rivoli; a concierge had denounced them after the woman became ill and asked if she could enter the building to rest. A shabbily dressed, fifty-six-year-old Dutch Jew, Tribels was carrying a sack with 15,000 to 20,000 florins, as well as annuity bonds worth about 50,000 francs, two gold watches, and a diamond ring. A search also yielded a book containing the addresses of various Parisian bankers and jewelers. The Versaillais took all this as evidence that he was pillaging the homes of wealthy families. After his wife was released, Tribels was taken to the *cour prévôtale* at Châtelet and condemned to death; the next day he marched the short distance to the Caserne Lobau, where he was shot.[40]

EDMOND DE GONCOURT, no friend of the Communards, would never forget what he saw as rain pounded down on Paris: "I am going along the railroad line near the Passy station when I see some men and women escorted by soldiers. I go through the broken barrier and am on the edge of a path where the prisoners are waiting to set out for Versailles. There are a lot of them, for I hear an officer say in a low voice as he gives a paper to the colonel: Four hundred and seven, of whom sixty-six are women." Men had been arranged in rows of eight, bound to each other by a rope linking their wrists. They were

> as they were when caught, most without hats or caps, their hair plastered on their foreheads and faces by the fine rain which has been falling since morning. There are men of the common people who have made a covering for their heads with blue-checked handkerchiefs. Others, thoroughly soaked by the rain, draw thin overcoats around their chests under which a piece of bread makes a hump. It is a crowd from every social level, workmen with hard faces, artisans in loose-fitting jackets, bourgeois with socialist hats, National Guards who have had no time to change their trousers,

two infantrymen pale as corpses—stupid, ferocious, indifferent, mute faces.

Goncourt's attention fell in particular on one young woman, "especially beautiful, beautiful with the implacable fury of a young Fate. She is a brunette with wiry hair that sticks out, with eyes of steel, with cheeks reddened by dried tears. She is planted in an attitude of defiance, spewing out insults at the officers from a throat and lips so contracted by anger that they cannot form sounds and words. Her furious, mute mouth chews the insults without being able to make them heard. 'She is like the one who killed Barbier with a dagger!' a young officer says to one of his friends."

A colonel took his place at the side of the column, "announcing in a loud voice with a brutality which I think [he] put on to induce fear: 'Any man who lets go of his neighbor's arm will be killed!' And that terrible 'will be killed!' is repeated four or five times." In the background, Goncourt and the other observers could hear "the dull sound of rifles being loaded by the infantry escort."[41]

When a barricade on the boulevard Prince Eugène defended by 180 people fell, fighters took refuge in a nearby house. An English medical student watched in horror as Versaillais immediately lined up and shot fifty-two captured women, along with about sixty men. The student heard an officer interrogate one of the women, telling her that two of his soldiers had been killed. "May God punish me for not having killed more of them," she shouted. "I had two sons at Issy, and both were killed, and two more at Neuilly, who suffered the same fate. My husband died at this barricade, and now you can do with me what you want."[42]

EVEN WITH VERSAILLAIS troops moving rapidly into eastern Paris, remaining hostages in La Roquette still had much to fear. A policeman and four national guardsmen went to the prison and took away the banker Jean-Baptiste Jecker, whom chance had spared two days earlier; they took him to a ditch near Père Lachaise Cemetery and killed him.[43] About 3 P.M. that same day, Friday, National Guard colonel Émile Gois and about sixty national guardsmen from various battalions arrived at La Roquette, where about nine hundred prisoners were still being held. Prison director Jean-Baptiste François, still wearing his red belt, had been at the *mairie* of the Eleventh Arrondissement. When he returned to La Roquette, he received an order signed by Théophile Ferré and brandished by Gois, ordering him to turn over about fifty prisoners, including ten imprisoned priests, four men accused of spying for Versailles, two gendarmes, and thirty-three *sergents-de-ville* (the two later groups were closely identified with Napoleon III and the Second Empire).[44]

François ordered Antoine Ramain, the head guard, to bring down all the gendarmes and gave him a list of twelve to fifteen other names. When Ramain asked for an explanation, François told him that with Versaillais shells falling, better security would be available at the *mairie* in Belleville. Ramain entered the corridor of the fourth section and announced, "Attention! I need 15 [prisoners]. . . . Get in line!"[45]

Guardsmen piled the prisoners into wagons. At about 4 P.M. they left, following the rue de la Roquette to the Père Lachaise Cemetery and then the boulevard Ménilmontant to the boulevard de Belleville. At the bottom of the chaussée Ménilmontant, they passed a barricade held by guardsmen. There a battalion commander ordered Captain Louis-François Dalivons, a twenty-six-year-old roofer from the rue Ménilmontant, to lead an escort of eight men. The wagons reached the rue de Puebla. A crowd formed, and curiosity turned into abuse as the escort drew near the *mairie* in Belleville. Then the wagons rattled into the rue Haxo, the crowd reached a point of fury, such that Eugène Varlin and Communard colonel Hippolyte Parent could not hold off those calling for the deaths of the gendarmes, policemen, and priests they could see in the open wagons. At the back of a small garden on the rue Haxo in Belleville, national guardsmen placed the prisoners against a wall and shot them dead with the help of other men and women who fired repeatedly into the bodies. Thirty-seven gendarmes, ten priests, and two Versaillais informers perished.[46]

On Saturday morning, Ferré arrived at La Roquette in the rain. According to one of the incarcerated priests, Abbé Pierre-Henri Lamazou, he "rushed and sprang about like a panther afraid of losing its prey," carrying a rifle and waving a pistol. There seemed little hope for the remaining hostages. But with the battle drawing nearer, Ferré suddenly left. In the afternoon, a prison guard began opening up the cells on the second floor; apparently under orders to send down two prisoners at a time for execution, the guard had finally had enough. The ten priests, forty gendarmes, and eighty or so Versaillais troops he freed began to improvise barricades, using beds, chairs, and whatever else they could find. National guardsmen arrived and tried to overcome the suddenly mobilized hostages with smoke, setting fire to mattresses.

Some prisoners managed to get down to the ground floor. Abbé Paul Perny, a few priests, and several others decided to take their chances and leave the prison, its big door now standing open. The risks were great. Some suspected a trap—that they would be slaughtered upon leaving the relative safety of their now protected prison corridor. Moreover, dressed in ecclesiastical garb, they risked attack by panicked Communards as the Versailles troops drew within blocks of the prison. Perny and some of the others did not know the neighborhood around La Roquette. Where to go? To turn left after passing through the prison gate or right? Perny knocked on the doors of several houses and hotels. None opened. To the priest, the ordinary Communards he encountered were "modern Redskins." As for the women, they "surpass[ed] the men in their frenzy and determination." Like so many others opposed to the Commune, he reserved special contempt for Belleville and other plebeian neighborhoods.[47]

Several people whom Perny encountered in the streets were kinder, asking what he was doing. Did he not hear the sound of nearby gunfire? He decided that his best chance was to return to La Roquette. Perhaps the guards, some of whom he now knew well and trusted, would protect him. Several other priests, the seminarian, and a few gendarmes had made the same choice after getting a sense of the chaos and dangers outside. They hid in the infirmary, even as Communards entered La Roquette and looked for them. Within hours the arrival of Versaillais troops had saved them.

Monseigneur Auguste Alexis Surat was not so fortunate. When he asked a woman for help, she spat, "Here you go, I will give you nothing!" The priest was shot as he tried to find his way through the maze of streets. Another missionary perished in the same way. In all, between May 24 and 26, sixty-six or sixty-eight hostages died.[48]

NOW THAT MOST OF the Eleventh Arrondissement had fallen, Versaillais troops attacked the major remaining points of defense: Belleville, Buttes-Chaumont, and Père Lachaise Cemetery. On Friday night, Versaillais troops encountered stiff resistance near Belleville and on streets leading to Père Lachaise, where two Communard batteries and several hundred national guardsmen prepared to fight. The next morning line troops gathered at Porte de Lilas and then moved into Belleville, Ménilmontant, and Charonne, isolating resisters. At the base of the rue de Belleville, soldiers overwhelmed the last concentrated resistance. Versaillais troops took 1,500 Communard prisoners on the rue Haxo

and at least 800 at the place des Fêtes in the Nineteenth Arrondissement in Belleville. The Communard resisters had turned their attention
toward a column of 1,300 line soldiers captured on March 18 whom,
for whatever reason, Ferré had ordered moved under guard from the
barracks of Prince Eugène to the church of Belleville. When a nearby
battery fell, twenty-three Communards were immediately shot. On the
rue de Puebla, sixty perished behind one barricade. Behind the barricade of the place de la Rotonde, after the bodies had been carted away,
W. Pembroke Fetridge described blood running "in streams through
the gutters." Dead horses lay about.[49]

General Joseph Vinoy's army moved toward Père Lachaise Cemetery very early Saturday morning. Ladmirault's army overcame Communard resistance and captured Buttes-Chaumont. That morning,
four hundred Communards came down slowly from Belleville to surrender, all carrying their guns upside down. They were soon on their
way to Versailles. MacMahon had promised to make Belleville pay.
With Buttes-Chaumont taken and Père Lachaise Cemetery under attack and about to fall, MacMahon's army did just that. Line troops
fired shell after shell into the *quartier*, igniting flames. Versaillais
convinced defenders behind one barricade to surrender in exchange
for their lives, then gunned them down from behind on the rue de
Bagnolet. On the rue de Belleville, a concierge denounced several
residents to line troops. An officer ordered them shot, then shot the
concierge as well for good measure—after all, he lived in Belleville.
One resident went to find a doctor for wounded *fédérés* hiding in a
cellar. A soldier grabbed him while marching a group of prisoners
past and said, "Let's go, you can join the dance!" His widow did not
learn for three months what had happened to him. As the London
Times related, Versaillais troops considered "anyone who cared in any
way for the wounded as sympathizing with them and thus meriting
the same fate."[50]

ON SATURDAY, Élie Reclus could hear around the Gare de Lyon "several volleys of fire from the [execution] squads, about a dozen or two
dozen shots." The victims were prisoners captured in the basements
and attics of nearby buildings or simply picked up because Versaillais
soldiers, police, or spies did not like their looks. Police detachments
assigned to each army corps searched buildings and arrested suspected
Communards. The Friends of Order wreaked vengeance on Paris. Taking refuge in a friend's apartment, Reclus could see, as he peered out

from behind a curtain, "these poor disarmed [Communards], bour-geois or workers, in civilian clothes or wearing some part of a uniform, marched straight ahead, with firm and proud steps, but with faces so pale. In an hour, they would be dead." Bodies were tossed into wagons, to be buried in deep ditches, covered with lime, or burned. Reclus had seen a convoy of ten to twelve omnibuses filled with human remains. A red ribbon of blood marked the riverbanks along both sides of the Seine.[51]

After destroying the gates to the Père Lachaise Cemetery on Saturday evening, Versaillais troops stormed in. Many of the Com-munard fighters there fell, some in hand-to-hand bayonet combat amid the tombs. Soldiers captured the rest and executed hundreds en masse, lining *fédéré* prisoners up in two rows against a wall, next to a very deep ditch. Machine guns did the rest, and most prisoners fell or were thrown into the mass grave. Georges Clemenceau later recalled that machine guns mowed down Communards for thirty minutes without a pause. On Sunday, the Versaillais brought more prisoners for execution. They arrived in groups of 150, 200, or even 300 to be shot, many of them falling into the same wide and deep ditch that contained the bodies of Communards killed in or after the fighting the day before.[52]

Albert Hans insisted that officers had not ordered the executions. The fate of the Communards thus often depended on sheer chance: a humanitarian gesture by one of the soldiers could save a prisoner—at least for a while. Some Volunteers showed mercy. They would take prisoners to the corner of the rues des Lilas and Belleville, with the trench of death nearby, and according to their assessment of the cap-tives' pleas, attitudes, and, in some cases, "their prayers," they might spare them. Yet Hans admitted that some ended up dead in a ditch on the way. Inevitably, at Père Lachaise, "a *faux pas*, a protest, a pause in a step, any incident, would irritate a guard and that was the end of the *fédéré*."[53]

Few could forget what they witnessed at Père Lachaise. Denis Ar-thur Bingham went to look at the cemetery after the massacre and found tombs broken open by shells. Bodies of those summarily shot lay fully exposed for all to see. Bingham estimated eight hundred in one long trench and three hundred in another, many near one of the cemetery's walls. "Most of them," he noted, "wore an expression of an-ger and hatred which rendered their faces perfectly hideous. It was a ghastly spectacle, from which I turned away with horror, and which

long haunted me."[54] A young American woman described the cemetery as "the ghastliest sight." The bodies of Communards killed along a
wall filled "a natural hollow." Among them were "many women. There,
thrown up in the sunlight, was a well-rounded arm with a ring on one
of the fingers; there again was a bust shapely in death; and there were
faces which to look upon made one shudder, faces distorted out of humanity with ferocity and agony combined. The ghastly effect of the
dusky white powder on the dulled eyes, the gnashed teeth, and the jag-
ged beards cannot be described."[55]

Journalist and Commune member Pierre Vésinier recalled the final
moments of the Communard fighters at Père Lachaise and elsewhere,
describing thousands of bodies that "strewed the avenues and tombs.
Many were murdered in the graves where they had sought shelter, and
dyed the coffins with their blood. . . . [T]errible fusillades, frightful platoon fires, intermingled with the crackling noise of *mitrailleuses*, plainly
told of the wholesale massacre." Vésinier reflected on the rationale of
the Versaillais with justified sarcasm: "Property, religion, and society
were once more saved."[56]

News of the mass executions of priests and gendarmes at the rue
Haxo kept hatred of the Communards burning among Thiers's troops,
and the Versaillais quickly went there to see the piles of bodies "horri-
bly mutilated, blue, swollen, black, totally in the state of decomposi-
tion." This sight stoked the murderous frenzy of some of the Versaillais
troops, angry that many prisoners had not been immediately gunned
down. A priest accompanying the convoy tried to calm them, telling
them that they should forgive their enemies. Such advice fell on deaf
ears. The good priest was fortunately able to convince the soldiers not
to chase and kill a man who had refused to bow his head as the wagons
filled with corpses passed by.[57]

By Sunday, the fighting was almost over. The Communards held
only a small area in the Eleventh Arrondissement south of Père Lachaise
Cemetery, where the Versaillais were still killing prisoners they had first
incarcerated in Mazas and La Roquette prisons. The struggle continued
briefly at the bottom of the rue de Belleville. Early in the morning,
Varlin and Ferré were among those leading a desperate column in an
attack on Versaillais forces near the place du Château d'Eau. They were
soon running for their lives. The Versaillais had taken all of Belleville,
the last Communard stronghold, by II A.M. Goncourt went up to Belleville to view the *quartiers* of the conquered enemy: "Empty streets.

People drinking in cabarets with faces of ugly silence. The appearance of a vanquished but unsubjugated district."[58]

Hearing that 2,000 Communards had just surrendered in Belleville, Hans hurried to catch a glimpse of them. That most of the Communard prisoners there appeared to be deserters from the French army accentuated the anger of the Versaillais forces. "So, here are the heroes of March 18!" they shouted. "Ah, scoundrels, I guess you won't be turning upside down your rifles now!" Vengeurs de Paris, a few sailors, and Parisian Mobile Guards were among the glum group of young men under heavy guard. Prisoners were herded inside a church; others began the long, painful, humiliating trek to Versailles, fortunate, for the moment, to have survived.

Hans and the other Versaillais soldiers expected no welcome in Belleville, but the bourgeois there greeted them with "energetic" excuses for their neighborhood—protesting that the radicals of Charonne, the faubourg du Temple, and adjoining Ménilmontant had given Belleville its undeserved reputation. Some shopkeepers seemed particularly pleased with the outcome; during the last days they had confronted increasing Communard requisitions, including for the civilian clothes some *fédéré* fighters needed to don quickly after tossing away their compromising uniforms. Shoes posed a major problem for the Communards as these were far less available than basic clothing, and combat boots (*godillots*) provided by the Commune were a dead giveaway ("Okay, *les godillots*, to the wall!" was an oft-heard command). Yet Hans and the others met with a welcome in the neighboring *quartiers* that was anything but warm: "Written all over the men was utter hatred, constrained only by fear. Women had red eyes; more than one of these awful women gave us a look of burning, concentrated rage." Their hatred was not always constrained, however; isolated attacks on Versaillais sentinels, soldiers, and guards did occur.

SCATTERED GROUPS OF COMMUNARDS continued to fight back on Sunday morning. The Versaillais took the remainder of the boulevard Voltaire and crushed the last resistance in Belleville, "the revolutionary den" in the eyes of the middle-classes. Soldiers executed fifty Communards at one barricade on the rue Voltaire and amused themselves by scrawling "Murderer," "Thief," or "a Drunk" near the bodies. Near the Gare d'Orléans along the Seine, where two Versaillais had been shot in the final hours of the Commune, Julien Poirier and his company came upon a woman with a chassepot and a sword standing on a stump of wood and killed her.[59]

That morning, May 28, Louise Michel could sense "the raging band of wolves approaching." All that remained of the Commune was a stretch of Paris from the rue du faubourg du Temple to the boulevard de Belleville. Soon, at the rue Ramponneau at the corner of the rue Tourtille, a single man defended the last Communard barricade until he had fired his last remaining bullet.[60]

VERSAILLAIS KILLED Eugène Varlin that day after the fighting had ended. He was seated at a café on the rue Lafayette when a priest denounced him to a Versaillais officer. Ordered shot, Varlin was battered by a hostile crowd and beaten with rifle butts by soldiers until, according to one witness, "his face was smashed to jelly, one eye out of the socket." Dragged to the wall of the garden on the rue des Rosiers where Generals Claude Lecomte and Clément Thomas had died on March 18, he was shot as he tried to shout, "Long live the Commune!" Forty-two men, three women, and four children, forced to kneel in repentance for the shooting of the generals, met their ends there after Varlin.[61]

Communards who tried to escape Belleville that Sunday had little chance of succeeding. The Versaillais held the rest of Paris, and those attempting to flee the city ran into the Prussian army. German troops had expanded their cordon around northern Paris, preventing Communards from getting out. They escorted several hundred *fédérés* to the fortress of Vincennes, thinking it held by government forces. Realizing their mistake, they instead turned them over to the Versaillais at Montreuil, where many were executed.[62]

Convoys of prisoners continued to march to Versailles, some dying on the journey. When a young woman collapsed, unable to go on, a soldier cut her stomach open with his bayonet. He then threw her into a store, shouting, "Go die in there!" In another convoy, an officer saw a woman carrying a very sick child; he took it from her, but his charge died along the way. When a pregnant woman, a prisoner from Montmartre, managed to free herself from the cords that bound her, a soldier supposedly cut her down with his sword.[63]

Troops forced prisoners to kneel as they passed the Church of Saint-Augustin "in expiation for their crimes"; others captives had to do the same at the Chapel of Expiation of Louis XVI, which the Commune had planned to level. Prisoners died along the way because, in addition to experiencing heat, fatigue, and fear, many had not eaten in well over two days. W. Gibson, a British Protestant minister who generally found the Communards distasteful, related that "one of our local preachers saw a man coolly [stabbed] to death by a soldier, and then lifted up on the point of the bayonet for the inspection of the lookers on. No sympathy was evinced for the poor old prisoner, and the two ladies suggested that the soldier should 'chop the rat's head off.'"[64]

AS THE WORLD OF THE COMMUNE collapsed, Maxime Vuillaume hoped to escape with his life. Replacing his National Guard kepi with a round little hat, the journalist avoided *brassards* (men wearing the armbands reflecting allegiance to Versailles) who were turning two men over to a platoon of soldiers. At the place de la Sorbonne, very different clients from a few days earlier filled the Café d'Harcourt. Vuillaume thought of a possible place of refuge, however temporary: Benjamin Flotte's apartment in the rue Saint-Séverin, where a day earlier he had taken the Archbishop Georges Darboy's letters. Vuillaume headed there, avoiding looking at the bodies of three women, half covered with straw.

With Versaillais troops now virtually everywhere on May 24, Vuillaume had to go to great lengths to avoid arrest in the Latin Quarter. He encountered a medical student friend who provided him with a Red Cross armband, which, according to the Geneva Convention of 1864, ensured his protection, at least in principle. As they walked up the rue Tournon to the rue de Vaugirard, several soldiers asked them where they were going, then took them to the prevotal court in the Senate. Vuillaume could hear the volleys of a firing squad beyond some trees. An officer asked about his armband. Vuillaume replied that it represented protection by the International Geneva Convention. "The International! The International!" came the furious retort. "So then, you are of the International! Oh, God damn it!" Then Vuillaume made a potentially fatal gaffe: he called a gendarme "citizen."

Vuillaume frantically considered what alias to give, coming up with "a really ordinary name: Langlois," that of a student he knew. He then tried to think of exactly what his interrogators would find in his pockets. Alas, he carried a watch on which he had engraved "Long live the Commune!" He managed to let it drop behind a bench without the two gendarmes noticing. At noon, the military judge passed by the prisoners, a cigar dangling from lips: "Hats off, miserable scum!" Vuillaume silently went over the names of medical school professors so he could recite them if asked. He listened to interrogations, which almost always ended with one of two death sentences: "To the line" (i.e., in the line to go up against the wall) or "Take him to the brigade!" A bit later, a priest, summoned to give consolation to those about to die, walked in, old, thin, wearing a thin smile, the Legion of Honor attached to his cassock.

The officer presiding over the court-martial returned from his meal. The interrogations went on. When Vuillaume's turn came, the officer asked what he had done during the insurrection. He had done nothing for the Commune, Vuillaume replied. Despite his claim to be a doctor helping the wounded, the sentence was unavoidable. He admitted to helping wounded on both sides (even if this was not true, he had borrowed the Red Cross insignia): "Take him to the line." Soldiers waited until six condemned were ready to go, bound together with ropes, and took them into the Luxembourg Gardens for execution. As Vuillaume waited, a soldier shouted something about "your *Père Duchêne*," the radical newspaper, but the target was another man. But what difference did it make now?

A sergeant guarding the condemned asked Vuillaume what he did in life and, seeing the Red Cross insignia, concluded that he was a medical student. Taking pity on him, since he too was a medical student, the sergeant pushed him back toward the end of the line—so that Vuillaume might live an hour or so longer—and left to find the chief medical officer to plead the case of his "colleague." The young guard returned an hour later, a seeming eternity given the murderous sound of more volleys, to say that he could not find the medical officer. But he had an idea. He told Vuillaume to *tutoyer* him (to address him familiarly)—they would be cousins. The sergeant left again, then returned to tell him to follow him—and quickly. Incredibly enough, with the sergeant were the two Versaillais who had arrested Vuillaume. They took him into the Café l'Enseigne de la Comète at the corner of the rue Servandoni. Over a glass of wine, the sergeant-savior gave Vuillaume a new name and, after dining near Odéon, took him to the apartment of a female friend, who, although quite terrified, took him in. Three days later, on Saturday, the sergeant returned, describing the latest rounds of executions in detail. He advised Vuillaume to find a new place to hide, warning that if he was taken prisoner again, the sergeant could nothing do to save him.

Hiding in an apartment on the rue Richelieu, across from the fountain of Molière, Maxime Vuillaume tried to think of a way to get out of Paris. For that, he needed a passport. A friend from school on whom he hoped to rely refused to help. Versaillais newspapers had carried stories reporting him already under arrest. A search of the building seemed inevitable. He considered one move, and then another. By luck he got out of Paris on a train without being stopped. In a village, a rural guard became suspicious of Vuillaume, who had clearly arrived from the capital. "Parisian" probably meant "fleeing Communard." But the mayor was sympathetic, urging Vuillaume to leave immediately, which he did. When he and a friend reached Troyes and boarded a train, police asked for all passengers' passports. They had none. Vuillaume was arrested once again but managed to slip away, thanks to an unobservant gendarme, and ultimately reached sanctuary in Geneva.[65]

WITH THE COMMUNE completely crushed, one needed a place to hide to survive in Paris with Versaillais line troops, gendarmes, police, and police spies now virtually everywhere, above all, in "suspect" neighborhoods. Reclus knew "a liberal bourgeois," a friend of his family for years, and an "excellent man, besides." On Tuesday, May 30, he went to ask this man for help and was refused. The old family friend told him that, in his view, other than the Friends of Order, there were now only three types of people: those who should be shot; those who should be sent to Cayenne, the infamous "dry guillotine," where death was certain but came slowly and painfully; and those who should be sent to Nouka-Hiva in the South Seas, which was, if anything, even worse. Élie noted bitterly that a fourth category might be added—those on the run: "Wandering in the street, going here, going there, trying not to give ourselves away and keeping police spies and those wearing tricolor armbands, or young zealous officers taking me for a rabid dog." This was real terror.

The next day, a republican family offered lodging. Élie wisely assumed another name. But he believed that now his best chance was to move from *quartier* to *quartier*, going quietly into neighborhoods already thoroughly searched for Communards and thereby "slipping through the mesh of the net." He eventually managed to escape Paris, reaching Zurich.[66]

In Versailles, Henri Vignon, who had remained in the old capital of the Bourbon monarchy during most of the Commune, watched convoy after convoy of prisoners arrive from the capital. Each time one or two tried to escape, they were gunned down. Armed with a pass from Versailles, Henri went into Paris and reported to his mother that their building had escaped harm. When Henri saw Paris burning, he added, "Certainly death is not too much for these *misérables*."[67] Such a view became prevalent among the *honnêtes gens*. Communards could expect no sympathy from people whose hatred of them was unrestrained.

CHAPTER 10

PRISONERS OF VERSAILLES

V ERSAILLAIS REPRISALS CONTINUED long after the last Communard defenses fell. Adolphe Thiers's army had taken thousands of
prisoners during the long Bloody Week; most were marched to Versailles for court-martial. The question now was what fate awaited those
who had survived the reprisals. Indeed, Versaillais forces gunned down
at least 1,900 people on Sunday alone.

An Englishman present would never forget "the angry ring of the
volleys of execution; the strings of men and women hurried off to their
doom; the curses of an infuriated populace; the brutal violence of an
exasperated soldiery." The anxious visitor saw a man supposedly caught
with combustible items in his pockets stumbling ahead of soldiers with
bayonets they had just used to stab him. A small crowd of Parisians
followed, hoping to seeing him shot, which they "loudly" demanded.
The Englishman had every reason to believe that "the bitterness of the
belligerents against each other is of a far more intense and sanguinary
kind than that which ordinarily exists between combatants."

The prisoners marched, tied together by rope, with a "hang-dog
look." Among them was a thin person in a National Guard uniform,
"long, fair hair floating over the shoulders, a bright blue eye, and a
handsome, bold, young face that seemed to know neither shame nor
fear." A crowd "howled and hooted." When the women in the crowd
realized that the youthful national guardsman was female, they shouted
abuse. Their target glared "right and left with heightened colour and
flashing eyes, in marked contrast to the cowardly crew that followed
her." At a bridge not far from the place Vendôme, where thirteen
women "caught in the act of spreading petroleum" had supposedly
been killed, the Englishman came upon twenty-four insurgent corpses,

"laid out in a row, waiting to be buried under the neighboring paving stones," with the "gaunt shell" of the Tuileries looming above.[1]

The Englishman reflected that "the rebels" had neither asked for nor given quarter. They had "made up their minds that death, whether as combatants or as prisoners, is their only alternative, and men and women seem to be lashed up to a frenzy which has converted them into a set of wild beasts caught in a trap." This, in his view, "render[ed] their extermination a necessity."

The Englishman made his way to the neighborhoods between the Père Lachaise Cemetery and Montmartre. In such places "it was evident from the looks and tone of the inhabitants . . . that their sympathies were strongly with the Commune. They muttered gloomily and savagely to each other, scarcely daring to raise their suspicious glances from the ground, for they knew not which of their neighbors might have denounced them." Indeed, it saddened him to see the children in the groups of prisoners being taken away. He managed to obtain access to the court-martial, where he found a dozen prisoners, all male, "cowering at one end of the corridor . . . waiting to know their fate." Prisoners were marched down from Buttes-Chaumont, where they had been held for two days without food. The Englishman was not exactly sympathetic. They were so common: "A more villainous collection of faces I never beheld. There were many women, among them some in men's clothes, some dressed as *cantinières* or *ambulancières*, and very young boys and old men."

As executions proceeded, the Englishman changed his tune: "It sounds like trifling for M. Thiers to be denouncing the Insurgents for having shot a captive officer 'without respect for the laws of war.' The laws of war! They are mild and Christian compared with the inhuman laws of revenge under which the Versailles troops have been shooting, bayoneting, ripping up prisoners, women and children, during the last six days. . . . So far as we can recollect there has been nothing like it in history."[2]

Up in Ménilmontant, stacks of guns stood here and there, along with piles of hastily abandoned National Guard pants and coats. Soldiers and residents did not speak to each other. The foreigner had been able to obtain a military pass that allowed him to move about as he pleased, and when people from the neighborhood saw this, they made him and his companions feel "that we were their enemies." In Belleville in particular, it was easy to understand "the scowling looks and stifled curses of the men and women glaring from doorways and windows at the execution of a friend before their eyes."

When night came, Paris fell dark, in part due to the lack of gas. In the poorer neighborhoods, people stayed at home for fear of being arrested because of how they looked. Several Versaillais roughed up the Englishman after someone claimed that he had shot at someone else. Such a vague denunciation could cost him his life, but his upper-class dress, at a time when clothes told much, and his British accent, impossible to hide, undoubtedly saved him. Back in central Paris, the stench of countless rotting bodies buried beneath the ruins drove him from the rue Royale.[3]

John Leighton went out to look at Paris on Sunday and came upon "corpses in the streets, corpses within the houses, corpses everywhere!" He believed those who had been killed were "terribly guilty . . . [and] horrible criminals, those women who poured brandy into the glasses and petroleum on the houses!" But "were those that were shot all guilty? Then the sight of these executions, however merited, was cruelly painful. The innocent shuddered at the doom of justice. . . . An unsupportable uneasiness oppresses us."[4]

The streets and gutters ran red with blood. Soldiers forced residents to throw chlorine on corpses, making the streets appear covered with snow. Thousands of bodies had already been tossed into mass graves, taken to the Carrières (Quarries) de l'Amérique, or buried in the catacombs or beyond the ramparts. The bodies that remained may have been left there intentionally, at Thiers's orders, to show ordinary people the cost of their defiance.

Count Arthur de Grandeffe, who had served in the Volunteers of the Seine, passed a Communard medical facility that day. Despite his hatred of the Commune, he asked if a priest could be found to give last rights to two dying men; he was told that in the neighborhood "there was little contact with those people." But he insisted, and a priest was indeed located. As he approached the two men, one gave the priest "the look of a wounded viper still looking for a way to bite you." Both had in their eyes "the seeds of hell." Grandeffe had limited sympathy for the dying Communards and concluded that he could lay what he had seen at the doors of "modern education." He believed that the time had come to enlighten Parisians about the dangers ahead if they rose up again. Summary executions, Grandeffe decided, were a good start.[5]

Even Edmond de Goncourt was unprepared for what he saw. Nearing Châtelet, he suddenly saw "the crowd head over heels in flight like a mob being charged on a day of a riot. Horsemen appear, threatening, swords in hand, rearing up their horses and forcing the promenaders from the street to the sidewalks." The soldiers pushed along a bearded man, his forehead bound by a handkerchief. Two other soldiers practically carried another prisoner in a state of collapse. This man had "a special pallor and a vague look which remains in my memory. I hear a woman shout as she takes herself off: 'How sorry I am I came this far!' Next to me a placid bourgeois is counting: 'One, two, three.' . . . There were twenty six. Their armed escort marches them rapidly into the Lobau Barracks, where the gate closes after them with a strange violence and precipitation."

Goncourt still did not understand but felt "an indefinable anxiety. My bourgeois companion, who had just been counting them, then says to a neighbor: 'It won't be long, you'll soon hear the first volley.' 'What volley?' 'Why, they're going to shoot them!'" Immediately they heard a violent explosion within the closed gates and walls, followed by "a fusillade having something of the mechanical regularity of a machine gun. There is a first, a second, a third, a fourth, a fifth murderous *rrarra*—then a long interval—and then a sixth, and still two more volleys, one right after the other."

The shooting seemed to go on forever. When it finally stopped, "everybody feels relieved and is beginning to breathe when there is a shattering sound which makes the sprung door of the barracks move on its hinges; then another; then finally the last." These were the coups de grâce to finish off those who were still alive. "At that moment, like a band of drunken men, the execution squad comes out of the door with blood on the end of some of their bayonets. And while two closed vans go into the courtyard, a priest slips out, and for a long time you see his thin back, his umbrella, his legs walking unsteadily along the outer wall of the barracks."[6]

PARIS NOW CAME UNDER MILITARY RULE and was divided into four sections commanded by Joseph Vinoy, Ernest de Cissey, Paul de Ladmirault, and Félix Douay. Searches of houses, often sparked by denunciations, continued unabated. As journalist Marc-André Gromier put it, "each denunciation was a decree of death." The red flags were gone. The tricolor flag had become the "flag of massacre." On Monday, the fort of Vincennes surrendered, Prussian troops having isolated it

The Fate of the Communards
(CORBIS)

from Paris. Versaillais forces promised to spare the lives of Communard fighters there, then shot nine officers, tossing their bodies into the giant moat.[7]

The convoys of prisoners marching to Versailles grew longer. Gromier was arrested at 5 A.M. on Sunday and thrown into the basement of a barracks on the rue du faubourg Poissonnière, not far from his home. As for so many others, the trip there was brutal. Angry shouts and rocks greeted the captured, and "a dog . . . dressed as a prostitute, tried to strike me with the end of her umbrella." When several onlookers from his *quartier* saluted him, others jumped them, fists flying. A soldier took care to crush Gromier's hat with his rifle. In the barracks, five hundred men, women, and children waited, some dead, others dying, including a man missing both legs. He saw a boy of about fifteen tied by rope to window bars. A Versaillais asked Gromier if he knew the boy. Before he could answer, the boy cried out that he did not know him, for he lived in the *quartier* of Cligancourt. Soldiers stabbed the boy repeatedly with bayonets.

Gromier and a convoy of twenty-six other prisoners then marched under heavy guard to the parc Monceau, starving and thirsty. Gromier saw a former surgeon from his National Guard battalion, now resplendent in a tricolored armband. They next trekked to Versailles. At the pont Saint-Cloud, a women fell and was shot. Three older men said they could go no further and were hit with rifles, then pushed off to the side and executed. Another five men and a woman were killed along the way. Gromier had no idea why. In Versailles, two little girls, three women, and an old man were taken from the convoy. They too were probably shot. Finally, after a forced march of many hours, Gromier and the others reached Satory, a Versaillais prison on the plateau of the same name, where they saw a machine gun prepped and ready. They could see two huge ditches—one full of bodies, the other used as a latrine. Troops occasionally fired at groups of prisoners. Not far away, they heard "an intermittent fusillade. Those who protested in any way: shot. Those who demanded to be able to go to the bathroom: shot. Those who a fever had made crazy: shot." On June 6 and 7, seven of twenty-seven of Gromier's group perished. Each morning, bodies were taken away. Guards shot some prisoners who displeased them with their responses to being asked their names or who refused at first to give up personal items, fearing, with reason, that they would be stolen. One evening, Gromier was taken to an improvised court-martial in Versailles and sentenced to six months in prison—but at least was alive.[8]

Another young Englishman was very lucky to escape the Versaillais rampage. In the wrong place at the wrong time, he found himself taken prisoner in a roundup. From some direction came the sound of shooting, "and then a whisper went around, 'They're going to shoot us all!'" He would never forget "the agonized look on the faces of some. . . . It was a complete index of what was passing in their minds. To die thus, and leave wife, children, parents, brothers, or sister, without one word of farewell . . . is fearful. . . . Soon it will be over. A rifle shot and that's it!" A boy of fifteen had with him documents that he said would prove his innocence. A Versaillais officer hit him: "Shut-up, bastard!" In contrast, a boy of about nine years "never uttered a word of complaint." He took the young Englishman's hand, "and from that time till the close of that terrible day we marched hand in hand, he never relaxing his grasp except when absolutely necessary. Meanwhile, the executions went on." The convoy marched to the Church of the Madeleine and down the rue Royale to the place de la Concorde, then up the Champs-Élysées to the Arc de Triomphe. The sun beat down, and the captives received nothing to eat or drink.[9]

General Gaston Galliffet showed up, heaping abuse on the prisoners. He ordered, "Step out of that line, you old bastards! And you . . . you're wounded! Well, we will take care of you!" leaving no doubt about what would happen next. A young man waved an American passport: "Shut up, we have more than enough foreigners and rabble here. We have to get rid of them."[10]

Some old men and wounded prisoners were shot, and more volleys in the distance signaled that men in that convoy had fallen and could not go on. The Englishman and the others reached Versailles and then Satory at 8 P.M. There, elegantly dressed crowds called for their execution: "Ah ha! We have some of those petrol bombs that you know so well reserved for you. There are [also] machine guns, miserable scoundrels [*sacrés coquins*]." The young foreigner got lucky and was finally released. What he had seen changed his view of the Communards, for whom he now felt sympathy.[11]

About 35,000 to 40,000 prisoners made the awful trek from Paris—most from eastern districts—to Versailles. Prisoners who refused to move any further or who could not because of wounds, infirmity, or age were gunned down. In one incident, a prisoner sat down, unable to go on. Soldiers prodded him with bayonets, then placed him on a horse, from which he immediately fell. The troops then attached him to the horse's tail and dragged him until he lost consciousness from loss of blood. The soldiers showed a little mercy: instead of simply shooting him, they tossed him onto a wagon for the remainder of the journey.[12] The convoy included many women and no small number of children—most between twelve and sixteen but some even younger. A Versaillais crowd assailed the editor of the *Journal des Débats* for daring to express sympathy for the prisoners chained together in the sun. Troops had to rescue him.[13]

Most of the "voyagers" to Satory were not combatants at all—many of those had already perished. Instead, they were Parisians who happened to be in the wrong place at the wrong time, rounded up by Versaillais troops. Some women carried their children in their arms or on their shoulders as they walked; others had their arms so tightly tied that they bled, escorted by "gendarmes ready become hangmen." In Camille Pelletan's opinion, the worst abuses along the way occurred in the faubourg Saint-Honoré, where "the aristocratic hangers-on came down into the streets to insult, threaten, and mistreat prisoners." In some other neighborhoods, observers were more respectful, some making the sign of the cross as the prisoners passed. This was not the case on the rue de la Chaussée d'Antin, where a furious elderly woman threw herself at a convoy of prisoners, flailing away at them with her umbrella.[14]

In Versailles, *tout Paris* awaited the arrival of prisoners, preparing for the spectacle as if anticipating the start of a horse race. Officers told one convoy to stop so the fancy folks could have a good look at them. One well-dressed woman, carrying a prayer book, demanded that a young *cantinière* salute God. When she refused, the woman hit her, breaking a tooth. Here was Christian charity at work in Versailles.[15]

A journalist for *Figaro*, a pro-Thiers newspaper, focused on the "disrespect" for hostile onlookers shown by several prisoners among the "hideous troops" heading to an uncertain future. A *cantinière* waved what was left of her bloody hand, having lost several fingers in the fighting, in the direction of those heaping insults on her and the others. Fashionable women struck at Communards with their parasols, shouting for their execution. Guards forced prisoners in at least one convoy to doff any caps they might be wearing: "Let's go! Rabble! Hats off before *les honnêtes gens!*"[16]

Eager upper-class people peppered soldiers who had returned from Paris with questions. One Versaillais line soldier bragged that he had killed a woman. Another one-upped him: "Me, I killed a child incendiary with my bayonet." A "respectable" lady, her Mass missal in her hands, interrupted to ask, "Really, my friend?" She reached into her purse and gave him money. Some soldiers reportedly sold as souvenirs objects taken from the bodies of Communards.[17]

Reaching Versailles, the women went to the prison of Chantiers, the men to the hellhole of Satory, where 3,000 to 4,000 prisoners were virtually piled one on top of another, with barely enough room to turn around or lie down. Disease, infection, and gangrene took hold while guards pointed their rifles at the prisoners, threatening to shoot anyone for any act of defiance. Some soldiers may have amused themselves by doing just that. Desperately thirsty, prisoners drank rainwater, sometimes tinted red with the blood of the wounded and the dead. Life—and death—at the Chantiers was almost as bad. Prisoners slept on straw or on the bare ground, sharing space with lice. Clothing and food brought by relatives aware of their family members' location remained stacked up outside, generally never reaching the women. Some prisoners held temporarily in the Orangerie amused themselves by taking care of plants, looking back at curious onlookers who came to gape at them from beyond the guards.[18]

Louise Michel was in one of the Versailles prisoner camps. Soldiers told her that she would be shot. She remembered, "Above us the lights of the fires [in the distance in Paris] floated like red crepe. And always we could hear the cannon. . . . In the middle of the night the soldiers would call out groups of prisoners, who got up from the mud to follow the soldier's lantern that led their way. They'd be given a pick and shovel to dig their own graves, and then they'd be shot. The echoes of volleys shattered the silence of the night." Michel was "insolent" to the soldiers and did not know why she was not shot. Millions of lice "made little silver nets as they meandered about, going to their nests that resembles anthills. They were enormous." Prisoners had the impression that they could actually hear the "noise of their swarming."[19]

As more and more prisoners arrived in Versailles, *les honnêtes gens* found new ways of condemning the defeated Communards. The claim that the riffraff from Paris were drunks emerged in Versaillais discourse, with references to the dependence of "drunken commoners" on absinthe, which was already ravaging the French population. Communards often received from their enemies the designation *crapule*, a term of extreme denigration derived from the Latin word for drunkenness.[20]

Versaillais lore had insurgents storming into a restaurant on the boulevard Saint-Martin, plunging into fine wines and liqueurs found in the cellar. When they had had their fill, the intruders announced that they planned to shoot "the brave soldiers" attacking Paris. A loyal anti-Communard stepped forward and slapped "one of those bastards," or so went the story. The Communards then pillaged the house, killing the *honnêtes gens* who opposed "their orgies" and set fire to the establishment. When a panicked woman managed to extract her daughter from the flames, the Communards pushed both back in, and they burned to death. That this never occurred mattered little to the *honnêtes gens*. Ironically, some of the rampaging Versaillais line soldiers may have been drunk, the effects of alcohol compounded by sun and fatigue.[21]

AS THOUSANDS OF PRISONERS awaited their fate in Versailles, "liberated" Paris suffered "the sickness of denunciations." Of all the horrendous statistics surrounding Bloody Week, among the most chilling is that, between May 22 and June 13, the prefecture of police received 379,823 denunciations accusing others of serving the Commune. Of these, only 5 percent were actually signed. Of course, this number is so astonishing because those who denounced neighbors knew very well that if the Versailles authorities took them seriously and the accusation was grave—simply being in favor of the Commune was a significant offense—execution could follow. To be sure, some were attempting to settle personal debts or conflicts. Others may have hoped to receive the rumored five hundred francs for turning in a Communard. Indeed, some denunciations did lead to executions; for instance, the marquis de Forbin-Janson denounced some of his neighbors and tenants, one of whom was shot. One Parisian, acquitted by a court-martial, had been denounced seventeen times.[22]

On June 1, two men, one wounded, turned up at the door of the house next door to Pastor Eugène Bersier and Marie Holland. Only the domestic was at home. They asked to be taken in, claiming to know the nephew of the owner. The woman let them inside and provided a bed for the wounded man. She then denounced them to the police. Soldiers arrived to take them away, one on a stretcher, the other walking head down, very pale. Marie Holland was sickened. The pastor's wife received a visit from a certain M. Bockairy, who told her that she would be happy to learn that a Communard officer had been shot and that, of his men, "not one escaped." The smug bourgeois seemed to her for a moment even more odious than the Communards she despised.[23]

With the return of the old civil police, police spies were everywhere, proudly sporting tricolor armbands. Jacques Durant, a fifty-three-year-old shoemaker elected to the Commune from the Second Arrondissement, was denounced and hauled off to the *mairie*. After an interrogation lasting not more than two minutes, he was shot in a courtyard adjoining the Church of the Petits-Pères. Édouard Moreau, who had opposed burning the Grenier d'Abondance, was arrested after being denounced while hiding near the rue Saint-Antoine. At Châtelet, Louis Vabre, the provost marshal, asked him if he was indeed M. Édouard Moreau, member of the Commune. Moreau replied, "No, of the Central Committee [of the National Guard]." The response came immediately: "It's the same thing!" He was taken to Caserne Lobau and shot with another batch of victims.[24]

The denunciations primarily targeted ordinary people, reflecting the Versaillais assumption that social class adequately marked involvement in the Commune. General Louis Valentin, serving Thiers as prefect of police, said, "The simple fact of having stayed in Paris under the Commune is a crime. Everyone there is to blame, and if I had my way everyone would be punished."[25] Many working-class Parisians had indeed supported the Commune, but even those who had not were at risk. Those who remained in Paris during the Commune were overwhelmingly working-class, unable to get out and with nowhere to go.

Prisoners identified as foreigners were singled out for particularly vociferous contempt, primarily because foreigners who had remained in Paris during the Commune were assumed to be part of the International. One rumor had 10,000 Poles among the Communards. Denis Arthur Bingham noted that "virtuous Parisians claimed that the insurrection was the work of foreigners," such as Italians and Poles. The conservative historian Hippolyte Taine subscribed to this belief, insisting that half of the 100,000 insurgents were not French. The literary critic Paul de Saint-Victor denounced "Polish forgers, 'gallant' Garibaldians [followers of the nationalist Italian revolutionary Giuseppe Garibaldi], mercenary Slavic soldiers, Prussian agents, Yankee buccaneers stampeding in from one of their battalions. . . . Paris has become the sewer collecting the dregs and scum of two worlds." Some of the Poles had fought courageously but futilely against Russian rule in Congress Poland in 1863. For her part, Louise Lacroix insisted, "To love France, one has to be French."[26]

Versaillais killed two Poles after shots rang out from a building on the rue de Tournon. They were arrested and accused of "spread[ing] terror in the entire quartier of Luxembourg" during the Commune. After their execution, Count Czartoryski, president of the Polish Committee, complained; the "incendiary tools" suspected by the Versaillais were simply lights for the Polish library on that street. One of the men had fought for the Commune, but the other, from Lithuania, had not—he ran the library and lived in the house. In any case, the role played by General Jaroslaw Dombrowski in the Communard resistance helped fuel anger among Versaillais against Poles. One officer, on hearing that prisoners brought before him were Polish, said, "Well, they're Polish. That's enough right there."[27]

Contemporaries were virtually unanimous that the Communards about to be shot accepted their fate with heads held high. A Belgian journalist quoted soldiers who had served on execution squads. One related that he had killed "forty of this rabble" in Passy. They all died "as soldiers," proudly, with arms folded across their chests. Some even opened their uniforms and shouted, "Go ahead and fire! We are not afraid of death."[28]

A Versailles official went to have a look for himself. He saw prisoners under escort and, counting twenty-eight of them, recognized men with whom he had fought during the Prussian siege. Almost all of them were workers. Their faces "betrayed neither despair, nor despondence, nor emotion. . . . They knew where they were being taken." The Versaillais had not taken more than four steps walking away when he heard the execution squad's volley. The twenty-eight "insurgents" fell. What he heard made him dizzy, but then came the series of individual shots that followed, the coups de grâce. He ran in the other direction, but "around me, the crowd seemed impassible." Parisians were now used to this.

Even if the Communards died "as soldiers," they were certainly not afforded the rights owed to combatants and even prisoners according to international conventions. The Communard Prosper-Olivier Lissaga-ray came across young sailors in a bar on the place Voltaire. He asked, rather coyly, if there had been many dead among the "enemy." "Ah," one replied, "we were given orders by the general to take no prisoners." Officers pressed young soldiers from the provinces to kill anyone who had fought for the Commune. Versaillais soldiers with rural origins who might have resisted such an order had been inundated with propa-ganda claiming that Parisians were evil-doers, scoundrels, liars, thieves, and degenerates who had turned their back on the Church.

Little more than two months earlier, line troops captured by in-surgents on Montmartre had received good treatment. Now, Versail-lais gunned down thousands of Communard prisoners. They shot a few men who had the misfortune of somewhat resembling a prom-inent figure from the Commune. Such was the case of a shoemaker called Constant who lived in the bourgeois *quartier* of Gros-Caillou in the Seventh Arrondissement and resembled Alfred-Édouard Bil-lioray, a member of the Commune. A certain Martin, taken to be Jules Vallès, was killed near Saint-Germain l'Auxerrois, while a crowd roared its approval.[29]

The Versaillais discourse openly encouraged the policy of killing Communards, comparing the insurgents and their supporters with brigands or wild animals, thereby dehumanizing them and justifying mass executions. Watching the lugubrious procession of prisoners on their way to Versailles, Augustine Blanchecotte castigated "these wild beasts, savage, raging. . . . These are monsters who should be classified by zoologists. These are not men." According to *Figaro,* "One cannot have any illusions. More than 50,000 insurgents remain in Paris. . . . What is a republican? A wild animal."[30]

Théophile Gautier agreed: "In all the great cities there are lion pits, caverns closed with thick bars where all the wild beasts, smelly animals, venomous snakes and all the perverted resisters whom civilization could not tame are to be found; those who love blood and adore fire as one does holiday fireworks, all those delighted by theft, those for whom attacks on decency represent love, all those who are monsters to the core, all those with deformities of the soul, a filthy population, unknown to this day, who swarm ominously in the depths of underground darkness." One day, he went on, a guard loses the keys to the zoo, "and the ferocious animals scatter throughout the terrified city with terrifying savage shrieks. Their cages now open, the hyenas of 1793 and the gorillas of the Commune rush out."[31]

Female Communard prisoners resembled to Gautier "the bearded and mustached sorcerers of Shakespeare, a hideous variety of hermaphrodite, formed by ugliness drawn from both sexes." He mocked "the horrible, inextinguishable, burning thirst of these scoundrels, infected by alcohol, combat, their journey, intense heat, the fever of intense situations and the torment of their coming death . . . crying out with husky and hoarse voices now lubricated only by saliva: Water! Water! Water!"[32]

Henri Opper de Blowitz, a German journalist who after becoming naturalized worked for Thiers, visited a Versailles prison during the Commune. He became obsessed with a young woman he observed from a safe distance beyond a fence, describing what he saw with animal imagery, as if he had returned from a zoo. She was "one of the most beautiful women" he had ever beheld. "Her long black tresses fell over her bare shoulders, and as she had torn her dress to shreds, not to wear the clothes of the 'accursed Versaillaise,' one could see her naked body through the rents. She was tall and graceful, and on the approach of visitors she reared her head proudly, like a horse about to neigh. . . . Her bright eyes glisten[ed]; a blush tint took over her face. She compressed her lips, ground her teeth, and burst into a shrill, defiant, vindictive laugh when she recognized the officer of the prison who accompanied us." In the final hours of the Commune, the young woman had apparently fought alongside her lover. When he died, or so the story went, she attacked a Versaillais officer and "furiously stabbed him, plunging her weapon again and again into her victim. Before she could be removed from his body, she had cut, bitten and torn it with all the fury of a hyena." The young woman arrived in Versailles covered with blood and "had to be bound and gagged before she would allow the blood to be washed off. Hideous!"[33]

Maxime du Camp, writer and friend of Gustave Flaubert, nuanced this biological discourse, blending analogies to human disease and animals. The Commune, he explained, had arisen out of "furious envy and social epilepsy." It reflected conditions that had always existed, "a Manichean struggle between Good and Evil, civilization and barbarism, order against anarchy, and intelligence opposed to stupidity . . . and finally the very idea of the elite of society against the jumble of all that is evil, perverse, and bestial."

Women were particularly suspect in these accounts. *Le Gaulois* quoted a doctor, who insisted that the female incendiaries acted "under the epidemic influence of the incendiary mania. . . . Their brain is weaker and their sensibility more lively. They also are one hundred times more dangerous, and they have caused without any doubt much more evil." Some accounts emphasized that "female incendiaries," as well as other female insurgents, wore men's clothing, including parts of National Guard uniforms. Such descriptions aimed to point out how unnatural and thus subversive these women were.[34]

A bourgeois who visited the Chantiers prison distinguished between women who had "an honest and proper appearance" and others whose rags and wild hair indicated "their moral state and social position." Journalists and curious bourgeois obsessed over women's physical appearance, particularly when it came to unflattering characteristics.[35]

Louise Lacroix stared at female prisoners. Some "dressed modestly" were clearly workers, and some very young ones who had probably passed their childhoods in workshops or factories looked old before their time. In her view, these were not the women "who would be going out preaching insanities on the rights of women." At the head of this particular group strode "a large creature, about forty or forty-five years of age, with two large headbands." To the hostile onlooker, she seemed more masculine than feminine, with robust arms. Next to her was a small, pale, blonde woman, about eighteen to twenty years old, "slender, gracious," in a skirt of gray silk, who had to walk rapidly to keep up. On her right cheek, black gunpowder and strands of hair partially covered a touch of blood. Lacroix had certainly never before seen "women marching with such determination toward certain death." A tall brown-haired woman raised her arms above her head and shouted in a voice both calm and convincing, "They killed my man and I avenged him. I die content. Long live the Commune!"[36]

The widespread belief among the Versaillais that the Commune had in part been the work of "uppity" and "unnatural" women may help explain the brutal treatment some women faced after their arrest. Rapes were reported in the First, Eighth, and Ninth Arrondissements.

Georges Jeanneret saw women "treated almost like the poor Arabs of an insurgent tribe: after they had killed them, they stripped them, while they were still in their death throes, of part of their clothing. Sometimes they went event further, as at the foot of the faubourg Montmartre and in the place Vendôme, where women were left naked and defiled on the sidewalks." Versaillais soldiers ripped away the blouses of women and corpses to reveal their breasts to the amusement of hostile onlookers. In one instance, troops bayonetted a young woman about eighteen to twenty years of age, then removed all her clothes and "cynically toss[ed] her beautiful body, still throbbing, in the corner of the street, after having odiously insulted all of her charms."[37] Undressing served as the kind of humiliation some believed putting things back in their proper order required. The fury of upper-class onlookers, particularly women, toward women assumed to be female insurgents reflected a desire to point out the potential danger of women forgetting their place.

Versaillais newspapers shouted for more vengeance to rid the city of the Communard contagion. *Le Figaro* demanded a complete purge of Paris: "Never has such an opportunity presented itself to cure Paris of the moral gangrene which has eaten away at it for the last twenty years. . . . Today clemency would be completely crazy. . . . Let's go, *honnêtes gens!* Help us finish with the democratic and socialist vermin." Goncourt compared the repression to a therapeutic bleeding. *Le Bien Public* called for a "hunt for the Communards," and that was what it got. The *Journal des Débats* reasoned that the army had now "avenged its incalculable disasters [in the Franco-Prussian War] by a victory." *Figaro* saluted the "general enterprise of sweeping Paris clean." All the guilty "should be executed." Similar calls came from overseas. The *New York Herald* advised "no cessation of summary judgment and summary execution. . . . Root them out, destroy them utterly, M. Thiers, if you would save France. No mistaken humanity."[38]

The goal now was to protect and restore Paris so that it might again deserve the *honnêtes gens* who had once flourished there. "Honesty" became the word of the day. *La Patrie*, for one, made clear that if Paris "wants to conserve its privilege of being the rendezvous of the honest and fashionable *beau monde*, it owes it to itself and to its invited visitors a security that nothing can trouble. . . . Examples are indispensable, a fatal necessity, but a necessity." Marshal Patrice de MacMahon made the point that, now that Versailles had crushed the Commune, he could finally "address [himself] to the honest population of Paris," by which he meant the upper classes on whose behalf Versaillais forces were conducting the massacre.[39] Those who had supported the Commune had no illusions about Paris's future, knowing full well that Thiers, along with his army and government, would cleanse the city of any traces of the Commune or its ideals. When Henri Rochefort arrived in a convoy of prisoners in Versailles, a man "in a cinnamon colored frock-coat . . . waving a beautiful red umbrella, shouted at the top of his lungs: 'It's Rochefort! He must be skinned alive!'" Rochefort had to stifle a laugh; the man was indeed "the type of ferocious bourgeois such as Daumier painted for us." Jules Simon identified civilization with the power of the bourgeoisie: "One overturns aristocracy, which is a privilege. . . . One does not overturn the bourgeoisie, one attains it." Pierre Vésinier, a journalist and Communard who survived, wrote, "The victorious bourgeoisie showed neither pity nor mercy. It had sworn to annihilate the revolutionary and socialist proletariat forever—to drown it in its own blood. Never had a better occasion presented itself; and it profited by it with ferocious joy."

It was clear, too, that Thiers intended the bloody repression not only to destroy the Commune but also to prevent the possibility of any future revolution in France. On May 31 Goncourt concluded, "It is good that there was neither conciliation nor bargain. The solution was brutal. It was achieved by pure force. . . . The solution has restored confidence to the army, which learned in the blood of the Communards that it was still able to fight. Finally, the bloodletting was a bleeding white; such a purge, by killing off the combative part of the population, defers the next revolution by a whole generation."[40]

FOR HIS PART, JULES FERRY was not shocked by "the reprisals taken by vengeful soldiers, the peasant in good order dishing out punishment. . . . I saw these things and accepted them as if I beheld the sword of the Archangel at work." The journalist Francisque Sarcey insisted that no compromise was possible: "If the scaffold is ever to be done away with, it should be kept for those who build barricades." The *honnêtes gens* counted on the *conseils de guerre* to finish the work.

The murderous discourse of "delivered" elites during and after Bloody Week included the belief that the march of Versaillais "justice" following "the red orgy" would "purify" French society, a concept, of course, with considerable bloody resonance in the twentieth century. After Bloody Week, the *honnêtes gens* were willing to go to great lengths to purify the city, even if this entailed more mass executions. Sébastien Commissaire remembered hearing groups talking on the boulevards

Montmartre and des Italiens: "The capital must be purged. Paris needs a good bleeding. We have to get rid of 50,000 men. . . . There are some who say 100,000." A policeman in Auteuil did not mince words either: "The soldiers of Versailles are saying . . . that they will spare no one, not women, not children, not old people, given that they are nothing more than Parisian scum and that France must get rid of them."[41]

Some elites were even willing to destroy Paris itself—in order to save it, of course. Louis Énault, obsessed with the fires that had devastated parts of the capital, used the image of purification through fire to justify the repression: "They say that flames purify! Oh! If this is the case, on the funerary pyre of Paris, let's throw all those who have cost us, all those among us who are scoundrels and evil, and all those who have brought about this dire debasement of our national character! Yes! . . . and then we will soon see our France, just like the phoenix of the old fable, be reborn out of the ashes that will still be warm."[42] Énault and others imagined that the restored Paris would be much like the city that had existed before the Commune, with the monumental public buildings that had burned rebuilt. But Paris would lack any hint of the revolutionary ideas that had given rise to the Commune in the first place. In the name of muscular religion, one could not strike hard enough. Eugène Hennebert, for one, demanded the banning of "this unhealthy literature that begins with *Les Misérables* of Monsieur Hugo." Theaters where performances "fall into the mud" should be shut down, as should "innumerable cafés, drinking places or shady bars that have given us the reputation as a people of drunks and imbeciles." "Triumphant" atheism had to be destroyed too, and religion would be the order of the day once more. In other words, as Élie Reclus noted wryly, "order, family, property again reign"—and would for the foreseeable future.[43]

Elegant Parisians return to their city after the Commune had been crushed. (BRIDGEMAN ART)

CHAPTER 11

REMEMBERING

Le cadavre est à terre, et l'idée est debout.
(The corpse lies on the ground, and the idea still stands.)

—VICTOR HUGO[1]

L ITTLE BY LITTLE, Paris returned to normal, at least for people of means. The Parisian upper classes returned in style to proudly stroll the grand boulevards of their capital, thrilled with the victory of Versailles. A journalist described the scene on May 28: "Along the towing path along the Seine fifty bodies of insurgents were stretched out." Workers were digging through the pavement to bury them, while "a large crowd looked on indifferently," including "young, elegant and radiant girls showing off their springtime umbrellas in the sunshine." For them, the good life began again. Yet with decomposing bodies still strewn about, calls to dispose of the remaining corpses in the streets of Paris came fast and furious. One could not have "these scoundrels who have done so much evil" cause more harm after death.[2] Such a sight could keep tourists away. The gates of the city were reopened on June 6, although police inspected the papers of all travelers. Barricades slowly disappeared as shops reopened. Sidewalks once covered with bodies and blood were cleared and cleaned.

Yet Paris was a city in ruins, the result of Versaillais shelling and seven days of pitched battles, however one-sided. Only gutted shells of the Tuileries Palace, the Ministry of Finance, and the Hôtel-de-Ville remained. Other monumental buildings, such as the Palais-Royal, Palace of Justice, and Louvre, had been badly damaged; the Grenier d'Abondance and the docks of La Villette had been destroyed. Along the Champs-Élysées and in other parts of western Paris, hundreds of houses lay in ruins. Burned out buildings lined the rues Royale, du faubourg Saint-Honoré, de Bac, and de Lille, as well as considerably less fancy streets in Montmartre and Belleville. Shells and bullets had riddled countless buildings that still stood. The shattered remnants of the Victory Column stretched across the place Vendôme. Rubble from barricades lay almost everywhere in central and eastern Paris, particularly Montmartre and Belleville. The City of Light had become the City of Blood. However almost immediately following the fall of the Commune, Thomas Cook in London organized trips to view the ruins of the French capital. Tourists could again "circulate joyously in the elegant Paris of pleasures."[3]

THE COMMUNE HAD BEEN CRUSHED, but public mourning for its bloody demise never took place. Te Deums echoed in the churches of Paris not for the thousands of dead Parisians but for the city's archbishop. Georges Darboy's body lay in the chapel of the archbishop's palace for ten days, viewed by streams of well-heeled Parisians. Arriving at the Gare de Montparnasse for the funeral on June 7, Vicomte Camille de Meaux, a member of the National Assembly, came upon yet another convoy of prisoners headed for Versailles. He would never forget the angry, proud looks directed at observers, expressing a confidence that revenge would one day come. Even around Notre Dame, the population seemed hostile. Meaux expressed surprise that anti-Communards were not greeted as liberators.[4]

The oration by priest P. Adolphe Perraud, describing the "Holy Martyr of La Roquette" as the most "universally loved archbishop who ever served in Paris," would have perplexed the late Darboy. In fact, as the eulogy noted, he had endured the constant opposition of those Perraud referred to as "demagogues, Legitimists, ultra-papists." Once he had been buried in Notre-Dame in all solemnity, attacks by Ultramontanes, those unconditionally loyal to the Vatican and thus determined enemies of French Gallicans, on Archbishop Darboy resumed.[5]

Karl Marx was among those to insist that Adolphe Thiers was "the real murderer of Archbishop Darboy." The head of the Versailles government may well have assumed that the Communards would not dare shoot the archbishop, but he had been willing to take the risk. If anything, the execution of the archbishop of Paris strengthened Thiers's position in orchestrating a vigorous repression. Wickham Hoffman, American Ambassador Elihu B. Washburne's secretary, concluded that if Darboy had not been a Gallican, the extreme Right of the assembly would "have exerted themselves that his life would have been saved."[6]

The Catholic Church wasted no time in trying to reassert itself in France after the Commune, using Darboy's death to promote a more conservative brand of Catholicism. On June 18, Pius IX denounced Catholic liberalism, after evoking the martyrdom of Georges Darboy at the hands of "the Commune and its men escaped from hell." Masses were celebrated as an expiation or even exorcism of the Communards. A marble plaque went up at La Roquette in honor of Darboy and the other hostages killed there, and the next year a pilgrimage was made to the spot on the rue Haxo where other hostages had been killed; a church was also soon built there.[7]

In 1875, the Church began constructing a more permanent monument: the basilica of Sacré-Coeur on Montmartre, near the spot where Eugène Varlin was battered and then shot to death. It stood as a symbol of penance—for France must have sinned to suffer such a crushing defeat in the Franco-Prussian War and then an uprising by ordinary people. Sacré-Coeur represented the close ties between the Church, which still anticipated a monarchical restoration, and the conservative republic that followed the Commune's defeat. It became an object of passionate hatred among men and women of the political Left.[8] The Church, ironically, lost even more ground with ordinary people, who did not fill the new houses of worship built in working-class districts on the margins of urban life.

THE MINISTRY OF WAR DISBANDED THE Volunteers of the Seine, who had returned to Versailles. But it feted them for their service: a banquet and a triumphant review at Longchamps on June 29 in the presence of Thiers, still carrying the title "chief of executive power of the French Republic," marked the end of the force. Albert Hans proudly believed that he and his colleagues had done their duty "under the eyes of an enemy which watched us agonize with a cruel joy." The Volunteers' losses had amounted to a few killed, including Gustave Durieu, the murderous battalion commander, with about ten wounded.[9]

Hans had been eager for war against the Prussians and confident of a French victory. Now, in the wake of the Commune, he promised to fight again "for the national and conservative cause" against "the turbulent masses" if revolutionaries dared rise up again. He would eagerly await the day when France could retake Metz from her "implacable enemies" across the Rhine. The victory of the Versailles forces, he believed, had restored France's "national dignity." For Hans, "the *patrie* is divinity."[10]

Adolphe Thiers and the Versaillais were surprised and angered by growing hostile international reaction to the repression. A Geneva newspaper denounced the massacres carried out in Paris. If so many bodies were necessary for "the reign of order," it argued, then "the civilized world will collapse even more rapidly." Other foreign newspapers began to describe Parisian workers as "martyrs." In London, the *Times*, kept well informed throughout by its correspondents in Paris, concluded that "the laws of war are soft and Christian when compared with the inhuman laws of vengeance by which the soldiers of Versailles shot, stabbed with bayonets, and ripped open the bodies of men, women, and children taken prisoner over the past six days. History has never seen anything like this before."[11]

Executions continued at least until June 7 in Satory, the Bois-de-Boulogne, and the prison of Cherche-Midi. In Père Lachaise Cemetery, workers rushed to clean up, carrying away debris and signs of what had happened. But they could only pile up the multitudes of corpses. Bodies had to be cleared from the streets, however much Thiers might have preferred that they remain as a warning, rather like the gallows that stood near Russian manor houses in the age of serfdom. In the Palais-Royal, bodies of women remained for days in the garden and under the arches of the structure. Decomposing corpses created a horrendous stench.[12]

The Versaillais attempted to cover up some mass graves to make it appear that fewer Communards had died. A Parisian newspaper published an official decree forbidding people from going into the Bois-de-Boulogne, where the killing continued. The notice ended, "Whenever the number of condemned exceeds ten men, the execution squad will be replaced by a machine gun" in the interest of efficiency. On June 16, the *Journal Officiel* announced that any newspaper that republished the chilling decree would be prosecuted. But it did not deny its authenticity.[13]

Thiers, whom Henri Rochefort called a "sanguinary Tom Thumb," triumphantly wrote France's prefects of the Communards, "The ground is covered with their cadavers; this awful sight will serve as a lesson." Élie Reclus noted that the verb "to shoot" had become "the core of

Communard corpses
(HULTON-DEUTSCH COLLECTION/CORBIS)

our language: 'we shoot, he was shot, we will be shot.'" The word had become "the great word of order in French society." The Communards may have been mortal, but their cause was not.[14]

THE VERSAILLES GOVERNMENT DID NOT content itself with arresting Communards in Paris. It also sent out orders to departmental prefects calling for the arrest of those who had managed to get out of Paris alive. Several *départements* were placed in a state of siege. About 1,500 accused Communards managed to get to Belgium, many of them ordinary laborers; 2,000 to 3,000 went to Switzerland, about 500 to England, and a few to Spain, the Netherlands, and South America. Most would live in abject poverty. Communard leaders were far more likely to escape than the rank and file because they had connections and travel experience. Here, too, the poorest Parisians were at a disadvantage, as they had been during the repression and bloodletting. Léo Frankel escaped, thanks to a coach driver who got him out disguised as a cabinetmaker. He and Élisabeth Dmitrieff reached Switzerland disguised as a Prussian couple as both spoke German well. Returning to Russia, she took up the cause of revolution and married the administrator of her legal husband's estate—this first one had been a marriage of convenience. When he was arrested and sent to Siberia, she followed him, never learning of her amnesty in 1879 after the Third Republic had been well established. She died in Siberia in 1910.[15]

The French government pressured authorities in Britain, Spain, Belgium, and Switzerland to arrest and extradite those who had participated in the Commune. From Belgium, Victor Hugo, who had at first opposed the Commune, now outraged Thiers and his entourage by attacking the Belgian government for its compliance with Thiers's directives. He denounced the execution without trial by the Versaillais of Raoul Rigault and others. Expelled from Belgium on May 30 for condemning its government, Hugo found refuge in the Netherlands.[16]

In July 1870, Sutter-Laumann's Communard past began to catch up with him. Technically he was a deserter, at least from the Versaillais point of view, because he had fought in the Franco-Prussian War. An officer attached to the *mairie* of the Eighteenth Arrondissement where he worked took him aside and told him that it was time to leave Paris. The officer wrote a letter recommending him for paid service as a guard on one of the pontoons—floating prisons—full of Communards sentenced to remain in captivity there or to be sent to prison in Cayenne or some other distant, tropical place. He went to Cherbourg, ironically guarding some of those with whom he had fought. For the rest of his life, Sutter-Laumann, who became a writer, poet, and critic, had nightmares about the horrors of Bloody Week.[17]

AS THE VERSAILLAIS DREW CLOSER and shells began to fall near his atelier, Gustave Courbet accepted the invitation of Demoiselle Girard, later described by the police as his mistress. She offered the painter a room in her apartment on the third floor and space for thirty-five paintings in her basement at 14, passage du Saumon in central Paris. Courbet had incurred great wrath among anti-Communards—newspapers invariably referred to him as "the dismantler" of the Vendôme Column. Eugène Delessert went further, insisting that he would have wanted the painter—"this Prussian vandal!"—shot.[18]

Police pillaged Courbet's atelier on the rue d'Hautefeuille. The painter had already lost two ateliers, one in Ornans at the time of the Prussian invasion and another at pont d'Alma. Rumors circulated as to Courbet's whereabouts. The *Paris-Journal* claimed he had been discovered hiding in the Ministry of the Navy, having stuffed "his *grosse personne*" into a closet, and when he resisted, a soldier had purportedly blown him apart with a rifle.[19]

Shortly before Bloody Week began, Courbet, aware that he was a wanted man, made a surprise visit to Arsène Lecomte, who made musical instruments and lived on the rue Saint-Gilles in the Marais. They had known each other for twenty years, but not well. Lecomte knew the painter had become involved in politics but not much about his role in the Commune. The artist said that he feared falling into the hands of the Versaillais and asked if he could stay one night in Lecomte's apartment while another was being prepared for him near Charenton. Lecomte's wife did not want him there, but Courbet simply showed up, carrying absolutely nothing with him. He hid there from May 23 to June 7, when police raided the apartment at night.[20]

Courbet had cut his hair and shaved his recognizable beard. A policeman said that his Franc-Comtois accent gave him away. At the Palace of Justice, another policeman asked him why he had associated with "these bandits." On July 4, Courbet was imprisoned in Mazas. The municipal council of Ornans removed a statue he had created from a fountain in the square. One arm had been broken off.[21]

On August 15, Courbet stood before a court-martial accused of trying to overthrow the government, inciting hatred, usurping public functions (for having served on the Commune), and being responsible for the demolition of the Vendôme Column. Courbet contended that the column had obstructed circulation, that he had opposed setting fire to the Palais-Royal, and that he had helped preserve the Louvre's artistic treasures. He insisted that he had tried to use his reputation to bring the Commune toward conciliation. The Versailles government did not see things that way but could not really shoot the famous artist.

On September 2, a court-martial sentenced Courbet to six months in prison. In 1873, the government, presided over by Marshal Patrice de MacMahon, condemned the painter to pay the costs of his trial and of rebuilding the Vendôme Column. Courbet left for exile in Switzerland. The government seized the artist's property, including paintings, in Paris and Ornans. The *maître d'Ornans* passed away on the last day of 1877, just before his first payment was due.[22]

Show trials like Courbet's were intended to reassure the upper classes about the efficiency of the repression. A lawyer called before a court-martial expressed outrage at what he had seen: "men led like worthless livestock; chained, insulted by a cowardly and idiotic crowd."

He was proud to defend defeated Communards, who, for the most part, did nothing more than raise up a flag, "that of Misery."[23]

In trials of suspected female incendiaries, "moral" considerations—"living in sin," bearing children out of wedlock, lacking a "good" family background, and so on—undoubtedly influenced the harshness of the sentences. Moreover, the Versaillais image of the militant female insurrectionary would linger. Along with that of the "drunken commoner," it would influence the emergence of crowd psychology—crowds were ascribed as having characteristics drawn from anti-Communard discourse, as individual identities were subsumed in and overwhelmed by irrational, emotional, flighty behavior, the way female incendiaries supposedly behaved, or lurching irrationally like drunks.[24]

During her trial, Louise Michel proudly faced the judges, telling them that although she always dressed in black, she had never been without her red belt since the proclamation of the republic on September 4. Looking as severe as always, Michel denounced the execution of hostages, insisting that the Commune "had had absolutely nothing to do with assassinations or burning." Social revolution had been its goal. She flatly stated that she would "have had no hesitation about shooting people who gave orders" to execute Communard prisoners, having resolved at one point to assassinate Thiers. She was "honored to be singled out as one of the promoters of the Commune" and swore "by our martyrs who fell on the field of Satory" that if the judges did not condemn her to death, she would "not stop crying for vengeance. . . . If you are not cowards, then kill me." The judges condemned her to deportation instead, probably believing that execution would make her a martyr. When asked at the court-martial if she had ever had an intimate relationship with a man—the goal apparently being to see if she had been involved with Théophile Ferré—the "Red Virgin" replied, "No, my only passion is the revolution."[25]

Disguised as a woman, Ferré had managed to avoid arrest for several days after the Commune fell, before being taken in a house on the rue Montorgueil. He refused to answer interrogators' questions and was condemned to death and shot that same day on the plain of Satory. Gustave Genton and Jean-Baptiste François were both condemned and shot there as well. The following summer, prisoners were still being dispatched at Satory. Communard general Louis Rossel was recognized in disguise on the boulevard Saint-Germain on June 7. He, too, was shot at Satory in November. Before dying, he wrote, "I shall never regret having tried to demolish that bastard oligarchy, the French bourgeoisie." On June 29, 1872, in a perfect example of a show trial at work, a court-martial sentenced Raoul Rigault to death, although he had been executed thirteen months before; another court-martial in November sentenced Eugène Varlin to death, although he had already died brutally eighteen months earlier.[26]

THE OFFICIAL GOVERNMENT INQUEST into the Commune predictably blamed Socialists (and specifically the International Workingmen's Association), anarchists, and the weakening influence of the Church for the "moral disorder" of the Commune. It exuded conservative hostility to Paris, noting that immigration brought together masses of people ready for revolution and suggesting that the city should cease to be the capital of France. Paris would not again have the right to elect a mayor for over a century, until 1977. The government dissolved the National Guard and the next year banned the International. Thiers insisted that the strength of France was inseparable from "a nation that believes" in God. The government report saluted the repression as "a painful necessity. Society is obliged to defend itself." But this was not enough. France had to "again rejoin the path of civilization." The elimination of the "unhealthy" parts of society played an important role in this effort. A massacre was a good start.[27]

Between the end of the Commune and 1873, some three hundred books appeared in support of the official version of events. These accounts saluted the Versaillais victory and castigated the "vandals" and "barbarians" of the Commune. Théophile Gautier, Alphonse Daudet, and other literary figures also published their attacks on the Communards. The Versaillais interpretation of the Commune, seeking to justify the bloody repression, remained dominant through the time of the "Republic of Moral Order," which lasted until 1877. Twenty-one years later, an anti-Semitic priest, horrified by the rise to power in France of people who had once supported the Commune, argued that the repression in 1871 had been "perhaps still too mild!"[28]

Unsurprisingly, the government account dominated in the years immediately following the Commune during the conservative "Republic of Moral Order." In fact, Communards were still being persecuted: twenty-four military courts continued to meet, some as late as four years after the Commune fell. In all, an official government report noted 36,309 arrests and 10,137 condemnations, which included exile to New Caledonia, the French penal colony in the southwestern Pacific

Ocean. "Deserters"—that is, former soldiers who fought with the Commune—who had not already been shot faced particularly harsh sentences. Again, specific *quartiers* identified with the Left were targeted; military courts condemned to deportation more than seven hundred Communards who lived in Montmartre. Many more than that were shot or simply disappeared.[29]

Thousands of prisoners endured long, miserable trips in animal wagons to fort and ship prisons and to the pontoons at Brest, La Rochelle, Rochefort, Cherbourg, Oléron, Lorient, and Ile-de-Ré. Prisoners received only a piece of bread to eat and water from two tin cans and had no opportunity "to get down in order to take care of the most legitimate need!" This was better than being gunned down, but prisoners still suffered greatly, and not all believed they were lucky. A song the prisoners sang included the line "Prison is worse than death."[30]

Louise Michel and Nathalie Le Mel were among more than 4,500 people deported to the South Seas. After two years' incarceration, they were transported in August 1873 from Paris to Rochefort, where they boarded the *Virginie*. Aboard ship they and as many as 150 prisoners were kept in steel cages with neither natural light nor fresh air and weighted down by a suffocating tropical humidity. There were several small children of prisoners, including one child born in the Versailles prison of Chantiers. The prisoners received little in the way of rations and were limited to a liter of water per day. Le Mel was among those violently ill on the long voyage to hell. Michel penned poetry describing the awful trip of more than five months.

Finally, the *Virginie* arrived in the Bay of Nouméa, which Michel noted with irony had, like Rome, seven bluish hills. Those prisoners condemned to forced labor were taken to the island of Noua four kilometers away, where they endured exhausting work and punishments inflicted by brutal guards. Louise Michel went with a group of prisoners condemned to exile within a fortified compound to the island of Ducos, six miles from Tomo, New Caledonia. Guards made the prisoners' conditions even worse, depriving them of bread and inflicting other calculated cruelties upon them. There the prisoners did the best they could, digging small gardens and building a small school, surviving without a doctor and lacking even the most basic medications and bandages to care for wounds and injuries. By the end of 1873, forty of them had died.[31]

Michel's complaints about the conditions and the suffering of Le Mel brought no improvement. She took the side of the Kanaks, the indigenous people of New Caledonia who rebelled against French rule in 1878. A year later Michel won the right to move to Nouméa, the capital of the largest island, and teach the children of prisoners there. During her seven years in New Caledonia, Michel, having seen the repressive might of the French state up close there and in France, became an anarchist.

HISTORIANS CONTINUE TO DEBATE the number of Communards who perished at the hands of Versaillais forces.[32] Conservative accounts accuse the Communards of mass murder, estimating that sixty-six or perhaps sixty-eight hostages were killed. The Versaillais, on the other hand, summarily executed without any real trial perhaps as many as 17,000 people, a figure given by the official government report that followed. The municipal council paid for that number of burials after Bloody Week. Some estimates have reached as high as 35,000. Montmartre and Belleville were prominent among *quartiers* specifically targeted because of their identification with Communard militancy; at least 2,000 people perished in the Twentieth Arrondissement alone.

Bodies were left in vacant lots, immense ditches, construction sites, and abandoned or torched buildings; others were tossed into the Seine, into mass graves such as those at the Square Saint-Jacques near the Lobau barracks—or beyond the city walls. Thousands of bodies simply disappeared, covered with lime or disposed of in other ways. For example, some were hauled to cemeteries outside Paris or buried at the gas factory; others ended up in the cemeteries of Montparnasse, Montmartre, or Père Lachaise. Many were burned, as at Buttes-Chaumont. More than 1,500 corpses were buried in the Nineteenth Arrondissement.[33]

When newspapers asked to publish lists of those executed by order of the prevotal courts, they were told that these instant courts-martial kept no records. Many people simply disappeared, becoming nameless victims. When identification of executed Communards was possible, authorities refused to allow family members to place flowers on their graves for four months.[34]

A subsequent survey carried out by members of the municipal council of Paris concluded improbably that more than 100,000 workers had been killed or imprisoned or had fled. The estimate may have been high, but the working class of Paris was inarguably depleted. In a comparison of the 1866 and 1872 censuses, half of the 24,000 shoemakers, 10,000 of 30,000 tailors, 6,000 of 20,000 cabinetmakers, and 1,500 of 8,500 bronze workers were not to be found; the number of plumbers, roofers, and other trades that provided militant Communards had also fallen dramatically. Well after the Commune, industrialists and small employers complained about the paucity of artisans and skilled workers.[35]

Maxime Vuillaume got it right when trying to assess the number of those massacred by the Versaillais, asking, "Who will ever know?" Louise Michel wondered, "But how many were there that we know nothing of? From time to time, the earth disgorges its corpses." Paris had become "an immense slaughterhouse and . . . we will never know the names nor the number" of victims.[36] This remains true today.

SOON AFTER THE CRUSHING of the Commune, class hatred intensified. The social question came to dominate politics in France and other countries, and contemporaries attributed this to the short-lived Paris Commune. From London Karl Marx concluded that the Paris Commune had not been the anticipated social revolution that would free the proletariat. That, he insisted, was still to come. Yet workers had risen up spontaneously, so he was reassured. Lenin would add to the equation the leadership of the avant-garde of the proletariat, ultimately the Bolsheviks, thereby turning away from an emphasis on the revolutionary spontaneity of workers. For his part, the British positivist Frederic Harrison, writing just after the Commune had fallen, concluded that for the first time in modern European history, "the workmen of the chief city of the Continent [had] organized a regular government in the name of a new social order" in opposition to the rich and powerful who benefited from state centralization to consolidate "vast and ever-increasing hoards of wealth, opening to the wealthy enchanted realms of idleness, luxury, and waste—laying on the labourer, generation after generation, increasing burdens of toil, destitution, and despair." To Jean Allemane, the massacres during Bloody Week sadly demonstrated "that the bourgeois soul contains egotism and cold cruelty." A short history of the Commune published after its demise noted that for the victorious bourgeoisie, "extermination" had been "the only word." The British authors argued that history would ultimately salute the overall humanity of the Communards, which still today seems true enough. For sixty-four days, ordinary Parisians had been "masters of their own destinies."[37] Their dream was not to be.

THIERS HAD MANAGED TO DESTROY the Commune. But the massacre perpetuated by his troops during and after Bloody Week would cast a long shadow over the next century. Despite the execution of hostages and the massacre of the Dominican priests—totaling up to sixty-eight killed—the acts of the Communards pale in comparison with the 12,000 to 15,000 executions carried out by the Army of Versailles. Indeed, despite their level of verbal violence, the Communards were overall very careful to show they were not going to behave like the Versaillais. State violence was organized and systematic, as the cruel, bloody events of the twentieth century would demonstrate to an even greater degree.[38] For the *hommes d'ordre*, as a Versaillais magistrate memorably thundered, "In Paris, the whole population was guilty!" Anti-Communards shouted, "The brigands! We must exterminate them to the last one!" One dreamed of "an immense furnace in which we will cook each of them in turn."[39] Nothing would come close to the slaughter perpetuated by the Versaillais until the atrocities against the Armenians in 1915 during World War I, and such language would not be heard again until the Nazi Holocaust and other genocides, including the tragic events in the Balkans during the 1990s.

ADOLPHE THIERS, whom the National Assembly named the first president of the Third Republic on August 31, 1871, got back most of his works of art taken to the Tuileries; the government also paid him a huge sum for the loss of his house. Jules Ducatel, who had signaled to Versaillais troops on May 21 that no one was guarding the Point-du-Jour, received government honors. In 1877 he lost a job when accused of theft. Colonel Louis Vabre, who oversaw mass murder at the court-martial at Châtelet, was awarded the Legion of Honor.[40]

Thiers died in 1873. Paris remained under martial law until early 1876. Workers' associations struggled under the repression that followed the Commune and only slowly revived. The French Third Republic survived the attempt by the monarchist president Marshal Patrice de MacMahon to bring about its destruction by parliamentary coup d'état, the so-called Crisis of May 16, 1877. He dismissed the moderate republican prime minister Jules Simon, but the Chamber of Deputies refused to support the appointment of a prominent monarchist to head the new government. New elections brought a republican majority.

Gradually the French Third Republic took root in provincial France, and statues celebrating it were raised in village squares. In Paris

the place du Château-d'Eau became the place de la République, centered on a grand monument celebrating the new government. The
Hôtel-de-Ville purchased one of Gustave Courbet's paintings. "La
Marseillaise" again became the national anthem of France in 1879. A
highly contested partial amnesty for Communards came that same
year, followed by a complete amnesty on July 11, 1880. Thousands of
French men and women returned from exile and imprisonment in distant places, including many of those condemned for years to impossi-
bly harsh conditions in New Caledonia.[41]

That year, July 14, Bastille Day, was celebrated as a national holiday
for the first time. Thousands of people greeted Louise Michel at the
Gare Saint-Lazare when she returned to France in November 1880. The
first French mass socialist parties took shape during the following two
decades. French unions grew in strength following their legalization in
1881. Gradually the dominance of the Versaillais discourse in the collective memory of the Paris Commune ebbed. With the entrenchment
of the Third Republic, above all with the national elections of the early
1880s, the Commune gradually came be seen as a founding moment,
however contested.[42] Today the French see it as major, positive event in
their national history.

But even after these developments, there were still moments of
bloody repression. On May 1, 1890, Louise Michel led the first demonstration of French workers on what became an international holiday.
A year later, French troops gunned down demonstrators supporting a
strike in the small northern working-class town of Fourmies. Ten people died, including four young women, the youngest just sixteen, and
twenty-four people were wounded, including children. The power of
the centralized French state endured, as did its capacity for extreme
violence, in France and in its colonies. If the Paris Commune of 1871
may be seen as the last of the nineteenth-century revolutions, the murderous, systematic, state repression that followed helped unleash the
demons of the twentieth century. This is sadly perhaps a greater legacy
of the Paris Commune than the experience of a movement for freedom
undertaken by ordinary people. The centralized French state added to
its arsenal. The *rafle*, or police roundup of "suspects," took shape in
working-class neighborhoods like Montmartre, Buttes-Chaumont, and
Belleville during the 1890s. By 1900 Paris was presented in guidebooks
as "pacified" and well policed—the "forces of order" stood ready to intervene at any instant.

THE WALL OF THE FÉDÉRÉS in Père Lachaise Cemetery, where so many Communards were gunned down, emerged as a site of memory symbolizing the massacres of Bloody Week. The wall drew visitors on July 14, 1880, the first time that date could be celebrated as a national holiday under the republic; some left commemorative wreaths. Gradually small crowds defied police by marching silently up to the wall, leading to confrontations. Eugène Pottier's revolutionary song "The Monument to the *Fédérés*" recalled what had occurred at Père Lachaise and in many other places in Paris: "Here was the slaughterhouse, the charnel house. The victims rolled down from the corner of this wall into the great ditch below." Police increasingly tolerated demonstrations at the wall on May 1. A simple marble plaque went up in 1908: "To the dead of the Commune, May 21–28, 1871."

Today the Wall of the *Fédérés* remains a somber, bracing monument to those massacred by the forces of "the men of order." Demonstrations there grew in size and intensity during the confrontations of May 1968 and again three years later on the centenary of the Commune. In 1983, the wall was classified as a historical monument, commemorating the ultimate victory of the French Republic for which the Communards fought.[43]

The former Communard Jules Vallès dedicated his *L'Insurgé*, an autobiographical novel,

> *To all those,*
> *Victims of social injustice,*
> *Who take up arms against the evil in the world*
> *And who formed,*
> *Under the flag of the Commune,*
> *A great federation of those who suffer.*[44]

Jean-Baptiste Clément, who managed to escape to Belgium and then London and was condemned to death by Versailles, wrote "*Le temps de cérises*" in 1866. Parisians had sung it during both the Prussian and Versaillais sieges. He now dedicated it "to valiant Citizen Louise, the volunteer doctor's assistant of rue Fontaine-au-Roi, Sunday, May 28, 1871":

> *I will always love the time of the cherries*
> *I will keep this time, in my heart,*
> *An open wound.*[45]

Le temps de cérises were now the good old days, when Parisians were free.[46]

WHEN I GO UP TO the Wall of the Fédérés, as nightfall approaches, the leaves are falling, and all is still, I can almost hear the words of Thomas Wolfe: "Oh lost, and by the wind grieved, ghost, come back again."[47]

ACKNOWLEDGMENTS

For as long as I can remember, I have been fascinated by the Paris Commune of 1871. My previous book focused on Émile Henry, a young intellectual and anarchist who threw a bomb into the Café Terminus near the Gare Saint-Lazare in the French capital in February 1894. He aimed to kill as many people as possible. Henry's targets were ordinary bourgeois drinking beer and listening to music before they returned to their homes to sleep. I argued that Henry's bomb represented the origins of modern terrorism. But there was a subtext: state terrorism. The French state, like that of Italy and Spain, used the fear of anarchists—and most anarchists were not terrorists at all—to suppress its political opponents. Émile Henry was the son of a militant in the Paris Commune of 1871, condemned to death in absentia by the French provisional government of Adolphe Thiers. Fortuné Henry had seen state terrorism up close. Soldiers fighting for the government of Versailles gunned down or executed thousands of ordinary people.

About six or seven years ago, the Bibliothèque historique de la ville de Paris organized an exposition of photos taken during the Franco-Prussian War of 1870–1871, in which Prussia and its other German allies crushed the Second Empire of Napoleon III, and during the Commune. One of these photos stuck in my mind—that of elegant upper-class Parisians returning to the French capital after their armies had crushed the Paris Commune during Bloody Week (May 21–28, 1871). They applauded the terror organized by the French state, which had crushed Parisians aspiring to freedom. One day, while walking to my office in Branford College at Yale, I decided to research and write a book about the life and death of the Paris Commune, focusing on the representative experiences of Communards and also on some of those who opposed them.

The MacMillan Center and the Whitney Griswold Fund at Yale University offered research support for this book. Bertrand Fonck, with whom Caroline Piketty put me in touch, made it possible for me to access otherwise unavailable dossiers in the Archives de la défense in Vincennes.

In writing about the Paris Commune of 1871, I have benefited greatly from the important studies of Stewart Edwards, Laure Godineau, Éric Fournier, Carolyn Eichner, David Shafer, Gay Gullickson, Quentin Deleurmoz, and Marc César. I have long admired and particularly learned from the superb scholarship of Robert Tombs and Jacques Rougerie, essential for anyone interested in the Commune. Tom Kselman, Colin Foss, and Joe Peterson also offered suggestions drawn from their knowledge of the period. Thanks also to someone I have never met, Olivier Marion, whose fine unpublished *mémoire de maîtrise* on the Catholic Church during the Commune (available in the Archives départementales des Hauts-de-Seine) merits wider exposure. In Fayl-Billot, Haute-Marne, where Archbishop Georges Darboy was born, I would like to thank Philippe Robert, until recently *curé* of that parish, and Jean-Remy Compain.

I was incredibly fortunate at the University of Michigan to have had the chance to study with Charles Tilly, who directed my dissertation long ago, and to have had him as a friend. And is the case with so many people in many fields, Chuck's death in 2008 remains an enormous loss. *Pour leur amitié et la manière dont ils ont inspiré mes travaux, je tiens à remercier chaleureusement* Michelle Perrot, Alain Corbin, Jean-François Chanet, Dominique Kalifa, Sylvain Venayre, Maurice Garden, and Yves Lequin. If the research for this book took place in Paris, most of it was written in Balazuc (Ardèche). There I am fortunate to have as friends Lucien and Catherine Mollier, Hervé and Françoise Parain, Eric Fruleux, and Mathieu Fruleux. Thanks also there to William Clavaroyet of La Fenière and Lionel Pélerin of Chez Paulette and to Paulette Balazuc. In Poland, where I have had the pleasure of spending a great amount of time over the past eight years, thanks to Andrzej Kamiński, Wojciech Falkowski, Krzysztof Łazarski, Adam Kożuchowski, and Eulalia Łazarska, as well as Jim Collins; in Rouen, to Jean Sion; in Paris, to Jean-Claude Petilon and Sven Wanegffelen; in the United States, to Bruno, Flora, Gabrielle and Constance Cabanes, Charles Keith, Mark Lawrence, Gene Tempest, Joe Malloure, Jim Read, Steve Shirley, Dick and Sandy Simon, Mike Johnson, Gil Joseph, Steve Pincus, Sue Stokes, and Peter Gay. Our family owes Victoria Johnson so much.

Peter McPhee and I have been talking about French history and much more since we first met in 1974—ça passe vite, le temps. He read the first draft of this book and offered his usual extremely helpful comments. At the Fletcher Company, I am indebted to Christy Fletcher, Melissa Chincillo, and Donald Lamm, who has supported this project from the beginning. Again Don contributed his unparalleled editing skills to one of my books. Melissa, with the assistance of Anne van den Heuvel, obtained the publication rights for the images in the book, greatly helping out in a complex eleventh hour. At Basic Books, I am grateful to Lara Heimert, the publisher, who took on this book when it was only an idea and offered insightful suggestions along the way. Katy O'Donnell's developmental reading of the manuscript was brilliant, and Jennifer Kelland provided wonderful copyediting. Thanks also to Rachel King, the project editor at Basic Books, for her excellent work.

Laura Merriman has spent much of her life in France, in Balazuc, but is often in Paris, where this tragic story took place. Chris Merriman first arrived in Balazuc at the age of ten days and also spent years in school in France; thus he also knows Paris very well. My spouse, Carol Merriman, contributed her editing skills to this book and has brought so much happiness into my life, including Laura and Chris.

Donald and Jean Lamm have been our friends for decades. Don has always represented the very best in publishing. This book is dedicated to him in gratitude and friendship and with great admiration.

NOTES

Prologue

1. Theodore Zeldin, *France, 1848–1945* (Oxford: Oxford University Press, 1973), 1:511; Roger Price, "Napoleon III," in *Europe 1789 to 1914*, edited by John Merriman and Jay Winter (Detroit: Charles Scribner's Sons, 2006), 3:1590.

2. Ted W. Margadant, *French Peasants in Revolt: The Insurrection of 1851* (Princeton, NJ: Princeton University Press, 1979); John M. Merriman, *Agony of the Republic: The Repression of the Left in Revolutionary France, 1848–51* (New Haven, CT: Yale University Press, 1978).

3. Theodore Zeldin, *The Political System of Napoleon III* (New York: Saint Martin's Press, 1958).

4. Geoffrey Warwo, *The Franco-Prussian War: The German Conquest of France in 1870–1871* (New York: Cambridge University Press, 2003), 25; David Jordan, *Transforming Paris: The Life and Labors of Baron Haussmann* (New York: The Free Press, 1995), 255; Jeanne Gaillard, *Paris, la ville 1852–1871* (Paris: Honoré Champion, 1997), 12–14, 135.

5. Gaillard, *Paris*, 14.

6. Gaillard, *Paris*, 191; Patrice Higonnet, *Paris: Capital of the World* (Cambridge, MA: Harvard University Press, 2002), 180–181; Dominique Kalifa, *Les Bas-fonds: Histoire d'un imaginaire* (Paris: Éditions du Seuil, 2013), 27, quoting Jules Janin, *L'été à Paris* (1843) and *Mémoires de M. Claude* (1881–1885), 47 and 52ff. See Louis Chevalier, *Dangerous Classes and Laboring Classes in Paris During the First Half of the Nineteenth Century* (New York: Howard Fertig, 1973).

7. Jordan, *Transforming Paris*, 7, 224, 259–260.

8. See Vanessa R. Schwartz, *Spectacular Realities: Early Mass Culture in Fin-de-Siècle Paris* (Berkeley: University of California Press, 1999).

9. Jordan, *Transforming Paris*, 109.

10. Jordan, *Transforming Paris*, 109–110, 188–189; Gaillard, *Paris*, 537–553, 568–571.

11. Higonnet, *Paris*, 174, 353.

12. Roger V. Gould, *Insurgent Identities: Class, Community, and Protest in Paris from 1848 to the Commune* (Chicago: University of Chicago Press, 1995), 71–72; see Jordan, "Money," in *Transforming Paris*, 227–245.

13. John Merriman, *Aux marges de la ville: Faubourgs et banlieues en France 1815–1870* (Paris: Éditions du Seuil, 1994), 292; Eric Fournier, *Paris en ruines: Du Paris haussmannien au Paris communard* (Paris: Imago, 2008), 22–26; John Merriman, *Police Stories* (New York: Oxford University Press, 2005); Gaillard, *Paris*, 204–205, 568–571. Between 1852 and 1859, 4,349 houses were destroyed, comprising 13 percent of old Paris. Families forced from their apartments received little more than the equivalent of a few dollars by virtue of a law in 1841 and an imperial decree in 1852.

14. Higonnet, *Paris*, 196–197, 250–252, 268; Walter Benjamin, *The Arcades Project* (Cambridge, MA: Harvard University Press, 1999).

15. Jacques Hillairet, ed., *Dictionnaire historique des rues de Paris*, 2 vols. (Paris: Éditions de minuit, 1979).

16. Émile Zola, *L'Assommoir* (New York: Penguin, 1970), 59.

17. Gaillard, *Paris*, 41–44, 61, 393–399; Jordan, *Transforming Paris*, 206–207; Robert Tombs, *The Paris Commune, 1871* (New York: Longman, 1999), 24.

18. Georges Duveau, *La vie ouvrière sous le Second Empire* (Paris: Gallimard, 1946), 203; Gaillard, *Paris*, 47; Merriman, *Aux marges de la ville*, 280.

19. John Merriman, *The Margins of City Life: Explorations on the French Urban Frontier, 1815–1851* (New York: Oxford University Press, 1991), 76.

20. Jacques Rougerie, *Paris libre 1871* (Paris: Éditions du Seuil, 1971), 19; Merriman, *Aux marges de la ville*, 301–303.

21. Louis Lazare, *Les quartiers de l'est de Paris et les communes suburbaines* (Paris: Au bureau de la Bibliothèque municipale, 1870), 102, 243.

22. Higonnet, *Paris*, 91.

23. Olivier Marion, "La vie religieuse pendant la Commune de Paris 1871" (unpublished master's thesis, Paris-X Nanterre, 1981), 20–22; Jacques-Olivier Boudon, *Monseigneur Darboy (1813–1871)* (Paris: Éditions du Cerf, 2011), 77–80; Charles Chauvin, *Mgr Darboy, archêveque de Paris, otage de la Commune (1813–1871)* (Paris: Desclée de Brouwer, 2011), 86. The Church would later classify as a "missionary" area any locale where less than 20 percent of the population fulfilled their Easter obligations.

24. Boudon, *Monseigneur Darboy*, 82; S. Sakharov, *Lettres au Père Duchêne pendant la Commune de Paris* (Paris: Bureau d'éditions, 1934), 18; Marion, "La vie religieuse," 23–26; S. Froumov, *La Commune de Paris et la démocratisation de l'école* (Moscow: Éditions du progrès, 1964), 30–31, 86–90; Carolyn Eichner, "'We Must Shoot the Priests': Revolutionary Women and Anti-clericalism in the Paris Commune of 1871, " in *Cities Under Siege/Situazioni d'assedio/États de siège*, edited by Lucia Carle and Antoinette Fauve-Chamoux (Florence, IT: Pagnini and Martinelli, 2002), 267–268.

25. Jacques Rougerie, *Procès des Communards* (Paris: Julliard, 1964), 33; Stewart Edwards, *The Paris Commune, 1871* (New York: Quadrangle, 1972), 12–13. See Duveau, *La vie ouvrière.*

26. Eichner, "We Must Shoot the Priests," 269.

27. Laure Godineau, *La Commune de Paris par ceux qui l'ont vécue* (Paris: Parigramme, 2010), 16–18.

28. Luc Willette, *Raoul Rigault, 25 ans, Communard, chef de police* (Paris: Syros, 1984), 121; Gaston Da Costa, *Mémoires d'un Communard: La Commune vécue* (Paris: Larousse, 2009), 256; Tombs, *The Paris Commune, 1871,* 38.

29. Maxime Vuillaume, *Mes cahiers rouges au temps de la Commune* (Paris: A. Michel, 1971), 219–222; Auguste Lepage, *Les cafés artistiques et littéraires de Paris* (Paris: M. Boursin, 1882), 79; Pierre Courthion, *Courbet raconté par lui-même et par ses amis* (Geneva: P. Cailler, 1948), 1:249.

30. Robert Boudry, "Courbet et la fédération des artistes," *Europe* 29, nos. 64–65 (April–May 1951): 122; Ernest A. Vizetelly, *My Adventures in the Commune* (London: Chatto and Windus, 2009; originally published 1914), 55; Denis Arthur Bingham, *Recollections of Paris* (London: Chapman and Hall, 1896), 2:117.

31. Boudry, "Courbet et la fédération des artistes," 122–123.

32. Archives of the Prefecture of Police (hereafter "APP"), Ba 1020, reports of June 27 and July 4, 1870; Jean Péridier, *La Commune et les artistes: Pottier, Courbet, Vallès, J. B. Clément* (Paris: Nouvelles editions latines, 1980), 59–61.

33. Frederic Harrison, "The Revolution and the Commune," *Fortnightly Review* 53, no. 9 (May 1871): 563; Alain Dalotel, Alain Faure, and Jean-Claude Freiermuth, *Aux origines de la Commune: Le mouvement des réunions publics à Paris, 1868–70* (Paris: F. Maspero, 1980), 295–296; S. Hollis Clayson, *Paris in Despair: Art and Everyday Life Under Siege (1870–71)* (Chicago: University of Chicago Press, 2002), 190; Gould, *Insurgent Identities,* 123–131. Legitimists, who wanted a restoration of the Bourbon monarchy, shared republican and socialist rejection of imperial centralized authoritarianism.

34. Maxime Vuillaume, *Mes cahiers rouges au temps de la Commune* (Paris: A. Michel, 1971), 189–190.

35. Archives de la Défense, 8J 3e, conseil de guerre 3, dossier 554 (all subsequent 8J dossiers are from these archives in Vincennes); APP, Ba 892; Willette, *Raoul Rigault,* 13–16, 21–28, 32–36; Charles Prolès, *Raoul Rigault: La préfecture de police sous la Commune, les otages* (Paris: Chamuel, 1898), 11–15; Jules Forni, *Raoul Rigault, procureur de la Commune* (Paris: Librairie centrale, 1871), 3–13; Lepage, *Les cafés artistiques,* 61–64, 78–79, 155; Robert Courtine, *La vie parisienne: Cafés et restaurants des boulevards, 1814–1914* (Paris: Perrin, 1984), 267.

36. Forni, *Raoul Rigault,* 41–51; Henry Bauer, *Mémoires d'un jeune homme* (Paris: G. Charpentier et E. Fasquelle, 1895), 89–92.

37. Willette, *Raoul Rigault*, 33–35; Patrick H. Hutton, *The Cult of the Revolutionary Tradition: The Blanquists in French Politics, 1864–1892* (Berkeley: University of California Press, 1981), 33.

38. Willette, *Raoul Rigault*, 33–48; Maurice Choury, *Les damnés de la terre, 1871* (Paris: Tchou, 1970), 80; Forni, *Raoul Rigault*, 20, 77; Prolès, *Raoul Rigault*, 18–22, 28.

39. Jean Renoir, *Pierre-Auguste Renoir, mon père* (Paris: Gallimard, 1981), 143–144.

40. Forni, *Raoul Rigault*, 16–17; Prolès, *Raoul Rigault*, 25–26; Willette, *Raoul Rigault*, 42–48.

41. Dalotel, Faure, and Freiermuth, *Aux origines de la Commune.*

42. Edwards, *The Paris Commune*, 30; Sutter-Laumann, *Histoire d'un trente sous (1870–1871)* (Paris: A. Savine, 1891), 14–15. I have never come across his first name.

43. Tombs, *The Paris Commune, 1871,* 36.

CHAPTER 1:
WAR AND THE COLLAPSE OF THE EMPIRE

1. Geoffrey Warwo, *The Franco-Prussian War: The German Conquest of France in 1870–1871* (New York: Cambridge University Press, 2003), 23.

2. Warwo, *The Franco-Prussian War,* 32.

3. Alistair Horne, *The Fall of Paris: The Siege and the Commune, 1870–71* (New York: Penguin, 1965), 62.

4. Robert Tombs, *The War Against Paris, 1871* (Cambridge: Cambridge University Press, 1981), 113–114.

5. Horne, *The Fall of Paris,* 66; Tombs, *The War Against Paris,* 13–15.

6. Michael Howard, *The Franco-Prussian War* (London: Hart-Davis, 1961), 40–71; Wawro, *The Franco-Prussian War,* 46–64, 74–80.

7. Warwo, *The Franco-Prussian War,* 67–68, 85–91.

8. Horne, *The Fall of Paris,* 72. Trochu's warning came on August 10.

9. Stewart Edwards, *The Paris Commune, 1871* (New York: Quadrangle, 1972), 47–48; Horne, *The Fall of Paris,* 71–74. Eudes was subsequently condemned to death for his part, then sent to prison instead.

10. Horne, *The Fall of Paris,* 67–70; Tombs, *The War Against Paris,* 15–21.

11. Pascal Chambon, "1871, la fin de la Garde nationale," in *La Commune de 1871. L'événement les hommes et la mémoire,* edited by Claude Latta (Saint-Étienne: Publications de l'Université de Saint-Étienne, 2004), 79; Robert Tombs, *The Paris Commune, 1871* (New York: Longman, 1999), 46.

12. Stéphane Rials, *Nouvelle histoire de Paris de Trochu à Thiers 1870–1873* (Paris: Hachette, 1985), 55.

13. Carolyn Eichner, *Surmounting the Barricades: Women in the Paris Commune* (Bloomington: Indiana University Press, 2004), 19–21.

14. Sutter-Laumann, *Histoire d'un trente sous (1870–1871)* (Paris: A. Savine, 1891), 27–30, 33, 45–49.

15. This account draws on Rials, *Nouvelle histoire*, 56–69.

16. Rials, *Nouvelle histoire*, 69. The republic had already been proclaimed in Lyon and Marseille.

17. Edwards, *The Paris Commune*, 59–60.

18. Horne, *The Fall of Paris*, 84; Rials, *Nouvelle histoire*, 73. Napoleon III died in exile in England in January 1873.

19. Luc Willette, *Raoul Rigault, 25 ans, Communard, chef de police* (Paris: Syros, 1984), 52–58; Patrick H. Hutton, *The Cult of the Revolutionary Tradition: The Blanquists in French Politics, 1864–1892* (Berkeley: University of California Press, 1981), 33–34.

20. Gérard Dittmar, *Belleville de l'annexation à la Commune* (Paris: Dittmar, 2007), 57; Edwards, *The Paris Commune*, 87; Odile Krakovitch, "Les femmes de Montmartre et Clemenceau durant le siège de Paris: De l'action sociale à l'action politique," in Latta, *La Commune de 1871*, 43–58.

21. Jacques Rougerie, *Paris libre 1871* (Paris: Éditions du Seuil, 1971), 74; Hutton, *The Cult of the Revolutionary Tradition*, 55, 64.

22. See Robert Tombs's excellent analysis in *The Paris Commune, 1871*, 73–77.

23. Willette, *Raoul Rigault*, 54; Tombs, *The Paris Commune, 1871*, 56.

24. Howard, *The Franco-Prussian War*, 286–288; Horne, *The Fall of Paris*, 140–146.

25. Villiers du Terrage (B[ar]on Marc de), *Histoire des clubs de femmes et des Légions d'Amazones 1793–1848–1871* (Paris: Plon-Nourrit, 1910), 383–386.

26. Sutter-Laumann, *Histoire*, 75–77, 201–209.

27. Sutter-Laumann, *Histoire*, 75–77, 201–209; Martin Phillip Johnson, *The Paradise of Association: Political Culture and Popular Organizations in the Paris Commune of 1871* (Ann Arbor: University of Michigan Press, 1996), 29–34; Willette, *Raoul Rigault*, 60–64. Louis Blanc and Alexandre Ledru-Rollin, important personages in 1848, were also there.

28. Tombs, *The Paris Commune, 1871*, 52, 73; Edwards, *The Paris Commune*, 75–76.

29. Alistair Horne, *The Fall of Paris* (New York: Penguin, 2007), 131–134.

30. Horne, *The Fall of Paris*, 220–224.

31. Jean Dubois, *À travers les oeuvres des écrivains, les revues et les journaux. Vocabulaire politique et social en France de 1869 à 1872* (Paris: Larousse, 1962), 179–180.

32. Choury, *Les damnés de la terre*, 36; Dittmar, *Belleville*, 188–189, 199–200, 206; Dubois, *À travers les oeuvres*, 265; Edwards, *The Paris Commune*, 73.

33. Tombs, *The Paris Commune, 1871*, 59; Willette, *Raoul Rigault*, 68–70.

34. Tombs, *The Paris Commune, 1871*, 60. The commanders of thirty-five National Guard battalions attempted to generate resistance to German armies but to no avail.

35. Johnson, *The Paradise of Association*, 55–64.

36. Pierre Lévêque, "Les courants politiques de la Commune de Paris" in Latta, ed., *La Commune de 1871*, 33; Tombs, *The Paris Commune, 1871*, 62.

37. Maurice Reclus, *Monsieur Thiers* (Paris: Plon, 1929), 12–25, 53; Camille de Meaux, *Souvenirs politiques, 1871–1877* (Paris: Plont-Nourrit et c^ie., 1905), 48.

38. Joseph-Alfred Foulon, *Histoire de la vie et des oeuvres de Mgr Darboy, archevêque de Paris* (Paris: Possielgue frères, 1889), 509; Joseph Abel Guillermin, *Vie de Mgr Darboy, archevêque de Paris, mis à mort en haine de la foi le 24 mai 1871* (Paris: Bloud et Barral, 1888), 313.

39. Eichner, *Surmounting the Barricades*, 21; Johnson, *The Paradise of Association*, 67–70.

40. Robert Tombs, "L'année terrible, 1870–71," *Historical Journal* 35, no. 3 (1992): 717–718; Bernard Accoyer, ed., *De l'Empire à la République: Les comités secrets au Parlement, 1870–1871* (Paris: Le grand livre du mois, 2011), 33–38.

41. Élie Reclus, *La Commune de Paris au jour le jour* (Saint-Martin-de-Bonfossé: Théolib, 2001), 174–175. Thiers famously said that the republic "will be conservative or it will not be."

42. Quentin Deluermoz, *Policiers dans la ville: La construction d'un ordre public à Paris 1854–1914* (Paris: Publications de la Sorbonne, 2012), 151–153; Denis Arthur Bingham, *Recollections of Paris* (London: Chapman and Hall, 1896), 2:19.

43. Dale Lothrop Clifford, "Aux armes citoyens! The National Guard in the Paris Commune of 1871" (unpublished PhD diss., University of Tennessee, 1975), 116.

44. Clifford, "Aux armes citoyens!" 125; Pierre Guiral, *Adolphe Thiers* (Paris: Fayard, 1986), 376, 393; Jules Simon, *The Governement of M. Thiers* (New York, 1879), 1:291.

45. Jean-François Lecaillon, ed., *La Commune de Paris racontée par les Parisiens* (Paris: B. Giovanangeli, 2009), 19; Tombs, "L'année terrible, 1870–71," 719–721.

46. Vuillaume, *Mes cahiers rouges*, 158.

47. Edwards, *The Paris Commune*, 118–119.

48. Adolphe Thiers, *Memoirs of M. Thiers, 1870–1873* (New York: Howard Fertig, 1973), 121, 136.

49. Simon, *The Government of M. Thiers*, 1:286–290.

50. de Meaux, *Souvenirs politiques*, 43–45; Léonce Dupont, *Souvenirs de Versailles pendant la Commune* (Paris: E. Dentu, 1881), 21; Edwards, *The Paris Commune*, 166; Maurice Garçon, "Journal d'un bourgeois de Paris," *Revue de Paris* 12 (December 1955): 26.

51. Dupont, *Souvenirs de Versailles*, 85–90, 110–111; Hector Pessard, *Mes petits papiers, 1871–73* (Paris: Quintin, 1887), 11, 40–42.

CHAPTER 2:
THE BIRTH OF THE COMMUNE

1. Dale Lothrop Clifford, "Aux armes citoyens! The National Guard in the Paris Commune of 1871" (unpublished PhD diss., University of Tennessee, 1975), 125; Pierre Guiral, *Adolphe Thiers* (Paris: Fayard, 1986), 376, 393; Jules Simon, *The Government of M. Thiers* (New York: C. Scribner's Sons, 1879), 1:291.

2. Jean-Claude Freiermuth, "L'armée et l'ordre en 1870–71: le cas Vinoy," in *Maintien de l'ordre et police en France et en Europe au XIXe siècle*, edited by Philippe Vigier et al. (Paris: Créaphis, 1987), 42–47; Elihu Benjamin Washburne, *Franco-German War and Insurrection of the Commune: Correspondence of E. B. Washburne* (Washington, DC: Government Printing Office, 1878).

3. Clifford, "Aux armes citoyens!" 119–127; Martin Phillip Johnson, *The Paradise of Association: Political Culture and Popular Organizations in the Paris Commune of 1871* (Ann Arbor: University of Michigan Press, 1996), 2–3, 277–279; Jean Baronnet, ed., *Enquête sur la Commune de Paris (La Revue Blanche)* (Paris: Les éditions de l'amateur, 2011), 93; Stewart Edwards, *The Paris Commune, 1871* (New York: Quadrangle, 1972), 129; Robert Tombs, *The War Against Paris, 1871* (Cambridge: Cambridge University Press, 1981), 39–43.

4. Edwards, *The Paris Commune*, 137–140; Stéphane Rials, *Nouvelle histoire de Paris de Trochu à Thiers 1870–1873* (Paris: Hachette, 1985), 251–252.

5. Gay Gullickson, *Unruly Women of Paris: Images of the Commune* (Ithaca, NY: Cornell University Press, 1996), 25.

6. Robert Tombs, *The War Against Paris, 1871*, 43–44.

7. François du Barail (Général), *Mes souvenirs* (Paris: E. Plon, 1898), 3:246–247.

8. Stewart Edwards, ed., *The Communards of Paris, 1871* (Ithaca, NY, 1973), 56–62.

9. Edwards, *The Paris Commune*, 140.

10. Carolyn Eichner, *Surmounting the Barricades: Women in the Paris Commune* (Bloomington: Indiana University Press, 2004), 22; Gullickson, *Unruly Women*, 25–28; Edwards, *The Paris Commune*, 137–139.

11. Edith Thomas, *Louise Michel* (Montreal: Black Rose Books, 1980), 21, 77–78, 87–88; Louise Michel, Lowry Bullitt, and Elizabeth Ellington Gunter, *The Red Virgin: Memoirs of Louise Michel* (University: University of Alabama Press, 1981); William Serman, *La Commune de Paris* (Paris: Fayard, 1986), 290; Eichner, *Surmounting the Barricades*, 2–3, 22, 48–49.

12. Edwards, *The Communards of Paris*, 62–63; Sutter-Laumann, *Histoire d'un trente sous (1870–1871)* (Paris: A. Savine, 1891), 225.

13. Gullickson, *Unruly Women*, 35–36; Edwards, *The Communards of Paris*, 63–65.

14. Gullickson, *Unruly Women*, 43; Tombs, *The War Against Paris*, 46–47.

15. Edwards, *The Paris Commune*, 137–142.

16. Jacques Rougerie, *La Commune de 1871* (Paris: Presses universitaires de France, 1988), 53; Rials, *Nouvelle histoire*, 255–256; Clifford, "Aux armes citoyens!" 145–163; Eugène Varlin, *Pratique militante et écrits d'un ouvrier communard*, edited by Paule Lejeune (Paris: F. Maspero, 1977), 155; Benoît Malon, *La troisième défaite du prolétariat français* (Neuchâtel: G. Guillaume fils, 1871), 74; Michel, Bullitt, and Gunter, *The Red Virgin*, 64–65.

17. Adolphe Thiers, *Déposition de M. Thiers sur le dix-huit mars* (Paris: Librarie générale, 1871), 33–43; Quentin Deluermoz, *Policiers dans la ville: La construction d'un ordre public à Paris 1854–1914* (Paris: Publications de la Sorbonne, 2012), 141–144, 154–155; Edwards, *The Paris Commune*, 148–150; Philippe Riviale, *Sur la Commune: Cerises de sang* (Paris: L'Harmattan, 2003), 194.

18. Jean-François Lecaillon, ed., *La Commune de Paris racontée par les Parisiens* (Paris: B. Giovanangeli, 2009), 38–39; Johnson, *The Paradise of Association*, 6.

19. George J. Becker, ed., *Paris Under Siege, 1870–71: From the Goncourt Journal* (Ithaca, NY: Cornell University Press, 1969), 228–237.

20. Ernest Vizetelly, *My Adventures in The Commune* (London: Chatto and Windus, 1914), 36; Lecaillon, *La Commune de Paris*, 37.

21. Christiane Demeulenaere-Douyère, "Un témoin de la Commune de Paris: Eugène Bersier," *Bulletin de la Société d'Histoire de Paris et de l'Ile de France* 108 (1981): 247; J. Rocher, ed., *Lettres de Communards et de militants de la Première Internationale à Marx, Engels et autres dans les journées de la Commune de Paris en 1871* (Paris: Bureau d'éditions, 1934), March 29; Lecaillon, *La Commune de Paris*, 39–41.

22. Paul Vignon, *Rien que ce que j'ai vu! Le siège de Paris—la Commune* (Paris: E. Capiomont, 1913), 87–92.

23. Serman, *La Commune de Paris*, 214–215; Riviale, *Sur la Commune*, 219–220; Alistair Horne, *The Fall of Paris: The Siege and the Commune, 1870–71* (New York: Penguin, 1965), 347.

24. Jacques Rougerie, *Paris libre 1871* (Paris: Éditions du Seuil, 1971), 114; Edwards, *The Paris Commune*, 151.

25. Maurice Dommanget, *Blanqui, Guerre de 1870–71 et la Commune* (Paris: Domat-Montchrestien, 1947), 114; Marcel Cerf, *Édouard Moreau, l'âme du Comité central de la Commune* (Paris: Les lettres nouvelles, 1971), 11; Edwards, *The Paris Commune*, 213.

26. Jacques Rougerie, "Autour de quelques livres étrangers," in Claude Latta, ed., *La Commune de 1871. L'événement les hommes et la mémoire* (Saint-Étienne: Publications de l'Université de Saint-Étienne, 2004), 58; Claude Latta, "Benoit Malon pendant la Commune," in Latta, *La Commune de 1871*, 112–113; Jacques Rougerie, *Procès des Communards* (Paris: Julliard, 1964), 142–143; Horne, *The Fall of Paris*, 359; Edwards, *The Paris Commune*, 155.

27. Malon, *La troisième défaite*, 93–98; Da Costa, *Mémoires d'un Communard: la Commune vécue* (Paris: Larousse, 2009), 91–98; Edwards, *The Paris Commune*, 162–164. Louis M. Greenberg, in *Sisters of Liberty: Marseille, Lyon, Paris and the Reaction to a Centralized State, 1868–1871* (Cambridge, MA: Harvard

University Press, 1971), seriously underestimates essential economic and social dimensions of the Commune.

28. Bernard Accoyer, ed., *De l'Empire à la République: Les comités secrets au Parlement, 1870–1871* (Paris: Le grand livre du mois, 2011), 54–63, 201, 205, 221, 229; Édouard Lockroy, *La Commune et l'Assemblée* (Paris: A. Chevalier, 1871), 26–29, 38.

29. Serman, *La Commune de Paris*, 371; Jean Dubois, *À travers les oeuvres des écrivains, les revues et les journaux. Vocabulaire politique et social en France de 1869 à 1872* (Paris: Larousse, 1962), 136, 163, 179–180; Adolphe Thiers, *Histoire de la Révolution du 4 septembre et de l'insurrection du 18 mars* (Paris: Garnier frères, 1875), 156.

30. Malon, *La troisième défaite*, 99; Élie Reclus, *La Commune de Paris au jour le jour* (Saint-Martin-de-Bonfossé: Théolib, 2001), 30; Gaston Cerfbeer, "Une nuit de la semaine sanglante," *Revue Hebdomadaire* 25 (May 23, 1903), 416.

31. Reclus, *La Commune de Paris*, 143–147.

32. Rougerie, *Paris libre 1871*, 128–130, 140; Peter McPhee, *A Social History of France, 1780–1880* (New York: Routledge, 1992), 214; Jeanne Gaillard, *Communes de province, commune de Paris 1870–1871* (Paris: Flammarion, 1971), 34; Latta, "Benoit Malon," 114; Carolyn Eichner, *Surmounting the Barricades*, 30; David Barry, *Women and Political Insurgency: France in the Mid-Nineteenth Century* (Basingstoke, UK: Macmillan, 1996), 108–111.

33. J. P. T. Bury and R. P. Tombs, *Thiers—a Political Life, 1797–1877* (London: Allen and Unwin, 1986), 200.

34. Philip Nord, "The Party of Conciliation and the Paris Commune," *French Historical Studies* 15, no. 1 (1987): 5, 9–12.

35. Rougerie, *Procès des Communards*, 147–151.

36. Sébastien Commissaire, *Mémoires et souvenirs* (Lyon: Meton, 1888), 2:369–370; Jean Dautry and Lucien Scheler, *Le Comité central républicain des vingt arrondissements de Paris (septembre 1870–mai 1871), d'après les papiers inédits de Constant Martin et les sources imprimées* (Paris: Éditions sociales, 1960), 236–238.

37. Edwards, *The Communards of Paris*, 69–71; Edwards, *The Paris Commune*, 173; Johnson, *The Paradise of Association*, 21. There were probably about 1,000 members of the International in Paris.

38. Reclus, *La Commune de Paris*, 82–83; Paul Reclus, *Les frères Élie et Élisée Reclus* (Paris: Les amis d'Élisée Reclus, 1964), 161–181, 188; Rougerie, *Procès des Communards*, 217–222; Edwards, *The Paris Commune*, 11–14. See Eugene Schulkind, "The Activity of Popular Organizations During the Paris Commune of 1871," *French Historical Studies*, no. 4 (1960): 408.

39. Louis Barron, *Sous la drapeau rouge* (Paris: A. Savine, 1889), 2.

40. Rials, *Nouvelle histoire*, 283–289; Luc Willette, *Raoul Rigault, 25 ans, Communard, chef de police* (Paris: Syros, 1984), 93–94.

41. Rials, *Nouvelle histoire*, 303–307; Willette, *Raoul Rigault*, 100–101; Alain Dalotel, *Gabriel Ranvier, le Christ de Belleville: Blanquiste, Franc-maçon, Communard et maire du XXe arrondissement* (Paris: Éditions Dittmar, 2005), 29–44; Maxime Jourdan, *Le cri du peuple* (Paris: L'Harmattan, 2005), 63–74, esp. February 22.

42. Johnson, *The Paradise of Association*, 6, 93–108; Clifford, "Aux armes citoyens!" 188; Tombs, *The Paris Commune, 1871*, 7.

43. R. D. Price, "Ideology and Motivation in the Paris Commune of 1871," *Historical Journal* 15 (1972): 76; Edwards, *The Communards of Paris*, 78–79; Camille Pelletan, *Questions d'histoire. Le Comité central et la Commune* (Paris: M. Dreyfous, 1879), 51; Jules Andrieu, "The Paris Commune: A Chapter Towards Its Theory and History," *Fortnightly* X (new series) (November 1871): 597.

44. Jourdan, *Le cri*, 107 (March 30); Prosper-Olivier Lissagaray, *History of the Paris Commune of 1871* (New York: New Park Publications, 1976), 128; Edwards, *The Paris Commune*, 186.

45. Da Costa, *Mémoires d'un Communard*, 109; Georges Bourgin, *La Commune de Paris* (Paris: Presses universitaires de France, 1971), 31–32, 40; Rials, *Nouvelle histoire*, 320–322; Malon, *La troisième défaite*, 130. A by-election took place on April 16 to replace the thirty-one men who had resigned, been elected from several arrondissements, been killed in early fighting, or, as in the case of Blanqui, been imprisoned. These elections, which had a low turnout, increased the number of radicals in the Commune (Laure Godineau, *La Commune de Paris par ceux qui l'ont vécue* [Paris: Parigramme, 2010], 45–51).

46. Varlin, *Pratique militante*, 164; Adolphe Thiers, *Notes et souvenirs de M. Thiers 1870–1873* (Paris: Calmann-Lévy, 1903), 145; Rougerie, *La Commune de 1871*, 72.

47. Riviale, *Sur la Commune*, 217; Paul Lidsky, *Les écrivains contre la Commune* (Paris: F. Maspero, 1970), 69; Johnson, *The Paradise of Association*, 224; Edwards, *The Paris Commune*, 190–191; Clifford, "Aux armes citoyens!" 164; Godineau, *La Commune de Paris*, 82; Maxime Vuillaume, *Mes cahiers rouges au temps de la Commune* (Paris: A. Michel, 1971), 286–292.

48. Tombs, *The Paris Commune, 1871*, 820–883.

49. Rougerie, *Procès des Communards*, 160–161, 241. Rougerie insists that these two conceptions of the Commune were not necessarily always contradictory and that the influence of Proudhon on the Commune has been exaggerated. Beginning April 20, the Executive Commission consisted of the delegates of the nine commissions as elected.

50. Reclus, *La Commune de Paris*, 235–236; Varlin, *Pratique militante*, 169–170.

51. Wickham Hoffman, *Camp, Court, and Siege: A Narrative of Personal Adventure and Observation During Two Wars, 1861–1865, 1870–1871* (New York: Harper and Brothers, 1877), 252; Rials, *Nouvelle histoire*, 345; Rougerie, *Paris libre 1871*, 187; Rocher, *Lettres de Communards*; E. Tersen, "Léo Frankel," *Europe* 29, nos. 64–65 (April–May 1951): 157–158.

52. Bury and Tombs, *Thiers*, 203. The other challenges were to prevent Bismarck and the newly unified German Empire from taking advantage of the provisional government's difficult situation and to maintain support in the

provinces, particularly in major centers of republicanism, such as Lyon and Marseille. See Greenberg, *Sisters of Liberty*.

53. Godineau, *La Commune de Paris*, 178.

54. William Serman, *Les officiers français dans la nation* (Paris: Aubier Montaigne, 1982), 15–18, 54; William Serman, *Les origines des officiers français 1848–1870* (Paris: Publications de la Sorbonne, 1979), 4–6.

55. Tombs, *The War Against Paris*, 110–123; Simon, *The Government*, 1:290; Riviale, *Sur la Commune*, 236.

56. Jacques Silvestre de Sacy, *Le Maréchal de Mac-Mahon* (Paris: Éditions inter-nationale, 1960), 255; Tombs, *The War Against Paris*, 96–100; Gabriel de Broglie, *Mac-Mahon* (Paris: Perrin, 2000), 175.

57. Tombs, *The War Against Paris*, 126–127.

58. Clifford, "Aux armes citoyens!" 106–107; Rougerie, *Procès des Communards*, 256–270.

59. 8J conseil de guerre 3, dossier 571, Gustave Cluseret, order of April 16, court-martial session April 17; Ernest A. Vizetelly, *My Adventures in the Commune*, 54; Rials, *Nouvelle histoire*, 326–327, 459; Jules Bourelly (Général), *Le ministère de la guerre sous la Commune* (Paris: Combet, 1911), 84; Clifford, "Aux armes citoyens!" 197–198.

60. 8J conseil de guerre 3, dossier 571, Gustave Cluseret, orders April 16, 21, and 23; Gaston Da Costa, *Mémoires d'un Communard*, 203–208; Vizetelly, *My Adventures*, 117, 132; Rials, *Nouvelle histoire*, 199–218, 326–327; Pascal Chambon, "1871, la fin de la Garde nationale," in *La Commune de 1871*. Latta, 81–83. Prosper-Olivier Lissagaray estimated the number at 100,000 men for active duty and another 103,500 for "sedentary" activity, including manning the ramparts and two hundred available cannon.

61. John Leighton, *Paris Under the Commune* (London: Bradbury, Evans and Company, 1871), 208.

62. Bury and Tombs, *Thiers*, 203; Thiers, *Déposition*, 53; Thiers, *Notes et souvenirs*, 162–165.

63. Louis Thomas, *Le général de Galliffet (1830–1909)* (Paris: Aux armes de France, 1941), 92; Albert de Mun (Count), "Galliffet," *Écho de Paris*, July 10, 1909; Tombs, *The War Against Paris*, 79; Simon, *The Government*, 363; Edwards, *The Paris Commune*, 192–194. In the wake of the first encounter, Rossel found himself arrested and in prison for one night for reasons that are not clear.

64. Edwards, *The Paris Commune*, 196; Tombs, *The War Against Paris*, 79; A. Balland, *La guerre de 1870 et la Commune* (Bourg-en-Bresse, FR: Imprimerie du Courrier de l'Ain, 1916), 151–152.

65. Rials, *Nouvelle histoire*, 262.

66. Godelier (colonel), "La guerre de 1870 et la Commune: Journal d'un officier d'état-major," *Nouvelle revue rétrospective* 17 (July–December 1902): 18–20.

67. Leighton, *Paris Under the Commune*, 85; Rials, *Nouvelle histoire*, 262–263.

68. Jean-Pierre Béneytou, *Vinoy: Général du Second Empire* (Paris: Éditions Christian, 2003), 182; Charles Prolès, *G. Flourens* (Paris: Chamuel, 1898), 89; Tombs, *The War Against Paris*, 85–86; Edwards, *The Paris Commune*, 199–200.

69. Sutter-Laumann, *Histoire*, 243–264. 8J conseil de guerre 3, dossier 571, Gustave Cluseret, copies of dispatches.

70. Sutter-Laumann, *Histoire*, 264–273.

71. Edwards, *The Communards of Paris*, 142–143.

CHAPTER 3:
MASTERS OF THEIR OWN LIVES

1. Ernest A. Vizetelly, *My Adventures in the Commune* (London: Chatto and Windus, 2009), 95, 136.

2. Louis Barron, *Sous la drapeau rouge* (Paris: A. Savine, 1889), 112–116; Laure Godineau, *La Commune de Paris par ceux qui l'ont vécue* (Paris: Parigramme, 2010), 112–114.

3. Albert Boime, *Art and the French Commune: Imagining Paris After War and Revolution* (Princeton, NJ: Princeton University Press, 1995), 17; Kathleen Jones and Françoise Vergès, "'Aux citoyennes!': Women, Politics, and the Paris Commune of 1871," *History of European Ideas* 13 (1991): 725. Some historians have perhaps overemphasized the festive aspects of daily life during the Commune. See Robert Tombs, *The Paris Commune, 1871* (New York: Longman, 1999), 105–107.

4. John Leighton, *Paris Under the Commune* (London: Bradbury, Evans and Company, 1871), 128; Stéphane Rials, *Nouvelle histoire de Paris de Trochu à Thiers 1870–1873* (Paris: Hachette, 1985), 403; Henri Dubief, "Défense de Gustave Courbet par lui-même," *L'Actualité de l'Histoire* 30 (January–March 1960): 32.

5. Kristin Ross, *The Emergence of the Social Space: Rimbaud and the Paris Commune* (Minneapolis: University of Minnesota Press, 1988), 136–137; Janine Bouissounouse and Louis de Villefosse, "La presse parisienne pendant la Commune," *Europe* (April–May 1951): 50; Maxime Jourdan, *Le cri du peuple* (Paris: L'Harmattan, 2005), 17, 123; Firmin Maillard, *Histoire des journaux publiés à Paris pendant le siege et sous la Commune* (Paris: E. Dentu, 1871), 195–212.

6. Marcel Cerf, *Les 'Cahiers rouges' de Maxime Vuillaume* (Paris: J. Braire, 1988), 2–9; Jacques Rougerie, *La Commune de 1871* (Paris: Presses universitaires de France, 1988), 96–98; Élie Reclus, *La Commune de Paris au jour le jour* (Saint-Martin-de-Bonfossé: Théolib, 2011), 225. In late April *Père Duchêne* organized an undisciplined battalion of paid *francs-tireurs* known as the Enfants du Père Duchêne, which consisted of seventy men wearing grey pants, a red flannel shirt, a jacket, and the National Guard kepi.

7. Reclus, *La Commune de Paris*, 243–245; Elihu Benjamin Washburne, *Franco-German War and Insurrection of the Commune: Correspondence of E. B. Washburne* (Washington, DC: Government Printing Office, 1878), May 19; Vizetelly, *My Adventures*, 135.

8. John Milner, *Art, War, and Revolution in France, 1870–71* (New Haven, CT: Yale University Press, 2000), 140; Martin Phillip Johnson, *The Paradise of Association: Political Culture and Popular Organizations in the Paris Commune of 1871* (Ann Arbor: University of Michigan Press, 1996), v.

9. Maurice Choury, *Bonjour Monsieur Courbet!* (Paris: Éditions sociales, 1969), 96.

10. Barron, *Sous la drapeau rouge*, 5–8.

11. APP, Ba 1020, dossier Courbet; Gonzolo J. Sánchez, *Organizing Independence: The Artists Federation of the Paris Commune and Its Legacy, 1871–1889* (Lincoln: University of Nebraska Press, 1997), 57, 65.

12. Choury, *Bonjour Monsieur Courbet!* 91–94; Sánchez, *Organizing Independence*, 43–56; Robert Boudry, "Courbet et la fédération des artistes," *Europe* 29, nos. 64–65 (April–May 1951): 124–125; Dubief, "Défense de Gustave Courbet," 32.

13. Gérald Dittmar, *Gustave Courbet et la Commune, le politique* (Paris: Dittmar, 2007), 99.

14. Paul Reclus, *Les frères Élie et Élisée Reclus* (Paris: Les amis d'Élisée Reclus, 1964), 181–182, 189.

15. Sylvie Chevalley, "La Comédie-française pendant la Commune," *Europe* 48 (November–December 1970): 499–500; Catulle Mendès, *Les 73 jours de la Commune* (Paris: Lachaud, 1871), 182. The Commune issued only one decree on theaters, suppressing "all monopolies," dated 1er prairial en 79 (May 20), 198; André Tissier, "Les spectacles pendant la Commune," *Europe* 48 (November–December 1970): 180.

16. Mendès, *Les 73 jours de la Commune*, 181.

17. Guy Tréal, "La musique et la Commune," *Europe* 29 (April–May 1951): 112–121.

18. Vizetelly, *My Adventures*, 61, 65.

19. Vizetelly, *My Adventures*, 56, 61, 63, 65; R. D. Price, "Ideology and Motivation in the Paris Commune of 1871," *Historical Journal* 15 (1972): 80–81; Godineau, *La Commune de Paris*, 65.

20. Luc Willette, *Raoul Rigault, 25 ans, Communard, chef de police* (Paris: Syros, 1984), 96–102; Tombs, *The Paris Commune, 1871*, 76–81.

21. Georges Bourgin, *La Commune de Paris* (Paris: Presses universitaires de France, 1971), 81; Édith Thomas, *Les pétroleuses* (Paris: Gallimard, 1963), 213; Achille Dalseme, *Histoire des conspirations sous la Commune* (Paris: Dentu, 1872), 100, 117.

22. Adolphe Thiers, *Notes et souvenirs de M. Thiers 1870–1873* (Paris: Calmann-Lévy, 1903), 157–159; Adolphe Thiers, *Memoirs of M. Thiers, 1870–1873* (New York: Howard Fertig, 1973), 138–139; Gaston de Galliffet (Général), "Mes souvenirs," *Journal des Débats*, July 19, 22, and 25, 1902.

23. 8J 3e conseil de guerre 6, dossier 29/8 Théophile Ferré; Sutter-Laumann, *Histoire d'un trente sous (1870–1871)* (Paris: A. Savine, 1891), 221; Denis Arthur Bingham, *Recollections of Paris* (London: Chapman and Hall, 1896), 2:116;

Johnson, *The Paradise of Association*, 210; P.-P. Cattelain, *Mémoires inédits du chef de la sûreté sous la Commune* (Paris: F. Juven, 1900), 115–120.

24. Edgar Rodriguès, *Le carnaval rouge* (Paris: E. Dentu, 1872), 113; 8J 3e conseil de guerre 26, dossier 535 Gaston Da Costa; W. Pembroke Fetridge, *The Rise and Fall of the Paris Commune in 1871* (New York: Harper Brothers, 1871), 382–387.

25. Willette, *Raoul Rigault*, 122–125; Fetridge, *The Rise and Fall of the Paris Commune in 1871*, 387.

26. Gustave Cluseret (general), *Mémoires du Général Cluseret* (Paris: J. Lévy, 1887), 2:213–215; Philip M. Katz, *From Appomattox to Montmartre: Americans and the Paris Commune* (Cambridge, MA: Harvard University Press, 1998), 51–52; Gaston Da Costa, *Mémoires d'un Communard: La Commune vécue* (Paris: Larousse, 2009), 245.

27. Cattelain, *Mémoires inédits*, III; Philip Nord, *Les Impressionistes et la politique* (Paris: Tallandier, 2009), 68.

28. Henri Rochefort, *The Adventures of My Life* (London: E. Arnold, 1896), 391.

29. Tombs, *The Paris Commune, 1871*, 88–90; Alistair Horne, *The Fall of Paris: The Siege and the Commune, 1870–71* (New York: Penguin, 1965), 367.

30. Willette, *Raoul Rigault*, 127–129. Ferré replaced Rigault as chief delegate at the prefecture of police on May 13.

31. Pierre Courthion, *Courbet raconté par lui-même et par ses amis*, vol. 1 (Geneva: P. Cailler, 1948); Willette, *Raoul Rigault*, 154–155; Reclus, *La Commune de Paris*, 137–138.

32. Frederic Harrison, "The Revolution and the Commune," *Fortnightly Review* 53, no. 4 (May 1871): 559, 573.

33. Jacques Rougerie, *Procès des Communards* (Paris: Julliard, 1964), 33–35, 125–134; Rougerie, *La Commune de 1871*, 99–102; Jacques Rougerie, "Composition d'une population insurgée: L'exemple de la Commune," *Mouvement Social* 48 (July–September 1964): 34, 46; Carolyn Eichner, *Surmounting the Barricades: Women in the Paris Commune* (Bloomington: Indiana University Press, 2004), 29. The median age was thirty-two; General Appert, "Rapport d'ensemble . . . sur les opérations de la justice militaire relatives à l'insurrection de 1871," *Annales de l'Assemblée nationale*, t. 43, du 1er au 17 décembre 1875 (Paris, 1876), t. 43, 117.

34. Rougerie, *La Commune de 1871*, 99–102; Rougerie, "Composition d'une population insurgée," 46.

35. David Shafer, "*Plus que des ambulancières*: Women in Articulation and Defence of Their Ideals During the Paris Commune," *French History* 7, no. 1 (1993): 97; Rougerie, "Composition d'une population insurgée," 33–46; Appert, "Rapport d'ensemble," 117; William Serman, *La Commune de Paris* (Paris: Fayard, 1986), 282–283. Among the professions: masons, 2,293; shoemakers, 1,491; domestics, 1,402; coachmen, 1,024; cabinetmakers, 1,657; day laborers, 2,901; locksmiths/mechanics, 2,664; building painters, 863, etc.; Jones and Vergès, "Aux citoyennes!" 716–719.

36. Wickham Hoffman, *Camp, Court, and Siege: A Narrative of Personal Adventure and Observation During Two Wars, 1861–1865, 1870–1871* (New York: Harper and Brothers, 1877), 246, 261.

37. Paul Lidsky, *Les écrivains contre la Commune* (Paris: F. Maspero, 1970), 48.

38. George J. Becker, ed., *Paris Under Siege, 1870–71: From the Goncourt Journal* (Ithaca, NY: Cornell University Press, 1969), 263.

39. Price, "Ideology and Motivation," 84; Robert Tombs, "Prudent Rebels: The 2nd Arrondissement During the Paris Commune of 1871," *French History* 5, no. 4 (1991): 393–413.

40. Horne, *The Fall of Paris*, 106; Stewart Edwards, ed., *The Communards of Paris, 1871* (Ithaca, NY: Cornell University Press, 1973), 81–83; Godineau, *La Commune de Paris*, 91–93; Rials, *Nouvelle histoire*, 422–423.

41. Pierre Lévêque, "Les courants politiques de la Commune de Paris," in *La Commune de 1871. L'événement les hommes et la mémoire*, edited by Claude Latta (Saint-Etienne: Publications de l'Université de Saint-Étienne, 2004), 32–35; Johnson, *The Paradise of Association*, 138–144.

42. Edwards, *The Communards of Paris*, 127–130.

43. Bourgin, *La Commune de Paris*, 55–56; Robert Tombs, "Harbingers or Entrepreneurs? A Worker's Cooperative During the Paris Commune," *Historical Journal* 27, no. 4 (1984): 970–977. The Association des Ouvriers de la Métallurgie was the other major cooperative.

44. Edwards, *The Communards of Paris*, 138–139; Rials, *Nouvelle histoire*, 419; Sébastien Commissaire, *Mémoires et souvenirs* (Lyon: Meton, 1888), 2:370–372. The salary decree was approved on May 21.

45. Rougerie, *Paris libre 1871* (Paris: Éditions du Seuil, 1971), 78.

46. Jones and Vergès, "Aux citoyennes!" 711–713; Gay Gullickson, *Unruly Women of Paris: Images of the Commune* (Ithaca, NY: Cornell University Press, 1996), 122–123; Eichner, *Surmounting the Barricades*, 1; Johnson, *The Paradise of Association*, 235.

47. Shafer, "*Plus que des ambulancières*," 91.

48. Eugene Schulkind, "Socialist Women During the 1871 Paris Commune," *Past and Present* 106 (February 1985): 133–134; Robert Tombs, "Les Communeuses," *Sociétés et Représentations* (June 1998): 6:54; Jones and Vergès, "Aux citoyennes!" 716–719; Rougerie, *Procès des Communards*, 214.

49. 8J 6e conseil de guerre, 683; Sylvie Braibant, ed., *Elisabeth Dmitrieff* (Paris: Belfond, 1993), 162; Eichner, *Surmounting the Barricades*, 29; Godineau, *La Commune de Paris*, 153–155; David Barry, *Women and Political Insurgency: France in the Mid-Nineteenth Century* (Basingstoke, UK: Macmillan, 1996), 130–131.

50. Jones and Vergès, "Aux citoyennes!" 728; Eichner, *Surmounting the Barricades*, 111–115.

51. 8J 6e conseil de guerre, 683; Gullickson, *Unruly Women*, 121–125; Eichner, *Surmounting the Barricades*, 69.

52. 8J, 4e conseil de guerre 131, dossier 688; Eichner, *Surmounting the Barricades*, 36–37, 63–65, 91–93; Braibant, *Elisabeth Dmitrieff*, 126, 141–142, 146–147.

53. Edwards, *The Communards of Paris*, 130–133.

54. Schulkind, "Socialist Women During the 1871 Paris Commune," 136, 154–58, 162; Jones and Vergès, "Aux citoyennes!" 714–715; Eichner, *Surmounting the Barricades*, 69–78, 87. One document suggests that in the Seventh Arrondissement, 365 women were members.

55. Katz, *From Appomattox to Montmartre*, 15–16, 26, 52–53, 354, 364, 426, 478.

56. René Bidouze, *72 jours qui changèrent la cité. La Commune de Paris dans l'histoire des services publics* (Pantin: Le Temps des cerises, 2001), 7, 88–89, 93, 100–101, 121, 130–131, 144.

57. Bidouze, *72 jours*, 108–114, 127; Archibald Forbes, "What an American Girl Saw of the Commune," *Century Illustrated Magazine* 45, no. 1 (November 1892): 66. The Commune's Commission des Finances oversaw income: bank of France, 15 million; *octrois*, just over 12.2 million; direct taxes, 373,813; industry and tobacco, 2.629 million; stamps and registrations of documents, 800,000; markets, 814,323; railways, 2 million; reimbursements by the National Guard, 1 million; various other revenues, 50,000; money seized, just under 6,609 million; total: nearly 41.95 million. The Commune spent about 42 million francs, 33 million of which went to the War Delegation, mostly to pay National Guard salaries, or to the arrondissements (Tombs, *The Paris Commune*, 90–93); Rials, *Nouvelle histoire*, 380–382.

58. Rials, *Nouvelle histoire*, 411–413; Willette, *Raoul Rigault*, 125–126.

59. Reclus, *La Commune de Paris*, 278; W. Gibson, *Paris During the Commune* (London: Methodist Book Room, 1895), 196, 206–207; Jean-François Lecaillon, ed., *La Commune de Paris racontée par les Parisiens* (Paris: B. Giovanangeli, 2009), 112; Choury, *Bonjour Monsieur Courbet!* 86; Rougerie, *Procès des Communards*, 197, 206–207; 8J 3e conseil de guerre 36, dossier Fortuné Henry.

60. Paul Martine, *Souvenirs d'insurgé. La Commune de 1871* (Paris: Perrin, 1971), 103–105. After the Commune, the *hommes d'ordre* declared such marriages null and void; one would have thought these individuals would have been pleased that such people were no longer in *unions libres*, so common among working people, of which they disapproved.

61. Stewart Edwards, *The Paris Commune, 1871* (London: Eyre and Spottiswoode, 1971), 289 and ch. 9.

62. Johnson, *The Paradise of Association*, 153–155, 171–184; Eugene Schulkind, "The Activity of Popular Organizations During the Paris Commune of 1871," *French Historical Studies*, no. 4 (1960): 400, 408. They were more likely to have had some sort of prior conviction for an offense against "public order," thus a political offense under the Second Empire.

63. Sutter-Laumann, *Histoire*, 274–289.

64. Vizetelly, *My Adventures*, 115; Becker, *Paris Under Siege*, 246, 248–250, 258, 265.

65. Jules Bourelly (Général), *Le ministère de la guerre sous la Commune* (Paris: Combet, 1911), 243; Mendès, *Les 73 jours de la Commune*, 193.

66. Paul Vignon, *Rien que ce que j'ai vu! Le siège de Paris—la Commune* (Paris: E. Capiomont, 1913), 97–100, 114 (Édouard's letters of March 22, 24, and 30; Paul, March 22 and 28), 137, 154–155 (Henri, April 14, 19).

67. Vignon, *Rien que ce que j'ai vu!* 184–185 (domestics, May 7).

68. Vignon, *Rien que ce que j'ai vu!* 109–119, 137, 145–146, 157 (Henri, April 10; Édouard, March 28 and 30; Paul, March 29, April 2).

69. Vignon, *Rien que ce que j'ai vu!* 146 (Paul, April 15).

70. Reclus, *La Commune de Paris*, 246.

71. Vignon, *Rien que ce que j'ai vu!* 121–125 (Édouard and Henri, April 4).

72. Vignon, *Rien que ce que j'ai vu!* 130–132 (Henri, April 8), 154–155 (Henri, April 19).

73. Vignon, *Rien que ce que j'ai vu!* 190–191 (Henri, May 13).

74. Gullickson, *Unruly Women*, 144–147.

75. Washburne, *Franco-German War*, April 4, 13, 14, 16, 20.

76. Tombs, *The Paris Commune, 1871*, 130–131; Leighton, *Paris Under the Commune*, 215–216.

77. Hoffman, *Camp, Court, and Siege*, 260.

78. Vignon, *Rien que ce que j'ai vu!* 160–172.

79. Sutter-Laumann, *Histoire*, 275–276.

80. Charles Beslay, *Mes souvenirs 1830–1848–1870* (Geneva: Slatkine, 1979), 374–380 (letter of April 24).

81. Eric Fournier, *Paris en ruines: Du Paris haussmannien au Paris communard* (Paris: Imago, 2008), 65–67; Vizetelly, *My Adventures*, 105–106; 8J 3e conseil de guerre 6, dossier 29/5 (Gustave Courbet), interrogation, July 3, 1871; Dittmar, *Gustave Courbet*, 147; Léonce Dupont, *Souvenirs de Versailles pendant la Commune* (Paris: E. Dentu, 1881), 146–147.

82. Edwards, *The Communards of Paris*, 134.

Chapter 4:
The Commune Versus the Cross

1. Jean Baronnet, ed., *Enquête sur la Commune de Paris (La Revue Blanche)* (Paris: Les éditions de l'amateur, 2011), 140; Jacques-Olivier Boudon, *Monseigneur Darboy (1813–1871)* (Paris: Éditions du Cerf, 2011), 144.

2. Joseph-Alfred Foulon, *Histoire de la vie et des oeuvres de Mgr Darboy, archevêque de Paris* (Paris: Possielgue frères, 1889), 1–25; Archives Nationales, F19 2555; Joseph Abel Guillermin, *Vie de Mgr Darboy, archevêque de Paris, mis à mort en haine de la foi le 24 mai 1871* (Paris: Bloud et Barral, 1888), 13; Boudon, *Monseigneur Darboy*, 11–15, 23–24; Jacques-Olivier Boudon, "Une nomination épiscopale sous le Second Empire: L'abbé Darboy à l'assaut de Paris," *Revue de l'Histoire Moderne et Contemporaine*, t. 39–3 (1992): 467; Archives Nationales, F19 2555; L'Abbé Omer Maurette, *Monseigneur Georges Darboy, archévêque de*

Paris, sa vie, ses œuvres (Paris: Bureau de la Tribune sacrée, 1863); Charles Chauvin, *Mgr Darboy, archevêque de Paris, otage de la Commune (1813–1871)* (Paris: Desclée de Brouwer, 2011), 12–13. A survey undertaken by Monseigneur Pierre-Louis Parisis revealed that between 8 and 16 percent of men practiced their religion in Haute-Marne; among women, the proportion was more than 60 percent (Boudon, *Monseigneur Darboy*, 18). The demolition of Notre-Dame-du-Fayl-Billot began in 1878, but parishioners expressed sufficient opposition that the choir remains, along with two very small lateral chapels and the sacristy. Élie-Jean-Baptiste was born in 1815 and became a merchant in Nancy; Eugénie married a merchant in Fayl-Billot.

3. Maurette, *Monseigneur Georges Darboy*, 1–11; Lewis C. Price, *Archbishop Darboy and Some French Tragedies, 1813–1871* (London: G. Allen and Unwin, [1918]), 144.

4. Boudon, *Monseigneur Darboy*, 26–31; Boudon, "Une nomination épiscopale," 470–472; Jacques Gadille, "Georges Darboy Archevêque de Paris," in *Mélanges offerts à M. le doyen André Latreille* (Lyon: Audin, 1972), 187–197. He soon published *les Femmes de la Bible* and *La vie des saints illustré, Saint-Augustin*.

5. George Darboy, *Statistique religieuse du diocèse de Paris mémoire sur l'etat present du diocese* (Paris: Morizot, 1856); Boudon, "Une promotion épiscopal," 474–475; Foulon, *Histoire*, 170–181. On January 3, 1857, Sibour became the second consecutive archbishop of Paris to meet a violent end, stabbed to death by a priest whom the pope had barred from the priesthood because he was an outspoken opponent of the doctrine of the immaculate conception.

6. Imbert de Saint-Amand, *Deux victimes de la Commune* (Paris: E. Dentu, 1888), 13–25; Price, *Archbishop Darboy*, 146; Boudon, *Monseigneur Darboy*, 45; Élie Reclus, *La Commune de Paris au jour le jour* (Saint-Martin-de-Bonfossé: Théolib, 2011), 76.

7. Archives Nationales, F19 2555, letter of the prefect of Meurthe-et-Moselle, March 1, 1862.

8. Alexis Pierron, *Mgr Darboy: Esquisses familières* (Paris: Laplace, Sanchez et cie., 1872), 8; Archives Nationales, F19 1954, ministre des cultes to ministre des affaires étrangères, January 13, 1863; Boudon, *Monseigneur Darboy*, 41, 64–66, 110–111, 103–104, 117–120. Empress Eugénie, however, strongly supported Deguerry's candidacy. With their son's ascension to his new post, the most important in the French Catholic Church, Darboy's parents began to "*vous-vous*" him.

9. Foulon, *Histoire*, 380, 414–421, 430, 435, 616; anonymous, *La vérité sur Mgr Darboy* (Gien, FR: P. Pigelet, 1889), 58; Price, *Archbishop Darboy*, 145; Pierron, *Mgr Darboy*, 191.

10. Adrien Dansette, *Religious History of Modern France* (New York: Herder and Herder, 1961), 1:303–306; Foulon, *Histoire*, 438–443, 460–465, 501, 505; Price, *Archbishop Darboy*, 125–127; Boudon, *Monseigneur Darboy*, 127–137; Chauvin, *Mgr Darboy*, 115, 306. Darboy presided over the funeral of a leading

figure among France's freemasons, seemingly oblivious of the presence of Masonic signs.

11. Foulon, *Histoire*, 509; Guillermin, *Vie de Mgr Darboy*, 313–317; Gustave Gautherot, *Thiers et Mgr Darboy* (Paris: Plon, 1910), 4–6.

12. Foulon, *Histoire*, 515–522; Gautherot, *Thiers et Mgr Darboy*, 11–12; Abbé [Henri-Pierre] Lamazou, *La place Vendôme et la Roquette* (Paris: C. Douniol et cie., 1876), 226; Olivier Marion, "La vie religieuse pendant la Commune de Paris 1871" (unpublished master's thesis, Paris-X Nanterre, 1981), 262. Rigault's inclination was to have Darboy and others shot immediately in retaliation for the Versaillais execution of Duval and Flourens (Luc Willette, *Raoul Rigault, 25 ans, Communard, chef de police* [Paris: Syros, 1984], 141).

13. Jean-Baptiste Clément, *La revanche des Communeux* (Paris: J. Marie, 1886–1887), 178; Pierre Vésinier, *History of the Commune of Paris* (London: Chapman and Hall, 1872), 309; L. P. Guénin, *Assassinat des otages. Sixième conseil de guerre* (Paris: Librarie de l'echo de la Sorbonne, 1871), 295–296. An article by Rigault in *La Sociale* accused the clergy of having aided the Prussians.

14. Paul Perny (R. P.), *Deux mois de prison sous la Commune, suivi de détails authentiques sur l'assassinat de Mgr l'archevêque de Paris* (Paris: Lainé, 1871), 35, 38; Willette, *Raoul Rigault*, 136; A. Rastoul, A. Rastoul, *L'Église de Paris sous la Commune* (Paris: Dillet, 1871), 25–26, 39, 55–56, 85–86, 117–118; Ernest A. Vizetelly, *My Adventures in the Commune* (London: Chatto and Windus, 2009), 109; Gaston Da Costa, *Mémoires d'un Communard: La Commune vécue* (Paris: Larousse, 2009), 158–159; Stéphane Rials, *Nouvelle histoire de Paris de Trochu à Thiers 1870–1873* (Paris: Hachette, 1985), 450; Marion, "La vie religieuse," 70–71, counts 148 priests arrested. Thirty-six of sixty-six curés were taken to prison, although some were held only briefly; twenty-five were described as "in flight."

15. de Saint-Amand, *Deux victimes*, 83; Antoine-Auguste Vidieu (abbé), *Histoire de la Commune de Paris en 1871* (Paris: E. Dentu, 1876), 1:232.

16. Clément, *La revanche des Communeux*, 168.

17. *Procès-Verbaux de la Commune de 1871* (Paris: E. Leroux, 1924), 1:145–148; Willette, *Raoul Rigault*, 109–113, 143–144; Vizetelly, *My Adventures*, 118–119. Willette (*Raoul Rigault*, 128) notes that the total number of arrests carried out during the Commune was 3,632. However, this number includes arrests for crimes and misdemeanors—the total number of "political" arrests, including of those freed quite quickly, was probably no more than several hundred (ibid., 129).

18. Stewart Edwards, *The Paris Commune, 1871* (New York: Quadrangle, 1972), 268–269; Gérard Dittmar, *Histoire des femmes dans la Commune de Paris* (Paris: Dittmar, 2003), 89; William Serman, *La Commune de Paris* (Paris: Fayard, 1986), 387–389; S. Froumov, *La Commune de Paris et la démocratisation de l'école* (Moscow: Éditions du progrès, 1964), 16–17, 113; Marion, "La vie religieuse," 54–57.

19. Marion, "La vie religieuse," 52–53; Eugene Schulkind, "Socialist Women During the 1871 Paris Commune," *Past and Present* 106 (February 1985): 136; Froumov, *La Commune de Paris*, 48–49, 70, 148.

20. Stewart Edwards, ed., *The Communards of Paris, 1871* (Ithaca, NY: Cornell University Press, 1973), 117–120. On May 21, the Commune appointed a commission to organize the education of girls.

21. Georges Bourgin, *La Commune de Paris* (Paris: Presses universitaires de France, 1971), 46–47.

22. Édouard Moriac, *Paris sous la Commune* (Paris: E. Dentu, 1871), 336–337.

23. Marion, "La vie religieuse," 59–61; Bertrand Taithe, *Defeated Flesh: Medicine, Welfare, and Warfare in the Making of Modern France* (Manchester, UK: University of Manchester Press, 1999), 131–135, 150–152.

24. Carolyn Eichner, *Surmounting the Barricades: Women in the Paris Commune* (Bloomington: Indiana University Press, 2004), 136; Marion, "La vie religieuse," 245–249; S. Sakharov, *Lettres au Père Duchêne pendant la Commune de Paris* (Paris: Bureau d'éditions, 1934), 51–52, 55 (April 30 and 27, 1871); Jacques Rougerie, *Paris libre 1871* (Paris: Éditions du Seuil, 1971), 195.

25. Rials, *Nouvelle histoire*, 456–457; Serman, *La Commune de Paris*, 292; Edwards, *The Paris Commune*, 282–283; Martin Phillip Johnson, *The Paradise of Association: Political Culture and Popular Organizations in the Paris Commune of 1871* (Ann Arbor: University of Michigan Press, 1996), 197–200.

26. Carolyn Eichner, "'We Must Shoot the Priests': Revolutionary Women and Anti-clericalism in the Paris Commune of 1871," in *Cities Under Siege/Situazioni d'Assedio/États de Siège*, edited by Lucia Carle and Antoinette Fauve-Chamoux (Florence, IT: Pagnini and Martinelli, 2002), 268.

27. Jacques Rougerie, *Paris libre 1871,* (Paris: Seuil, 1971), 210; Rougerie, *Procès des Communards* (Paris: Julliard, 1964), 182; David Barry, *Women and Political Insurgency: France in the Mid-Nineteenth Century* (Basingstoke, UK: Macmillan, 1996), 122; Carolyn Eichner, *Surmounting the Barricades*, 138, 146–147; Kathleen Jones and Françoise Vergès, "'Aux citoyennes!': Women, Politics, and the Paris Commune of 1871," *History of European Ideas* 13 (1991): 721.

28. Eichner, "We Must Shoot the Priests," 65–67.

29. Johnson, *The Paradise of Association*, 208, 217; Rougerie, *Paris libre 1871,* 229, 237, 246; Robert Tombs, *The Paris Commune, 1871* (New York: Longman, 1999), 121, 123.

30. François Bournand, *Le clergé pendant la Commune* (Paris: Tolra, 1892), 135–139; Maurice Choury, *Les damnés de la terre, 1871* (Paris: Tchou, 1970), 81–82; Eichner, *Surmounting the Barricades*, 142.

31. Maxime Vuillaume, *Mes cahiers rouges au temps de la Commune* (Paris: A. Michel, 1971), 274–278.

32. 8J 4e conseil de guerre 131 dossier 688, report on Duval, femme Le Mel, June 21, 1872; commissaire de police Pédezert, June 21, 1871; commissaire de police, Notre-Dame-des-Champs, July 22, 1872; Quimper gendarmerie captain, July

24, 1872; gendarmerie, Brest, July 21 and 29, 1872; renseignements de police, August 19, 1872; commissaire de police Pédezert, June 21, 1871.

33. Gay Gullickson, *Unruly Women of Paris: Images of the Commune* (Ithaca, NY: Cornell University Press, 1996), 109; Edwards, *The Communards of Paris*, 105–108.

34. George J. Becker, ed., *Paris Under Siege, 1870–71: From the Goncourt Journal* (Ithaca, NY: Cornell University Press, 1969), 280.

35. Marion, "La vie religieuse," 120–122; Rougerie, *Procès des Communards*, 201.

36. Marion, "La vie religieuse," 118; Stéphane Rials (*Nouvelle histoire*, 456–457) writes that in Paris some sort of pillaging occurred in thirty-one churches, profanation occurred in twelve, and vandalism took place in nineteen; thirteen churches were definitively or temporarily closed during the Commune.

37. Marion, "La vie religieuse," 79, 162–172. Baptisms fell from 3,513 in May 1870 to 823 the same month a year later.

38. Marion, "La vie religieuse," 43–45, 88–89, 224–238 (*Père Duchêne*, April 1, 3, and 20).

39. Rastoul, *L'Église de Paris*, 341–351; Edward S. Mason, *The Paris Commune: An Episode in the History of the Socialist Movement* (New York: Macmillan, 1930), 272–273.

40. Archives de la Défense, Ly 140, July 20, 1871.

41. Denis Arthur Bingham, *Recollections of Paris* (London: Chapman and Hall, 1896), 257–259.

42. Marion, "La vie religieuse," 97–103.

43. Vizetelly, *My Adventures*, 121–123.

44. Marion, "La vie religieuse," 104–105, 149–153.

45. Foulon, *Histoire*, 520–530; Price, *Archbishop Darboy*, 213–222; Gautherot, *Thiers et Mgr Darboy*, 9–14; Da Costa, *Mémoires d'un Communard*, 157–158; Willette, *Raoul Rigault*, 129. Bonjean was well known for his support of Gallicans.

46. Pierron, *Mgr Darboy*, 73; Chauvin, *Mgr Darboy*, 133.

47. Da Costa, *Mémoires d'un Communard*, 162; Willette, *Raoul Rigault*, 139.

48. Foulon, *Histoire*, 534–536.

49. Chauvin, *Mgr Darboy*, 133–140; Benjamin Flotte, *Blanqui et les otages en 1871* (Paris: Imprimerie de Jeanette, 1885), 6–14; Gautherot, *Thiers et Mgr Darboy*, 40–60, 104, 126–135; Boudon, *Monseigneur Darboy*, 146; Foulon, *Histoire*, 536–544.

50. Philip M. Katz, *From Appomattox to Montmartre: Americans and the Paris Commune* (Cambridge, MA: Harvard University Press, 1998), 47–48.

51. Gustave Cluseret (Général), *Mémoires du Général Cluseret* (Paris: J. Lévy, 1887), 2:213–215.

52. Katz, *From Appomattox to Montmartre*, 20–22, 40–43; Patrick H. Hutton, *The Cult of the Revolutionary Tradition: The Blanquists in French Politics, 1864–1893* (Berkeley: University of California Press, 1981), 87–88.

53. Gautherot, *Thiers et Mgr Darboy*, 73–90, 123, 143, 150–166; E. B. Washburne, *Account of the Sufferings and Death of the Most Reverend George Darboy, Late Archbishop of Paris* (New York: Catholic Union of New York, 1873), 26–29 (letters of April 25 and May 2).

54. Washburne, *Account of the Sufferings*, 34–38; Chauvin, *Mgr Darboy*, 139; Foulon, *Histoire*, 626.

55. Washburne, *Account of the Sufferings*, 40 (Plou to Washburne, May 11, 1871); Elihu Benjamin Washburne, *Franco-German War and Insurrection of the Commune: Correspondence of E. B. Washburne* (Washington, DC: Government Printing Office, 1878), April 23. After being released, Justine went to join another brother in Nancy (Chauvin, *Mgr Darboy*, 141).

56. Flotte, *Blanqui et les otages*, 24–29.

57. Flotte, *Blanqui et les otages*, 24–28; Gautherot, *Thiers et Mgr Darboy*, 44–46.

58. Foulon, *Histoire*, 546–555; Perny, *Deux mois de prison*, 132–239.

59. Foulon, *Histoire*, 551–555.

CHAPTER 5:
THE BATTLE TURNS AGAINST THE COMMUNARDS

1. W. Gibson, *Paris During the Commune* (London: Methodist Book Room, 1895), 164.

2. Gay Gullickson, *Unruly Women of Paris: Images of the Commune* (Ithaca, NY: Cornell University Press, 1996), 75.

3. Gibson, *Paris During the Commune*, 166, 180, 193; John Leighton, *Paris Under the Commune*, (New York: Scribner, 1871), 116; Wickham Hoffman, *Camp, Court, and Siege: A Narrative of Personal Adventure and Observation During Two Wars, 1861–1865, 1870–1871* (New York: Harper and Brothers, 1877), 264.

4. Henri Rochefort, *The Adventures of My Life* (London: E. Arnold, 1896), 377–378; Pierre Vésinier, *History of the Commune of Paris* (London: Chapman and Hall, 1872), 231.

5. Leighton, *Paris Under the Commune*, 84.

6. Gullickson, *Unruly Women*, 83–85.

7. S. Froumov, *La Commune de Paris et la démocratisation de l'école* (Moscow: Éditions du progrès, 1964), 222.

8. Leighton, *Paris Under the Commune*, 171.

9. Vizetelly, *My Adventures in the Paris Commune* (London: Chatto and Windus, 1874), 111.

10. John Murray, MD, "Four Days in the Ambulances and Hospitals of Paris Under the Commune," *British Medical Journal* (January–June 1871): 541–542, 621.

11. Henri Ameline, ed., *Enquête parlementaire sur l'insurrection du 18 mars* (Versailles: Cerf, 1872), 3:23–24.

12. Gullickson, *Unruly Women*, 99–103.

13. Gullickson, *Unruly Women*, 96–98.

14. Gullickson, *Unruly Women*, 89–96.

15. Edith Thomas, *Louise Michel* (Montreal: Black Rose Books, 1980), 83; Gérard Dittmar, *Belleville de l'annexation à la Commune* (Paris: Dittmar, 2007), 45.

16. 8J 6, dossier 135 Louise Michel, interrogation September 19, 1871; Élie Reclus, *La Commune de Paris au jour le jour*, (Saint-Martin-de-Bonfussé: Théolib, 2011), 298–299.

17. Godelier (Colonel), "La guerre de 1870 et la Commune: Journal d'un officier d'état-major," *Nouvelle revue rétrospective* 17 (July–December 1902): 24; Clifford, "Aux armes citoyens!" "The National Guard in the Paris Commune of 1871" (PhD diss., University of Tennessee, 1975), 241–246; Leighton, *Paris Under the Commune*, 208; Rials, *Nouvelle histoire* de Paris de Trochu à Thiers 1870–1873 (Paris: Imprimerie Nationale, 1985), 266. See above all Robert Tombs, *The War Against Paris, 1871* (Cambridge: Cambridge University Press, 1981), ch. 8.

18. Émile Maury, *Mes souvenirs sur les événements des années 1870–1871*, edited by Alain Dalotel (Paris: La boutique de l'histoire, 2001), 55–58.

19. Reclus, *La Commune de Paris*, 219–220; Philip Nord, "The Party of Conciliation and the Paris Commune," *French Historical Studies* 15, no. 1 (1987): 22–25; Laure Godineau, *La Commune de Paris par ceux qui l'ont vécue* (Paris: Parigramme, 2010), 169–175; Gullickson, *Unruly Women*, 127–128.

20. Jacques Silvestre de Sacy, *Le Maréchal de Mac-Mahon* (Paris: Éditions Inter-nationale, 1960), 257.

21. Georges Riat, *Gustave Courbet, peintre* (Paris: H. Floury, 1906), 302; Stewart Edwards, *The Paris Commune, 1871* (New York: Quadrangle, 1972), 22–28; Edwards, ed., *The Communards of Paris, 1871* (London, 1973), 98; Stéphane Rials, *Nouvelle histoire de Paris de Trochu à Thiers 1870–1873* (Paris: Hachette, 1985), 368–369.

22. 8J conseil de guerre 3, dossier 571, Gustave Cluseret; Dale Lothrop Clifford, "Aux armes citoyens! 106–107; Jacques Rougerie, *Procès des Communards* (Paris: Julliard, 1964), 285, 301–302; Edwards, *The Paris Commune*, 226–227; Cerf, *de Maxime Vuillame*, 7–8, Prolès, *le Colonel Rossel*, 61–65, 81–93.

23. Charles Prolès, *Le colonel Rossel* (Paris: Chamuel, 1898), 82–83; Ernest A. Vizetelly, *My Adventures in the Commune* (London: Chatto and Windus, 2009), 67; Louis-Nathaniel Rossel, *Rossel's Posthumous Papers* (London: Chapman and Hall, 1872), 80–83, 95–115; Clifford, "Aux armes citoyens!" 234; Gaston Da Costa, *Mémoires d'un Communard: La Commune vécue* (Paris: Larousse, 2009), 213–228; Rials, *Nouvelle histoire*, 329–330; Luc Willette, *Raoul Rigault, 25 ans, Communard, chef de police* (Paris: Syros, 1984), 116–119.

24. Edwards, *The Communards of Paris*, 162, and *The Paris Commune, 1871*, 314–315; Jean-François Lecaillon, ed., *La Commune de Paris racontée par les Parisiens* (Paris: B. Giovanangeli, 2009), 95; Archibald Forbes, "What an American Girl Saw of the Commune," *Century Illustrated Magazine* 45, no. 1 (November 1892): 65.

25. Tombs, *The War Against Paris*, 137–138.

26. Adolphe Hippolyte Clémence (known as Roussel), *De l'antagonisme social, ses causes et ses effets* (Neuchâtel, 1871), 17–20; William Serman, *La Commune de Paris* (Paris: Fayard, 1986), 491.

27. Alistair Horne, *The Fall of Paris: The Siege and the Commune, 1870–71* (New York: Penguin, 1965), 407–409.

28. Gérard Conte, *Éléments pour une histoire de la Commune dans le XIIIe arrondissement—5 mars–25 mai 1871* (Paris: Éditions de la butte aux Cailles, 1981), 75–88; Tombs, *The War Against Paris*, 120–121, 129–133, 137; Elihu Benjamin Washburne, *Franco-German War and Insurrection of the Commune: Correspondence of E. B. Washburne* (Washington, DC: Government Printing Office, 1878), dispatch of May 11; Vizetelly, *My Adventures*, 138, 142; Da Costa, *Mémoires d'un Communard*, 240; Gaston Bouniols, *Thiers au pouvoir (1871–1873)* (Paris: Delagrave, 1922), 63 (letter of Thiers to duc de Broglie, May 10); Maurice Choury, *Les damnés de la terre, 1871* (Paris: Tchou, 1970), 145.

29. Clifford, "Aux armes citoyens!" 106–107; Jacques Rougerie, *Procès des Communards* (Paris: Gallimard, 1978), 294; Tombs, *The War Against Paris*, 142.

30. Edwards, *The Paris Commune*, 239–242.

31. Rossel, *Rossel's Posthumous Papers*, 162; Jules Bourelly (Général), *Le ministère de la guerre sous la Commune* (Paris: Combet, 1911), 151–152, 157; Charles Prolès, *Les hommes de la révolution de 1871: Charles Delescluze 1830–1848–1871* (Paris: 111 rue Réaumur, 1898), 101–102, 106–110.

32. Godineau, *La Commune de Paris*, 74–77; Edwards, *The Paris Commune*, 93–94; Jacques Rougerie, *La Commune de 1871* (Paris: Presses universitaires de France, 1988), 75; Eugène Varlin, *Pratique militante et écrits d'un ouvrier communard*, edited by Paule Lejeune (Paris: F. Maspero, 1977), 171–173; Marcel Cerf, *Les 'Cahiers rouges' de Maxime Vuillaume* (Paris: J. Braire, 1988), 8–9.

33. J. Rocher, ed., *Lettres de Communards et de militants de la Première Internationale à Marx, Engels et autres dans les journées de la Commune de Paris en 1871* (Paris: Bureau d'éditions, 1934), Jenny to Doctor Kugelmann, May 12, 1871.

34. Janine Bouissounouse and Louis de Villefosse, "La presse parisienne pendant la Commune," *Europe* (April–May 1951): 55; Gustave Gautherot, *Thiers et Mgr Darboy* (Paris: Plon, 1910), 111–113; Jacques Gadille, "Georges Darboy, archevêque de Paris," in *Mélanges offerts à M. le doyen André Latreille* (Lyon: Audin, 1972), 195; Villiers du Terrage (B[ar]on Marc de), *Histoire des clubs de femmes et des Légions d'Amazones 1793–1848–1871* (Paris: Plon-Nourrit, 1910), 404; Rougerie, *Procès des Communards*, 194.

35. Maurice Garçon, "Journal d'un bourgeois de Paris," *Revue de Paris* 12 (December 1955): 14–33.

36. Albert Hans, *Souvenirs d'un volontaire versaillais* (Paris: Dentu, 1873), 6.

37. Serman, *La Commune de Paris*, 459.

38. Hans, *Souvenirs*, 9, 19, 22–33, 34–38, 41, 47, 53–55. Delclos was the commander, Valette, the colonel, and Gustave Durieu, the battalion commander.

39. Henri Malo, *Thiers, 1797–1877* (Paris: Payot, 1932), 506; J. P. T. Bury and R. P. Tombs, *Thiers—a Political Life, 1797–1877* (London: Allen and Unwin, 1986), 206.

40. Sutter-Laumann, *Histoire d'un trente sous (1870–1871)* (Paris: A. Savine, 1891), 290; Serman, *La Commune de Paris*, 458; Gordon Wright, "The Anti-Commune 1871," *French Historical Studies* 10, no. 1 (spring 1977): 159–164.

41. Bronislaw Wolowski, *Dombrowski et Versailles* (Geneva: Carey Frères, 1871), 67–68, 92–114.

42. John Leighton, *Paris Under the Commune*, 224; Maurice Choury, *Bonjour Monsieur Courbet!* (Paris: Éditions sociales, 1969), 110; Riat, *Gustave Courbet*, 304.

43. APP, Ba 1020, session of the Commune of April 27.

44. Vizetelly, *My Adventures*, 145; Forbes, "What an American Girl Saw," 66.

45. Riat, *Gustave Courbet*, 304–305.

46. Auguste Lepage, *Histoire de la Commune* (Paris: A. Lemerre, 1871), 249–250.

47. Christianne Lapostolle, "Plus vrai que le vrai: Stratégie photographique et la Commune de Paris," *Actes de la Recherche en Sciences Sociales* 73 (June 1988): 67–76. For example, she cites the 1872 Liebert album *Les ruines de Paris et de ses environs, 1870–71*. Kathleen Jones and Françoise Vergès also make the point that photos distributed by the Versaillais showed destroyed building to reinforce their insistence that the Communards were modern barbarians: "'Aux citoyennes!': Women, Politics, and the Paris Commune of 1871," *History of European Ideas* 13 (1991): 726.

48. Serman, *La Commune*, 490–496.

50. Élie Reclus, *La Commune de Paris au jour le jour* (Saint-Martin-de-Bonfossé: Théolib, 2011), 319–320, 343–345; François Bournand, *Le clergé pendant la Commune* (Paris: Tolra, 1892), 244–250; Olivier Marion, "La vie religieuse pendant la Commune de Paris 1871" (unpublished master's thesis, Paris-X Nanterre, 1981), 214–221.

51. Willette, *Raoul Rigault*, 145–150; Da Costa, *Mémoires d'un Communard*, 174–175; Alistair Horne, *The Terrible Year: The Paris Commune, 1871* (New York: Viking Press, 2004), 114.

52. Laurent Amodru (Abbé), *La Roquette, journées des 24, 25, 26, 27, et 28 mai 1871* (Paris: Laroche, 1873), 29.

53. Joseph Abel Guillermin, *Vie de Mgr Darboy, archevêque de Paris, mis à mort en haine de la foi le 24 mai 1871* (Paris: Bloud et Barral, 1888), 327; Gautherot, *Thiers et Mgr Darboy*, 174; Joseph-Alfred Foulon, *Histoire de la vie et des oeuvres de Mgr Darboy, archevêque de Paris* (Paris: Possielgue frères, 1889), 564; Washburne, *Franco-German War*, 29 (letter of May 19, 1871).

54. Reclus, *La Commune de Paris*, 343, 351–352.

55. Maury, *Mes Souvenirs*, 66–67.

56. Gullickson, *Unruly Women*, 75.

57. Philippe Riviale, *Sur la Commune: Cerises de sang* (Paris: L'Harmattan, 2003), 299–300; Serman, *La Commune de Paris*, 491.

58. W. Pembroke Fetridge, *The Rise and Fall of the Paris Commune in 1871* (New York: Harper Brothers, 1871), 224.

59. Athanase Josué Coquerel *fils* Athanase Josué, *Sous la Commune: Récits et souvenirs d'un Parisien* (Paris: E. Dentu, 1873), 76–77; Vizetelly, *My Adventures*, 137; Edwards, *The Communards of Paris*, 144–146; Maxime Vuillaume, *Mes cahiers rouges au temps de la Commune* (Paris: A. Michel, 1971), 281–285; Philip M. Katz, *From Appomattox to Montmartre: Americans and the Paris Commune* (Cambridge, MA: Harvard University Press, 1998), 20–22.

60. Prosper-Olivier Lissagaray, *Les huit journées de mai derrière les barricades* (Bruxelles: Bureau du "Petit Journal," 1978), 41–43; Robert Tombs, *The Paris Commune, 1871* (New York: Longman, 1999), 164–165.

61. Maury, *Mes Souvenirs*, 6–10, 69–70.

62. Forbes, "What an American Girl Saw," 48–61.

63. Arthur de Grandeffe, *Mobiles et volontaires de la Seine pendant la guerre et les deux sieges* (Paris: E. Dentu, 1871), 254–255.

64. Hans, *Souvenirs*, 57–60.

65. Camille Pelletan, *La semaine de mai* (Paris: M. Dreyfous, 1880), 24–30; Tombs, *The War Against Paris*, 170–171.

66. Hans, *Souvenirs*, 61–79, 88–89.

67. George J. Becker, ed., *Paris Under Siege, 1870–71: From the Goncourt Journal* (Ithaca, NY: Cornell University Press, 1969), 293–294.

68. Reclus, *La Commune de Paris*, 353.

69. Leighton, *Paris Under the Commune*, 238–239; Tombs, *The War Against Paris*, 146.

70. "Souvenirs d'un habitant de la Porte Saint-Denis, du 21 au 25 mai 1871," Bibliothèque de l'Hôtel-de-Ville, ms. 1031.

71. "Souvenirs d'un habitant de la Porte Saint-Denis."

72. Lissagaray, *Les huit journées de mai*, 313; Tombs, *The War Against Paris*, 145–149; Adolphe Thiers, *Déposition de M. Thiers sur le dix-huit mars* (Paris: Librarie générale, 1871), 53.

73. Marquis de Compiègne, "Souvenirs d'un Versaillais pendant le second siege de Paris," *Le Correspondant*, 10 aout, 1875, 633; Charles des Cognets, *Les bretons et la Commune de Paris 1870–71* (Paris: L'Harmattan, 2012); Da Costa, *Mémoires d'un Communard*, 207; Joseph Vinoy (Général), *L'Armistice et la Commune* (Paris: H. Plon, 1872), 310; Papiers Eugène Balleyguier *dit* (known as) Eugène Loudun (Fidus), Bibliothèque Historique de la Ville de Paris, ms. 1284, 2e cahier, Notes sur la Politique, la Litérature, etc., 1870–1871; Tombs, *The War Against Paris*, 247–249.

74. Lecaillon, *La Commune de Paris*, 166.

75. Forbes, "What an American Girl Saw."

76. Edwards, *The Paris Commune*, 314–315.

77. Thomas, *Louise Michel*, 90; Joseph Vinoy, *L'Armistice et la Commune* (Paris: Plon, 1872), 310; Lissagaray, *Les huit journées de mai*, 316–319; Edwards, *The Paris Commune*, 316.

78. Leighton, *Paris Under the Commune*, 240.

79. Lissagaray, *Les huit journées de mai*, 56–59, 63; Edwards, *The Paris Commune*, 320; Lecaillon, *La Commune de Paris*, 172–173.

80. Forbes, "What an American Girl Saw," 61–66.

81. Marquis de Compiègne, "Souvenirs d'un Versaillais pendant le second siège de Paris," *Le Correspondant*, 10 augustio 1875.

CHAPTER 6:
BLOODY WEEK BEGINS

1. L. P. Guénin, *Assassinat des otages. Sixième conseil de guerre* (Paris: Librarie de l'echo de la Sorbonne, 1871), 196–205.

2. Olivier Marion, "La vie religieuse pendant la Commune de Paris 1871" (unpublished master's thesis, Paris-X Nanterre, 1981), 130; Jean Baronnet, ed., *Enquête sur la Commune de Paris (La Revue Blanche)* (Paris: Les éditions de l'amateur, 2011), 132; William Serman, *La Commune de Paris* (Paris: Fayard, 1986), 313.

3. Joseph-Alfred Foulon, *Histoire de la vie et des oeuvres de Mgr Darboy, archevêque de Paris* (Paris: Possieglue frères, 1889), 568–573; Paul Perny (R. P.), *Deux mois de prison sous la Commune, suivi de détails authentiques sur l'assassinat de Mgr l'archevêque de Paris* (Paris: Lainé, 1871), 132–133, 144–145; Charles Chauvin, *Mgr Darboy, archêveque de Paris, otage de la Commune (1813–1871)* (Paris: Desclée de Brouwer, 2011), 143; Gaston Da Costa, *Mémoires d'un Communard: La Commune vécue* (Paris: Larousse, 2009), 185–190; Abbé [Henri-Pierre] Lamazou, *La place Vendôme et la Roquette* (Paris: C. Douniol et cie., 1876), 215; AG Ly 137 (6e conseil de guerre, 297), interrogation of June 29, 1871.

4. R. P. Prosper Malige, *Picpus pendant la Commune, par un prêtre de la congrégation du Sacré-Coeur (dite de Picpus)* (Evreux: Imprimerie de l'Eure, 1898), 111–112; Lamazou, *La place Vendôme*, 220–221; Perny, *Deux mois de prison*, 154–155.

5. Foulon, *Histoire*, 575.

6. Vizetelly, *My Adventures in the Commune* (London: Chatto and Windus, 2009), 159–163.

7. Michel Robida, *Ces bourgeois de Paris, trois siècles de chronique familiale de 1675 à nos jours* (Paris: R. Julliard, 1955), 170; Jean-François Lecaillon, ed., *La Commune de Paris racontée par les Parisiens* (Paris: B. Giovanangeli, 2009), 167–168; Jules Andrieu, *Notes pour servir à l'histoire de la Commune de Paris en 1871* (Paris: Payot, 1971), 132–133.

8. Fetridge, *The Rise and Fall of the Paris Commune in 1871* (New York: Harper Brothers, 1871), 291–294.

9. Marcel Cerf, "La barricade de 1871," in *La Barricade*, edited by Alain Corbin and J.-M. Mayeur (Paris: Publications de la Sorbonne, 1997), 331–332; Serman, *La Commune de Paris*, 492; W. Pembroke Fetridge, *The Rise and Fall of the Paris Commune in 1871* (New York: Harper Brothers, 1871), 301–302; Gay Gullickson, *Unruly Women of Paris: Images of the Commune* (Ithaca, NY: Cornell University Press, 1996), 161.

10. Wickham Hoffman, *Camp, Court, and Siege: A Narrative of Personal Adventure and Observation During Two Wars, 1861–1865, 1870–1871* (New York: Harper and Brothers, 1877), 279; Stewart Edwards, *The Paris Commune, 1871* (New York: Quadrangle, 1972), 163–164; Eric Fournier, *Paris en ruines: Du Paris haussmannien au Paris communard* (Paris: Imago, 2008), 58, 90–91; Robert Tombs, "La lutte finale des barricades: Spontanéité révolutionnaire et organisation militaire en mai 1871," in Corbin and Mayeur, *La Barricade*, 362.

11. John Leighton, *Paris Under the Commune* (London: Bradbury, Evans and Company, 1871), 222, 236–237.

12. Élie Reclus, *La Commune de Paris au jour le jour* (Saint-Martin-de-Bonfossé: Théolib, 2011), 252–253.

13. Hoffman, *Camp, Court, and Siege*, 279–280; Prosper-Olivier Lissagaray, *Les huit journées de mai derrière les barricades* (Bruxelles: Bureau du "Petit Journal," 1871), 77–78.

14. Ernest A. Vizetelly, *My Adventures in the Commune* (London: Chatto and Windus, 2009), 136; Athanase Josué Coquerel *fils* Athanase Josué, *Sous la Commune: Récits et souvenirs d'un Parisien* (Paris: E. Dentu, 1873), 79–80.

15. See Robert Tombs, *The Paris Commune, 1871* (New York: Longman, 1999), 2, 166–173.

16. Lecaillon, *La Commune de Paris*, 168; Laure Godineau, "Les barricades de mai 1871 chez Jules Vallès" (la Commune de Paris, l'Insurgé), in Corbin and Mayeur, *La Barricade*, 173; Laure Godineau, *La Commune de Paris par ceux qui l'ont vécue* (Paris: Parigramme, 2010), 190–191; Robert Tombs, *The War Against Paris, 1871* (Cambridge: Cambridge University Press, 1981), 152–153; Jules Bergeret, *Le 18 mars: Journal hebdomadaire* (London: n.p., 1871), 21; Guy Tréal, "La musique et la Commune," *Europe* 29 (April–May 1951): 121.

17. George J. Becker, ed., *Paris Under Siege, 1870–71: From the Goncourt Journal* (Ithaca, NY: Cornell University Press, 1969), 298–299, 300–301.

18. Paul Martine, *Souvenirs d'insurgé. La Commune de 1871* (Paris: Perrin, 1971), 236.

19. Maurice Garçon, "Journal d'un bourgeois de Paris," *Revue de Paris*, 12 (December 1955): 28–30.

20. Leighton, *Paris Under the Commune*, 241–242.

21. Hans Ludovic and J. J. Blanc, *Guide à travers les ruines* (Paris: A. Lemerre, 1871), 17; Lissagaray, *Les huit journées de mai*, 84–85; Martine, *Souvenirs*, 244; Joseph Vinoy (Général), *L'Armistice et la Commune* (Paris: H. Plon, 1872), 316–317; Vizetelly, *My Adventures*, 158; Eugène Delessert, *Épisodes pendant la Commune, souvenirs d'un délégué de la Société de secours aux blessés militaires des armées de terre et de mer* (Paris: C. Noblet, 1872), 52.

22. Denis Arthur Bingham, *Recollections of Paris* (London: Chapman and Hall, 1896), 2:88–91, 103.

23. Gaston Cerfbeer, "Une nuit de la semaine sanglante," *Revue Hebdomadaire* 25 (May 23, 1903), 416–423.

24. Lecaillon, *La Commune de Paris*, 174.

25. Vizetelly, *My Adventures*, 172; Fournier, *Paris en ruines*, 96–99; Martine, *Souvenirs*, 241. The Versaillais were convinced that the Communards, on the verge of defeat, planned to destroy Paris, perhaps turning to science to invent new terrible weapons. A scientific delegation of the Commune met to consider the development of new, bizarre weapons (Fournier, *Paris en ruines*, 81–88).

26. Frédéric Fort, *Paris brûlé* (Paris: E. Lachaud, 1871), 15–21; Édith Thomas, *Les pétroleuses* (Paris: Gallimard, 1963), 190–193. Yet, article 14 of the Union des Femmes did state, "Monies that remain will be used . . . to purchase petrol and arms for the *citoyennes* fighting on the barricades."

27. Gullickson, *Unruly Women*, 205–209; David Barry, *Women and Political Insurgency: France in the Mid-Nineteenth Century* (Basingstoke, UK: Macmillan, 1996), 127; Thomas, *Les pétroleuses*, 164–166.

28. Camille Pelletan, *La semaine de mai* (Paris: M. Dreyfous, 1880), 111–113; Thomas, *Les pétroleuses*, 190–193 (quote from *Gazette des Tribunaux,* September 23, 1871).

29. Leighton, *Paris Under the Commune*, 258–261; Elihu Benjamin Washburne, *Franco-German War and Insurrection of the Commune: Correspondence of E. B. Washburne* (Washington, DC: Government Printing Office, 1878), May 25.

30. Lissagaray, *Les huit journées de mai*, 171–172; François Jourde, *Souvenirs d'un membre de la Commune* (Bruxelles: Kistemaechers, 1877), 104.

31. Fournier, *Paris en ruines*, 59, 103.

32. Serman, *La Commune de Paris*, 503; Edwards, *The Paris Commune*, 325–327; 8J 3e conseil de guerre 6, dossier 29/8 Théophile Ferré.

33. Archives de la Défense, 4e conseil de guerre 131, dossier 688, Reports of July 29, August 17, 19, 23, 26, 1872; renseignements du commissaire de police, n.d.; Fournier, *Paris en ruines*, 43, 52–56, 96–99; Martine, *Souvenirs*, 241; Godineau, *La Commune de Paris par ceux qui l'ont vécue*, 204; 8J 6, dossier 135 Louise Michel, interrogation December 3, 1871; Gustave Lefrançais, *Études sur le mouvement communaliste à Paris, en 1871* (Neuchâtel: G. Guillaume fils, 1871), 326–327.

34. Louis Enault, *Paris brûlé par la Commune* (Paris: H. Plon, 1871), 4, 150; papiers Eugène Balleyguier *dit* (known as) Eugène Loudun (Fidus), Bibliothèque Historique de la Ville de Paris, ms. 1284, 2e cahier, Notes sur la Politique, la Littérature, etc., 1870–1871; Fournier, *Paris en ruines*, 112–113, 118–119, 125; Coquerel, *Sous la Commune*, 99–100.

35. Reclus, *La Commune de Paris*, 354–355, 358–360.

36. Reclus, *La Commune de Paris*, 356.

37. Paul Lanjalley and Paul Corriez, *Histoire de la révolution du 18 mars* (Paris: Lacroix, 1871), 542; Lissagaray, *Les huit journées de mai*, 55n1.

38. A point made by Tombs, *The War Against Paris*, 164–165; René Héron de Villefosse, *Les graves heures de la Commune* (Paris: Perrin, 1970), 252.

39. André Zeller, *Les hommes de la Commune* (Paris: Perrin, 1969), 371–372; Pelletan, *La semaine de mai*, 24–30; Tombs, *The War Against Paris*, 148–149, 171.

40. Pelletan, *La semaine de mai*, 35; Serman, *La Commune de Paris*, 517.

41. Jacquelynn Baas, "Edouard Manet and 'Civil War,'" *Art Journal* 45, no. 1 (spring 1985): 36–42; Philip Nord, *The Republican Moment: Struggles for Democracy in Nineteenth-Century France* (Cambridge, MA: Harvard University Press, 1995), 170; Philip Nord, *Les Impressionistes et la politique* (Paris: Tallandier, 2009), 54–56, 67–68. Manet's sympathies lay, as in 1848, with ordinary people. Like Courbet, Manet turned down the imperial Legion of Honor, and his canvas of the execution of "Emperor" Maximilian in Mexico outraged the emperor and Bonapartists. The Salon des Refusés in 1863 that launched Impressionism stood as a provocative rejection of imperial artistic tastes, patronage, and authoritarianism. Manet, a republican who hated "that little Thiers," once said that he hoped the "demented old man" would one day drop dead at the podium. Like Camille Pissarro, Manet castigated the bloody repression even if he had not originally supported the insurrection and condemned the execution of Generals Lecomte and Thomas.

42. Alphonse Vergès d'Esboeufs (viscount), *La vérité sur le gouvernement de la défense nationale, la Commune et les Versaillais* (Geneva: Imprimerie coopérative, 1871), 14–15; Pelletan, *La semaine de mai*, 123.

43. Jean Allemane, *Mémoires d'un Communard* (Paris: Librairie socialiste, 1910), 137–38. The devastation highlighted in Ludovic and Blanc, *Guide à travers les ruines*, 55.

44. John Murray, MD, "Four Days in the Ambulances and Hospitals of Paris Under the Commune," *British Medical Journal* (January–June 1871): 622.

45. Lissagaray, *Les huit journées de mai*, 64–65; J. A. Faucher, *Les carnets d'un fédéré: 1871*, edited by Martial Senisse (Paris: Saint-Just, 1965), 139; Henri Ameline, ed., *Enquête parlementaire sur l'insurrection du 18 mars* (Versailles: Cerf, 1872), 3:13.

46. Allemane, *Mémoires*, 137–150; Maurice Choury, *Bonjour Monsieur Courbet!* (Paris: Éditions sociales, 1969), 111–113; Gérald Dittmar, *Gustave Courbet et la Commune, le politique* (Paris: Dittmar, 2007), 151–152.

47. Maxime Vuillaume, *Mes cahiers rouges au temps de la Commune* (Paris: A. Michel, 1971), 236–238.

48. Allemane, *Mémoires*, 161–170, 178–179.

49. Philippe Riviale, *Sur la Commune: Cerises de sang* (Paris: L'Harmattan, 2003), 300.

50. Roger Gould, "Trade Cohesion, Class Unity, and Urban Insurrection: Artisanal Activism in the Paris Commune," *American Journal of Sociology* 98, no. 4 (January 1993): 721, 728–729, 735–751; Jacques Rougerie, "Autour de quelques livres étrangers. Réflexions sur la citoyenneté populaire en 1871," in *La Commune de 1871. L'événement les hommes et la mémoire*, edited by Claude Latta (Saint-Étienne: Publications de l'Université de Saint-Étienne, 2004), esp. 221–229, 233–235. Gould argues that social relations within neighborhoods, more

than solidarities of work and class consciousness (in contrast, he insists, to 1848), were the most important factor in explaining attachment to the Commune and resistance in its name. In his view, this accounts for the overrepresentation of textile, construction, and machine workers and the presence of middle-class neighbors and allies among participants in the Commune. Rougerie contends that Gould ignores the wider sense of linkage and solidarity formed by work and class experience that developed in the late Second Empire.

51. Barry, *Women and Political Insurgency*, 123–128, 136–139; Jean-Baptiste Clément, *La revanche des Communeux* (Paris: J. Marie, 1886–1887), 159.

52. Sutter-Laumann, *Histoire d'un trente sous (1870–1871)* (Paris: A. Savine, 1891), 292; Da Costa, *Mémoires d'un Communard*, 267–269; Edwards, *The Paris Commune*, 321.

53. Louis Barron, *Sous la drapeau rouge* (Paris: A. Savine, 1889), 75–81.

54. Alistair Horne, *The Fall of Paris: The Siege and the Commune, 1870–71* (New York: Penguin, 1965), 443; Reclus, *La Commune de Paris*, 354.

55. Serman, *La Commune de Paris*, 499.

56. Georges Jeanneret, *Paris pendant la Commune révolutionnaire de 1871* (Paris: Éditions d'histoire sociale, 1871), 222.

57. Albert Hans, *Souvenirs d'un volontaire versaillais* (Paris: Dentu, 1873), 90–91, 97–101; Leighton, *Paris Under the Commune*, 251.

58. Marquis de Compiègne, "Souvenirs d'un Versaillais pendant le second siège de Paris," *Le Correspondant*, August 10, 1875.

59. Jourde, *Souvenirs*, 73.

60. Martine, *Souvenirs*, 231.

61. Prosper-Olivier Lissagaray, *History of the Paris Commune of 1871* (New York: New Park Publications, 1976), 329, 339; Gullickson, *Unruly Women*, 162–163; Robert Tombs, "Les Communeuses," *Sociétés et Représentations* (June 1998): 6:55. Tombs argues that the story of a battalion of women is a myth in *The Paris Commune*, 139.

62. 8J, 4e conseil de guerre 131, dossier 688. Le Mel would deny entering the pharmacy, insisting that they had enough bandages and medications (reports of July 29 and August 17, 19, 23, and 26, 1872; renseignements du commissaire de police, n.d.).

63. 8J 6, dossier 135; Edith Thomas, *Louise Michel* (Montreal: Black Rose Books, 1980), 90; Edwards, *The Paris Commune*, 321–322; Bingham, *Recollections*, 2:108.

64. Christiane Demeulenaere-Douyère, "Journal de l'entrée des troupes versaillaises dans Paris," *Bulletin de la Société d'Histoire de Paris et de l'Ile de France* 108 (1981): 301–303.

65. Sutter-Laumann, *Histoire*, 302–310; Lissagaray, *History*, 360.

66. Sutter-Laumann, *Histoire*, 327–352. Alcide was sent as a soldier to Algeria and saved, more or less, by having been wounded during the Prussian siege.

67. Hans, *Souvenirs*, 158–159, 172–173; Sutter-Laumann, *Histoire*, 320; de Compiègne, "Souvenirs."

68. Vinoy, *L'armistice*, 320–321, 341; Lissagaray, *History*, 357.

69. 8J 6, dossier 554, "rapport sur l'affaire," May 31, 1872; Alistair Horne, *The Terrible Year: The Paris Commune, 1871* (New York: Viking Press, 2004), 129; Edwards, *The Paris Commune*, 328–329.

70. Charles Prolès, *Les hommes de la révolution de 1871: Charles Delescluze 1830–1848–1871* (Paris: 111 rue Réaumur, 1898), 114–118; Robert Tombs, "Paris and the Rural Hordes: An Exploration of Myth and Reality in the French Civil War of 1871," *Historical Journal* 29, no. 4 (1986): 807.

71. Reclus, *La Commune de Paris*, 357–358.

72. Bergeret, *Le 18 mars*, 45–48.

73. Edwards, *The Paris Commune*, 322; Serman, *La Commune de Paris*, 518.

74. "Souvenirs d'un habitant de la porte Saint-Denis, du 21 au 25 mai 1871," Bibliothèque de l'Hôtel-de-Ville, ms. 1031.

75. Edgar Monteil, *Souvenirs de la Commune, 1871* (Paris: Charavay frères, 1883), 106–113, 121–142. Monteil was condemned to a year in prison and the loss of civic rights for five years.

CHAPTER 7:
DEATH COMES FOR THE ARCHBISHOP

1. William Serman, *La Commune de Paris* (Paris: Fayard, 1986), 499–500. Moreau was condemned to death at Châtelet and shot.

2. Ludovic Hans and J. J. Blanc, *Guide à travers les ruines* (Paris: A. Lemerre, 1871), 13.

3. Prosper-Olivier Lissagaray, *Les huits journées derrière les barricades* (Paris: Bureau du Petit Journal, 1871), 79–83.

4. Stewart Edwards, ed., *The Communards of Paris, 1871* (London 1973), 161.

5. Paul Martine, *Souvenirs d'insurgé. La Commune de 1871* (Paris: Perrin, 1971), 233–234; Prosper-Olivier Lissagaray, *History of the Paris Commune of 1871* (New York: New Park Publications, 1976), 348.

6. Georges Bourgin, *La Commune de Paris* (Paris: Presses universitaires de France, 1971), 97.

7. Albert Hans, *Souvenirs d'un volontaire versaillais* (Paris: Dentu, 1873), 119–122.

8. Élie Reclus, *La Commune de Paris au jour le jour* (Saint-Martin-de-Bonfossé: Théolib, 2011), 361–362, 365–366.

9. Reclus, *La Commune de Paris*, 363.

10. Théophile Gautier, *Tableaux de siège de Paris* (Paris: G. Charpentier, 1881), 113; Maurice Garçon, "Journal d'un bourgeois de Paris," *Revue de Paris* 12 (December 1955): 31.

11. Georges Jeanneret, *Paris pendant la Commune révolutionnaire de 1871* (Paris: Éditions d'histoire sociale, 1871), 267; Ernest A. Vizetelly, *My Adventures in the Commune* (London: Chatto and Windus), 2009, 165.

12. Maxime Vuillaume, *Mes cahiers rouges au temps de la Commune* (Paris: A. Michel, 1971), 8–10, 300–306.

13. Hélène Haudebourg, ed., "Carnet de guerre d'un Vertarien en 1870 Julien Poirier," *Regards sur Vertou*, no. 7 (2003): 11–16.

14. Laure Godineau, *La Commune de Paris par ceux qui l'ont vécue* (Paris: Parigramme, 2010), 197; Eric Fournier, *Paris en ruines: Du Paris haussmannien au Paris communard* (Paris: Imago, 2008), 157–158; Camille Pelletan, *La semaine de mai* (Paris: M. Dreyfous, 1880), 104–105.

15. Robert Tombs, *The War Against Paris, 1871* (Cambridge: Cambridge University Press, 1981), 155; Serman, *La Commune de Paris*, 517; Edwards, *The Paris Commune*, 331.

16. Jean Baronnet, ed., *Enquête sur la Commune de Paris (La Revue Blanche)* (Paris: Les éditions de l'amateur, 2011), 169–170.

17. Reclus, *La Commune de Paris*, 360.

18. Martine, *Souvenirs*, 245–246; 8J 3e conseil de guerre 6, dossier 29/8 Théophile Ferré, tribunal report July 12.

19. Martine, *Souvenirs*, 250; Maurice Choury, *La Commune au Quartier latin* (Paris: Livre club Diderot, 1971), 286.

20. Lissagaray, *Les huit journées de mai*, 88–89; Luc Willette, *Raoul Rigault, 25 ans, Communard, chef de police* (Paris: Syros, 1984), 158–161.

21. Henri Dabot, *Griffonnages quotidiens d'un bourgeois du Quartier latin, du 14 mai 1869 au 2 décembre 1871* (Péronne: Imp. de E. Quentin, 1895), 228–229.

22. Jean Allemane, *Mémoires d'un Communard* (Paris: Librairie socialiste, 1910), 151–157; Edwards, *The Paris Commune*, 331–332.

23. Jeanneret, *Paris pendant la Commune*, 268, 318–321.

24. Bertrand Taithe, *Citizenship and Wars: France in Turmoil, 1870–1871* (London: Routledge, 2001), 138; Robert Tombs, "Les Communeuses," *Sociétés et Représentations* (June 1998): 6:63.

25. 8J 6e conseil de guerre 213, dossier 189, interrogations of Genton, August 6, 12, 16, 24, 29, 1871; testimony of Jean Costa, August 14; Romain, July 27 and August 16.

26. Gaston Da Costa, *Mémoires d'un Communard: La Commune vécue* (Paris: Larousse, 2009), 177–181, 191. Earlier that morning, Genton had gone to La Roquette prison on the matter of the incarceration of a troubled carpenter called Greffe, a Blanquist leader who had been arrested for insubordination and was being hidden in the prison apartment of Jean-Baptiste François, director of La Roquette.

27. Ly 140, rapport Alpert, nomination by Committee of Public Safety "25 floréal an 79"; 8J 6e conseil de guerre, dossier 189 (Genton); p.v., June 5 and August 24, 1871; Charles Chauvin, *Mgr Darboy, archêveque de Paris, otage de la Commune (1813–1871)* (Paris: Desclée de Brouwer, 2011), 144; Ly 137, dossier Jean-Baptiste François; Ly 132, "Rapport sur l'affaire des nommés Ramain, Genton, etc."; Joseph-Alfred Foulon, *Histoire de la vie et des oeuvres de Mgr Darboy,*

archevêque de Paris (Paris: Possielgue frères, 1889), 585; L. P. Guénin, *Assassinat des otages. Sixième conseil de guerre* (Paris: Librarie de l'echo de la Sorbonne, 1871), 303; Vuillaume, *Mes cahiers rouges*, 73. Jacques-Olivier Boudon (*Monseigneur Darboy [1813–1871]* [Paris: Éditions du cerf, 2011], 153) thinks that no such tribunal ever was constituted. In Da Costa's interpretation, orders for the execution of six hostages arrived at La Roquette but gave no names (ibid., 153–154). The names on the two lists, besides those of Darboy and Bonjean, remain unknown, amid confusing and sometimes contradictory accounts.

28. AG Ly 137, dossier Jean-Baptiste François.

29. Ferdinand Évrard, *Souvenirs d'un otage de la Commune* (Paris: P. Dupont, 1871), 5–6, 43, 58–64; Foulon, *Histoire*, 589–595; Abbé [Henri-Pierre] Lamazou, *La place Vendôme et la Roquette* (Paris: C. Douniol et cⁱᵉ·, 1876), 247; Guénin, *Assassinat des otages*, 303; Sempronius, *Histoire de la Commune de Paris en 1871* (Paris: Décembre-Alonnier, 1871), 226–227.

30. Guénin, *Assassinat des otages*, 210, 251–252.

31. Alexis Pierron, *Mgr Darboy: Esquisses familières* (Paris: Laplace, Sanchez et cie., 1872), 97–99; Guénin, *Assassinat des otages*, 303; Joseph Abel Guillermin, *Vie de Mgr Darboy, archevêque de Paris, mis à mort en haine de la foi le 24 mai 1871* (Paris: Bloud et Barral, 1888), 340.

32. 8J 3e conseil de guerre 6, dossier 29/8 Théophile Ferré; Guénin, *Assassinat des otages*, 14, 187–88, 303; AG Ly 132, report; Foulon, *Histoire*, 594; Ly 137, Affaire de la rue Haxo; 8J 6e conseil de guerre 213, dossier 189, interrogations of Genton, August 6, 12, 16, 24, 29, 1871; testimony of Jean Costa, August 14; Romain, July 27 and August 16; Lewis C. Price, *Archbishop Darboy and Some French Tragedies, 1813–1871* (London: G. Allen and Unwin, [1918]), 290. Several witnesses attested that they had indeed seen Ferré at La Roquette that day. According to one story, upon seeing Darboy bless the other hostages, one of the execution squad said, "So. You are giving a benediction. Well, I will give you mine!" Communards later claimed that Darboy tried to get up three times before being shot again. According to Maxime Vuillaume, *Mes cahiers rouges*, 76–78, Benjamin Sicard commanded the execution squad. Ramain, brigadier chef de la Roquette, formally identified Genton as having presided over the execution.

33. A. Rastoul, *L'Église de Paris sous la Commune* (Paris: Dillet, 1871), 191; Chauvin, *Mgr Darboy*, 149.

34. Baronnet, *Enquête*, 109; Serman, *La Commune de Paris*, 503; Edwards, *The Paris Commune*, 326.

35. Baronnet, *Enquête*, 109; Serman, *La Commune de Paris*, 503; Edwards, *The Paris Commune*, 319, 326.

36. Woodford McClellan, *Revolutionary Exiles: The Russians in the First International and the Paris Commune* (Totowa, NJ: Cass, 1979), 154–157; Godineau, *La Commune de Paris*, 156; 8J 6e conseil de guerre 230, dossier 683, Élisabeth Dmitrieff.

CHAPTER 8:
THE COURTS-MARTIAL AT WORK

1. Wickham Hoffman, *Camp, Court, and Siege: A Narrative of Personal Adventure and Observation During Two Wars, 1861–1865, 1870–1871* (New York: Harper and Brothers, 1877), 261, 281.

2. Robert Tombs, *The War Against Paris, 1871* (Cambridge: Cambridge University Press, 1981), 178–189; Prosper-Olivier Lissagaray, *Les huit journées de mai derrière les barricades* (Bruxelles: Bureau du "Petit Journal," 1871), 75; Laure Godineau, *La Commune de Paris par ceux qui l'ont vécue* (Paris: Parigramme, 2010), 218; Paul Martine, *Souvenirs d'insurgé. La Commune de 1871* (Paris: Perrin, 1971), 231.

3. René Héron de Villefosse, *Les graves heures de la Commune* (Paris: Perrin, 1970), 253; William Serman, *La Commune de Paris* (Paris: Fayard, 1986), 521; Maurice Choury, *Les damnés de la terre, 1871* (Paris: Tchou, 1970), 151; Camille Pelletan, *La semaine de mai* (Paris: M. Dreyfous, 1880), 336–337.

4. Pelletan, *La semaine de mai*, 213–227.

5. Henri Dabot, *Griffonnages quotidiens d'un bourgeois du Quartier latin, du 14 mai 1869 au 2 décembre 1871* (Péronne: Imp. de E. Quentin, 1895), 222, 227–233.

6. Maurice Garçon, "Journal d'un bourgeois de Paris," *Revue de Paris*, 12 (December 1955): 14–33.

7. "Souvenirs d'un habitant de la Porte Saint-Denis, du 21 au 25 mai 1871," Bibliothèque de l'Hôtel-de-Ville, ms. 1031.

8. Élie Reclus, *La Commune de Paris au jour le jour* (Saint-Martin-de-Bonfossé: Théolib, 2011), 366–367.

9. Alix Payen, "Une ambulancière de la Commune de Paris," in *Mémoires de femmes, mémoire du peuple*, edited by Louis Constant (Paris: F. Maspero, 1979), 86–87.

10. Hélène Haudebourg, ed., "Carnet de guerre d'un Vertarien en 1870 Julien Poirier," *Regards sur Vertou*, no. 7 (2003): 16–17.

11. Charles des Cognets, *Les bretons et la Commune de Paris 1870–1871* (Paris: L'Harmattan, 2012), 341–342; Tombs, *The War Against Paris*, 267; Stewart Edwards, *The Paris Commune, 1871* (New York: Quadrangle, 1972), 332–333; Robert Tombs, "La lutte finale des barricades: Spontanéité révolutionnaire et organisation militaire en mai 1871," in *La Barricade*, edited by Alain Corbin and J.-M. Mayeur (Paris: Publications de la Sorbonne, 1997), 360–364.

12. AG Ly 132, report; 6e conseil de guerre, affaire des Dominicains d'Arcueil, rapport du rapporteur, December 24, 1871; Gérard Conte, *Éléments pour une histoire de la Commune dans le XIIIe arrondissement—5 mars–25 mai 1871* (Paris: Éditions de la butte aux Cailles, 1981), 78, 90.

13. Haudebourg, "Carnet de guerre," 15–18.

14. W. Pembroke Fetridge, *The Rise and Fall of the Paris Commune in 1871* (New York: Harper Brothers, 1871), 395; des Cognets, *Les bretons et la Commune*,

342; Lissagaray, *Les huit journées de mai*, 96–98; Joseph Vinoy (Général), *L'armistice et la Commune* (Paris: H. Plon, 1872), 327–328.

15. Tombs, *The War Against Paris*, 140. The Prussians held everything between Charenton and Saint-Denis, including all forts except Vincennes. Tombs describes the tensions between Bismarck, eager to extend his influence, and the Thiers government (ibid., 136–140). The Versaillais entry into Paris removed any possibility of German intervention.

16. Alistair Horne, *The Fall of Paris: The Siege and the Commune, 1870–71* (New York: Penguin, 1990), 408.

17. Pelletan, *La semaine de mai*, 50–53.

18. Augustine Blanchecotte, *Tablettes d'une femme pendant la Commune* (Paris: Didier, 1872), 200, 204, 211–213.

19. Albert Hans, *Souvenirs d'un volontaire versaillais* (Paris: Dentu, 1873), 108–109; Tombs, *The War Against Paris*, 167.

20. Hans, *Souvenirs*, 128–138, 141–142, 148–153, 161–171.

21. Christiane Demeulenaere-Douyère, "Journal de l'entrée des troupes versaillaises dans Paris," *Bulletin de la Société d'Histoire de Paris et de l'Ile de France* 108 (1981): 301–303.

22. P. F. Borgella, *Justice! Par un officier de l'armée de Paris* (London: Imprimerie nationale, 1871), 11, 23.

23. Borgella, *Justice!* 33–34.

24. John Leighton, *Paris Under the Commune* (London: Bradbury, Evans and Company, 1871), 262–263.

25. Le Maréchal de Mac-Mahon, *L'armée de Versailles depuis sa formation jusqu'à la complète pacification de Paris* (Paris: A. Ghio, 1872), 40.

26. Blanchecotte, *Tablettes*, 263; Jules Bergeret, *Le 18 mars: Journal hebdomadaire* (London: n.p., 1871), 11, 86.

27. Reclus, *La Commune de Paris*, 364.

CHAPTER 9: MASSACRE

1. Élie Reclus, *La Commune de Paris au jour le jour* (Saint-Martin-de-Bonfossé: Théolib, 2011), 368.

2. Paul Martine, *Souvenirs d'insurgé. La Commune de 1871* (Paris: Perrin, 1971), 270; Stewart Edwards, *The Paris Commune, 1871* (New York: Quadrangle, 1972), 326; Vizetelly, *My Adventures in the Commune* (London: Chatto and Windus, 2009), 176.

3. Émile Maury, *Mes souvenirs sur les événements des années 1870–1871*, edited by Alain Dalotel (Paris: La boutique de l'histoire, 2001), 74.

4. Benoît Malon, *La troisième défaite du prolétariat français* (Neuchâtel: G. Guillaume fils, 1871), 473; Robert Tombs, *The Paris Commune, 1871* (New York: Longman, 1999), 168.

5. Edwards, *The Paris Commune*, 334–335. The previous day Édouard Moreau and two others had proposed reaching out to Thiers in an attempt to arrange a

truce, based improbably enough on the Versaillais army abandoning Paris, the dissolution of the National Assembly, and the holding of new elections. Thiers never would have accepted this, and in any case, there was no way of getting to Versailles (ibid., 333).

6. Edwards, *The Paris Commune*, 335; Alistair Horne, *The Fall of Paris: The Siege and the Commune, 1870–71* (New York: Penguin, 1965), 401; Robert Tombs, *The War Against Paris, 1871* (Cambridge: Cambridge University Press, 1981), 157.

7. Prosper-Olivier Lissagaray, *Les huit journées de mai derrière les barricades* (Bruxelles: Bureau du "Petit Journal," 1871), 101–102; Ernest A. Vizetelly, *My Adventures in the Commune*, 56; Charles Prolès, *Les hommes de la révolution de 1871: Charles Delescluze 1830–1848–1871* (Paris: 111 rue Réaumur, 1898), 120–123; Maxime Vuillaume, *Mes cahiers rouges au temps de la Commune* (Paris: A. Michel, 1971), 293–296; Jean Baronnet, ed., *Enquête sur la Commune de Paris (La Revue Blanche)* (Paris: Les éditions de l'amateur, 2011), 161–166. On June 20, Vermorel died of his wounds, which the Versaillais left untreated.

8. Vuillaume, *Mes cahiers rouges*, 49.

9. Benoît Malon, *La troisième défaite du prolétariat français* (Neuchâtel: G. Guillaume fils, 1871), 473; Jean-Pierre Béneytou, *Vinoy: Général du Second Empire* (Paris: Éditions Christian, 2003), 176–183; Tombs, *The War Against Paris*, 186–188.

10. Jacques de la Faye (Marie de Sardent), *Le général de Ladmirault, 1808–1898* (Paris: B. Bloud, 1901), xii, xxii–xxiii, 281–289.

11. Tombs, *The War Against Paris*, 112–113.

12. William Serman, *Les origines des officiers français 1848–1870* (Paris: Publications de la Sorbonne, 1979), 6; William Serman, *Les officiers français dans la nation* (Paris: Aubier Montaigne, 1982), 55–57, 85–88, 98–99; Robert Tombs, "Réflexions sur la Semaine sanglante," in *La Commune de 1871. L'événement les hommes et la mémoire*, edited by Claude Latta (Saint-Étienne: Publications de l'Université de Saint-Étienne, 2004), 238–239; Alexandre Montaudon (Général), *Souvenirs militaires* (Paris: C. Delagrave, 1898–1900), 2:420; Tombs, *The War Against Paris*, 172–176; On May 26, MacMahon ordered that any Communards who offered to surrender should be taken prisoner and not executed (ibid., 185–187).

13. Augustine Blanchecotte, *Tablettes d'une femme pendant la Commune* (Paris: Didier, 1872), 250–252; Jules Bergeret, *Le 18 mars: Journal hebdomadaire* (London: n.p., 1871), 11.

14. Camille Pelletan, *La semaine de mai* (Paris: M. Dreyfous, 1880), 269–275; Louis Thomas, *Le général de Galliffet (1830–1909)* (Paris: Aux armes de France, 1941), 102, 104; Pierre Guiral, *Adolphe Thiers* (Paris: Fayard, 1986), 402. Benoît Malon titled his Chapter 9 "The Tricolor Terror."

15. René Héron de Villefosse, *Les graves heures de la Commune* (Paris: Perrin, 1970), 256–257; Jean Bruhat, Jean Dautry, and Émile Tersen, *La Commune de 1871* (Paris: Éditions sociales, 1970), 283. The Ardennais poet Arthur Rimbaud,

who sympathized with the *fédérés*, compared oppressed workers to oppressed colonial peoples (Kristin Ross, *The Emergence of the Social Space: Rimbaud and the Paris Commune* [Minneapolis: University of Minnesota Press, 1988], 148–149).

16. Charles de Montrevel, *Nouvelle histoire de la Commune de Paris en 1871* (Paris: Bloud et Barral, 1885), 204, 208; Gustave de Molinari, *Les clubs rouges pendant le siège de Paris* (Paris: Garnier frères, 1871), x–xxvi.

17. Anonymous, *Réflexions sur les événements des dix derniers mois par un provincial habitant à Paris* (Paris: Dentu, 1871), 19, 48–49.

18. Jacques Silvestre de Sacy, *Le Maréchal de Mac-Mahon* (Paris: Éditions inter-nationale, 1960), 260–261.

19. Tombs, *The War Against Paris*, 186.

20. Tombs, *The War Against Paris*, 186–189.

21. Edith Thomas, *Louise Michel* (Montreal: Black Rose Books, 1980), 94.

22. Bruhat, Dautry, and Tersen, *La Commune de 1871*, 283; Pelletan, *La semaine de mai*, 39, 104; Serman, *La Commune de Paris*, 521; Tombs, *The War Against Paris*, 170–171.

23. Pelletan, *La semaine de mai*, vii, 2, 6–7, 17, 20–23, 32.

24. Maurice Choury, *La Commune au Quartier latin* (Paris: Livre club Diderot, 1971), 163–164; Pelletan, *La semaine de mai*, 191.

25. Arthur Adamov, *La Commune de Paris 18 mars–28 mai 1871. Anthologie* (Paris: Éditions sociales, 1959), 223–224.

26. Sutter-Laumann, *Histoire d'un trente sous (1870–1871)* (Paris: A. Savine, 1891), 312–321; Tristan Rémy, *La Commune à Montmartre: 23 mai 1871* (Paris: Éditions sociales, 1970), 64, 86.

27. Paul Perny (R. P.), *Deux mois de prison sous la Commune, suivi de détails authentiques sur l'assassinat de Mgr l'archevêque de Paris* (Paris: Lainé, 1871), 197.

28. Pelletan, *La semaine de mai*, 119–122.

29. Tombs, *The War Against Paris*, 183–185; Pelletan, *La semaine de mai*, 340–341.

30. Clémence (Adolphe Hippolyte, dit Roussel), *De l'antagonisme social, ses causes et ses effets* (Neuchâtel: G. Guillaume fils, 1871), 23–24.

31. Tombs, *The War Against Paris*, 178–182; Maurice Choury, *Les damnés de la terre, 1871* (Paris: Tchou, 1970), 151 (June 9); Serman, *La Commune de Paris*, 522.

32. Lissagaray, *Les huit journées de mai*, 161.

33. Serman, *La Commune de Paris*, 508.

34. Édgar Monteil, *Souvenirs de la Commune, 1871* (Paris: Charavay frères, 1883), 102–107; Charles des Cognets, *Les bretons et la Commune de Paris 1870–1871* (Paris: L'Harmattan, 2012) 334; 8J 3e conseil de guerre 6, dossier 29/8 Théophile Ferré, May 24; Pelletan, *La semaine de mai*, 306–307; Edwards, *The Paris Commune*, 337; Tombs, *The War Against Paris*, 159.

35. W. Pembroke Fetridge, *The Rise and Fall of the Paris Commune in 1871* (New York: Harper Brothers, 1871), 394.

36. Reclus, *La Commune de Paris*, 369–371; Eric Fournier, *Paris en ruines: Du Paris haussmannien au Paris communard* (Paris: Imago, 2008), 92, 96.

37. Fetridge, *The Rise and Fall of the Paris Commune in 1871*, 445–447; Edwards, *The Paris Commune*, 337.

38. des Cognets, *Les bretons et la Commune*, 351; Robert Tombs, *The War Against Paris*, 160–161.

39. Alain Dalotel, *Gabriel Ranvier, le Christ de Belleville: Blanquiste, Franc-maçon, Communard et maire du XXe arrondissement* (Paris: Éditions Dittmar, 2005), 52; John Leighton, *Paris Under the Commune* (London: Bradbury, Evans and Company, 1871), 227; Edwards, *The Paris Commune, 1871*, 336.

40. Pierre Angrand, "Un épisode de la répression versaillais. L'affaire Tribels (mai 1871–octobre 1872)," *La Pensée* 68 (July–August 1956): 126–133. Tribels earned a living selling gold and gold objects and dealt in income coupons. All the valuables had disappeared, undoubtedly into the hands of Vabre and other Versaillais. Madame Tribels later received an indemnity from the French government.

41. George J. Becker, ed., *Paris Under Siege, 1870–71: From the Goncourt Journal* (Ithaca, NY: Cornell University Press, 1969), 305–308.

42. Bergeret, *Le 18 mars*, 15–16; Malon, *La troisième défaite*, 462.

43. Martine, *Souvenirs*, 269; Edwards, *The Paris Commune*, 336–337.

44. Blanchecotte, *Tablettes*, 249–250; Serman, *La Commune de Paris*, 515–516; 8J 6e conseil dossier 189, Antoine Ramain.

45. AG Ly 137, "Rapport sur l'affaire des nommés . . . ," February 23, 1872; Ly 137, "Assassinations de la rue Haxo, Pourvois en Cassation," April 29, 1872; interrogation of Antoine Ramain, February 7, 1872; Fetridge, *The Rise and Fall of the Paris Commune in 1871*, 309.

46. AG Ly 137, dossier François, interrogation of February 3, 1872; A. Rastoul, *L'Église de Paris sous la Commune* (Paris: E. Dentu, 1871), 220–232; Jacques Rougerie, *Procès des Communards* (Paris: Julliard, 1964), 54; Serman, *La Commune de Paris,* 515–516. Those accused of involvement in the massacre of the prisoners on rue Haxo were workers, mostly from nearby quartiers. Six were condemned to death; Ramain received fifteen years' hard labor.

47. Rastoul, *L'Église de Paris*, 235–243; Horne, *The Fall of Paris*, 410. Rastoul relates, among other things, that Ferré came to La Roquette at about 3:00 P.M. and ordered the remaining prisoners who were serving time for criminal offenses freed if they would agree to fight against the Versaillais (ibid., 239–240).

48. Rastoul, *L'Église de Paris*, 243–256; Perny, *Deux mois de prison*, 227–229; Jacques-Olivier Boudon, *Monseigneur Darboy (1813–1871)* (Paris: Éditions du Cerf, 2011), 153; Robert Tombs, "Les Communeuses," *Sociétés et Représentations* (June 1998): 6:60–61.

49. Fetridge, *The Rise and Fall of the Paris Commune in 1871*, 437–441; Edwards, *The Paris Commune*, 338; Tombs, *The War Against Paris*, 159; Horne, *The Fall of Paris*, 411.

50. Pelletan, *La semaine de mai*, 320–327.

51. Reclus, *La Commune de Paris*, 370–371; Tombs, *The War Against Paris*, 165–166.

52. de Villefosse, *Les graves heures*, 253; Martine, *Souvenirs*, 288.

53. Albert Hans, *Souvenirs d'un volontaire versaillais* (Paris: Dentu, 1873), 160–165.

54. Denis Arthur Bingham, *Recollections of Paris* (London: Chapman and Hall, 1896), 2:110.

55. Archibald Forbes, "What an American Girl Saw of the Commune," *Century Illustrated Magazine* 45, no. 1 (November 1892): 61.

56. Pierre Vésinier, *History of the Commune of Paris* (London: Chapman and Hall, 1872), 312, 325–328, 334. During the June Days, between 1,500 and 3,000 were killed, and several hundred were summarily executed.

57. Hans, *Souvenirs*, 187–196.

58. Edwards, *The Paris Commune*, 338; Becker, *Paris Under Siege*, 313; Horne, *The Fall of Paris*, 412.

59. Gérard Dittmar, *Belleville de l'annexation à la Commune* (Paris: Dittmar, 2007), 76; Hélène Haudebourg, ed., "Carnet de guerre d'un Vertarien en 1870 Julien Poirier," *Regards sur Vertou*, no. 7 (2003): 18. Poirier remained in occupied Paris until September, then returned home to Vertou.

60. Louise Michel, *La Commune, histoire et souvenirs* (Paris: La découverte, 1970), 2:59; Edwards, *The Paris Commune*, 339; Robert Tombs, "La lutte finale des barricades: Spontanéité révolutionnaire et organisation militaire en mai 1871," in *La Barricade*, edited by Alain Corbin and J.-M. Mayeur (Paris: Publications de la Sorbonne, 1997), 364.

61. Edwards, *The Paris Commune*, 338–339.

62. Lissagaray, *Les huit journées de mai*, 108–110, 129–136; *Les martyrs de la Seconde Terreur ou Arrestation, captivité et martyre de Mgr Darboy, archevêque de Paris de M. Deguerry* (Paris: A. Josse, 1871), 197.

63. Pelletan, *La semaine de mai*, 276–282.

64. Bergeret, *Le 18 mars*, 9; W. Gibson, *Paris During the Commune* (London: Methodist Book Room, 1895), 297, 308–309.

65. Vuillaume, *Mes cahiers rouges*, 14–50, 308–317, 327–357.

66. Reclus, *La Commune de Paris*, 379; Paul Reclus, *Les frères Élie et Élisée Reclus* (Paris: Les amis d'Élisée Reclus, 1964), 189; 8J 3e conseil de guerre 82, dossier 2084. A military court-martial condemned Élie on October 6, 1875, to "deportation to the confines of a fortified enclosure." Four years later the condemnation was reduced. Élisée was condemned to deportation on September 15, 1871. Élie Reclus was arrested in 1894 at the time of the anarchist attacks in Paris.

67. Paul Vignon, *Rien que ce que j'ai vu! Le siège de Paris—la Commune* (Paris: E. Capiomont, 1913), 203.

CHAPTER 10:
PRISONERS OF VERSAILLES

1. [Davy], *The Insurrection in Paris, Related by an Englishmen* (Paris: A. Lemoigne, 1871), 102–114.

2. [Davy], *The Insurrection in Paris*, 123, 133, 141–143.

3. [Davy], *The Insurrection in Paris*, 153–154.

4. John Leighton, *Paris Under the Commune* (London: Bradbury, Evans and Company, 1871), 266.

5. Arthur de Grandeffe, *Mobiles et volontaires de la Seine pendant la guerre et les deux sieges* (Paris: E. Dentu, 1871), 255, 274; Jean Bruhat, Jean Dautry, and Émile Tersen, *La Commune de 1871* (Paris: Éditions sociales, 1970), 283.

6. George J. Becker, ed., *Paris Under Siege, 1870–71: From the Goncourt Journal* (Ithaca, NY: Cornell University Press, 1969), 306–311.

7. Pierre de Lano (Marc-André Gromier), *La Commune, journal d'un vaincu* (Paris: V. Havard, 1892), 38; Prosper-Olivier Lissagaray, *Les huit journées de mai derrière les barricades* (Bruxelles: Bureau du "Petit Journal," 1871), 122ff; Stewart Edwards, *The Paris Commune, 1871* (New York: Quadrangle, 1972), 339.

8. de Lano, *La Commune*, 39–55, 223; Eric Fournier, *La Commune n'est pas morte: Les usages politiques du presse de 1871 à nos jours* (Paris: Libertalia, 2013), 56.

9. Rupert Christiansen, *Paris Babylon* (New York: Viking, 1995), 360–365.

10. William Serman, *La Commune de Paris* (Paris: Fayard, 1986), 519.

11. Christiansen, *Paris Babylon*, 360–365.

12. David Barry, *Women and Political Insurgency: France in the Mid-Nineteenth Century* (Basingstoke, UK: Macmillan, 1996), 143.

13. Léonce Dupont, *Souvenirs de Versailles pendant la Commune* (Paris: E. Dentu, 1881), 93–95.

14. Camille Pelletan, *La semaine de mai* (Paris: M. Dreyfous, 1880), 265–268.

15. Pelletan, *La semaine de mai*, 282, 288.

16. Lissagaray, *Les huit journées de mai*, 148–149.

17. Paul Lidsky, *Les écrivains contre la Commune* (Paris: F. Maspero, 1970), 75; Robert Tombs, "How Bloody Was *La Semaine Sanglante* of 1871? A Revision," *Historical Journal* 55, no. 3 (September 2012): 33.

18. Gullickson, *Unruly Women*, 195–198; Dupont, *Souvenirs de Versailles*, 104–106.

19. Louise Michel, Lowry Bullitt, and Elizabeth Ellington Gunter, *The Red Virgin: Memoirs of Louise Michel* (University: University of Alabama Press, 1981), 69–73.

20. Susanna Barrows, "After the Commune: Alcoholism, Temperance, and Literature in the Early Third Republic," in *Consciousness and Class Experience in Nineteenth-Century Europe*, edited by John M. Merriman (New York: Holmes and Meier, 1979); Susanna Barrows, *Distorting Mirrors: Visions of the Crowd in*

Late Nineteenth-Century France (New Haven, CT: Yale University Press, 1981); Kristin Ross, *The Emergence of the Social Space: Rimbaud and the Paris Commune* (Minneapolis: University of Minnesota Press, 1988), 148.

21. On the rue du Cherche-Midi, a drunken corporal allegedly gunned down a woman standing in front of her store, then a passing dog, then a child of seven, and then a woman (Pelletan, *La semaine de mai*, 123, 257–262).

22. Sébastien Commissaire, *Mémoires et souvenirs* (Lyon: Meton, 1888), 2:384; Lissagaray, *Les huit journées de mai*, 156; Pelletan, *La semaine de mai*, 102–103. In the end, there were 399,823 denunciations.

23. Christiane Demeulenaere-Douyère, "Journal de l'entrée des troupes versaillaises dans Paris," *Bulletin de la Société d'Histoire de Paris et de l'Ile de France* 108 (1981): 309.

24. Marcel Cerf, *Édouard Moreau, l'âme du Comité central de la Commune* (Paris: Les lettres nouvelles, 1971), 207.

25. Edwards, *The Paris Commune*, 343.

26. Lidsky, *Les écrivains*, 66; Marforio (Louise Lacroix), *Les écharpes rouges: Souvenirs de la commune* (Paris: A. Laporte, 1872), 96; Woodford McClellan, *Revolutionary Exiles: The Russians in the First International and the Paris Commune* (Totowa, NJ: Cass, 1979), 167–168.

27. Bronislas Wolowski, *Dombrowski et Versailles* (Geneva: Carey Frères, 1871), 140–142; Denis Arthur Bingham, *Recollections of Paris* (London: Chapman and Hall, 1896), 2:122; Pelletan, *La semaine de mai*, 130–133.

28. René Héron de Villefosse, *Les graves heures de la Commune* (Paris: Perrin, 1970), 253.

29. Pelletan, *La semaine de mai*, 129.

30. Augustine Blanchecotte, *Tablettes d'une femme pendant la Commune* (Paris: Didier, 1872), 225; Lissagaray, *Les huit journées de mai*, 132–133.

31. Lidsky, *Les écrivains*, 46.

32. Gautier, *Tableaux de siège*, 242–244.

33. Henri Opper de Blowitz, *My Memoirs* (London: E. Arnold, 1903), 40.

34. Lidsky, *Les écrivains*, 47–48; Gay Gullickson, *Unruly Women of Paris: Images of the Commune* (Ithaca, NY: Cornell University Press, 1996), 176–177. Gustave Flaubert, who had served in the National Guard during the Franco-Prussian War, wrote to George Sand, who was hostile to the Commune, that the latter was "repugnant" (Michelle Perrot, "George Sand: Une républicaine contre la Commune," in *La Commune de 1871. L'événement les hommes et la mémoire*, edited by Claude Latta [Saint-Étienne: Publications de l'Université de Saint-Étienne, 2004], 147, 154).

35. Gullickson, *Unruly Women*, 197, 205; Dupont, *Souvenirs de Versailles*, 255, 267, 286. Gullickson shows that during the ensuing trials at Versailles, Communards' physical appearance remained almost an obsession.

36. Marforio, *Les écharpes rouges*, 147–152.

37. Gullickson, *Unruly Women*, 180–183; Georges Jeanneret, *Paris pendant la Commune révolutionnaire de 1871* (Paris: Éditions d'histoire sociale, 1871), 250; Jules Bergeret, *Le 18 mars: Journal hebdomadaire* (London: n.p., 1871), 7–8.

38. Bruhat, Dautry, and Tersen, *La Commune de 1871*, 285; Gullickson, *Unruly Women*, 169; Maurice Choury, *Les damnés de la terre, 1871* (Paris: Tchou, 1970), 151; Lissagaray, *Les huit journées de mai*, 132–133; Pelletan, *La semaine de mai*, 351–358.

39. Laure Godineau, *La Commune de Paris par ceux qui l'ont vécue* (Paris: Parigramme, 2010), 218; Frédéric Fort, *Paris brûlé* (Paris: E. Lachaud, 1871), 124.

40. Becker, *Paris Under Siege*, 312.

41. Georges Valance, *Thiers: Bourgeois et révolutionnaire* (Paris: Flammarion, 2007), 344; Lidsky, *Les écrivains*, 76; Commissaire, *Mémoires et souvenirs*, 2:383; Bruhat, Dautry, and Tersen, *La Commune de 1871*, 288.

42. Louis Énault, *Paris brûlé par la Commune* (Paris: H. Plon, 1871), 266.

43. Henri Rochefort, *Les aventures de ma vie*, edited by Paul Lidsky (Paris: Mercure de France, 2005), 215; Pierre Vésinier, *History of the Commune of Paris* (London: Chapman and Hall, 1872), 344–345; Élie Reclus, *La Commune de Paris au jour le jour* (Saint-Martin-de-Bonfossé: Théolib, 2011), 380–382; H. Sarrepont (Eugène Hennebert), *Guerre des Communeux de Paris: 18 mars–28 mai 1871* (Paris: Librarie de Firmin Didot frères, fils et cie., 1871), 363–366.

CHAPTER 11:
REMEMBERING

1. Prosper-Olivier Lissagaray, *Les huit journées de mai derrière les barricades* (Bruxelles: Bureau du "Petit Journal," 1871), 34.

2. Lissagaray, *Les huit journées de mai*, 138–139.

3. Georges Bell, "Les ruines," in *Paris Incendié: Histoire de la Commune de 1871* (Paris: E. Martinet, 1872); [Davy], *The Insurrection in Paris, Related by an Englishmen* (Paris: A. Lemoigne, 1871), 118, 122–159; Robert Tombs, *The Paris Commune, 1871* (New York: Longman, 1999), 12; Jules Bergeret, *Le 18 mars: Journal hebdomadaire* (London: n.p., 1871), 14–15; Camille Pelletan, *La semaine de mai* (Paris: M. Dreyfous, 1880), 301, 344–350.

4. Camille de Meaux, *Souvenirs politiques, 1871–1877* (Paris: Plont-Nourrit et cie., 1905), 54–56.

5. Alexis Pierron, *Mgr Darboy: Esquisses familières* (Paris: Laplace, Sanchez et cie., 1872), 111–112. The new archbishop restored Lagarde to his status as first vicar. Pius IX saluted Darboy in his *Lettre encyclique* of June 4. The Versaillais shot Vérig at La Roquette immediately on their arrival. Various campaigns to obtain Darboy's beatification began in the late 1880s and lasted into the late 1960s. A statue of Darboy, sculpted in 1873 by Jean-Marie Bienaimé (Bonassieux), stands in Notre-Dame. Streets in the Eleventh Arrondissement were renamed for Darboy and Deguerry.

6. Jacques-Olivier Boudon, *Monseigneur Darboy (1813–1871)* (Paris: Éditions du Cerf, 2011), 146; Wickham Hoffman, *Camp, Court, and Siege: A Narrative of Personal Adventure and Observation During Two Wars, 1861–1865, 1870–1871* (New York: Harper and Brothers, 1877), 264.

7. Fournier, *La Commune*, 22–25. The Church of Notre-Dame des Otages today stands at 81, rue Haxo.

8. Olivier Marion, "La vie religieuse pendant la Commune de Paris 1871" (unpublished master's thesis, Paris-X Nanterre, 1981), 262; John Merriman, *Dynamite Club* (New York: Houghton Mifflin, 2009), 88–89; Fournier, *La Commune*, 26–27.

9. Albert Hans, *Souvenirs d'un volontaire versaillais* (Paris: Dentu, 1873), 213, 239–240.

10. Hans, *Souvenirs*, 213, 229–232.

11. Henri Ameline, ed., *Enquête parlementaire sur l'insurrection du 18 mars* (Versailles: Cerf, 1872), 1:227–228; René Héron de Villefosse, *Les graves heures de la Commune* (Paris: Perrin, 1970), 249.

12. Frédéric Chauvaud, "L'élision des traces, l'effacement des marques de la barricade à Paris (1830–1871)," in *La Barricade*, edited by Alain Corbin and J.-M. Mayeur (Paris: Publications de la Sorbonne, 1997), 272–279.

13. Lissagaray, *Les huit journées de mai*, 142–143.

14. Georges Valance, *Thiers: Bourgeois et révolutionnaire* (Paris: Flammarion, 2007), 325; Élie Reclus, *La Commune de Paris au jour le jour* (Saint-Martin-de-Bonfossé: Théolib, 2011), 374–376, 378.

15. William Serman, *La Commune de Paris* (Paris: Fayard, 1986), 529–537; 8J 6e conseil de guerre, 683; E. Tersen, "Léo Frankel," *Europe* 29, nos. 64–65 (April–May 1951): 166; Carolyn Eichner, *Surmounting the Barricades* (Bloomington: Indiana University Press, 2004), 154–62.

16. Louise Michel, *La Commune* (Paris: Stock, 1978), 328–329; Serman, *La Commune de Paris*, 536.

17. Sutter-Laumann, *Histoire d'un trente sous (1870–1871)* (Paris: A. Savine, 1891), 356–357.

18. 8J 3e conseil de guerre 6, dossier 29/5 (Gustave Courbet), reports of May 31 and June 1, 1871, and interrogation of Courbet, July 25, 1871; Eugène Delessert, *Épisodes pendant la Commune, souvenirs d'un délégué de la Société de secours aux blessés militaires des armées de terre et de mer* (Paris: C. Noblet, 1872), 51.

19. APP, Ba 1020, for example, report of July 7, 1871.

20. 8J 3e conseil de guerre 6, dossier 29/5 (Gustave Courbet), p.v., June 8, 13, and 14, 1871.

21. Pierre Courthion, *Courbet raconté par lui-même et par ses amis* (Geneva: P. Cailler, 1948), 1:267–269; Gerstle Mack, *Gustave Courbet* (New York: A. Knopf, 1951), 272; Jean Péridier, *La Commune et les artistes: Pottier, Courbet, Vallès, J. B. Clément* (Paris: Nouvelles éditions latines, 1980), 70–71.

22. 8J 3e conseil de guerre 6, dossier 29/5 (Gustave Courbet); Péridier, *La Commune*, 72–75; Henri Dubief, "Défense de Gustave Courbet par lui-même," *L'Actualité de l'Histoire* 30 (January–March 1960): 32–33; Édouard Moriac, *Les conseils de guerre de Versailles* (Paris: E. Dentu, 1871), 95–100, 222–223; Robert Boudry, "Courbet et la fédération des artistes," *Europe* 29, nos. 64–65 (April–May 1951): 126; (Jules) Castagnary, *Gustave Courbet et la Colonne Vendôme: Plaidoyer pour un ami mort* (Paris: E. Dentu, 1883), 2:77–83. Courbet was fined 323,091 francs for the rebuilding of the column and 6,850 francs for the trial.

23. L. Bigot, *Dossier d'un condamné à mort. Procès de Gustave Maroteau* (Paris: A. Chevalier, 1871), 163.

24. Gay Gullickson, *Unruly Women of Paris: Images of the Commune* (Ithaca, NY: Cornell University Press, 1996), 206–209; Susanna Barrows, *Distorting Mirrors: Visions of the Crowd in Late Nineteenth-Century France* (New Haven, CT: Yale University Press, 1981). Three women, Élisabeth Rétiffe, Joséphine Marchais, and Léotine Suétens, were condemned to death, despite a lack of evidence that they had set fire to anything, but they were subsequently spared.

25. 8J 6, dossier 135 Louise Michel, interrogation June 28, 1871; Louise Michel, Lowry Bullitt, and Elizabeth Ellington Gunter, *The Red Virgin: Memoirs of Louise Michel* (University: University of Alabama Press, 1981), 85–86; Gullickson, *Unruly Women*, 210–214; Kathleen Jones and Françoise Vergès, "'Aux citoyennes!': Women, Politics, and the Paris Commune of 1871," *History of European Ideas* 13 (1991): 725.

26. Louis-Nathaniel Rossel, *Rossel's Posthumous Papers* (London: Chapman and Hall, 1872), 203; Jules Bourelly (Général), *Le ministère de la guerre sous la Commune* (Paris: Combet, 1911), 154; Ly 137; Michel, Bullitt, and Gunter, *The Red Virgin*, 77–79; 8J 3e conseil de guerre 6, dossier 29/8 Théophile Ferré, interrogation July 16, 1871; 8J 6, dossier 554; Pelletan, *La semaine de mai*, 154–155.

27. Louis Énault, *Paris brûlé par la Commune* (Paris: H. Plon, 1871), 25; Ameline, *Enquête*, 1:127, 243, 264; J. M. Roberts, "La Commune considérée par la droite, dimensions d'une mythologie," *Revue de l'Histoire Moderne et Contemporaine* 19 (April–June 1972): 200–201. Alain Corbin suggests, "It is as if no regime could establish itself firmly until it had proved its capacity to bathe in the blood of the monster: the angry populace, the frenzied mob" (*Village of Cannibals: Rage and Murder in France, 1870* [Cambridge, MA: Harvard University Press, 1992], 98).

28. Eric Fournier, *La Commune n'est pas morte: Les usages politiques du presse de 1871 à nos jours* (Paris: Libertalia, 2013), 16–17, 30; François Bournand, *Le clergé pendant la Commune* (Paris: Tolra, 1892), 10.

29. Robert Tombs, *The War Against Paris* (Cambridge: Cambridge University Press, 1871), 191–192; Tristan Rémy, *La Commune à Montmartre: 23 mai 1871* (Paris: Éditions sociales, 1970), 125. According to another report, the Versaillais forces claimed to have arrested 38,578 people, including 1,054 women and 615 boys and girls under sixteen. Of these, about 20,000 were

released without charges, and more than 10,000 were condemned to a variety of penalties. Others ended up in well-guarded prison forts in the provinces (Valance, *Thiers*, 344–345; General Appert, "Rapport d'ensemble . . . sur les opérations de la justice militaire relatives à l'insurrection de 1871," *Annales de l'Assemblée nationale*, tome 43, du 1er au 17 décembre 1875 [Paris, 1876]; Stewart Edwards, *The Paris Commune*, 347–348). By early 1875, the cases of 50,559 prisoners had been heard. Twenty-two courts-martial tried 10,448 people, bringing 13,440 condemnations, 3,313 of them *par contumace*, between 1871 and 1874. Of the 270 condemned to death, 26 men were executed; 410 Communards (20 women) were sentenced to *travaux forces*; 3,989 (16 women) were deported, and 1,269 were sent to prison (Gérard Milhaud, "De la calomnie à l'histoire," *Europe* 48 [November–December 1970]: 42–56). They were not the "dangerous classes" imagined by elites; yet compared to other workers, they were poorer and, by virtue of the transient nature of their work, arguably less integrated into the city, younger, less likely to be married, and more likely to be "illegitimate" (*enfants naturels*) and illiterate. Twenty-one percent had had some sort of encounter with the law, the vast majority of these involving quite minor judicial proceedings. Of those condemned, 64.2 percent were between twenty-one and forty years of age; 25.6 percent were between forty-one and sixty. Those aged twenty-one to twenty-five were more likely to be deported. Of those arrested, 24.5 percent were born in the *département* of the Seine (that of Paris). The Seine led the way with 8,938 facing charges, followed by the neighboring Seine-et-Oise, with 1,267. Among 1,725 foreigners arrested at the end of the Commune, Belgians led the way with 737, followed by 215 Italians, 201 Swiss, 154 Dutch, and 110 Poles (Appert, "Rapport d'ensemble," 117). The Musée d'Art et d'Histoire in Saint-Denis gives a total of 34,952 arrests, including 819 women and 538 children, of whom 2,455 were acquitted; in 22,727 cases, charges were dropped; 93 people were condemned to death, with 23 executed; 251 were sentenced to hard labor for specific terms or for life; 3,417 were deported to New Caledonia; 1,247 were sentenced to life in prison, and 3,359 received shorter prison terms; 3,313 were condemned in absentia.

30. Arthur Monnanteuil, *Neuf mois de Ponton: Paroles d'un détenu* (Paris: A. Sagnier, 1873), 6–9; Maurice Choury, *Les damnés de la terre, 1871* (Paris: Tchou, 1970), 160.

31. Michel, *La Commune*, 395ff; Serman, *La Commune de Paris*, 531–535. Henri Rochefort and Francis Jourde managed to escape in March 1874, bribing the captain of a British vessel carrying coal to take them to the Australian port of Newcastle, from which they eventually reached Europe. Roger L. Williams, *Henri Rochefort: Prince of the Gutter Press* (New York: Scribner, 1966), 135–137.

32. Robert Tombs has argued that fewer Communards perished than suggested by other historians, including Tombs himself, who had earlier posited 10,000 ("Victimes et bourreaux de la Semaine sanglante," *1848: Révolutions et Mutations au XIX siècle* 1, no. 10 [1994], 81–96). He argues against Rougerie's contention that outward migration, including the departure of foreigners who

could no longer find work and residents who had managed to flee during the siege, can in part explain the precipitous decline—a drop of 10,000—in population among workers, particularly in certain radical trades, with the next official census. Tombs estimates the number of those buried within Paris during and right after Bloody Week at 5,700 and 7,400, respectively ("How Bloody Was *La Semaine Sanglante* of 1871? A Revision," *Historical Journal* 55, no. 3 [September 2012], 679–704). He concludes that Bloody Week was neither "an act of unprecedented violence" nor as violent as the French Revolution. However, many bodies were not buried until after May 30, and lime, cremation, and mass graves discovered subsequently likely account for thousands more deaths, which could not turn up in Tombs's new total of 7,400 executions.

33. Appert, "Rapport d'ensemble"; Jacques Rougerie, "Composition d'une population insurgée: L'exemple de la Commune," *Mouvement Social* 48 (July–September 1964): 32. Camille Pelletan, who was there, figured 30,000; Benoît Malon estimated about 25,000 (Benoît Malon, *La troisième défaite du prolétariat français* [Neuchâtel: G. Guillaume fils, 1871], 475; Pelletan, *La semaine de mai*, 5); Robert Tombs, "La lutte finale des barricades: Spontanéité révolutionnaire et organisation militaire en mai 1871," in Corbin and Mayeur, *La Barricade*, 364. Wickham Hoffmann (*Camp, Court, and Siege*, 280) relates that the huge, sixteen-foot-deep ditch had been dug in front of Napoleon Gaillard's barricade at the place de la Concorde.

34. Lissagaray, *Les huit journées de mai*, 140–143; Serman, *La Commune de Paris*, 521.

35. Rougerie, "Composition d'une population insurgée," 31; Pelletan, *La semaine de mai*, 398; Lissagaray, *Les huit journées de mai*, 160–161; Tombs, "How Bloody Was *La Semaine Sanglante* of 1871?" 13–14.

36. Maxime Vuillaume, *Mes cahiers rouges au temps de la Commune* (Paris: A. Michel, 1971), 58; Michel, Bullitt, and Gunter, *The Red Virgin*, 68; Jean Baronnet, ed., *Enquête sur la Commune de Paris (La Revue Blanche)* (Paris: Les éditions de l'amateur, 2011), 146.

37. Frederic Harrison, "The Revolution and the Commune," *Fortnightly Review* 53, no. 9 (May 1871): 577–578; Jean Allemane, *Mémoires d'un Communard* (Paris: Librairie socialiste, 1910), 136; E. Belfort Bax, Victor Dave, and William Morris, *A Short History of the Paris Commune* (London: Socialist League Office, 1886), 63–65, 72–79; Jacques Rougerie, *Procès des Communards* (Paris: Julliard, 1964), 7; Peter McPhee, *A Social History of France, 1780–1889* (New York: Routledge, 1992), 214–215. From London, Karl Marx asserted that the Paris Commune was the first socialist revolution in history, intoning memorably, "Working-man's Paris, with its Commune, will forever be celebrated as the glorious harbinger of a new society. Its martyrs are enshrined in the great heart of the working class. Its exterminators' history has already been nailed to the eternal pillory from which all the prayers of their priests will not avail to redeem them" (*The Civil War in France* [Chicago: C. H. Herr, 1934], 81–82). Marx concluded that the Paris Commune was not the anticipated social revolution that

would free the proletariat. Yet workers had risen up spontaneously, so he was reassured. Lenin would point to the revolutionary role during the Commune of the leadership of the avant-garde of the proletariat. In this he was thinking of the organization of his own Bolsheviks, thereby turning away from an emphasis on the revolutionary spontaneity of ordinary people.

38. Robert Tombs, "L'année terrible, 1870–71," *Historical Journal* 35, no. 3 (1992): 724, anticipating "the chilly bureaucratic carnage of the twentieth century."

39. Henri d'Alméras, *La vie quotidienne pendant le siège et sous la Commune* (Paris: Michel, 1927), 514–515.

40. Denis Arthur Bingham, *Recollections of Paris* (London: Chapman and Hall, 1896), 2:126–133.

41. Paschal Grousset, Francis Jourde, and Henri Brissac, *La bagne en Nouvelle-Calédonie . . . l'enfer au paradis* (Nouméa, New Caledonia, FR: Éditions footprint pacifique, 2009), 13.

42. Malon, *La troisième défaite*; Gustave Lefrançais, *Études sur le mouvement communaliste à Paris*, en 1871 (Neuchâtel: G. Guillaume fils, 1871). See Fournier, *La Commune*, 32–40, 147–174.

43. Madeleine Réberioux, "Le mur des fédérés," in *Les lieux de mémoire*, ed. Pierre Nora (Paris: Gallimard, 1984), 1:619–649. See also Danielle Tartakowsky, "Le mur des fédérés ou l'apprentissage de la manifestation," *Cahiers d'histoire de l'Institut de recherches marxistes* 44 (1991): 70–79; Danielle Tartakowsky, *Manifester à Paris: 1880–2010* (Seyssel: Champ Vallon, 2010).

44. Jules Vallès, *L'Insurgé* (Paris: G. et A. Mornay, 1923).

45. Remy Cazals in Gilbert Larguier and Jérôme Guaretti, eds., *La Commune de 1871: utopie ou modernité?* (Perpignan, FR: Presses Universitaires de Perpignan, 2001), 389–390. Clément wrote "La Semaine sanglante" (Bloody Week) while in hiding in Paris.

46. Jean Varloot, ed., *Les poètes de la Commune* (Paris: Les éditeurs français réunis, 1951), 95–98.

47. Thomas Wolfe, *Look Homeward, Angel: A Story of the Buried Life* (New York: Modern Library, 1929).

INDEX